# LOVE AND RESPONSIBILITY

# LOVE AND RESPONSIBILITY

## Karol Wojtyła

### Translation, Endnotes, and Foreword
by Grzegorz Ignatik

Pauline
BOOKS & MEDIA
Boston

Library of Congress Cataloging-in-Publication Data

John Paul II, Pope, 1920-2005.
  [Milosc i odpowiedzialnosc. English]
  Love and responsibility / Karol Wojtyla ; translation and foreword by Grzegorz Ignatik.
    p. cm.
  Includes bibliographical references.
  ISBN-13: 978-0-8198-4558-0
  ISBN-10: 0-8198-4558-2
  1. Sex--Religious aspects--Catholic Church. 2. Sexual ethics. 3. Catholic Church--Doctrines. I. Title.
  BT708.J6313 2013
  241'.66--dc23

                      2012042267

Scripture references and other quotations are translated from Karol Wojtyła's (Pope John Paul II's) own wording of the text as he wrote in Polish.

Cover design by Rosana Usselmann

"P" and PAULINE are registered trademarks of the Daughters of St. Paul.

Originally published in Polish as *Miłość i odpowiedzialność* by Towarzystwo Naukowe KUL, Lublin, copyright © 2001. First published by Towarzystwo Naukowe KUL, Lublin, copyright © 1960.

Published by Pauline Books & Media, 50 Saint Pauls Avenue, Boston, MA 02130-3491.

Printed in the U.S.A.

www.pauline.org

Pauline Books & Media is the publishing house of the Daughters of St. Paul, an international congregation of women religious serving the Church with the communications media.

2 3 4 5 6 7 8 9                                                    20 19 18 17 16

*To my wife, Christine*
G. I.

# Contents

# Translator's Foreword

The main goal of this new English translation of Bishop Karol Wojtyła's masterpiece *Love and Responsibility* is to allow the English reader to enter into the thought of Wojtyła in a more profound way so as to encounter the reality he examined, the reality of the human person in the order of love. Being created in and for love, man in his freedom is unintelligible without love. Wojtyła himself wished that this encounter might bring the fruit of transformation and cultivation of the reader (see especially his introduction to the second Polish edition). At the same time, however, this encounter is a meeting with Karol Wojtyła, a loving man or rather a loving father who shares with his children the truth and beauty of the human person and of human nature.

This translation achieves its goal, or at least attempts to do so, by meticulous attention to the original Polish text, which is rendered into English faithfully and clearly. What made this possible is not only that I am a native speaker of Polish but also that most of my higher education has taken place in the United States after emigrating from Poland. In addition, the task of translating *Love and Responsibility* demanded from me a familiarity with other writings of Karol Wojtyła. This includes the knowledge of philosophical and theological presuppositions and contexts contributing to his thought expressed in this book, and of the philosophical method he used. Due to the philosophical nature of the book and its Polish origin, I provide notes at the end of this English edition.*

The first English publication of then-Cardinal Wojtyła's article *On the Meaning of Spousal Love* accompanies this translation (pp. 273ff.). Although published in 1974, some years after the first Polish publication of *Love and Responsibility* in 1960, the article is a fruit of Wojtyła's renewed reflection on certain themes presented in the book. This reflection was prompted by a discussion concerning the problems of conjugal morality (see my opening note to the article). That is why this article belongs to the book in an organic way.

Lastly, the Polish edition used as a basis for this translation is the Lublin 2001 publication of the book by Towarzystwo Naukowe KUL. However, in some instances I referred to the second Polish edition of *Love and Responsibility* from 1962, which was published in Kraków by Społeczny Instytut Wydawniczy Znak, and which carried the imprimatur of Archbishop Eugeniusz Kuczkowski. Although my translation is not meant to be a critical edition of the book, in the notes I indicate several noteworthy differences between the 1962 and 2001 editions. There is no doubt that Wojtyła himself introduced the changes. Besides simple deletions from the 1962 edition, the most recent edition contains rewritten or added paragraphs (especially in chapter V) that bear the full weight of Wojtyła's thought, method, and style. Without stipulating the reasons why he made the changes, I have included the deleted material in my notes because it contributes significantly to a more integral grasp of his intention and word, hence to a deeper encounter with the human person and his love.

I wish to express my sincere thanks to several people for assisting with this translation project. First, I would like to thank Fr. Josef Spindelböck for offering me his always enthusiastic encouragement, his German translation of *Love and Responsibility*, and his valuable comments concerning my notes and translation. I am particularly grateful to Dr. David L. Schindler for reviewing and discussing my notes with

---

* The translator's notes (numbered references within text) clarify the meaning of various words and concepts Wojtyła employed and, in several cases, present a broader context to the issues at hand. The reader will also find English translations of all foreign phrases (mostly Latin) that were left untranslated or unexplained in the text. — Ed.

me. I consider his sound advice invaluable. Furthermore, I wish to thank Sr. Marianne Lorraine Trouvé from the Daughters of St. Paul for her editing help, which contributed greatly to the legibility of this translation. My gratitude is also extended to Sr. Bonita Sajnóg from the Congregation of the Sister Servants of the Most Sacred Heart of Jesus, and to my brother, Adam Ignatik, for procuring the indispensable and needed versions of Polish texts used for this project. Finally, I am indebted to Ellen Roderick and Fr. Pietro Rossotti for their translation of the French and Italian quotations respectively.

GRZEGORZ IGNATIK

Reynoldsburg, Ohio

June 12, 2012

# Editors' Introduction
# to the Polish Edition (1979)

This book, which presently finds its way to the hands of the reader, has its history. It appeared for the first time twenty years ago.[1] At the present rate of literary and publishing production this signifies a long period, even for the field of philosophy where works age more slowly. Yet, this book also has a long prehistory. This prehistory was written by the experience of many people, which in a way was becoming the experience of the author himself as their pastor and friend co-experiencing (*współprzeżywać*) their most intimate matters. This experience converged with and in a sense met his own intuition regarding these matters. It provoked reflections and considerations which, over time, gave rise to a need to bear testimony to them. At first, this testimony found its expression in the form of lectures given in 1958–1959 at the Catholic University of Lublin. Then it finally assumed the form of the book *Love and Responsibility*, published in Lublin by TN KUL (the Academic Society of the Catholic University of Lublin) in 1960.

From that moment, the work started to live its own, independent life. Since then, in a sense, it has been writing its history by itself. *Habent sua fata libelli* . . .[2] It writes its history for itself and, in a way, also for its author.

This history is mainly a history of an encounter between, on the one hand, the experiences and the testimony expressed in this book and, on the other hand, the conceptions and suggestions which want to appeal to the same source, or at least in the same source they seek their legitimation and validation. How well has *Love and Responsibility* fared in this confrontation? This question imposes itself in a natural way in reference to this book, which happened to exist in a time so preoccupied by the problems the book deals with. Thus, understandably, the reader also poses this question and expects an answer to it. But answering this question here would discredit the very presupposition of the work. After all, this work was intended as a call to "experience the experience"—something that can be summoned as a testimony of experience and at any moment submitted again to the judgment of experience, as soon as the need to appeal to the very sources and foundations of the validity of our judgments emerges or intensifies anew. So, *tolle et lege!*[3] But above all, *vide!*[4] "Possessing that character, the book," as the author himself confesses in the Introduction to the Second Edition, "counts on further co-authorship: it counts on the fact that it will be continually created, as it were, by those who will thoroughly—both in theory and in practice—ponder or implement its main formulations." Hence, being open to every echo of experience that originates from any side, this work at the same time appeals to the reader to let experience speak in its entire scope, both in its breadth and depth.

When we speak of depth here, we mean all that which sometimes does not appear directly and in the foreground as a content of experience, but which, in a hidden way, as it were, belongs to experience in such a manner that it is impossible not to consider it when identifying the contents of experience. For otherwise, some of this content would be diminished, depleted, thereby canceling the authority of the integrally understood experience—experience as the only source of information and the basis for genuine knowledge about anything. Taking this methodological foundation as a basis, *Love and Responsibility* does not need to be apprehensive about anything that can provide its credentials by experience. Experience that is properly interpreted is not threatened by any further experiences. Truth can only benefit from this confrontation.

The history of *Love and Responsibility* seen precisely from that perspective manifests a peculiar vitality of this book. Of course, speaking about its "triumphant march" would be a simplification. It is known that the "rediscovery" or "resurrection" of the book was not simply due to the circumstance that its author became the pope. *Love and Responsibility* has lived and lives not only by the editions that came to be: three Polish (including two in Poland, which is remarkable due to the publishing difficulties!) and a few in foreign languages: French, Italian, and Spanish.* It also lives in a certain way by the editions that were to be published but never have been.

Although, twenty years after its publication, the work does not need a recommendation, it is obvious that it needs, in a sense, to be presented in a new context. What determines this context? Speaking most generally, two complementary "coordinates" determine it.

On the one hand, this context is determined by the discussion about the central problems that Pope Paul VI took up in the encyclical *Humanae Vitae*. As is known, this discussion—which in its first phase concentrated on the sometimes uncoordinated search for arguments for and against contraception in order to win over supporters in the dispute—over time turned into a methodologically deepened self-reflection. The discussion became centered on the way of substantiating moral norms in the aspect of their rightness.† Hence, from that point on, without fundamentally questioning the rightness of the norms of *Humanae Vitae*, some discussed the scope of their force. The decision concerning this particular problem was made dependent on resolving the issue between the deontological and the teleological theory of ethical argumentation. A deeper analysis of the object of this dispute, however, manifests a greater complexity of the problems in question

---

* The current list of editions: Polish: Lublin 1960, Kraków 1962, London 1965; French: Paris 1965, 1978; Spanish: Madrid 1969, 1978—eight editions, 1979—two editions; Italian: Torino 1969, 1978, 1979; German: Munich 1979; English: London 1979; Portugal: Saõ Paulo 1979; Swedish: Uppsala 1979; Japanese: Tokyo 1979. [*The current list of editions*: Of course, this list was up-to-date in 1979. The following major editions have appeared since then: Polish: Lublin 1979, 1982, 1986, 2001; French: Paris 1985; Spanish: Madrid 1980, 1983, Barcelona 1996; English: London 1981, San Francisco 1993, 1994; German: Munich 1981, Kleinhain (Austria) 2010, 2011 (Fr. Josef Spindelböck's translation) — Trans.].

† Cf. footnote, p. 146.

and at the same time a possibility—or even a necessity—of an intermediary position, which could surprise the two parties contending with each other. It also manifested that at the basis of a solution that could find full acceptance, there must appear, on the one hand, a genuine anthropology: a theory of the human person, and, on the other hand, a deepened vision of the act itself. It manifested in particular that the moment of the rightness of the act must not become isolated, so that it ends up separated from the fundamental function of the act in the interpersonal relations: the function of expressing* love, that is, of affirming the person due to the dignity proper to him in an inalienable way. It is by all means interesting to look at this whole discussion ten years after the appearance of the encyclical *Humanae Vitae* from the perspective of the work that preceded it by almost ten years—the work which is completely alien to any atmosphere of animosity, contestation, or contention, the work whose atmosphere is defined completely by one and only one concern: to let the truth of experience express itself fully on the theme of love worthy of the human person.[5] But precisely for this very reason there exists a need of situating this work in that context and of presenting it against the background of that context. This very need demands the introduction of the notes, which fulfill the role of a commentary linking the text of *Love and Responsibility* with the aforementioned context. A commentary of this kind becomes simply indispensable here.

On the other hand, we must not overlook the fact that during these twenty years the author of *Love and Responsibility* published many articles in which he developed the themes of the book in various directions, in particular in the direction of family ethics and of the philosophy and theology of the body. The need to consider this strictly authorial context seems completely obvious. At first it even suggested an idea of adding an appendix to *Love and Responsibility* containing the aforementioned publications. However, besides the fact that such an appendix would have greatly increased the size of the book, another reason was brought forward against this idea. Actually, this appendix would have excluded another work of the author, a work of exceptional significance for

---

* Cf. footnote †, p. 211.

forming this context. This work is *Person and Act* (*Osoba i czyn*), in which the author expressed himself most fully—although in a fundamentally extra-ethical way—on the theme of the human person. There is no need to waste words in order to convince anyone how much the issues covered by that work are related to the problem of responsible love, the main problem of *Love and Responsibility*. After all, precisely the person in his act and through his act becomes the subject and recipient of this responsible love. The person is an actor of this drama—persona dramatis—in which he himself writes "his truest history," the history of love or of its negation, and hence of his fulfillment or nonfulfillment. The text of *Love and Responsibility* would be impoverished in its fundamental framework if it was not at least in some way linked to the text of *Person and Act*, if it was not presented in the context of Karol Wojtyła's "treatise on man." This is the second reason contributing to both the necessity of introducing a commentary and the character of the commentary.

In the notes we placed below the text of *Love and Responsibility*,[6] the reader will find, on the one hand, references to works by the author himself and, on the other hand, references that will present his work as a call to confront the propositions and notions that differ not so much from the author's work, but rather through it—as if through a *medium quo*[7]—from the eloquence of the integral, ethical experience of one person's love for another person. And love—as is constantly confirmed precisely by experience—is what it is only when it rises to the level of affirmation of the personal dignity of both the subject of love and its recipient in everything whence this dignity proceeds, what it permeates, and in which it is ultimately rooted.

Fr. Tadeusz Styczeń
Jerzy Gałkowski
Adam Rodziński
Fr. Andrzej Szostek[*]

Lublin, May 18, 1979

---

[*] A note from the Polish editors: At the author's request, the word division in some cases has been preserved by using a hyphen (-) instead of forming compound words.[8]

# Author's Introduction to the First Polish Edition (1960)

There exists a view that only married people may speak about marriage, and that only persons who experience (*przeżywać*) love between a man and a woman may speak about such love.[1] This view demands personal and direct experience as the basis for speaking in a given field. Thus, priests, the religious, and celibate persons cannot have anything to say on matters of love and marriage.[2] Nevertheless, they often speak and write on those topics. A lack of their own personal experience does not hinder them since they possess a very rich indirect experience proceeding from pastoral work. For in pastoral work they encounter precisely these problems so often and in such a variety of ways and situations that another experience is created, experience that is undoubtedly more indirect and "alien," but at the same time much more extensive. Indeed, the abundance of facts from this field prompts all the more a general reflection and a search for synthesis.

That is how this book came into being. It is not an exposition of doctrine. Instead, it is above all the fruit of constant confrontation of doctrine with life (and the work of a pastor consists precisely in this). The doctrine—the teaching of the Church—in the field of "sexual" morality is based on the Gospel, whose statements on that topic are both concise and sufficient. One wonders that a system so complete can be built on the basis of so few statements. They apparently concern the cruces of the problem, the decisive points, which determine all the remaining moral principles and norms. It is sufficient to be familiar with texts such as Matthew 5:27–28, Matthew 19:1–13, Mark 10:1–12, Luke 20:27–35, John 8:1–11, 1 Corinthians 7 (the entire chapter), and Ephesians 5:22–33 in order to form quite clear views on the given topic. In this book (which does not constitute an exegetical study) we refer to these most important statements.

Although simply compiling the norms of Catholic ethics regarding "sexual" morality is easy, the need to substantiate these norms arises with every step. For these norms often encounter resistance, perhaps more so in practice than in theory, but a pastor, who above all deals with practice, must seek the reasons for them. For his task is not only to command or to prohibit, but also to substantiate, interpret, and explain. This book was born principally from the need to substantiate the norms of Catholic sexual ethics—and to do so as definitively as possible while appealing to the most elementary and undeniable moral truths and to the most fundamental values or goods. Such a good is the person, and the moral truth most closely connected to the world of persons in particular is the "commandment to love"—for love is the good proper to the world of persons. And therefore the most fundamental grasp of sexual morality is to grasp it on the basis of "love and responsibility"— hence the title of the whole book.

Such a grasp demands a number of analyses. Notwithstanding its synthetic character, the book is strongly analytical. The object of the analysis is at first the person in relation to the sexual drive, then love which grows between a man and a woman on the foundation of this drive, then the virtue of chastity as an unavoidable factor of that love, and finally the issue of marriage and vocation. All these problems are the object of analyses and not of descriptions, for the point is precisely to explicate the rationale to which the rules and norms of the Catholic "sexual" ethics owe their *raison d'être*.[3] This book has a philosophical character throughout, for ethics is (and can only be) a part of philosophy.

Is the book practical and "relevant to real life"? In principle it is, although nowhere does it endeavor to present some ready-made formulas or punctilious prescriptions of conduct.[4] It is not casuistic, but attempts to create an integral vision of the problem rather than to provide particular solutions—for all of them in some way are included in this vision. The title of the book is its most proper expression: in reference to the relations that occur among persons of different sex, when we speak of "sexual ethics" we actually think about "love and responsibility."

The main concept here is the concept of love, to which we devote most analyses—and in a sense even all the analyses contained in this book. For particularly on the basis of the Christian ethics born of the Gospel, a problem exists, which can be described as an "introduction of love into love."[5] In the first instance the word "love" signifies the content of the greatest commandment, whereas in the second instance all that is formed on the basis of the sexual drive between a man and a woman. Proceeding in the opposite direction, one can say that a problem exists of reducing the latter love to the former one, i.e., to the love of which the Gospel speaks.

This is an open problem. The manuals of ethics and of moral theology grasp these two loves somewhat separately: they speak of the former in the treatise on the theological virtues, because love is the greatest of these virtues, whereas they speak of the latter chiefly within the treatise on the cardinal virtue of temperance, since sexual chastity is linked to it. Consequently, what may arise in human consciousness is a certain hiatus, some sense of irreducibility of the latter love to the former one—or in any case an unawareness of the ways in which this can be realized. At the same time, observation of life (and especially pastoral experience) proves that an enormous demand exists for knowing those ways. And the moral teaching of the Gospel seems to create a clear inspiration for it. Both believers and nonbelievers read the Gospel. The former discover in the commandment to love the main bond of the whole supernatural order, but both believers and nonbelievers are able to discover in this commandment an affirmation of some great human good, in which persons can and should share. In this book it is rather on the latter that we place the main emphasis.

It is a common opinion that the problems of "sex" are *eo ipso*[6] above all the problems of the "body."[7] Hence, there arises a tendency to grant competency in that field almost exclusively to physiology and medicine, and secondarily to psychology. It is also supposed that these sciences will by themselves produce ethical norms. This book grasps this problem in a fundamentally different way. Sexual ethics is a domain of the person. Nothing in it can be comprehended without understanding the person, his being, action, and rights. The personal order is the only plane proper to all reflections in the field of sexual ethics. Physiology or medicine can only supplement these reflections. By themselves they do not constitute a full basis for understanding love and responsibility, yet this is precisely the point in the mutual relations between persons of different sex.

Therefore, all the reflections contained in this book possess a personalistic character. Physiological and medical details will be placed in the footnotes.[*] At this point, I take the opportunity to thank those persons who facilitated my organizing of those details as well as compiling and reviewing a certain number of bibliographical items.

THE AUTHOR

---

[*] Regardless of this announcement, the author introduced these details within the main text by using parentheses. Additionally, "some remarks on the relation of sexology to ethics" are presented in chapter V of this edition as a "supplementary view."

# Author's Introduction to the Second Polish Edition (1962)

The book titled *Love and Responsibility*, which was first printed in 1960 due to the efforts of Towarzystwo Naukowe KUL, is hereby published the second time by the Znak publishing house. Problems of sexual ethics are the subject of this book, which is therefore addressed to all those interested in these problems either theoretically or practically. At the beginning of the second edition, just as at the beginning of the first one, some explanations are due concerning the genesis of the book as well as its conception and structure. It is also proper to say right away that the book owes its existence to many co-authors. Some of them consciously supported the author in writing the book, helping him in various ways, for which I wish to thank them cordially. Others contributed to its creation unknowingly by providing incentives for writing it. This, however, is linked to the problem of the book's genesis.

*Love and Responsibility* came to be on the basis of two sources, which concurrently provided elements for it. In order to understand these sources and the whole mechanism of their cooperation, one must consider the fact that the author of the book is a priest. Yet priests, as well as the religious, are often denied the competency to speak on sexual matters, precisely on the grounds that they do not personally encounter them the way that lay married people do, that they do not possess personal experience in that field. Due to that fact it must be underscored that it is precisely experience—the indirect experience provided by pastoral work—that is one of the two sources of this book. This work so often places the priest or the religious face to face with sexual problems, in so many diverse moments or situations, that quite a specific experience ensues as a result. It is granted that this experience is not personal but "alien" instead, although at the same time it is more extensive than any exclusively personal experience. It must be added at once that this experience differs from the specialized experience of persons—such as physicians—who also encounter sexual problems in the wide sector of various facts. The point of view specifying this experience is different.

Concerning the genesis of the book, the function of experience is not in any case exclusive, or the only one. Precisely due to the state of the author, besides the experience—yet in a sense through the pastoral experience—a second source was at work. That superior source is the Gospel together with its extension, the teaching of the Church. This source fostered reflections, whereas experience provided facts for confrontation with doctrine. The Gospel contains relatively few texts that speak directly about sexual and conjugal ethics, for example Matthew 5:27–28, Matthew 19:1–13, Mark 10:1–12, Luke 20:27–35, John 8:1–11, 1 Corinthians 7 (the entire chapter), and Ephesians 5:22–33, not to mention extremely significant texts in the Old Testament, especially in Genesis.[1] All the above mentioned passages organically inhere in the whole of the Gospel and must be read in this whole as in their essential context. Read in this way, they give an incentive for philosophical reflection. After all, it is well known that not only theology, which employed philosophy as a tool of intellectual speculation, came to be on the basis of Revelation. Revelation also provided a powerful impetus for philosophy—it is sufficient only to mention the conception of being that St. Thomas developed. So it seems that in a somewhat similar manner the Gospel provides an impetus for philosophical reflections concerning sexual problems.

These problems pertain to morality, for this is how they appear in the Gospel and in the teaching of the Church. Therefore, philosophical reflections on them must assume the character of a certain study of ethics (or of "an ethical study," as the subtitle indicates).[2] After all, the aspect of morality is most essential in all sexual problems, as indicated indirectly even by sexology. Morality is a separate sphere of human existence, and especially of human action, that is connected with consciousness and free will. Based on consciousness and free will human acts possess a moral value; they are morally good or bad. As a separate sphere of philosophical reflection, ethics is based on the fact of morality in order to seek above all the rationale for moral good and evil. It is not content with a mere presentation of the norms that direct human morality, but attempts to penetrate more profoundly and explain why human acts in conformity with these norms are morally good or otherwise morally bad. In our case, one of the aforementioned sources, namely experience, draws us closer to the facts concerning a living sexual or conjugal morality. The other source, that is, the Gospel, not only provides ready-made norms, rules of conduct in the field of sexual and conjugal morality, but also considerably helps us in finding the proper rationale for these norms. Thanks to this, it enables philosophical reflection—that is, in our case, ethical reflection in particular—on the totality of sexual problems. The subtitle of the book, namely "an ethical study," is thereby justified.

Reflection based on the above mentioned sources leads to the personalistic grasp of sexual-conjugal problems, which essentially denotes the main conception of the book. This is evident from the very plan of the book, where chapter I is titled "The Person and the Drive," chapter II "The Person and Love," and chapter III "The Person and Chastity." Chapter IV, "Justice with Respect to the Creator," perhaps more than the others, concerns the religious presuppositions and consequences of personalism in the sector of sexual ethics. Finally, chapter V constitutes only an attempt (quite incomplete at that) to confront that position in ethics with propositions and recommendations of biological and medical sexology. One must admit that throughout the book biology and medicine occupy much less space than psychology—that is also a consequence of the personalistic conception adopted in the book. The person, even in the sexual sphere, is above all characterized by his "psyche." *Nota bene*,[3] this psychology possesses in the book a philosophical character, although we very often attempt to proceed by way of phenomenological analysis.

Already in the introduction it is difficult to answer the question whether this book is practical and "relevant to real life." The answer is important with respect to the recipients of the book. So, as in the first edition, in relation to which this edition is modified a little, I would like to emphasize that nowhere does the book endeavor to present some ready-made formulas or punctilious prescriptions of conduct. It is not casuistic, but attempts to create an integral vision of the problem rather than to provide particular solutions, which nonetheless are already in some way included in this integral vision. The title of the book, *Love and Responsibility*, seems to indicate this sufficiently. At the same time, while possessing that character, the book counts on further co-author-ship: it counts on the fact that it will be continually created, as it were, by those who will thoroughly—both in theory and in practice—ponder or implement its main formulations.

THE AUTHOR

## Chapter I

# The Person and the Drive

# Part One

# Analysis of the Verb "to use"

## *The person as the subject and object of action*

The world in which we live consists of many objects. The word "object" in this case signifies more or less the same as "a being" (*byt*).[1] This is not the proper meaning of this word, for properly speaking an "object" signifies what is posited in relation to some "subject." The subject is also a being—a being that in some way exists and acts. It can be said accordingly that the world in which we live consists of many subjects. It would even be suitable to speak about subjects before objects. If this order has been reversed here, this was done in order to emphasize from the first words of this book objectivity, and realism together with it. For when we start from the subject, and in particular from man as the subject, then it is easy to treat everything else that is located outside the subject, namely the whole world of objects, in a merely subjective way, that is, inasmuch as this world reaches the subject's consciousness, lives in it, and embeds itself in it. It must be clearly recognized from the beginning that every subject is at the same time an objective being, that it is an objective something or somebody.*

---

* "In the field of experience man appears as a particular '*suppositum*' and at the same time as a concrete 'I,' each time unique and unrepeatable. It is the experience of man in a twofold meaning at once, for the one *who* experiences is man, and he *whom* the subject of experience experiences is also man—man as the subject and the object at the same time. The objectivity of experience belongs to its essence, as experience is always of 'something' or of 'somebody,' and hence the man-subject is given in experience also in an objective way. Experience in a sense ousts in human cognition the notion of 'pure subjectivity' ('pure consciousness'), or rather it summons all this, which deepened our knowledge about man on the basis of this notion to the dimensions of objective reality" (K. Wojtyła, "Osoba: podmiot i wspólnota" [The Person: Subject and Community], *Roczniki Filozoficzne* 24, fasc. 2 [1976], 7. [Herein after cited as "Osoba: podmiot i wspólnota"].) In *Osoba i czyn* (*Person and Act*) the author takes up the analysis of many facts from the sphere of the dynamic whole "man acts," the facts that preserve their real objectivity only in man's subjectivity. Justified limits to the fear of falling into subjectivism must be set in the name of precisely these facts.

Man is objectively a "somebody"—and this distinguishes him from the rest of the beings of the visible world, the beings that objectively are always merely "something." This simple, elementary distinction conceals a deep abyss that divides the world of persons from the world of things. The objective world, to which we belong, consists of persons and things. A thing is customarily considered a being that is deprived not only of reason, but also of life; a thing is an inanimate object. We will hesitate to call an animal or even a plant a thing. However, nobody speaks convincingly about an animal person. Instead, one speaks about animal individuals, regarding them simply as specimens of a given animal species. And such a description suffices. Yet, it is not sufficient to speak of man as an individual of the species *Homo sapiens*. The word "person" has been coined in order to stress that man cannot be reduced wholly to what is contained in the concept of a "specimen of the species," but has in himself something more, some particular fullness and perfection of being. To emphasize this fullness and perfection the word "person" must necessarily be used.

The most proximate and the most proper reason for this is the fact that man possesses reason, that he is a rational being, which by no means can be stated about any other being of the visible world, for in none of them do we encounter any trace of conceptual thinking. What issued hence is the well-known definition of Boethius, according to which the person is simply an individual of a rational nature (*individua substantia rationalis naturae*).[2] This distinguishes the person in the whole world of objective beings; this constitutes the person's distinctness.

The fact that the person is an individual of a rational nature—that is, an individual to whose nature reason belongs—makes the person at the same time the only subject of its kind among the whole world of beings, a subject that differs completely from subjects such as animals, i.e., beings (especially some of them) that are relatively most similar to man with respect to their bodily constitution. Speaking somewhat descriptively, it must be said that the person as a subject differs from even the most perfect animals by his *interiority* and a specific life, which is concentrated in it, i.e., an interior life. One cannot speak about this life in the case of animals, even though bio-physiological processes, which are similar to man's and which are related to the constitution that is more or less similar to that of man, take place inside their organisms.

On the basis of this constitution a more or less abundant sensual life develops in them—a life whose functions extend far beyond the elementary vegetation of plants and sometimes deceptively resemble the typical functions of human life: cognition (*poznanie*) and desire (*pożądanie*), or, speaking somewhat more broadly about the former function, striving (*dążenie*).

Cognition and desire in man take on a spiritual character, and therefore they contribute to the formation of the true interior life, which does not occur in animals. The interior life is the spiritual life. It focuses on truth and the good. It also deals with a multitude of problems; it seems that the most central of these are the following two: what is the final cause of everything, and how to be good and possess the fullness of the good. The first of these central problems of man's interior life primarily engages cognition, whereas the other one engages desire, or rather striving. Besides, both of these functions seem to be something more than functions; they are rather some natural orientations of the whole man-being. It is remarkable that precisely through his interiority and interior life man not only is a person, but at the same time mostly through them inheres in the objective world, in the "external" world, where he inheres in the manner proper and characteristic to him. The person is an objective being, which, as a definite subject, most closely contacts the whole (external) world and most thoroughly inheres in it precisely through his interiority and interior life. It must be added that he contacts in this way not only the visible world, but also the invisible one, and above all God. And this is another manifestation of the person's distinctness in the visible world.

The contact of the person with the objective world, with reality, is not merely "biological" (*przyrodniczy*), physical, as is the case with all other creations of nature (*przyroda*), nor only sensual, as is the case with animals.[3] The human person, as a distinctly definite subject, establishes contact with other beings precisely through his interiority, whereas the whole "biological" contact, which also belongs to him—for the person possesses a body and even in a sense "is a body"—and the sensual contact in the likeness of animals do not constitute for him the characteristic ways of connecting with the world.[4] Although the connection of the human person with the world begins on the "biological" and sensual basis, it is nevertheless formed in the manner proper to man only in the orbit of the interior life. Here appears a moment characteristic of the person: man not only appropriates the content that reaches him from the external world and reacts to it in a spontaneous or even downright mechanical manner, but in all his relation to this world, to reality, he attempts to make his mark, to state his "I"—and he has to act this way since this is demanded by the nature of his being. Man has a fundamentally different nature from animals. His nature includes the power of self-determination based on reflection and manifested in the fact that, while acting, man chooses what he wants to do.* This power is called free will.[5]

Thanks to the fact that man—a person—possesses free will, he is also a master of himself, *sui iuris*, as the Latin phrase declares of the person.[6] A second characteristic property of the person remains closely linked to this distinctive feature of his. The Latin of philosophers grasped this property in the statement that the person is *alteri incommunicabilis*—nontransferable, incommunicable.[7] The point in this case is not to emphasize that the person is always some unique and unrepeatable being, as this can also be stated about any other being: about an animal, a plant, or a stone. This nontransferability or incommunicability of the person is most closely linked with his interiority, with self-determination, with free will. No one else can will in my stead.[8] No one can substitute his act of the will for mine. It happens that sometimes someone wants very much for me to want what he wants. What is then best made manifest is this impassable boundary between him and me, the boundary that is determined precisely by free will. I can not want what he wants me to want—and precisely in this I am *incommunicabilis*. I am and should be self-reliant in my actions.[9] All human interactions are based on this presupposition, and the truth about education (*wychowanie*) and about culture is reduced to it.[10]

---

* The author performed detailed analyses on the power of self-determination and its structure in his study *Person and Act*, part II, titled "Transcendence of the Person in the Act" (Kraków, 1969), 107–196. [*Person and Act*: The Polish editors reference the first Polish edition of Wojtyła's masterpiece *Person and Act* (*Osoba i czyn*) published by the Polish Theological Society in Kraków in 1969. I retained the page references, but also wherever possible I added additional description such as chapters and sections for ease of locating the cited passages in any edition of *Person and Act*. — Trans.]

For man is not only the subject of action, but he also at times is its object.[11] At every step acts occur that have the other man as their object. Within the theme of this book, which is sexual morality, we will continually speak precisely about such acts. In relations between persons of different sex, and especially in sexual intercourse, a woman is constantly an object of some action of a man, and a man, an object of a woman's action. Therefore, first it would be proper to become aware, at least briefly, of who is the one who acts—the subject, and who is the one toward whom the action turns—the object of action. It is already known that both the subject and the object of action are persons. Now, we need to consider well the principles that the action of man must comply with when the object of this action is another human person.*

## *The first meaning of the verb "to use"*

Precisely for this purpose we must thoroughly analyze the verb "to use." It signifies a certain objective form of action. To use means to employ some object of action as a means to an end, namely to the end for which the acting subject strives. The end is always that for the sake of which we act. The end also suggests the existence of means (by means we understand the objects on which our action centers for the sake of the end we intend to attain). By nature, then, a means is subordinated to an end, and, at the same time, it is also to a certain degree subordinated to the one who acts. It cannot be otherwise, since the one who acts makes use of means for the sake of his end—the very expression suggests a subordinate and, so to speak, "servile" relation of the means with respect to the acting subject: the means serves both the end and the subject.

---

*The term "object" in the expression "the human person as the object of action of another human person" is used in the broad sense, which corresponds to the objectivistic (objective) philosophical perspective that the author adopted from the beginning of the discourse (see footnote, p. 3). This meaning of the object should not be confused with another, more narrow meaning, which the author will apply when speaking about the possibility of treating the human person as an "object of use" (see p. 14). To treat somebody as an object of use means to treat him exclusively as a means to an end, as a thing, without respecting the person's own finality that belongs to him.

So, it seems beyond doubt that various things or beings, which are only individuals, that is, specimens of their species, can and should remain in such a relation to man-person. Man in his diverse activity makes use of the whole created world. He takes advantage of its resources for these ends, which he posits himself, because he alone understands them. This attitude of man toward inanimate nature (*przyroda*), whose riches mean so much to economic life, or toward animate nature (*przyroda*), whose energy and values man assimilates, in principle does not raise doubts. The only thing that is demanded from the rational human being is that he does not destroy and squander these natural resources, and that he uses them with the moderation that will not impede the personal development of man himself and will guarantee for human societies a just and harmonious coexistence. In particular, concerning the relation to animals—the beings endowed with sensation and sensibility to pain—it is demanded from man that the use of these beings never involves torment or physical torture.[*]

All these are simple principles that are easily understandable by every normal man. The problem begins when a relation to another man, to another human person is concerned. Is it permissible to treat this person as a means to an end and use him in this manner? The problem posited in this question possesses a very broad scope; it extends over many spheres of human life and interactions. Let us take, for example, such cases as the organization of work in a factory, the relation of a commanding officer to a soldier in an army, or even the relation of parents to a child in a family. Does not the employer use a worker, thus a human person, for the purpose of attaining the ends he chose himself?

---

[*] Thus, what generates duty in the moral sense with respect to the subject-person is not only persons due to their proper value called dignity, but also non-personal beings due to the inherent value proper to them, in particular living beings, especially those capable of suffering. These beings, however, not only may but even should be treated instrumentally (by becoming an object of use and consumption), whenever such treatment turns out to be the only way of effectively affirming a person or persons. However, purely instrumental treatment of one person for the sake ("for the good") of another or even of all the remaining ones would be impermissible. This essential difference allows us to define the chief ethical principle more narrowly, in relation to the whole scope of the field of moral duty, and to express it in the form of the "personalistic norm," that is, a postulate for the affirmation of the person. The intended narrowing of the scope of this principle is justified by the completely exceptional rank of the personal dignity, that is, of the value incomparable to anything in the world outside the world of persons.

Does not the commanding officer employ soldiers under his command for conducting certain military objectives, which are intended by him and sometimes known only by him? Do not parents, who alone understand the ends for which they educate their children, treat the children in a sense as means to an end, since the children themselves do not understand those ends and do not consciously strive for them? Yet both a worker and a soldier are adults and fully-mature (*pełnowartościowy*)[12] persons, and a child—even if unborn—cannot be denied personhood in the most objective ontological sense, even though it is true that the child is meant to acquire only gradually many characteristics that determine that personhood in the psychological and ethical senses.[13]

The same problem will emerge as we delve deeply into the analysis of the whole reciprocal woman-man relation, which is the basis for the reflections in the field of sexual ethics.* We will discover this problem in, so to speak, various layers of our analysis. Does not a woman in sexual intercourse serve for a man as something of a means for him to attain various ends of his, precisely those ends that he seeks to realize in sexual intercourse? Similarly, does not a man serve for a woman as a means of attaining her own ends?

For the time being let us be content with posing questions that implicate a very essential ethical problem—a problem that is not first of all psychological but precisely ethical.† For a person should not be

---

* The author specifies and develops the personalistic understanding of Catholic sexual ethics in a separate article titled "Zagadnienie katolickiej etyki seksualnej. Refleksje i postulaty" (The Problem of Catholic Sexual Ethics: Reflections and Postulates), *Roczniki Filozoficzne* 13, fasc. 2 (1965), 5–25; herein after cited as "Zagadnienie katolickiej etyki seksualnej," *Roczniki Filozoficzne*.

† The author has dealt a number of times with the distinction between the psychological and the ethical analyses. He took up the problem of the relation between psychology and ethics most extensively in the article "Zagadnienie woli w analizie aktu etycznego" (The Problem of the Will in the Analysis of the Ethical Act), *Roczniki Filozoficzne* 5, fasc. 1 (1955–57), 111–135. Psychology and ethics meet at the point of origin, which in this case is the fact of the interior experience of human efficacy (cf. *Person and Act*, 27–106, part I: "Consciousness and Efficacy"). The grasp of the fact of efficacy by contemporary psychology displays the validity of Thomas Aquinas' analyses in this area, as well as a certain shortcoming in the analyses by Immanuel Kant and Max Scheler. Psychology and ethics grasp efficacy as an essential element of the lived-experience of the will, and see the will as the core of experiencing (*przeżywać*) efficacy. At this point, the paths of these two disciplines part, although further analyses still manifest other points of convergence. By the experimental-inductive method, psychology strives for discovering particular mechanisms of the will's

merely a means to an end for another person.* This is excluded due to the very nature of the person, due to what every person simply is. For the person is a subject that is thinking and capable of self-determination—these are two properties that first of all we discover in the interiority of the person. Accordingly then, every person is capable by his nature to define his ends himself.[14] When someone else treats a person exclusively as a means to an end, then the person is violated in what belongs to his very essence and at the same time constitutes his natural right. It is clear that it must be demanded from the person, as a thinking individual, that those ends be truly good, for striving for evil ends is contrary to the rational nature of the person.† This also explains the sense of education, both the education of children as well as the reciprocal education of people in general. The point is precisely to seek true ends, that is, true goods as ends of action, and to find and show ways for their realization.

But in this educational activity, especially in the case of educating small children, a person must never be treated as a means to an end. This

---

action, for grasping concrete motives that provide a beginning for the realization of a chosen end. On the other hand, ethical analyses strive for a full explication of the lived-experience of efficacy through grasping and characterizing an end—a moral value. Efficacy here is understood as a source of the ethical value, i.e., that through which man becomes good or evil in the moral sense, which can be comprehended *sensu lato* (good or evil interiorly as man), or in a way that is personalistically qualified (true in attitudes and conduct to the value that is the person). [*Sensu lato*: In the broader sense. —Trans.]

* In accord with the intention of the author of this principle, Immanuel Kant (*Uzasadnienie metafizyki moralności* [*Groundwork of the Metaphysics of Morals*], Warsaw, 1953, 62), the "merely" here means that the person as the possessor of his nature (understood substantially) can undertake, without harm to himself, a role of, or even serve unknowingly a function of "a means to an end," on the condition that this end of another is honorable, and that the one who "uses" the person's physical or psychological forces is ready to put the person's inalienable value before an end he strives for in a given case, if an axiological conflict of this kind occurs. In the further course of his reflections, whenever the author has in mind the strictly personal (relational) subjectivity of man rather than the substantial one, then he omits the "merely" stating, for example, that "Kant demands that ( . . . ) we should never treat a person as a means to an end, but always only as an end" (see p. 21 in this book).

† The expression "the nature of the person" can be understood in a twofold sense: 1) "nature" as the essence of a human being that manifests itself in action that is innate to this being and hence in this sense proper; 2) "nature" as the specificity or constitution of the person's strictly personal subjectivity (possessing relational, axiological provenience) that is proper to the person as person (and not as substance). In the further course of his reflections, the author employs both meanings of "nature." Here, both of them come into play together and in solidarity, although each in its own way.

principle has the most universal scope; no one may use a person as a means to an end: neither any man nor even God the Creator.* Indeed, this is excluded most completely on the part of God, because he, by the very fact of giving a rational and free nature to the person, decided that the person himself will define the ends of action and will not serve as a tool for the ends of others. Therefore, if God intends to direct man to some ends, first and foremost he lets him know these ends, so that man can make them his own and strive for them on his own.[15] In this, among others, lies the deepest logic of Revelation: God lets man know the supernatural end, but the decision to strive for this end, its choice, is left to man's freedom.[16] Therefore, God does not save man against his will.

This elementary truth—that the person may not be a means of action as opposed to all other objects of action, which are not persons—is thus the exponent of the natural moral order. Thanks to this truth, this order acquires personalistic properties: the order of nature, which also includes personal beings, must possess such properties. Perhaps it is not irrelevant to add at this point that at the end of the eighteenth century Immanuel Kant formulated this elementary principle of the moral order in the following imperative: "Act in such a way so that the person is never a mere means of your action, but always an end."[17] In light of the previous reflections, this principle should not so much be formulated in the wording Kant gave to it, but rather as follows: "Whenever the person is an object of action in your conduct, remember that you may not treat him merely as a means to an end, as a tool, but [you must] take into account that the person himself has or at least should have his end."[18] The principle thus formulated stands at the basis of every properly comprehended freedom of man, especially freedom of conscience.†

---

* The author reflects in more detail on the proper interpretation of the laws of God the Creator with respect to the human person in the article "O znaczeniu miłości oblubieńczej" (On the Meaning of Spousal Love), *Roczniki Filozoficzne* 22, fasc. 2 (1974), especially 166–172 (see pp. 281–291 in this book).

† For conscience reveals essential *truth* about man as a person, and—according to the author—precisely the relation to truth belongs to the essence of freedom, and of conscience that binds freedom: "Freedom is due to the human person not as pure independence, but as self-dependence, which contains dependence on truth [ . . . ], and this is most vividly manifested in conscience [ . . . ]. The proper and complete function of conscience consists in making the act depend on truth" (*Person and Act*, 162–163, in section 2 of chapter IV).

## Love as the opposite of "using"

The whole previous reflection on the first meaning of the verb "to use" gives us only a negative solution to the problem of the proper relation to the person. The person may not be either exclusively or first and foremost an object of use, because the role of a blind tool or a means to an end intended by another subject is contrary to the nature of the person.

In turn, when we seek a positive solution to the same problem, then love appears—but only, so to speak, at first glance—as the only distinct opposite of using the person in the role of a means to an end or of a tool of one's own action. For it is evident that I can strive for the other person to will the same good that I will. Clearly, this other person must recognize this end of mine and acknowledge it as a good; he must make it also his own end. Then, between myself and this other person a particular bond is born: the bond of a *common good* and a common end, which binds us. This particular bond is not limited to the fact that we strive together for a common good, but unites the acting persons "from within"—and then it constitutes the essential core of every love. In any case, love between persons is unthinkable without some common good, which binds them.* This good precisely is at the same time the end which both of these persons choose. When different persons consciously choose an end together, this makes them equal to each other, thereby excluding a subordination of one person to another. So, both persons (although more than two persons can be bound by a common end) are in a sense uniformly and equally subordinated to that good, which constitutes a common end. When we look at man, then we perceive in him an elementary need for the good, a

---

*The common good is understood here basically in a personalistic way. "The point is the truly personalistic structure of human existence in the community to which man belongs. The common good is the good of the community precisely because it creates in the axiological sense the conditions of being together, and action follows that. It can be said that in the axiological order the common good determines a community, a society, or a commune. We define each of these on the basis of the common good that is proper to it. We then take action (*operari*) together with being (*esse*). However, the common good reaches above all to the area of being 'together with others.' The very acting 'together with others' does not yet reveal the common good in such fullness of reality, although it must be present here as well" (*Person and Act*, 308–309, section 6 of chapter VII). (See K. Wojtyła, "Osoba: podmiot i wspólnota," *Roczniki Filozoficzne* 24, fasc. 2 [1976], 23.)

natural urge and tendency toward it—although this does not yet manifest the capacity to love. In animals we observe manifestations of instinct that are analogically directed. But instinct itself does not yet determine the capacity to love. People, however, possess such a capacity linked to free will. The capacity to love is determined by the fact that man is ready to seek the good consciously with others, to subordinate himself to this good because of others, or to subordinate himself to others because of this good. Only persons can love.

Love in reciprocal relations between people is not something readily available. Love is first of all a principle or an idea, which people must live up to, so to speak, in their conduct if they want—and they should want—to liberate it from a utilitarian, i.e., consumer (Latin *consumere*—to use up), attitude toward other persons.[19] Let us return for a moment to the examples put forward previously. A serious danger of treating the worker merely as a means exists in the employer-worker relationship; this is demonstrated by various faulty ways of organizing labor. If, however, the employer and the worker arrange their whole interaction in such a way that the common good, which they both serve, will be clearly visible in it, then the danger of treating the person as less than what he truly is will be diminished and almost eliminated. For love will gradually eliminate in the conduct of both interested parties a purely utilitarian or consumer attitude toward the person of the worker. Much has been simplified in this example while retaining only the essential core of the issue. The case is similar with the second example regarding the relation of the commanding officer to the soldier. When both of them are bound by a certain basic attitude of love (of course, the point does not concern the very affection of love) evoked by the shared search for the common good, which in this case is the defense or safety of the homeland, this is simply because they both desire the same thing. We cannot speak merely about using the person of the soldier as a blind tool or a means to an end.

This whole reflection* must be applied in turn to the woman-man relationship, which constitutes the basis of sexual ethics. In this

---

* The author devoted the last chapter of the book *Person and Act* ("Outline of the Theory of Participation," 285–326) and the article "Osoba: podmiot i wspólnota" to the problem—treated here in a very cursory way—concerning the proper structure of the interpersonal community.

relationship as well—and indeed particularly in it—only love is able to exclude the use of one person by another. Love, as has been said, is conditioned by the common relation of persons to the same good that they choose as an end and to which they subordinate themselves. Marriage is one of the most important areas for realizing this principle. For in marriage, two persons, a woman and a man, unite in such a way that they become in a sense "one flesh" (to use the words of the Book of Genesis), that is, so to speak, one common subject of sexual life.[20] How can it be ensured that a person does not then become for the other—a woman for a man, and a man for a woman—merely a means to an end, that is, an object used to attain only one's own end? In order to exclude this possibility, both of them must then have a common end. Concerning marriage, this end is procreation, progeny, the family, and at the same time the whole constantly growing maturity of the relationship between both persons in all the spheres brought by the spousal relationship itself.

This whole objective finality of marriage fundamentally creates the possibility of love, and fundamentally excludes the possibility of treating the person as a means to an end and as an object of use. However, in order for the former possibility to be realized within the framework of the objective finality of marriage, we must consider more attentively the very principle that excludes the possibility of one person treating another person as an object of use in the whole sexual context. The very recognition of the objective finality of marriage does not yet completely solve the problem.

For it seems that the sexual sphere in particular presents many occasions to treat the person—even unknowingly*—as an object of use. In

---

* It is evident that for the corresponding act (of benevolence) to be also an act of love it is not enough merely to *want* to affirm the other. What is also needed is that the act taken up by the intention of affirming another person is objectively *suitable* for the role determined by the intention of the agent. Whether it is suitable for this role or not is decided by the objective structure of the person-recipient. Only an accurate recognition of this structure, and taking it into account in action, guarantees that a given act has the mark of a genuine act of love. On the other hand, a faulty recognition of the structure of the person-recipient must become the source of the unknowing and consequently unintentional action to his detriment. This action is all the more dangerous because in this case using the other occurs in the name of love. The agent is unaware of this pretense, and this safeguards him from fault. Nonetheless, he becomes a doer of the act of anti-love out of love! Only being aware

addition, it must be taken into account that the entire sphere of sexual morality is broader than the sphere of conjugal morality alone, and that it encompasses many issues from the area of interaction or even coexistence of men and women. So, within the framework of this interaction or coexistence, all must constantly with all the conscientiousness and with a full sense of responsibility attend to this fundamental good of each and every one—the good that is simply "humanity," or, in other words, the value of the human person. If we treat this fundamental woman-man relationship as broadly as possible and not only within the boundaries of marriage, then love in this relationship is identified with a particular readiness to subordinate oneself to the good that is "humanity," or speaking more precisely, the value of the person, despite the whole distinctiveness of sex. In fact, this subordination by all means obliges in marriage itself, and the objective ends of this institution can be realized only in accord with this broadest principle that results from acknowledging the value of the person in the whole expanded sexual context. This context creates an altogether specific sphere of morality—whereas with respect to science, a specific sphere of ethical problems—in reference to both marriage and many other forms of interaction or simply of coexistence concerning persons of different sex.[21]

## *The second meaning of the verb "to use"*

In order to comprehend these problems in their totality, it is necessary to reflect further on the second meaning that is quite often applied to the verb "to use." Various *emotional-affective* moments or states accompany our thinking and acts of the will, i.e., what constitutes the objective structure of human action. They precede the action itself, go hand in hand with it, or finally manifest themselves in the consciousness of man when the action is already complete.[*] The emotional-affective

---

of the possibility of the danger of such disintegration (emotionalization) of love can lead efficiently to excluding this danger. See the "Introduction to First Edition," where the author formulates a postulate of "introducing love into love."

[*] See *Person and Act*, 51–56 and 258–275, for a more extensive treatment concerning the relation between consciousness and emotions.

moments or states themselves are a separate theme, as it were, which weaves and forces itself sometimes with great strength and insistence into the whole objective structure of human acts. An objective act itself would at times be something pale and almost unnoticeable to the consciousness of man if it were not manifested and sharply delineated in that consciousness by variously colored emotional-affective lived-experiences.[22] Moreover, these emotional and affective moments or states usually exercise some influence on what determines the objective structure of human acts.

For the time being we shall not analyze this problem in detail, for we shall need to return to it repeatedly throughout the book. At this point, our attention must be directed to one thing only: the emotional-affective moments and states, which mean so much in the whole interior life of man, are in principle colored positively or negatively, as if they contained in themselves a positive or negative interior charge. The positive charge is *pleasure*, whereas the negative one is *pain*. Pleasure occurs in various shapes or shades, depending on the emotional-affective lived-experiences to which it is bound: either as sensual satisfaction, as affective contentment, or as a deep and thorough joy. Pain also depends on the character of the emotional-affective lived-experiences evoking it and occurs in various shapes, kinds, or shades: as sensual pain, as affective discontent, or as deep sorrow.

Here we must turn our attention to the particular richness, variety, and intensity of these emotional-affective moments and states occurring when a person of the other sex is an object of action. They then color this action in a specific way and confer on it some exceptional vividness. This pertains especially to some actions that are linked with the reciprocal relations between persons of different sex and with sexual intercourse itself between a woman and a man. And therefore, precisely within the scope of these actions, the second meaning of the verb "to use" is particularly sharply delineated. To use means to experience (*przeżywać*) pleasure—the pleasure that in various shades is linked to action and to the object of action. It is known that this object of action in the reciprocal relations of a woman and a man and in their sexual intercourse is always a person. And the person becomes a proper source of variously colored pleasure or even delight.

It is an easily understandable fact that precisely one person is for another the source of lived-experiences that have a particular emotional-affective charge. For it is a person who must be for another person an equal object—a "partner" of action. This equality of the subject and the object of action constitutes a particular basis for emotional-affective lived-experiences, and for the emotional-affective positive or negative charges in the form of pleasure or pain that are linked to these lived-experiences. Also, it should not be supposed that a pleasure that is purely and exclusively sensual comes into play here. Such a supposition would diminish the natural greatness of a contact that in every case retains its inter-personal, human character. Even purely "bodily" love, due to the nature of partners who participate in it, does not cease to be a fact of this kind. Hence, for this reason, the sexual life of animals and people cannot be properly compared, although it is clear that in animals this life also exists and constitutes the basis of procreation, thus the preservation and extension of species. In animals, however, it exists on the level of nature and the instinct linked to it, whereas in the case of people it exists on the level of the person and morality. Sexual morality results from the fact that persons not only have a consciousness of the finality of sexual life, but also a consciousness of being persons. The whole moral problem of using as the opposite of loving is linked to this consciousness.[23]

This problem has been delineated previously concerning the first meaning of the verb "to use." The second meaning of this verb is equally important for morality. For man, since he possesses reason, can in his action not only clearly distinguish pleasure or pain, but also in a sense separate them and treat them as a distinct end of action. Then his acts are formed with regard to pleasure alone, which he wants to acquire, or exclusively with regard to pain, which he wants to avoid. Since acts related to the person of the other sex will be formed exclusively or even first and foremost because of that, then that person will become in a particular way only a means to an end—hence, as we can see, the second meaning of the verb "to use" constitutes a particular case of the first meaning. This case, however, is very frequent and can easily occur in the conduct of the man-person. Yet, it does not occur in the sexual life of animals, which takes place exclusively on the level of nature and instinct and therefore tends solely toward the end which the sexual drive serves, that is, toward procreation, the preservation of species. On this level, sexual pleasure—purely animal, of course—cannot constitute a separate end. It is different with man. Here, it is clear how personhood and rationality generate morality. This morality is in this case subjectively and objectively personalistic—objectively, because what is at stake is the proper relation to the person in the context of sexual pleasure.

The person (of the different sex) may not be for another person merely a means to an end, which is constituted by this sexual pleasure or even delight. A conviction that man is a person leads to accepting the postulate that using should be subordinated to loving. "To use," not only in the first meaning, the broader and objective one, but also in the second meaning, the rather narrower and subjective one—for by its nature the experience (*przeżywanie*) of pleasure is something subjective—may be interiorly ordered and elevated to the level of the persons only by love. Only "loving" excludes "using," also in that second meaning. Therefore, if ethics intends to fulfill its proper task in the area of sexual morality, it must—in the whole abundance and variety of actions, and perhaps also of human lived-experiences linked to this area—accurately distinguish "loving" a person from what is but "using" him, even when it keeps the appearance of love and uses love's name as its own. Consequently, in order to investigate this issue even more thoroughly on the basis of ethics as a scientific system (which after all finds its confirmation in morality that corresponds to it), a critique of so-called utilitarianism is needed.

## *Critique of utilitarianism**

From the background of the previous reflections a critique of utilitarianism emerges—utilitarianism as a certain theoretical notion in ethics as well as a practical program of conduct. In this book we will

---

* Utilitarianism has undergone a significant and complex evolution since the time of its creators. Jeremy Bentham and John Stuart Mill are known above all for propagating the application of the balance of goods as the only proper method of determining the moral value of acts. However, to the question of *which* goods should be multiplied maximally,

often return to this critique, for utilitarianism is a characteristic property of contemporary man's mentality and his attitude toward life. In
any case, it is difficult to attribute this mentality and attitude only to
modern man—for utilitarianism constitutes a perennial bedrock, as it
were, on which the life of individuals and human collectives tends to
flow. Nonetheless, utilitarianism in the modern age is conscious, formulated in respect to its philosophical presuppositions, and specified with
scientific precision.

The name itself relates to the Latin verb *uti* (to use, to take advantage) and the adjective *utilis* (useful). In accord with this etymology,
utilitarianism emphasizes usefulness in the whole action of man. The
useful is what brings pleasure and excludes pain, for pleasure constitutes

---

various utilitarians answer differently. Many of them do not share the hedonistic
identification of the highest good (that signifies the morally entrusted end of human
aspirations) with pleasure (*bonum delectabile*), which was Bentham's position. They consider
this good to be the more broadly and objectively understood utility (*bonum utile*). Today
there is no shortage of those who consider themselves utilitarians although they understand
this good—the highest good—personalistically: they subordinate any calculation of goods
to the good (perfection, happiness) of the person treated always and above all as a morally
due end of action (*bonum honestum*). Also, to the question of *whose* good ought to be
considered while applying the balance of goods, individual utilitarians answer differently,
preferring either the variously understood (depending on the answer to the previous
question) individual advantage of the subject of action; or the advantage of a selected social
group (this group can be also a future generation of mankind, for the happiness of which
the people living today should make sacrifices—or be sacrificed); or finally the maximum
advantage of the maximum number of people.

The critique below refers to utilitarianism both in its hedonistic version as well as in any
other one, insofar as it allows treating the human person instrumentally and reductively (we
mean the reduction of the person as value to the value of a function that is served by the
person, i.e., to this or that—not necessarily hedonistic—usefulness of the person). This
critique, however, does not concern the aforementioned "personalistic" version of
utilitarianism.

The balance of goods (whose fundamental idea is, after all, not alien to the Thomistic
tradition: see there the issue of *ordo bonorum et caritatis*) has the lesser practical application,
the less sensually one comprehends the highest good that constitutes a measure of partial
goods. [*Ordo bonorum et caritatis*: The order of goods and of charity. —Trans.] It is no
wonder, then, that the first and so to speak classical version of utilitarianism was
hedonism.

The author performed an extensive critical presentation of utilitarianism during the
lectures conducted at the Philosophical Department of the Catholic University of Lublin
in the academic year 1956–57. See *Zagadnienia normy i szczęścia* (Problems of Norm and
Happiness). (The typescript in the possession of the Institute of Ethics of the Catholic
University of Lublin.)

the essential manifestation of man's happiness. To be happy according to the assumptions of utilitarianism means nothing else but to live pleasantly. It is well known that pleasure itself assumes various shapes and shades. However, there is no need to pay too much attention to that in order to affirm certain pleasures as spiritual or higher while depreciating others, such as sensual, bodily, or material ones. The utilitarian values pleasure as such, for his vision of a man does not discover in that man a distinct composition of matter and spirit as two factors constituting one personal being, which owes its whole specificity precisely to the spiritual soul. For the utilitarian, man is a subject endowed with sensibility and the ability to think. Sensibility makes him desire pleasure and compels him to shun pain. Furthermore, the ability to think, i.e., reason, is given to man for the purpose of directing his action in such a way so as to secure for himself the maximum possible pleasure with the minimum possible pain. The utilitarian considers the principle of maximizing pleasure while at the same time minimizing pain as the chief norm of human morality, adding that it should be applied not only individually, egoistically, but also collectively, socially. In its final formulation, the *principle of utility* (*principium utilitatis*) proclaims the maximum of pleasure for the greatest possible number of people with, of course, the simultaneous minimum of pain for that number.

At first sight this principle seems both right and attractive, for it is difficult to imagine that people could act otherwise, that is, that they could want to find more pain than pleasure both in their individual and collective lives. However, a somewhat more thorough analysis must reveal the weakness and superficiality of this way of thinking and of this principle of normalizing human acts.[24] The essential error lies in the recognition of pleasure alone as the only or the greatest good, to which everything else in the action of man and of human society should be subordinated. But pleasure in itself is not the only good; it is also not the proper end of man's action, as we will have the opportunity to affirm in the course of this work. Pleasure in its essence is something collateral, accidental, something that may occur when acting. Thus, undertaking to act for the sake of pleasure itself as the exclusive or highest end naturally clashes with the proper structure of human acts. I can will or do something that is linked to pleasure, and I can not will or not do something that is linked to pain. I can even will this or not will that, do this or not do that, because of this pleasure or that pain. This is all true. But I may not treat this pleasure (contrasting it with pain) as the only norm of action, and even less so as a principle based upon which I declare and judge what is morally good and morally evil in my acts or the acts of another person. For it is known that sometimes what is truly good, what morality and conscience command me, is accompanied precisely by some pain and demands forgoing some pleasure. This pain, however, or the pleasure that I forgo in a given case, is not the final criterion for my rational conduct. Besides, it is not something that can be fully determinable in advance. Pleasure and pain are always linked to a concrete act, hence there is no way to determine them in advance or much less to plan or even, as the utilitarians would want, to calculate them. For pleasure is actually something rather elusive.

We could indicate many difficulties and misunderstandings that utilitarianism conceals both in theory and in practice. We will disregard all others in order to pay particular attention to only one, namely to what was also indicated by the resolute opponent of utilitarianism, Immanuel Kant. His name has already been mentioned above in connection with the moral imperative, in which Kant demands that when we act we should never treat a person as a means to an end, but always only as an end. This demand exposes one of the weakest points in utilitarianism: if pleasure is the only and indispensable good and end of man, if it alone constitutes the whole basis of moral norms in human conduct, then consequently everything in that conduct must be treated as a means to this good and end. So even the human person, both my own as well as any other, every one, must be presented in that role. If I accept the presuppositions of utilitarianism, I must look at myself as a subject that wants to have as many sensations and lived-experiences possessing a positive emotional-affective charge as possible, and at the same time as an object that may be used in order to evoke these sensations and lived-experiences. As a result, I also must look at any other person besides myself from the same point of view, that is, inasmuch as he is a means to attain maximum pleasure.

In this form, the utilitarian mentality and attitude must influence various spheres of human life and interaction, although in particular they seem to threaten the sexual sphere. The essential danger consists in this, that with utilitarian presuppositions it is not clear how interaction and relations between persons of different sex can be placed on the plane of true love, thus liberated by love both from using the person (in the second and in the first meaning of the verb "to use") and from treating the person as a means to an end. Utilitarianism seems to be a program of consistent egoism without any possibility of turning into authentic altruism. For although in the declarations of the representatives of this system we meet with the principle of maximum pleasure ("happiness") for the greatest possible number of people, this principle nonetheless contains a deep interior contradiction. For pleasure by its very essence is a good that is merely temporary, belonging solely to a given subject—it is not a supra-subjective or transsubjective good. So as long as this good is considered to be the complete basis of the moral norm, there can be no way of transcending what is *good only for me*.

We can supplement this only with some fiction, an appearance of altruism. For if, presuming that pleasure is the only good, I strive for maximum pleasure also for the other—and not only for myself, which would then be plain egoism—then I assess this pleasure of the other person through my own pleasure; it brings me pleasure that somebody else feels pleasure. If, however, it brings me no more pleasure or if it does not follow from my "balance of happiness" (the term that the utilitarians very often use), then this pleasure of the other person ceases to be for me something binding, something good, and may even become something evil. Then, according to the presuppositions of utilitarianism, I will strive to eliminate the other person's pleasure because no pleasure of mine is linked to it, or at least I will be indifferent toward the pleasure of another and will not seek it. It is quite clearly visible that with the presuppositions of utilitarianism, the subjective attitude regarding the understanding of good (good as pleasure) leads on a straight path to egoism, even if this may be not deliberate. The only way out of this inevitable egoism is to recognize besides a purely subjective good, i.e., besides pleasure, an *objective good*, which can also unite persons—and then it acquires the characteristics of a common good. This objective common good is the foundation of love, and the persons choosing this common good together at the same time subordinate themselves to it. Thanks to this, they bind one another with the true, objective bond of love, the bond that enables them to liberate themselves from subjectivism and from egoism inherently concealed in it.* [25] Love is a union of persons.

Consistent utilitarianism can (and has to) counter this objection only with some harmonization of egoisms, which is furthermore questionable since, as we have seen, there is no way out of egoism once utilitarian presuppositions are accepted. Can various egoisms be harmonized? For example, can the egoism of a woman and that of a man be harmonized in the sexual sphere? Certainly, this can be done according to the principle of "maximum pleasure for each of the two persons," but nevertheless the realization of this principle will never lead us out of egoisms. In this harmonization, egoisms will still remain egoisms, with the only difference that these two egoisms, the feminine and masculine, will be for each other mutually useful and mutually advantageous. Once the mutual usefulness and advantage cease, nothing remains from this whole harmony. Love is then nothing in the persons and nothing between them; it is not an objective reality, for the objective good, which constitutes love, is missing. According to such understanding, "love" is a coming together of egoisms that are arranged in such a way so as not to appear to each other as something painful, as something contrary to two-sided pleasure. Hence, by virtue of this understanding, love is an appearance that must be painstakingly maintained in order not to reveal what it truly conceals: egoism—and an egoism that is most rapacious, using another person for one's own sake, for one's "maximum pleasure." Then, the person is and remains merely a means to an end, as Kant rightly observed in his critique of utilitarianism.

Thus, in place of love—love that as a reality present in various persons, for instance, in a concrete man X and in a concrete woman Y,[26] allows them to go beyond the attitude of two-sided and reciprocal use of themselves as means to a subjective end—utilitarianism introduces in their mutual relation the following paradoxical relationship: each person, Y as well as X, fundamentally disposes himself toward securing his own egoism while at the same time agreeing to serve the egoism of

---

* A more extensive definition of the difference between subjectivism and subjectivity is given below and in *Person and Act*, 56–60 in section 6 of chapter I.

the other person, because this gives him a chance to gratify his own egoism, but of course only inasmuch as this chance is given. This paradoxical relationship between Y and X, which is not only a possible relationship, but which must occur in reality when the utilitarian mentality and attitude are realized, demonstrates that indeed the person here, and not only one's own person, is reduced to the role of a means, a tool. This implicates some logically indispensable and penetrating necessity: I must treat myself as a means and a tool since for my own sake I treat the other in this way. This is the reverse, as it were, of the commandment to love.

## *The commandment to love and the personalistic norm*

The commandment formulated in the Gospel demands from man love for other people, for neighbors (*bliźni*); in its full reading, however, it demands love for persons. For God, whom the commandment to love names in the first place, is the most perfect personal Being. The whole world of created persons draws its distinctness and natural superiority in relation to the world of things (non-persons) from its more particular likeness to God. The commandment formulated in the Gospel, while demanding love in relation to persons, remains indirectly in opposition to the principle of utilitarianism, for this principle—as was demonstrated in the previous analysis—is incapable of ensuring love in the relation between human beings, between persons. The opposition between the evangelical commandment and the principle of utilitarianism is indirect inasmuch as the commandment to love does not formulate the very principle on which realizing this love in the relations between persons is possible. Christ's commandment, however, lies in a sense on a different level than the principle of utilitarianism; it is a norm of a different degree. It does not directly concern the same thing: the commandment speaks of love for persons, whereas the principle of utilitarianism indicates pleasure as the basis not only of action, but also of normalizing human actions. Yet, we have stated in the critique of utilitarianism that starting from this basis of normalizing, which that system adopts, we will never be able to arrive at love. For the very principle of "using," that is, of treating the person as a means to an end, and even to the end that is pleasure—the maximization of pleasure—will always stand in the way of love.

Thus, the opposition between the principle of utilitarianism and the commandment to love results from the fact that on the basis of this principle, the commandment to love simply loses its meaning. Of course, certain axiology is linked to the principle of utilitarianism; according to this axiology, pleasure is the only or the highest value. However, at this point we do not even have to analyze this further. For it becomes clear that if the commandment to love, and love that is the object of this commandment, are to possess meaning, then we must base them on a different principle from the principle of utilitarianism, on another axiology, and on another fundamental norm. In the given case it will be the personalistic principle and norm. As a principle formulated negatively, this norm states that the person is a kind of good that is incompatible with using, which may not be treated as an object of use and, in this sense, as a means to an end. Hand in hand with this goes the positive formulation of the personalistic norm: the person is a kind of good to which only love constitutes the proper and fully-mature relation. And this positive content of the personalistic norm is precisely what the commandment to love brings out.

Can we say in that case that the commandment to love is the personalistic norm? Strictly speaking, the commandment to love is only based on the personalistic norm as a principle containing the negative and positive content, thus—in the strict sense of the word—it is not the personalistic norm. It is only derived from this norm as from a principle (a fundamental norm) that constitutes the proper ground for the commandment to love, whereas the principle of utilitarianism does not constitute this ground. It is necessary to seek this ground of the commandment to love in a different axiology, in a different system of values than the system of utilitarianism—it must be precisely the personalistic axiology, within which the value of the person is always higher than the value of pleasure (and therefore the person cannot be subordinated to pleasure; he cannot serve as a means to the end which is pleasure). So, although strictly speaking the commandment to love is not identified with the personalistic norm, but only presupposes it and the personalistic axiology together with it, speaking more broadly, however, it is permissible to say that the commandment to love is the personalistic norm. Strictly speaking, the commandment declares: "Love persons," whereas the personalistic norm as a principle says: "The person is a kind of being such that only love constitutes the proper and fully-mature relation to it." It is evident then that the personalistic norm is a substantiation for the commandment of the Gospel. So, when we take the commandment together with this substantiation, we can say that the commandment is the personalistic norm.

This norm as a commandment defines and commends a certain way of relating toward God and people, that is, a certain attitude toward them. This way of relating, this attitude, is in conformity with what the person is, with the value he represents, and therefore it is honorable. Honorableness (*godziwość*) is superior to utility alone (which is the focus of the principle of utilitarianism) even though it does not cancel utility, but only subordinates it: everything that is honorably useful in relation to the person is contained within the scope of the commandment to love.[27]

By defining and commending a certain way of relating to beings that are persons, a certain attitude toward them, the personalistic norm, as the commandment to love, presupposes not only the honorableness of such a relation, of such an attitude, but also its justice. For it is always just to render what is rightly due to somebody. It is rightly due to the person to be treated as an object of love, and not as an object of use. In a certain sense it could be said that love is a requirement of justice, just as the use of a person as a means would be contrary to this justice. Essentially, the order of justice is more fundamental than the order of love—and in a certain measure even contains it—inasmuch as love can be a requirement of justice. For certainly to love man or God, to love a person, is something just. At the same time, however, love—if its very essence is taken into account—is something above and beyond justice; simply, the essence of love differs from the essence of justice. Justice pertains to things (material goods or also moral goods, e.g., a good name) for the sake of persons, so it pertains to persons rather indirectly, whereas love pertains to persons immediately and directly. The affirmation of the value of the person as such is contained in the essence of love. And if we may rightly say that the one who loves a person is thereby just toward him, it will not be true at all to state that loving a person consists in being only just toward him. In the course of the book we will attempt to analyze separately and more broadly what constitutes the love of the person. So far, we have explicated one thing, namely that the love of the person must consist in affirming his supra-material and supra-consumer (supra-utilitarian) value. Whoever loves will attempt to show this in his entire conduct. And there is no doubt that this way he will also be just toward the person as such.*

This aspect of the problem, this encounter of love with justice on the basis of the personalistic norm, is very important for the whole of our reflections, which have sexual morality for their object. Precisely here, the basic task is to develop the concept of love that is just to the person, that is, of love that is always ready to give every man what is rightly due to him on account of his being a person. For what is at times considered "love" in the sexual context can quite easily even be unjust for the person. This happens not because sensuality and affectivity take a particular part in the formation of this love between persons of different sex (which we will analyze separately), but rather because, partly unknowingly and partly even consciously, an interpretation based on the utilitarian principle is permitted for love in its sexual context.

This interpretation, in a sense, forces itself into this love by taking advantage of the natural gravitation toward pleasure of the sensual-affective factors contained in this love. There is an easy transition from experiencing (*przeżywanie*) pleasure to not only seeking this pleasure or even seeking it for its own sake, but also considering it as the superior value and the proper basis of a norm. This constitutes the very essence of the distortions that occur in love between a woman and a man.

Thus, because the sexual sphere happens to be so easily associated with the concept of "love," while at the same time being the field of constant attrition between two fundamentally different ways of valuating and two fundamentally different ways of normalizing, namely the personalistic and the utilitarian, it is then necessary in order to clarify

---

* The point here concerns so-called strict justice (because in the broad, biblical sense "a just man" is the same as "a man of good will"). Strict justice designates a certain minimum that satisfies one's right to certain personal or material benefits. However, since love is true as long as it is not minimalistic, benefits that are just in this strict sense constitute only a basis and a condition of full interpersonal affirmation. See Aristotle, *Nicomachean Ethics* VII 1–1955a26, and St. Thomas, *Summa Contra Gentiles* III 130.

the whole issue to state explicitly that this love, which is the content of the commandment in the Gospel, is connected only with the personalistic norm, and not with the utilitarian one.[28] Therefore, we must seek the proper solutions for sexual morality within the scope of the personalistic norm if these solutions are to be Christian. They must be based on the commandment to love. However, although man completely realizes the commandment to love in its full evangelical sense through supernatural love of God and neighbors, this love nonetheless does not conflict with the personalistic norm and is not realized in isolation from it.

Perhaps, at the end of these reflections, it is worth recalling the distinction St. Augustine made between *uti* and *frui*, by which he distinguished two attitudes.[29] The one that tends to pleasure alone, disregarding the object, is exactly *uti*. The other, which finds joy in the fully-mature relation to the object because this relation is precisely what the nature of this object demands, he called *frui*. The commandment to love indicates the path to this *frui* also in the mutual interaction of persons of different sex, both in marriage and outside of it.

# Part Two

# Interpretation of the Drive

## *Instinct or drive?*

In our reflections thus far we have attempted to define the position of the person as the subject and object of actions with respect to the specific context of these actions, namely the sexual context. The fact that a woman and a man are persons does not change the fact that these persons are a woman and a man. The sexual context, however, is not only about a "static" distinctiveness of sex, but about the real contribution in human actions of a dynamic element closely linked to the distinctiveness of sex in human persons. Should we call this element an instinct (*instynkt*) or a drive (*popęd*)?

The question refers to two words which, taken etymologically, actually have the same meaning. For "instinct" is derived from the Latin *instinguere*, which means more or less the same as "to urge," "to drive." [30] Hence, instinct means the same as drive. Concerning affective associations that are usually linked to some word, the associations connected with the word "drive" used in relation to man are rather negative. For the drive indicates an activity of urging on, and this activity performed in relation to man awakens in him a reflex of resistance. Man senses his freedom, the power of self-determination, and therefore he instinctively opposes everything that in any way violates this freedom. Thus, the drive remains in some detectable conflict with freedom.

By instinct, which is etymologically identified with drive, we understand a certain way of action, which at the same time indicates its source. Namely, what is meant is a spontaneous way of action, independent of reflection. It is remarkable that in instinctive action the means are undertaken without any consideration (reflection) regarding their relation to the end for which one strives. This way of action is not typical for man, who indeed possesses an ability to reflect on the relation of means to an end. He chooses the means depending on the end for which he strives. As a result, by acting in the way proper to himself, man chooses means consciously and adapts them consciously to the end, of which he is also conscious. Because the way of action sheds light on the very source of action, it must be acknowledged that there inheres in man a source that makes him capable of reflective conduct, that is, of self-determination. Man is by nature capable of supra-instinctive action. He is also capable of such action in the sexual sphere. If it were otherwise, then morality in this sphere would make no sense—simply, it would not exist—yet it is well known that sexual morality is something common, that it is a fact with a universally human scope. It is thus difficult to speak of the sexual instinct in man in the same sense as applied to animals; it is difficult to consider this instinct as the proper and definitive source of action in the sexual sphere.

The word "drive" means etymologically almost the same as the word "instinct," but affectively it evokes even more negative associations than the other word. However, another meaning may be attributed to it, a meaning that is better adapted to what man is. So, when we speak about the sexual drive in man, then we do not have in mind an interior source of certain actions that are "imposed in advance," as it were, but instead we mean a certain orientation, a certain direction of the whole human being linked to his very nature. According to this understanding, drive is a certain natural direction of tending, innate in every man, according to which man's whole being develops from within and perfects itself.[31]

Although the sexual drive is not some source of ready-made and interiorly complete actions in man, it is nevertheless a certain property of the human being, a property that is reflected in action, where it finds its expression. This property is something natural in man, and thus something ready-made. A consequence of this property is not so much that man acts in a certain way, but rather that something happens with man, that something starts to happen without any initiative on his part, and this interior "happening" creates a substratum, as it were, for certain actions, in fact for reflective actions, in which man determines himself; he himself determines his acts and takes responsibility for them. In this place, human freedom meets drive.[*]

---

[*] See the section "The Drive and the Integration of the Person in the Act" in chapter V of *Person and Act*, 230–235.

Man is not responsible for what happens in him in the sexual sphere, of course inasmuch as he has not evoked it himself, but he is by all means responsible for what he does in this sphere. The fact that the sexual drive is a source of what happens in man, of various events occurring in his sensual or affective life without a contribution of the will, demonstrates that this drive is a property of the whole human being, and not only of its sphere or power. This property permeating the whole being of man possesses the character of a force whose expression is not only what "happens" in the human body, the senses, or affections without a contribution of the will, but also what is formed with the will's contribution.

## The sexual drive as a property of the individual

Every man is by nature a sexual being, that is, from birth belonging to one of the two sexes.[32] This fact is not abolished by the phenomenon of so-called hermaphroditism, as in the same way every other disorder or even abnormality does not abolish the fact that human nature indeed exists, and that every human being, even one afflicted with an abnormality or a disorder, possesses this nature and is a human being precisely thanks to it. And so, in a similar way, every man is a sexual being, and, belonging to one of the two sexes, entails a certain orientation of the whole being itself, an orientation that is manifested in a concrete development of this being from within. This development, which is perceivable more easily in the organism than in the psyche, will be depicted in more detail in the final chapter of this book, which contains a certain amount of data from the field of sexology.

The orientation of the human being that is evoked by belonging to one of the sexes is not only manifested inside, but at the same time proceeds to the outside, and it ordinarily (again, we are not speaking about disorders or perversions) reveals itself through a certain natural tendency, a direction toward the other sex. To what does this direction turn? We will answer this question gradually. And so, this sexual direction, superficially speaking, turns to the "other sex" as a group of certain characteristic properties in the whole psycho-physiological structure of man.

Taking it in a purely exterior way, almost phenomenally, sex can be defined as a specific synthesis of properties that are clearly delineated in the psycho-physiological structure of man. The sexual drive emphasizes the fact that these properties correspond to one another, and thus they open before a woman and a man a possibility of being, so to speak, complemented (*uzupełniać się*) reciprocally.[33] A man does not possess the properties a woman possesses, and vice versa. Consequently, for each of them there exists not only the possibility of complementing (*uzupełnić*) one's properties with the properties of a person of the other sex, but also there even appears at times a lively felt need for such complementing (*uzupełnienie*). If man looked quite deeply into his essence through this need, then this could also help him in understanding his own limitations, insufficiency, and, indirectly, even what philosophy calls the contingency of being (*contingentia*). But in general people do not reach that far in their reflection on the fact of sex. For sexual distinctiveness by itself merely indicates, so to speak, a certain division of psycho-physiological properties within the species "man," similar to that of animal species. The resulting drive toward complementing (*uzupełnić*) each other indicates that these properties reciprocally possess for people of different sex some specific value. Thus, we could speak of sexual values, which are linked with the psycho-physiological structure of woman and man. Do these properties possess value for them reciprocally, therefore giving rise to what we call drive? Or—the other way round—do these properties possess value for them reciprocally because the sexual drive exists? The latter solution is more fitting. The drive is something more fundamental than the very psycho-physiological properties of woman and man, even though it neither manifests itself nor acts without them.

Besides, the sexual drive in woman and man is not exhausted in being directed toward the very psycho-physiological properties of the other sex. For these properties do not exist and cannot exist in separation, but they exist always in a concrete person, in a concrete woman or a man. Thus, as a matter of fact, the sexual drive in the human person is always by nature turned toward another human person—such is its normal formation. Its turning toward the sexual properties alone ought to be considered a diminishment or even distortion of the drive. When it turns toward these properties in the person of the same sex, then we speak of a homosexual perversion. We speak of perversion all the more when the sexual drive does not turn toward the sexual properties in the human person but toward those in animals. The natural direction of the sexual drive indicates a human being of the other sex, and not the "other sex" alone.[34] But precisely due to the fact that the drive turns toward man, the *possibility of love* grows within its scope and in a sense even on its substratum.

The sexual drive in man has a natural tendency to turn into love precisely because both objects, which differ in their sexual psycho-physiological properties, are people. The phenomenon of love characterizes the world of people; in the animal world only the sexual instinct operates.

Love, however, is not just either a biological or even a psycho-physiological crystallization of the sexual drive, but is something fundamentally different from the drive. For although love grows and is crystallized on the substratum of the sexual drive, in the orbit of the conditions the drive creates in the psycho-physiological life of concrete people, it is nevertheless formed thanks to acts of the will on the level of the person.

The sexual drive does not create in man ready-made, finished actions, but only provides material, as it were, for these actions by all that "happens" inside man under the influence of the drive. All this, however, does not deprive man of the capacity for self-determination, hence for this reason the drive is naturally dependent on the person. The drive is subordinated to the person, and the person can use it at his discretion; he has the drive at his disposal in accord with this discretion. It must be added that this situation does not at all diminish the force of the sexual drive, but quite the contrary; even though it does not possess the power to determine the acts of the will in man, the drive possesses the potency to use the will. The sexual drive is found in man as a completely different situation than in animals, where it constitutes a source of instinctive actions that are subject to nature itself. In man, the drive by nature is subordinated to the will, and thereby it is subject to the specific dynamic of freedom that is at the disposal of the will. The sexual drive rises above determinism of the biological order with an act of love. But precisely for this reason, symptoms of the sexual drive must be assessed in man on the level of love, and actualizations of the drive belong to the cycle of responsibility, precisely the responsibility for love. All this is possible because complete determination in the psychological sense is not bound together with the sexual drive, which leaves in man a field of operation for freedom.

Now, it is proper to state again that the sexual drive is a universal human property and a force that acts in every man, even though this force manifests itself in various ways in particular people, and even with different psycho-physiological intensity. However, the drive itself is something different from its manifestations. Because the drive itself is a common, universal human property, at every step its contribution to the interactions and coexistence between persons of different sex, men and women, must be taken into account. This coexistence belongs in the framework of social life. Man is a social being as well as a sexual being who belongs to a given sex. Consequently, the principles of coexistence and interaction between persons of different sex will also be a part of the principles that in general regulate the social intercourse among people. The social moment in sexual ethics must be taken into account with no less attention than the individual moment. For since at every step of social life we encounter manifestations of the coexistence of persons of different sex, the task of ethics is to arrange all these manifestations not only on the level that is worthy of persons, but also on the level of the common good of society. For human life is by nature in many sectors coeducational.

## *The sexual drive and existence*

The notion of determination is linked to the notion of necessity. That which is determined cannot be otherwise, but must be precisely in this way. It is possible to speak about necessity, thus about certain determination, in connection with the sexual drive from the point of view of the human species. Indeed, the existence of the whole species *Homo sapiens* depends most closely on this drive.[35] This species could not exist if there were no sexual drive and its natural effects. Here, a certain necessity is clearly visible. Humankind can be preserved in its existence only under the condition that individual people, individual men and women, human couples, follow the sexual drive. As we have seen, this drive provides, so to speak, material for the love of persons, of a woman and a man, but (inasmuch as we remain on the line of the very finality of the drive) this happens only in a sense collaterally, *per accidens*,[36] for the love of persons is properly speaking *per se* a work of human free will.[37] Persons can love one another even though the drive does not act between them. Thus, it is clear that the love of a man and a woman does not determine the proper finality of the drive. The proper end of the drive, the end per se, is something supra-personal; it is the existence of the species *Homo sapiens*, the constant extension of its existence.

This includes a distinct likeness to the animal world, to various biological species. The species *Homo sapiens* is a part of nature (*przyroda*), and the sexual drive acting within this species guarantees its existence. Existence is, in fact, the first and fundamental good of every being. The existence of the species *Homo sapiens* is the first and fundamental good of that species. All other goods proceed from this fundamental one. I can act only insofar as I am. Various works of man, creations of his genius, fruits of his holiness, are possible only insofar as this man, this genius, this saint, exists. In order to be, he must have come into being. The natural path for man to come into existence passes through the sexual drive.

Although we can think and say that the sexual drive is a specific biological force, we cannot think and say nonetheless that it possesses a merely biological meaning, for that is not true. The sexual drive possesses an existential meaning, for it is closely linked to the existence of man, to the existence of the species *Homo sapiens*, whereas it is not linked merely to man's physiology or even psycho-physiology, which are the objects of the natural sciences. Existence, however, does not constitute the proper and commensurate object of any natural science. Each of them presupposes existence as a concrete fact already contained in the object that it studies. Existence itself is the object of philosophy, which alone occupies itself with the problem of existence as such. Therefore, the full view on the sexual drive, which is most closely related to the existence of the species *Homo sapiens* and, as has been said, possesses an existential and not only "biological" character, belongs to philosophy. This is very important when the issue concerns the recognition of the proper greatness of this drive, as that also has distinct consequences in the field of sexual ethics. If the sexual drive has merely a "biological" meaning, then it can be considered an area of use, and it can be agreed that it constitutes for man an object of use no different from the various living or inanimate objects of nature (*przyroda*). But since the sexual drive possesses an existential character, since it is linked to the very existence of the human person, which is the person's first and most fundamental good, then it must be subject to the principles that apply in relation to the person. So even though the drive is at man's disposal and he may use it, it can never be used in isolation from or—even more so—against the love of the person.

Hence, by no means can we think that the sexual drive, which has its own finality in man, the finality determined in advance and independent from the will and self-determination of man, is something located below the person and below love.* The proper end of the sexual drive is the existence of the species *Homo sapiens*, its extension, *procreatio*; and the love of persons, of a man and a woman, is formed within this finality, in its bedrock, as it were; it is formed as if out of this material, which is provided by the drive.† So, this love can be correctly

---

* The drive is a form of natural human dynamism oriented toward a specified end. It results from the somatic structure, but in man it obtains its own proper fullness only through integration with the psychical and spiritual "layer." The very appearing of the drive is a certain objective necessity. This, however, only constitutes a basis of human lived-experience, because the content of the lived-experience also depends on these higher layers. The integration of somaticity, psychical emotivity, and spirituality on the level of the person occurs in the act, which constitutes the realization of this drive: "The tendency for being with another human person is based on the sexual drive, on the basis of at once the profound likeness and the difference resulting from the distinctness of sexes. This natural tendency constitutes a basis of marriage and—through conjugal intercourse—a basis of the family" (*Person and Act*, 233–234, section 8 of chapter V).

† The sexual drive—broadly understood—is valuable not only "procreatively" for man, but also as a factor in the reciprocal complementing (*uzupełniać się*) of a man and a woman in the course of their whole life, in many reciprocal relations that do not pertain—whether concretely or generally speaking—to the generation and education of children. However, for the spouses to honorably take advantage of the energy that is evoked by this drive and of the energy's natural tendencies, they must take into consideration what constitutes the drive's fundamental sense and its *raison d'être*. Once this condition (of not contradicting the proper finality of the drive) is fulfilled, then even if a new human being cannot be generated from the union or a specific act of intercourse between a man and a woman, the spouses themselves are renewed in love and generate, as it were, each other in the interpersonal community (*communio personarum*). See K. Wojtyła, "Zagadnienie katolickiej etyki seksualnej," *Roczniki Filozoficzne* 13, fasc. 2 (1965), 16; "O znaczeniu miłości oblubieńczej" (On the Meaning of Spousal Love), *Roczniki Filozoficzne* 22, fasc. 2 (1974), 169.

formed only inasmuch as it is formed in close harmony with the proper finality of the drive. A clear conflict with this finality will be at the same time a disturbance and undermining of the love of persons. This finality at times impedes man, so that some people attempt to evade it in an artificial way. However, this way must negatively affect the love of persons, which in this case is most thoroughly linked with using the drive.*

The fact that at times this finality impedes man is due to various causes; we will speak of them on the occasion of our further reflections contained in this book. Certainly, one of these causes is also the fact that man in his consciousness, in his reason, often confers on the sexual drive merely a "biological" meaning without quite deeply grasping its proper existential meaning—its connection with existence. Precisely this connection with the very existence of man and of the species *Homo sapiens* confers on the sexual drive its objective greatness and meaning. But this greatness appears in the consciousness only when with his love man takes up what is contained in the natural finality of the drive. However, is he not impeded in this by the determination that the existence of man and the existence of the species necessarily depend on the use of the sexual drive? In fact, the necessity and determination linked to the order of the existence of man and of the species can be known and consciously accepted by every person. They do not constitute a necessity in the psychological sense; hence they do not exclude love, but only confer on it a specific character. Precisely this character is possessed by the fully-mature conjugal love of two persons, of a man and a woman, who consciously decided to participate in the whole order of existence and serve the existence of the species *Homo sapiens*. Speaking more closely and more concretely, these two persons, a man and a woman, serve the existence of another concrete person, who is their own child—blood from their blood and flesh from their flesh. At the same time this person constitutes a confirmation and extension of their own love. The order of human existence, the order of being, does not remain in conflict with the love of persons, but is closely harmonized with it.

---

* See *Person and Act*, 78–94 and 197–235.

## The religious interpretation

The problem of the sexual drive is one of the cruces of ethics. In Catholic ethics it possesses a deeply religious meaning. The order of human existence, as well as of all existence, is a work of the Creator, not merely a one-time work performed in some distant past of the universe, but a constant work that is still being performed. God creates continuously, and only because he creates continuously, the world is preserved in existence (*conservatio est continua creatio*).[38] For the world consists of creatures, that is, of such beings that do not have their existence from themselves, for they do not have in themselves the ultimate reason and source of this existence. This source, and with it the ultimate reason for existence of all creatures, is invariably found in God. However, these creatures participate in the whole order of existence not only through the fact that they themselves exist, but also through the fact that at least some of them help transmit existence to new beings within their species. This is the case with man, with a man and a woman, who, by taking advantage of the drive in sexual intercourse, enter into the cosmic current, as it were, of the transmission of existence. Their distinct position lies in the fact that they themselves consciously direct their own action as well as foresee possible effects or fruits of this action.

However, this consciousness reaches further and is developed in this direction with the help of the religious truth contained in the Book of Genesis and the Gospel. Through procreation, through the fact of participating in the work of bringing a new human being into existence, a man and a woman participate at the same time, in their own way, in the work of creation. So then, they can look at themselves as the rational co-creators of a new human being. This new human being is a person. Parents take part in the genesis of a person. It is evident that the person is not only and not foremost an organism. The human body is the body of the person because it constitutes a substantial unity with the human spirit. The human spirit is not generated through bodily intercourse of a man and a woman. The spirit cannot at all emerge from the body nor be generated and come into being in accordance with the principles of the generation of the body. Sexual intercourse of a man and a woman is fundamentally a bodily intercourse, which nonetheless should also proceed from spiritual love. However, nothing is known in the order of nature about the kind of relation of spirits that would generate a new substantial spirit. The love of a man and a woman, even if the love happened to be in itself the strongest and the deepest, does not generate it either. Nevertheless, when a new human being is conceived, then a new spirit is also conceived, a spirit that is substantially united to the body and whose embryo begins to exist in the womb of the woman-mother. Without this, there is no way of comprehending how this embryo could later on develop precisely into a human being, a person.

Hence, the human being is—as the Church teaches—a work of God himself: God creates the spiritual and immortal soul of this being, whose organism begins to exist as a consequence of bodily intercourse between a man and a woman.* 39 Bodily intercourse should proceed from the love of persons and also there find its full justification. Although this love does not give existence to a new spirit—to the soul of a child—it nonetheless must be in full readiness to receive this new personal being, who in fact came into existence through bodily intercourse that is also an expression of the spiritual love of persons, and to ensure for this new being a full development, not only bodily but also spiritual. This full spiritual development of the human person constitutes the fruit of education. Procreation is the proper end of the sexual drive, which—as has been said—provides at the same time material for the love of persons, of a man and a woman. This love owes to the drive fertility in the biological sense, but it also should possess the fertility proper to itself in the spiritual, moral, and personal spheres. Precisely here, in the work of education of new persons, is concentrated the whole fertility of love of both persons, of a woman and a man. Here lies its proper end, its natural direction.

Education (*wychowanie*) is creativity concerning the most personal object—as always and only a person is educated, whereas an animal can

---

* God, as the only Being existing through himself and by all means perfect, creates man (makes him a contingent being), whose person is called by the Divine Persons to community with other persons, but at the same time first and foremost with themselves. Precisely by virtue of this "vocation," his strictly personal subjectivity in the natural and supernatural dimensions is constituted in man. In this way, God himself bestows on each man the dignity of "being a person." However, the parents' participation in the "genesis of the person" acquires a new content once they receive the child into the family as a community of persons and accept his relational subjectivity, which is oriented not only toward them and other people, but also toward God.

only be trained—and at the same time creativity in the material that is entirely human: everything that is by nature contained in the man being educated constitutes material for educators, material which their love should employ.[40] What God gives in the supernatural order, i.e., in the order of grace, also belongs to the whole of this material. For he does not leave the work of education, which is in a sense a continuous creation of personhood, entirely and exclusively to parents, but he himself personally takes part in it as well. Not only did love of the parents stand at the beginning of the new human person, as they were only co-creators, but the Creator's love decided about a person's coming to be in the womb of the mother. Grace is, so to speak, the further continuation of this work. God himself takes the highest part in creation of human personhood in the spiritual, moral, and strictly super-natural sphere. And parents, if they are not to forgo their proper role, the role of co-creators, also should help in this.

Evidently, this whole reality that we call the sexual drive is not something thoroughly dark and unintelligible, but is fundamentally accessible and, in a sense, permeable to the light of human thought, especially thought based on Revelation, which in turn conditions love, in which freedom of the person is expressed. The sexual drive is linked in a particular way with the order of existence, and the order of existence is the divine order inasmuch as it is realized under the continuous influence of God the Creator. A man and a woman through conjugal life, through full sexual intercourse, join in this order; they decide to take a particular part in the work of creation. The order of existence is the divine order, even though existence itself is not something super-natural. Indeed, not only the super-natural order, but also the order of nature, which remains in relation to God the Creator, is the divine order. The expression "order of nature" (*porządek natury*) cannot be confused nor identified with the expression "biological order" (*porządek przyrodniczy*), as the latter, even though also signifying the order of nature, denotes it only inasmuch as it is accessible for the empirical-descriptive methods of natural sciences, and not as a specific order of existence with a clear relation to the First Cause, to God the Creator.

Confusing the order of existence with the "biological order" in this way, or rather obscuring the former with the latter—which, together with all the empiricism, seems to loom greatly over the mentality of modern man, especially the modern intellectual—causes particular difficulties in understanding Catholic sexual ethics on the basis of its very presuppositions. According to these presuppositions, *sexus*, sex, and the sexual drive are not only and exclusively a specific sphere of man's psycho-physiology.[41] The sexual drive has its objective greatness precisely because of this link with the divine work of creation, a greatness that almost completely disappears in the field of vision of a mentality influenced by the "biological order" alone. In relation to that order, the sexual drive is only a sum of functions, which from the biological point of view undoubtedly tend to a biological end, to reproduction. So, since man is the master of nature (*przyroda*), should he not mold these functions—even in an artificial way, with the help of an appropriate technique—in a way that he deems fitting, that suits him? The "biological order," as a work of the human mind separating some elements of this order from what really exists, has man as its immediate author. From here it is easy to leap into autonomism in ethical views. The case is different with the "order of nature." It constitutes a group of cosmic relations that occur among beings that really exist. It is thus the order of existence, and the whole order present in existence finds its basis in the one who is the unceasing source of this existence, in God the Creator.*

---

* This particular ordination of the sexual drive to existence (or this particular bond of the sexual drive with the value of existence), which is expressed by this drive's contribution to the coming to be of a new personal life, decides the specific position and rank of the drive in the real structure of the human person. This position and rank, so easily evident, become particularly vivid especially when one looks from the metaphysical perspective at the existence of the human person as a work of unceasing creative initiative of Personal Love. This standpoint is sometimes charged with imparting normative meaning to fundamentally biological facts and processes (transition from "is" to "ought"), which allegedly leads to the *biologization* of ethics. From the position of the author's vision expounded here, this charge consists in misunderstanding this vision (*ignorantia elenchi*), because the need for a transition from the purely biological fact, which is the sexual drive, to the normativity of the drive is absolutely out of the question, since this drive can be adequately and cognitively identified and fully described only together with its existential-axiological dimension. [*Ignorantia elenchi*: Literally "the ignorance of proof" (another version is ignoratio elenchi), which describes a fallacy that consists in a presumption that an irrelevant argument proved the point and solved the problem at hand. — Trans.] So, in order to bring forth the charge of biologism, first it must be *presupposed* that man's sexual drive possesses only a biological sense, that is, that it is only a purely biological fact. This presupposition, however, in a purely dogmatic way deprives the drive of its due existential-axiological dimension (scientific empiricism is a deeper source of that), by reducing the full sense of this notion to the biological sense in order to bring the above mentioned charge. In fact, however, precisely this

## *The rigoristic interpretation*

Understanding the sexual drive, its proper interpretation, has no less fundamental significance for sexual ethics than the proper under-standing of the principles governing inter-personal relations. The first part of this chapter ("The analysis of the verb 'to use'") was devoted to this second issue, for it seems to be an element that is mentally earlier than the interpretation of the sexual drive. The drive in the world of persons is something different; it possesses another meaning than in the whole world of nature (*przyroda*). Thus, the interpretation of the drive must proceed correlatively to understanding the person and his elemen-tary rights in relation to other persons—the first part of this chapter prepared us for this.

Having before our eyes the principles formulated there (the person-alistic norm), we can in turn exclude erroneous interpretations of the sexual drive for being unilateral and unilaterally exaggerated. One of

---

reductionism deserves the name of biologism, because it obfuscates the totality of the depicted phenomenon with the (after all, important) biological aspect (*pars pro toto*) by absolutizing that selected aspect. [*Pars pro toto*: A part for the whole. — Trans.] The further logic of this reductionism and the charge of biologism formulated from its point of view are understandable. Nonetheless, it could be expected that these reductionists expound their presuppositions with complete openness. Among others, the point here concerns negating the validity of any other experience beyond exterior and interior perception, and that includes, of course, negating the validity of metaphysical cognition. Honesty toward the reader demands this much. However, the argumentation of some moral *theologians* is less understandable, if not even astounding, when they, perhaps unknowingly yielding to scientific sensualism, reduce man's sexual drive to a biological fact, so that consequently, which for this reason can deceive many, they grant to man the same degree of liberty in using the sexual drive that he possesses in relation to growing fingernails or hair.

These authors seem to be subject to the charge of reductionism for a different reason from the one mentioned above. Namely, they do not consider adequately the connection between the objective structure of the sexual drive and the Christian sense of spousal love. For since, in accord with the first commandment to love, man's self-giving in love is due to God alone, then any other self-gift to another human person should be at the same time a way and a form of giving self to God. Moreover, since in accord with the Catholic faith a new man that is being conceived is not only a fruit of intercourse between a man and a woman, but above all a work and a gift of God, the giver of all existence, then justice toward the Creator requires a particular respect toward the order of a new human life coming into existence, the order that is established by him. This theological substantiation of obedience to the natural law, so often omitted by some Catholic theologians, is developed by the author in chapter IV of this book.

these is the "libidinistic" interpretation (with this expression we refer to Freud and his notion of *libido*), which we will cover later. Another is the rigoristic or puritan interpretation, which we will attempt to present and assess right away, especially that the rigoristic, puritan interpretation may seem to express a view on sexual matters that was developed on the basis of Christian beliefs connected with the Gospel. In fact, however, this interpretation conceals in itself presuppositions of naturalism, and even sensualistic empiricism. It arose in its time probably in order to oppose in practice the presuppositions that it itself accepts in theory (for historically and geographically puritanism and sensualistic empiricism reside very close to each other; both grew mainly in England during the seventeenth century). But this fundamental contradiction between theoretical presuppositions and the ends intended in practice contributed to the fact that the rigoristic and puritan notions fall in different ways into utilitarianism, which so fundamentally opposes the way of valuating and normalizing developed on the basis of the Gospel. We will attempt to demonstrate this now by unmasking this utilitarian feature in rigorism.

This view would be formed in this way: because the Creator uses a man and a woman and their sexual intercourse to ensure the existence of the species *Homo sapiens,* he uses persons as means to his end. In consequence, marriage and sexual intercourse are good only when they serve procreation. Hence, a man acts well when he uses a woman as an indispensable means for producing offspring. The use of the person as a means to this objective end, which is procreation, belongs to the essence of marriage. This use in itself is something good (we mean the use according to the first meaning of the verb "to use"—I refer to the analysis conducted in the previous part of this chapter). Evil is only the use according to the second meaning, that is, seeking pleasure in sexual intercourse. Although that is an indispensable component of the use according to the first meaning, it is nevertheless a component that is in itself "unclean," some *sui generis* necessary evil.[42] This evil, however, must be tolerated, since it cannot be excluded.

This view refers to the tradition of Manichaeanism condemned by the Church already in the first centuries. Although this view does not reject marriage as something that in itself is evil and unclean due to being "bodily"—as was maintained by the Manichaeans—it contents itself with stating the permissibility of marriage for the sake of the good of the species. However, the interpretation of the sexual drive contained in this view can be shared by only very unilateral spiritualists. Precisely due to its one-sidedness and exaggeration in one direction, they fall into what the teaching of the Gospel and of the Church, thoroughly understood, attempts to exclude. At the basis of this erroneous view lies a faulty understanding of the relation of God—the First Cause—to the secondary causes that are persons. By joining in sexual intercourse, a man and a woman join themselves as rational and free persons, and their union possesses a moral value when it is justified by true conjugal love. Hence, if we can say that the Creator "uses" the sexual union of persons to realize the order of existence intended by him within the species *Homo sapiens*, it definitely may not be held that the Creator thereby uses persons merely as means to an end intended by himself.[*]

For the Creator, by giving man and woman a rational nature and the ability to determine consciously their acts, gave them thereby the power to choose by themselves the end to which sexual intercourse leads in a natural way. And where two persons can choose together a certain good as an end, there the possibility of love also exists. Therefore, the Creator does not use persons merely as means or tools of his creative power, but opens before them the possibility of a particular realization of love. It depends on them whether they will place their sexual intercourse on the

---

[*] The Creator inscribed in the nature of the personal being the potency and power of giving oneself, and this potency is closely joined with the structure of self-possession and self-governance proper to the person, with the fact that he is *"sui iuris et alteri incommunicabilis."* What is rooted precisely in this ontic "incommunicability" is a capacity for giving oneself, for becoming a gift for others (K. Wojtyła, "O znaczeniu miłości oblubieńczej" [On the Meaning of Spousal Love], *Roczniki Filozoficzne* 22, fasc. 2 [1974], 166. Herein after cited as "O znaczeniu miłości oblubieńczej," *Roczniki Filozoficzne.* See pp. 281–282, in this book).

The belonging of the human person to God as his Creator and Redeemer does not abolish the "law of the gift," which he himself inscribed in the personal being of man ( . . . ) The *"law of the gift,"* which God as the Creator inscribed in the being of the human person, of a man and a woman, ( . . . ) *constitutes the proper basis of that "communio personarum"* [emphasis original]. ( . . . ) From the very beginning, the Creator wills that marriage is this *"communio personarum,"* in which a man and a woman realize day by day and in the dimension of their whole life the ideal of the personal union by "giving and receiving each other" (see *Gaudium et Spes*, 48). Spousal love can be understood as the realization of this ideal (ibid., 170); (see pp. 287–288 in this book).

level of love, on the level proper to persons, or below this level. And the Creator wills not only the preservation of the species through sexual intercourse, but also its preservation based on love that is worthy of persons. The Gospel compels us to understand the will of the Creator in this way through the content contained in the commandment to love.

At the same time—and against what the unilateral spiritualism of puritan rigorists suggests—it is not contrary to the objective dignity of persons that sexual use is included in the love that persons realize in marriage. In this case, the point concerns all that we have gathered under the second meaning of the verb "to use." This is precisely what the rigoristic interpretation wants to limit or exclude in an artificial way. And therefore, this interpretation emphasizes all the more this second meaning of the verb "to use" as if it constituted an end in itself that should be separated, on the one hand, from the action of the drive, and, on the other hand, from the love of persons. As we have seen previously, this is also a fundamental thesis of utilitarianism: again, rigorism attempts to overcome in practice what it accepts completely on theoretical grounds. Yet, this manifold pleasure linked to the distinctness of the sexes, or even the sexual delight linked to conjugal intercourse, cannot be understood as a separate end of action, because then, even unknowingly, we begin to treat the person as a means to this end, and thus exclusively as an object of use.

Sexual use without treating the person as "an object of use" is an ethical problem.[43] Rigorism, which disposes itself unilaterally to overcome the sexual *uti*, inevitably leads precisely to it, at least in the sphere of intention. The only way to overcome this *uti* is to receive beside it the second, fundamentally distinct possibility that St. Augustine calls *frui*. For there exists a joy that is in conformity with the nature of the sexual drive and is at the same time adapted to the level of persons. In the whole vast area of love between a woman and a man, this joy proceeds from acting together, from the reciprocal understanding and the harmonious realization of the ends chosen together. This joy, this *frui*, can also be provided by the manifold pleasure connected to the distinctness of the sexes and the sexual delight that conjugal intercourse brings. The Creator intended this joy and bound it with the love of a woman and a man, insofar as this love is correctly formed on the substratum of the sexual drive, that is, in a way corresponding to man as person.

## *The "libidinistic" interpretation* [44]

The distortion in the direction of exaggerated rigorism—in which in fact we discovered a specific manifestation of utilitarian thinking (*extrema se tangunt!*)—is not, however, in general as frequent as the contrary distortion, which we will call here "libidinistic." [45] This name refers to the Latin word *libido* (delight resulting from use), which Sigmund Freud used in his interpretation of the sexual drive. At this point, let us pass over a more extensive description of Freudian psychoanalysis, of his theory of the subconscious. Freud is regarded as a representative of pansexualism, for he is willing to interpret all manifestations of human life, beginning from those already found in the newborn, as manifestations of the sexual drive. Even though only some of these manifestations are turned directly and explicitly toward sexual objects and values, all of them turn at least indirectly and implicitly toward delight, *libido*, and this delight always has a sexual meaning. Hence, Freud speaks above all about the drive toward delight (*libido-trieb*), and not about the sexual drive. What is important at this point is precisely that the sexual drive in his view is fundamentally the drive toward delight.

Putting things this way is a consequence of a particularistic and purely subjectivistic vision of man. According to this understanding, the essence of the sexual drive is determined by what constitutes the most vivid and imposing content of human lived-experiences in the sexual sphere. In Freud's opinion, this content is precisely the delight, *libido*. Man plunges into it when he encounters it, and he strives for it when he does not experience (*przeżywać*) it, so he is interiorly determined to seek it. He seeks it continually and, in a sense, in everything he does. This delight is, so to speak, the primary end of the sexual drive and even of the whole urge-related life in man—the end *per se*. [46] According to this understanding, the transmission of life, procreation, is only some collateral end—an end *per accidens*. Therefore, in the same view, the objective end of the drive is more remote and, so to say, nonessential. Psychoanalysis depicted man only as a subject, and not as an object, one of the objects of the objective world. This object is at the same time a subject—as has been said at the beginning of this chapter—and this subject possesses interiority and the interior life proper only to itself.

And a characteristic of this interiority is the ability to know, that is, to grasp the truth objectively and wholly. Thanks to it, man—the person—is also conscious of the objective end of the sexual drive, for he finds himself in the order of existence, and together with this he also finds in this order the role of the sexual drive. He is even capable to comprehend this role in relation to the Creator as participation in the work of creation.

However, when the sexual drive is understood fundamentally as the drive toward delight, then that whole interiority of the person is thereby canceled, as it were. In this understanding, the person remains only a subject that is "exteriorly" sensitized to sensory-sexual stimuli, which evoke the lived-experience of delight. This understanding places the human psyche—perhaps unknowingly—on the level of the animal psyche. An animal may be disposed toward seeking sensory-vital plea-sure and toward avoiding pain of the same kind, because the whole relation to the objective ends of its being is correctly developed in an instinctive way. However, in man this is not so. The correct development of the relation to the objective ends of his being remains in him in the power of reason, which directs the will, and therefore this development acquires a moral value—it is morally good or evil.[47] When man uses the sexual drive in some way, then he also develops—correctly or incor-rectly—the relation to the objective ends of his being, to these ends which are connected precisely with the drive. Thus, the sexual drive does not possess a purely libidinistic character, but it possesses an existential character. Man cannot seek in it only *libido* alone, for this contradicts his nature; this simply contradicts what man is. A subject equipped with "interiority" as man is, a subject that is a person, cannot leave to instinct the whole responsibility for the drive, disposing himself only toward delight, but he must take up full responsibility for the way he uses the sexual drive. This responsibility constitutes the fundamental, vital com-ponent of man's sexual morality.

It must be added that this "libidinistic" interpretation of the sexual drive correlates very closely with the utilitarian attitude in ethics. The point in this case concerns the second meaning of the verb "to use," namely, as was said earlier, the meaning possessing a distinct subjectiv-istic tint. That is precisely why treating the person exclusively as a means to an end, as an object of use, becomes linked with this meaning in an even more drastic degree. The "libidinistic" distortion constitutes an open form of utilitarianism, whereas exaggerated rigorism conceals in itself only some symptoms of utilitarian thinking. They occur in it, so to speak, in a roundabout way, whereas *libido* speaks about them immediately and directly.

This whole problem, however, possesses another background, the socio-economic background. Procreation is some function of the collective life of mankind; after all, the point is the existence of the species *Homo sapiens*. It is also a function of social life in various concrete communities, [political] systems, states, and families. The socio-economic problem of procreation appears on many levels. Simply, the point is that it is not enough only to generate children, but that later on they also have to be supported and educated. Contemporary mankind experiences (*przeżywać*) enormous apprehension about being unable to keep up economically with natural population growth. The sexual drive seemingly turns out to be a force that is more powerful than human forethought in the economic sphere. For some two hundred years mankind—especially in white, civilized societies—has grappled with the need to resist the sexual drive and its potential productivity. This need was crystallized in the doctrine usually linked with the name of Thomas Malthus, and thus known as Malthusianism or neo-Malthusianism. We will return to the problem of neo-Malthusianism in chapters III and IV. Malthusianism itself is a separate problem, which we will not consider in this book in more detail, since it belongs to the field of demography, which deals with the problem of the actual and potential number of people on the globe and in its particular parts. However, attention must be paid to the fact that Malthusianism has been associated with the purely "libidinistic" interpretation of the sexual drive. For since the earth is threatened with overpopulation, and economists complain about the "overproduction" of people so that the production of the means of living cannot keep up, then the goal must be to limit the use of the sexual drive regarding its objective finality. However, those who, like Freud, perceive above all the subjective finality of this drive, the finality linked to *libido* alone, and mainly emphasize that, will also consequently strive to fully preserve this subjective finality linked to the pleasure of sexual intercourse, while at the same time limiting or even eliminating the objective finality linked to procreation. A problem emerges, which the adherents of the utilitarian mentality want to regard as a problem of a purely technical nature, whereas Catholic ethics sees in it a problem of an utterly ethical nature. The utilitarian mentality remains in this case faithful to its presuppositions: after all, the point is to obtain the greatest possible pleasure, which the sexual sphere provides in such a prominent degree in the form of *libido*. Catholic ethics, however, protests in the name of its personalistic presuppositions: one may not be led by the "balance of pleasures" alone where relation to the person comes into play—the person may not in any way be an object of use. This is the proper crux of the conflict.

Catholic ethics is far from some one-sided forejudgment of the demographic problems posited by Malthusianism and supported by contemporary economists. The problem of the birth rate, the problem of the number of people on the globe or in its particular parts, are problems that in a natural way appeal to human prudence, to what in a sense is the providence, which man as a rational being must also be for himself in both the individual and collective life.[48] However, regardless of how correct the demographic difficulties posited by economists may be, the whole problem of sexual intercourse between a woman and a man should not be solved in a way that contradicts the personalistic norm. For in this case the point is the value of the person, since the person is the most proximate good for all mankind—a good more proximate and more important than economic goods.[49] Thus, the person himself cannot be in any way subordinated to economics, for his proper sphere of values is the sphere of moral values, the values that are linked in a particular way with love of the person. The conflict of the sexual drive with economics must be necessarily considered also, and even above all, from this perspective.

At the conclusion of this chapter, it is fitting to posit one thought, one reflection, that lies on the plane of our considerations about the drive. Namely, in the elementary structure of the human being—in fact, similar to the whole animal world—we observe two fundamental drives: the drive for self-preservation and the sexual drive. In accord with its name, the drive for self-preservation serves to preserve and maintain the existence of a given being, man or animal. We know many manifestations of this drive, which we will not analyze here in detail. Characterizing this drive, one could say that it possesses ego-centric marks inasmuch as it is by nature disposed toward the existence of the very "I" (of course, we mean the human "I," for it is difficult to speak of the animal "I"—"I" goes hand in hand with personhood). And by this, the drive for self-preservation differs fundamentally from the sexual drive. For the natural direction of the latter always proceeds outside its own "I" and has as its direct object some being of the other sex within the same species, and as its final end the existence of that species. That is the objective finality of the sexual drive, the drive whose nature— unlike the drive for self-preservation—contains something that we can call "alter-centrism," which is precisely what creates the basis for love.

Now, the "libidinistic" interpretation of the sexual drive introduces a very thorough confusion of these concepts. For it imparts to the sexual drive a purely ego-centric meaning, that is, the meaning naturally belonging to the drive for self-preservation. Therefore, the utilitarian- ism in sexual ethics that is linked to this interpretation bears in itself a danger deeper than generally thought: a danger of a certain confusion of fundamental and elementary lines of human tendencies, of ways of human existence. This confusion, of course, must affect the whole spiri- tual situation of man. After all, here on earth the human spirit constitutes a substantial unity with the body, so the spiritual life cannot develop correctly when the elementary lines of human existence are thoroughly tangled in the sphere of matters directly involving the body. Reflections and conclusions in sexual ethics must penetrate deeply, especially when the commandment to love is accepted as the orientation point of these reflections and conclusions.

## Final remarks

At the end of these reflections aimed at the proper interpretation of the sexual drive, partly by excluding improper interpretations of the drive, certain conclusions linked to the traditional teaching on the ends of marriage present themselves. Now, the Church, as already mentioned, teaches consistently that the primary end of marriage is *procreatio*, whereas the secondary end is what in the Latin terminology has been defined as *mutuum adiutorium*. Besides these, there is a tertiary end listed—*remedium concupiscentiae*. Objectively speaking, marriage is above all to serve existence, then the relationship between a man and a woman, and finally the correct direction of concupiscence. The ends of marriage ordered in this way oppose any subjectivistic interpretation of the sexual drive, and accordingly they demand from man as person objectivity in thinking about sexual themes and above all in conduct. This objectivity is the foundation of conjugal morality.

In light of all the reflections contained in this chapter, especially in its first part ("Analysis of the Verb 'to use'"), it must be stated that in marriage the point is the realization of the aforementioned ends on the basis of the personalistic norm. Because a man and a woman are persons, they must consciously realize the ends of marriage in accordance with the above defined order, for this is an objective order that is accessible to reason, and thus binding for persons. At the same time, the personalistic norm contained in the evangelical commandment to love indicates the fundamental way of realizing these ends, which in themselves also proceed from nature, and to which—as the previous analysis demonstrated—the sexual drive directs man. Sexual morality, or, speaking more strictly, conjugal morality, consists in the constant and most mature possible synthesis of the finality of nature with the personalistic norm.* If any of the mentioned ends of marriage was treated independently from the personalistic norm—that is, ignoring the fact that a man and a woman are persons—then this would have to lead to some form of utilitarianism (in the first or the second meaning of the verb "to use"). Procreation treated this way leads to the rigoristic distortion; the "libidinistic" distortion is based on a similar treatment of the tertiary end of marriage—*remedium concupiscentiae.*

---

* The synthesis that is at issue could be expressed in a concise formula, namely the fact *that* I should love has its objective basis in *the personal dignity* of the recipient of action (the personalistic norm); however, *how* I should love has its objective basis in *human nature.* One must constantly take into account that "*natura*" does not mean here "*przyroda.*" [As I have already indicated in a previous note (n. 3, p. 298), although the word *przyroda* is translated as "nature," its meaning is synonymous with the material or biological environment. The proper notion of nature is denoted by the Polish word *natura.* — Trans.] The author has in mind man's nature understood most deeply, that is, with taking into account or even placing into the foreground these contents of that nature that the physical or all the more physicalistic conceptions cannot grasp (because of not being able to do so). Although they are ethically reliable in their own way, these contents, as being theoretical-descriptive, do not by themselves give rise to moral duty but only in their axiologized shape, thanks to the aforementioned synthesis with the personalistic norm.

Of course, the personalistic norm itself is not one of the ends of marriage; in general a norm is never an end, and an end is not a norm. Namely, it is a principle that conditions the proper realization of each of the mentioned ends and all of them together—proper, i.e., corresponding to man as person. At the same time, this principle guarantees that these ends will be realized in accordance with the indicated hierarchy, for a deviation from it contradicts the objective dignity of the person. Thus, the realization of all the ends of marriage must be at the same time the fulfillment of love as virtue, for only as virtue does love correspond to the evangelical commandment and the demands of the personalistic norm contained in this commandment. The thought that the ends of marriage can be realized without being based on the personalistic norm would be fundamentally unchristian, for it would be incompatible with the fundamental ethical demand of the Gospel. Therefore, we must greatly beware of a shallow interpretation of the teaching on the ends of marriage.

Considering that, it also seems advisable not to translate this *mutuum adiutorium*—which in the teaching of the Church on the ends of marriage has been listed as the secondary end after procreation— with "mutual love," as it sometimes happens. For then there arises the following possibility of confusing the concepts: procreation as the primary end is something different from "love," and on the other hand the tertiary end, *remedium concupiscentiae*, is also something different from "love." Yet, both procreation and *remedium concupiscentiae* as ends of marriage should proceed from love as virtue and thereby fit within the personalistic norm. *Mutuum adiutorium* as an end of marriage is also only an effect of love-virtue. There is no basis for translating the phrase *mutuum adiutorium* as "love." For by prioritizing the objective ends of marriage, the Church wants to underscore that procreation in the objective, ontological order is an end that is more important than for a man and a woman to live together complementing and supporting each other (*mutuum adiutorium*).[50] Similarly, the latter is more important than the satisfaction of natural concupiscence. However, opposing love to procreation or indicating a primacy of procreation over love is out of the question.

Besides, the realization of these ends is a complex fact. A complete, positive exclusion of the possibility of procreation undoubtedly diminishes or even eliminates the possibility of durable, mutual co-education of the spouses themselves.[51] Procreation unaccompanied by precisely this co-education and co-striving for the highest good would also be in a certain sense incomplete and incompatible with the love of the person. Indeed, the point here is not only and exclusively the material multiplication of the headcount within the human species, but also education—whose natural substratum is the family based on marriage—cemented by *mutuum adiutorium*. If an interior cooperation between a woman and a man exists in marriage, and if they know how to educate and complement (*uzupełniać się*) each other, then their love matures to become the basis of the family. However, marriage is not identified with the family and always remains, above all, an intimate union of two people.

In turn, the third end—*remedium concupiscentiae*—depends for its human realization on the previous two. Again, it must be admitted that the absolute severance from the natural effects of conjugal intercourse violates somehow the spontaneity and depth of lived-experiences, especially when artificial means are employed for this end. What leads to that, perhaps even to a higher degree, is the lack of reciprocal understanding and of reasonable concern for the full good of the spouse. We will return to these matters in chapter V.

# CHAPTER II

# The Person and Love

# Part One

# Metaphysical Analysis of Love

## *The word "love"*

The word "love" is not univocal. In this book we consciously narrow down the scope of this word's meaning, for we mean love between two persons who differ with respect to sex.[1] It is known, however, that even with this narrowing down the word "love" still possesses various meanings, so we cannot think of using it univocally. A detailed analysis is needed in order to reveal at least in a certain measure the whole wealth of the reality often signified by the word "love." This reality is complex and multifaceted. For the starting point we shall accept that love is always some reciprocal relation of persons. In turn, this is based on a certain relation to the good. Each person remains in such a relation, and both of them also remain in it. This is the starting point for the first part of our analysis of love, the metaphysical analysis. The analysis also concerns the general characteristic of love between a woman and a man. In order to conduct it, we must distinguish the fundamental elements that are contained in love, both the content-related elements linked with the relation to the good, and the structural elements linked with the reciprocal relation of persons. These elements are included in every kind of love. Thus, for instance, every love contains fondness or benevolence. Love between a woman and a man is one concretization of love in general, in which these common elements of love are contained in a specific way. Therefore, this analysis is called metaphysical—the word "love" clearly possesses an analogical sense.

In turn, the metaphysical analysis will open a path to the psychological analysis. Love of a woman and a man is formed deeply in the psyche of both persons and is linked to the specific sexual vitality of man. Hence, in fact, there is a need for a psycho-physiological or biopsychological analysis. The bio-physiological moments will be discussed in the last chapter ("Sexology and Ethics"). Human love, the love of persons, is neither reduced to nor identified with them. If this were the case, it would not be love, unless perhaps in the broadest meaning when we speak, for instance, of *amor naturalis* or of cosmic love, perceiving the latter in all the final tendencies occurring in nature (*przyroda*).

The love of a man and a woman is a reciprocal relation of persons and possesses a personal character. This is linked most closely to its profound ethical meaning, and in this ethical meaning it constitutes the content of the greatest commandment of the Gospel. Our analysis must finally turn to precisely this meaning. Its object will then be love as virtue, and the greatest virtue at that, which in a sense encompasses all the other virtues and elevates them all to its own level, while impressing on them its own profile.

This threefold analysis of what unites a woman and a man is indispensable in order to explicate gradually the precise meaning that interests us from the multitude of meanings associated with the word "love."

## Love as fondness [2]

The first element in the general analysis of love is the element of fondness (*upodobanie*).[3] As has been said, love signifies a reciprocal relation of two people, of both a woman and a man, based on some relation to the good. This relation to the good begins precisely with fondness. To be the object of fondness (*podobać się*) means more or less to be presented as a certain good. A woman can easily enter a man's field of vision as a specific good, and he, also as a good, can enter her field of vision. This two-sided ease of fondness toward each other is a fruit of the sexual drive understood as a property and a force of human nature, but a force working in persons and demanding to be placed on the level of persons. Fondness toward a person of the other sex places this force of nature, i.e., the drive, on the level of the person's life.

For fondness is most closely linked to cognition (*poznanie*), and with intellectual cognition at that, even though the object of cognition—a woman or a man—is concrete and as such falls under the senses. Fondness is based on impression, but impression alone does not yet constitute it. For in fondness we already discover a certain cognitive commitment of the subject toward the object, a woman toward a man and vice versa. Knowledge itself, even the most thorough knowledge, and mere thinking about a given person are not yet fondness, which is often formed independently from thorough knowledge of the person and without prolonged thinking about him. Fondness does not possess a purely cognitive structure. It must be admitted that not only meta-intellectual but also meta-cognitive factors, namely affections and the will, take part in this cognitive commitment that has a character of fondness.

Fondness is not only thinking about some person as a good; fondness means a commitment of thinking about this person as a certain good, and this commitment can be brought forth ultimately only by the will. So, some element of "I want" is already contained in this "fondness" although this element is still very indirect, and as a result of this, fondness has first of all a cognitive character. This is, so to speak, cognition committing the will, and it commits because it is committed by the will. It is difficult to explain fondness without granting a reciprocal penetration of reason and will. The sphere of affections, which plays a great role in fondness, will be an object of a somewhat more insightful analysis in the next part of this chapter. However, already it is proper to say that affections are present at the birth of love precisely through the fact that they help to shape a man's fondness toward a woman and hers in relation to him. The whole affective sphere of man is not by nature disposed toward cognition but rather toward passion (*doznawanie*).[4] The natural attitude of this sphere is expressed in an emotional-affective reaction to a good. Such a reaction must possess a great significance for fondness, in which a person, for instance Y, stands in the field of vision of another person, X, precisely as a good.

Affectivity is an ability to react to a good of a certain quality, an ability to be moved in an encounter with it (in the psychological analysis we will assume more detailed meanings of affectivity when contrasting it with sensuality). This quality of a good that a concrete man or a concrete woman is particularly capable of reacting to depends in a certain measure on various innate and inherited factors, as well as on various factors acquired both as a result of various influences and also by the conscious effort of a given person, by his work on himself. And this is precisely whence the tint of the content of affective life originates, the life that comes to light in individual emotional-affective reactions and possesses a great significance for fondness. To a large extent this life conditions the direction that fondness will follow, which person it will turn to, and what in this person it will focus on above all.[5]

For every human person is a good that is complex beyond words and in a sense not unvarying. Both a man and a woman are by nature bodily-spiritual beings. They are also goods of such a kind. As such this good stands in the field of vision of another person and becomes an object of fondness. So, if we consider fondness, so to speak, on the film of the consciousness of the subject who is fond of another person, then without violating and without upsetting the fundamental uniformity of this fondness, we must discover in it the lived-experiences of various values. All these values experienced (*przeżywać*) by the person who feels fondness toward another person originate from the latter person. The subject of fondness, Y, finds them in X. Precisely because of this, X stands in the field of vision of Y as a good that has awakened fondness.

Nevertheless, fondness does not equal only a certain sum of lived-experiences born in the contact of person X with person Y. All these lived-experiences appear with fondness in the consciousness of the person who is its subject. Fondness, however, is something more than this state of consciousness experiencing (*przeżywać*) these or those values. It has for its object a person and also proceeds from the whole person. This relation to the person is nothing else but love, although still in its bud. Fondness belongs to the essence of love and, in a sense, it is already love, even though love is not just fondness. This in particular was expressed by medieval thinkers who spoke of *amor complacentiae*. Fondness is not only one of the elements of love, in a sense its part, but also it is one of the essential aspects of love as a whole. Applying the principle of analogy, we can already speak of fondness itself as love. Hence *amor complacentiae*. The lived-experience of various values, which at that point can be in a sense read in the consciousness, is symptomatic of fondness, inasmuch as the lived-experience places on it one chief accent, so to speak, or even many of them. Therefore, in Y's fondness toward the person X, this or that value, which Y finds in X and to which he reacts particularly strongly, is manifested most powerfully.

However, the value to which Y reacts (clearly, one could similarly speak about the fondness of X toward Y) depends not only on the fact that it resides in X, that X possesses it, but also on the fact that Y is particularly sensitive to it, particularly inclined to perceive and experience (*przeżyć*) this value. This has much significance especially for love between a woman and a man. Although the object of fondness in such love is always the person, nevertheless there is no doubt that someone can be fond of a person in various ways. When, for instance, a concrete Y [he] is capable of reacting only or simply first and foremost to sensory-sexual values, then all his fondness toward X [her], and indirectly all his love for her, will be formed differently than when Y is more capable of a lively reaction to the spiritual or moral values of the other person, for example, to her intelligence or virtues of character.[6]

The emotional-affective reaction plays a considerable part in fondness and impresses its own mark on it. By themselves affections do not have cognitive power, although they have the power of disposing and orienting cognitive acts, and this in fact is most clearly manifested in fondness. But this in particular creates a certain interior difficulty with regard to the personal-sexual sphere.

This difficulty exists in the relation of lived-experience to truth. For affections appear in a spontaneous way—hence fondness toward some person arises at times suddenly and unexpectedly—but properly speaking this reaction is "blind." The natural activity of affections does not tend to grasp the truth about the object. Truth is in man a function and a task of reason. And although some thinkers (such as Pascal and Scheler) have strongly emphasized the distinctive logic of affections (*logique du coeur*), nonetheless emotional-affective reactions can help as much as hinder fondness of the true good.[7] And this is an extremely important issue for the value of every fondness. It is because the value of fondness lies in the fact that the good to which it turns is truly the good that is sought. So, in fondness between Y and X, the truth about the value of the person of whom the other person is fond is something fundamental and decisive. And precisely here the emotional-affective reactions at times contribute to distorting or falsifying fondness, when through them one perceives values in a given person that in truth do not exist there. This can be very dangerous for love. For when the affective reaction passes away—and fluctuation belongs to its nature—then the subject who based his entire relation to a given person on this reaction, and not on the truth about the person, is left in a vacuum, so to speak, being deprived of the good that he thought he had found. And sometimes an affective reaction of the opposite coloring is born out of this vacuum and the sense of disappointment linked to it: a purely affective love often turns into an affective hate toward the same person.

Therefore, precisely already in fondness—and even mostly in it—the moment of truth about the person toward whom this fondness turns is of such great importance. One must then take into account the tendency born from the whole dynamic of affective life, the tendency that inclines to diverting this moment of truth from the object of fondness, from the person, and turning it precisely toward the subject, that is, strictly speaking, toward the affections alone. Then one does not consider whether the person truly possesses the values that are perceived in him with fondness, but above all whether the affection born for the other is a true affection. Here there is at least one of the sources of subjectivism so common in love (we will return to this in due time).

In people's opinion love is first of all reduced to the truth of affections. Although there is no way to deny this completely, for it follows at least from the analysis of fondness alone, nevertheless due to the value of both fondness and love as a whole, one must demand that the truth about the person, who is the object of fondness, plays at least no lesser role in that fondness than the very truth of affections. The proper culture of fondness, one of the elements of truly educated and truly good love, consists in the appropriate unification of these truths.

Fondness is linked very closely with the lived-experience of values. The person of the other sex can provide many lived-experiences of varied value. All of them play some role in fondness as a whole, which, as has been said, finds its chief accent thanks to one of these values, thanks to a value experienced (*przeżyć*) most strongly. Since we now speak of truth in fondness (and indirectly of truth in love), an effort must be necessarily made so that fondness is never limited to partial values, to something that only inheres in the person without being the person himself. The point is simply to feel fondness toward the person, that is, while experiencing (*przeżywać*) various values that inhere in him, to experience (*przeżywać*) always together with them in the act of fondness the value of the person as such—that the person himself is a value, and not only that he deserves fondness because of the various values contained in him. At this point we cannot yet indicate why this moment is so important for fondness, as it will be manifested above all in the part devoted to the ethical analysis of love. In any case, fondness, which among various values contained in the person knows how to capture acutely above all the very value of the person, possesses the value of full truth; the good to which it turns is precisely the person and not something else. And the person as a being—thus also as a good—differs from everything else that is not a person.

"To be the object of fondness" (*podobać się*) means to be presented as a certain good, moreover, as a good that it is (this must be added in the name of truth, so important for the structure of fondness). The object of fondness, which stands as a good in the field of vision of the subject, presents itself to him at the same time as the beautiful. This is very important for fondness, upon which love between a woman and a man is based. It is known that a separate and extensive issue exists: the problem of feminine and masculine beauty. The lived-experience of beauty goes hand in hand with the lived-experience of value, as if each of them contained an "additional" aesthetic value. "Charm," "glamour," "enchantment"—these and similar words serve to describe this important moment of the love of persons. Man is beautiful, and as beautiful he can "reveal" himself to another person. A woman is beautiful in her own way, and through her beauty she can stand in a man's field of vision. A man is beautiful in his own way, and through his beauty he can stand in a woman's field of vision. The beautiful finds its place precisely in fondness.

There is no time here to engage in an analysis of all of man's beauty. It is proper, however, to recall that man is a person, a being whose nature is determined by "interiority." Thus, besides exterior beauty one must also know to discover the interior beauty of man and be fond of each other in it, or perhaps even know how to be fond of each other first and foremost in it. This truth is in some particular way important for love between a man and a woman, since this love is, and in any case should be, the love of persons. Fondness, upon which this love is based, cannot be born merely from visible and sensual beauty, but should completely and thoroughly take into account the beauty of the person.

## *Love as desire*

Based on the same principle previously used to define fondness, we can in turn speak of desire as one of the aspects of love. Again, it translates the Latin phrase *amor concupiscentiae*, which indicates not so much that desire constitutes one of the elements of love, but that love is also contained in desire. It belongs to the essence of love, as fondness does, and sometimes is manifested in love most strongly. Thus, the medieval thinkers who spoke about love of desire (*amor concupiscentiae*), as they similarly spoke about love of fondness (*amor complacentiae*), were completely right. Desire also belongs to the very essence of this love that is established between a woman and a man. This proceeds from the fact that the human person is a limited being, and not self-sufficient, and therefore—speaking most objectively—he needs other beings. Acknowledging the limitations and insufficiency of the human being serves as a point of departure for understanding the relation of this being to God. Man needs God, just as any other creature does, simply in order to live.

At this point, however, something else is at stake. Man, the human person, is a woman or a man. Sex is also a certain limitation, a certain one-sidedness. Thus, a man needs a woman as if to complement (*uzupełnić*) his being, and in a similar way she needs a man.[8] This objective, ontic need is manifested through the sexual drive.[9] The love of the person X toward the person Y grows on the substratum of this drive. This love is love of desire, for it proceeds from a need and aims at finding the missing good. This good is a woman for a man, and a man for a woman. Thus, objectively speaking, their love is love of desire. However, a deep difference occurs between love of desire (*amor concupiscentiae*) and desire itself (*concupiscentia*), especially sensual desire. Desire presupposes a sensual feeling of some lack, and this unpleasant feeling could be removed by means of a certain good. In this way, for instance, a man can desire a woman. A person then becomes a means to satisfy desire, just as food is used to satisfy hunger (this comparison is quite deficient). Nevertheless, what is hidden in the word "desire" suggests a relation of utility, and in the given case the object of this relation would be a person of the other sex. This is precisely what Christ spoke about: "Whoever looks at a woman in order to desire her has already committed adultery with her in his heart" (Mt 5:28). This sentence explains much concerning the essence of love and sexual morality. This problem will be outlined more fully in the analysis of sensuality.

So, love of desire is not reduced to desires alone. What is crystallized in this love is merely an objective need of a being directed to another being, which is a good and an object of pursuit for the former. However, in the consciousness of the person who is the subject of this pursuit, love of desire is not manifested in the least as desire alone. This love is manifested only as *longing for the good for oneself*: "I want you, because you are a good for me." The object of love of desire is a good for the subject: a woman for a man, a man for a woman. Therefore, love is experienced (*przeżywać*) as a longing for a person and not as desire alone, *concupiscentia*. Desire goes hand in hand with this longing, though it rather remains, so to speak, in its shadow. The loving subject is conscious of its presence and knows that it is in a sense at his disposal, but if he works on his love for the other person, he does not allow desire alone to prevail; he prevents it from overpowering all that is above it and belongs to his love. For even if he does not understand, he nonetheless feels that this predominance of desire would in a certain way deform love and deprive them both of it.

Although love of desire is not identified with sensual desires alone, it nonetheless constitutes that aspect of love in which—especially concerning the man-woman relation—attitudes close to utilitarian ones can settle in most easily. For, as has been stated, love of desire presupposes a real need, thanks to which (to use the words just employed) "you are a good *for me*." The good that serves to satisfy a need is in some way beneficial or even useful. But to be useful or even beneficial is different from being an object of use. Thus, one can simply state that through its aspect manifested in love of desire, love closely approaches the field of utility, permeating it nonetheless with its own essence. Therefore, true love of desire never turns into a utilitarian attitude, for it always (even in desire) originates from the personalistic principle. Let us add that *amor concupiscentiae* comes to light also in love of God, for whom man can long and does long as the good for himself. This is also the case in love between persons Y and X—if we apply a remote though eloquent analogy. The problem of their relations precisely in this area requires a particular precision so as not to see in sensual desires alone the full equivalent of love of desire and, on the other hand, not to think that the essence of love—the love of which a human person is capable in relation to another human person (all the more in relation to God)—is exhausted completely in love of desire.

## Love as benevolence

At this point, it is proper to emphasize that love is the fullest realization of the possibilities that dwell in man. Potentiality (from Latin *potentia*: possibility, potency, power) that is proper to the person is actualized most fully through love (the word "actualize" comes from Latin *actus*: act, perfection). The person finds in love the greatest fullness of his being, of his objective existence. Love is such action, such an act, which most fully develops the existence of the person.[10] Of course, this has to be true love. What does true love mean? It means a love in which the true essence of love is realized, the love that turns to the true (and not merely apparent) good in a true way, that is, the way that corresponds to the nature of the good. This ought to be also applied to love between a man and a woman. In this field also, true love perfects the being of the person and develops his existence. False love, on the other hand, causes quite contrary effects. False love is a love that either turns to an apparent good or—as usually happens—turns to some true good, but in a way that does not correspond to the nature of the good, in a way contrary to it. At times this happens to be the love between a man and a woman either in its assumptions or—even despite (apparently) good assumptions—in its particular manifestations, in its realization. False love is, in fact, evil love.

Also, the love of a woman and a man would be evil, or in any case incomplete, if it did not transcend desire. However, love of desire alone does not exhaust fully the essence of love between persons. It is not enough only to desire the person as a good for oneself, but in addition—and above all—it is also necessary to desire his good. This utterly altruistic turning of the will and affections is called in the language of St. Thomas *amor benevolentiae*, or *benevolentia* for short, which corresponds in our language, not quite accurately, by the way, to the concept of benevolence (*życzliwość*).[11] Love of one person for another must be benevolent, otherwise it will not be true. Moreover, it will not be love at all, but it will be only egoism. In the nature of love not only is there no contradiction between desire and benevolence, but in fact a connection exists between them. Let us say that Y [he] wants X [her] as a good for himself. In that case, however, he must want X to be a good, since without this she cannot be a good for him. In this way a connection between desire and benevolence is manifested.

However, benevolence alone does not consist in the following configuration of wants: Y [he] wants X [her] to be a good as complete as possible in order to be a good all the more for him. Benevolence separates itself from any self-interest, whose elements still prominently inhere in love of desire. Benevolence is simply disinterestedness in love: "I do not long for you as a good," but "I long for your good," "I long for what is good for you." A benevolent person longs for this without any thought of himself, without any regard for himself. Therefore, benevolent love, *amor benevolentiae*, is love in a more absolute sense than love of desire. It is love that is most pure. Through benevolence we come as close as possible to what constitutes the "pure essence" of love. Such love perfects its object the most; it develops most fully both his existence and the existence of the person to whom it turns.

A man's love for a woman and hers for him cannot but be love of desire, although it should move in the direction of becoming more and more complete benevolence, *benevolentia*. It should tend to this in every state and in every manifestation of their coexistence and interaction. However, it should tend to this particularly in marriage, since that is where not only love of desire is somehow manifested most distinctly, but also desire alone comes most distinctly to light. A specific richness of conjugal love, but also a specific difficulty, lies in this. There is no need to conceal or hide it. For true love of benevolence can go hand in hand with love of desire, and even with desire alone, as long as the latter does not overpower all else that is contained in the love of a man and a woman, or does not become its exclusive content and sense.

## *The problem of reciprocity*

Now we must turn to the problem of reciprocity (*wzajemność*), which demands looking at the love of a man and a woman not so much as a love of X for Y and Y for X, but rather as something that exists *between* them. Reciprocity is closely linked with love "between" a man and a woman. It is worthwhile to pay attention to this preposition.[12] It suggests that love is not only something in a woman and something in a man—for in that case there would be two loves, properly speaking—but also it is something joined and one. Numerically and psychologically speaking, there are two loves, but these two distinct psychological facts join and create one objective whole—one being, as it were, in which two persons are involved.

The relation of "I" to "we" is connected with this. Every person is a unique and unrepeatable "I." This "I" possesses its interiority thanks to which it is, so to speak, a little world, which depends on God for its existence, while at the same time being self-reliant within the proper limits.[13] The path from one to another "I" leads, then, through free will, through its commitment. This path, however, can lead only in one direction, for example, from X to Y. Then, love for a person is one-sided. Even though it does possess its distinct and authentic psychological profile, it nevertheless does not possess the objective fullness that reciprocity imparts to it. In that case it is called unrequited love, and it is well known that unrequited love is linked with pain and suffering. Such love may sometimes remain very long in its subject, in the person who experiences (*przeżywać*) it, but this happens in virtue of interior obstinacy, as it were, which rather deforms love and deprives it of its proper character. Unrequited love is condemned first to vegetation in its subject and then to a gradual agony. Sometimes even by its agony it also causes the very ability to love to die with it. However, it does not always come to this extreme.

In any case it is quite evident that love by its nature is not something one-sided but something two-sided, something "between" persons, something social. Its full being is precisely inter-personal and not individual. It is closely linked with the force of joining and uniting, and by its nature opposes dividing and isolating. It is necessary for the fullness of love that the path from X to Y meets the path from Y to X. Two-sided love creates the most proximate basis for two "I's" to become one "we." Its natural dynamic dwells in that. In order for the "we" to exist, two-sided love itself is not enough because, after all, there are still two "I's" in it, although they are already fully predisposed to become one "we." Reciprocity is decisive precisely for this "we" to come into existence. Reciprocity reveals that love has matured, that it has become something "between" persons, that it created some community—in this its full nature is realized. Reciprocity belongs precisely to it.

This sheds new light on the whole problem. We have previously stated that fondness, longing (desire), and benevolence all belong to the nature of love. Love of desire and love of benevolence differ from each other, but not so much as to exclude each other: Y can long for X as a good for himself and at the same time long for a good for X, regardless of the fact that X is a good for him. This is understood in a new way in light of the truth about reciprocity. Namely, when Y [he] longs for love from X [her] as a response to his love, then he longs for the other person above all as a co-creator of love and not as an object of desire. The "self-interest" of love would then lie only in the fact that it seeks a response, and this response is reciprocal love. However, because reciprocity belongs to the nature of love, determines its inter-personal profile, it is difficult to speak of "self-interest." The longing for reciprocity does not exclude the disinterested character of love. Indeed, reciprocal love can be thoroughly disinterested; nonetheless, what constitutes the content of love of desire between a woman and a man finds full satisfaction in it. Reciprocity, however, brings a synthesis, as it were, of love of desire and of benevolent love. Love of desire manifests itself especially when one of the persons begins to be jealous "about the other," when he fears the other's infidelity.

This is a separate problem, so important in the entire love between a woman and a man, so important in marriage. It is worthwhile to recall here what Aristotle said on the topic of reciprocity in his treatise on friendship (books VIII and IX of *Nicomachean Ethics*). According to Aristotle, reciprocity can vary, and this is determined by the character of the good upon which reciprocity, along with the entire friendship, is based. If this good is true (the honorable good), reciprocity is something profound, mature, and in a sense immovable. When, on the other hand, only advantage, utility (the useful good), or pleasure determines reciprocity, then it is something shallow and unstable. Indeed, although reciprocity is essentially always something "between" persons, it principally depends on what both persons contribute to it. Hence arises the fact that each of the persons, both X and Y, treats reciprocity in love not as something supra-personal, but as something utterly personal.

So, in reference to Aristotle's thought, if both persons contribute to reciprocal love their personal love, but a love of full ethical value, love-virtue, then reciprocity itself acquires characteristics of thorough stability, of certainty. This explains trust in the other person, a trust that liberates from suspicion and from jealousy—a trust that determines that love is the true good of two people. The fact that one can rely on the other person, that one can think of the other as a friend who will not fail, is for the one who loves a source of peace and of joy. Peace and joy are fruits of love very closely linked to its very essence.

However, if two persons contribute to reciprocal love only or above all desire that is inclined to use, to seek pleasure, then the very reciprocity does not possess the characteristics we are now discussing. One cannot have trust in the other human person once one knows or at least feels that that person is disposed only toward using and pleasure as the only end. Also, one cannot have this trust while being first of all disposed toward that oneself. At this place, the particular property of love by virtue of which love creates an inter-personal community "takes its revenge," as it were. It is enough for one of the persons to contribute a utilitarian attitude, and already the problem of "reciprocal love" generates much suspicion and jealousy. Suspicions and spells of jealousy in fact often proceed from man's weakness. However, people who even with all their weakness contribute true good will to their love are those who attempt to base reciprocity on "the honorable good"—on virtue, perhaps still imperfect but nonetheless real. Their life together gives them a constant opportunity to test their good will and complement it through virtue. Life together becomes, so to speak, a school of perfection.

It is a different matter when two people, or at least one of them, contribute merely a consumer attitude to "reciprocal love." A woman and a man can provide pleasure of a sexual nature to each other; they can be for each other a source of various advantages. However, pleasure and sensual delight themselves are not goods that join and unite people in the long run, as Aristotle pointed out most accurately. If only pleasure or advantage determines their "reciprocal love," a woman and a man will be united to each other as long as they continue to be a source of this pleasure or advantage for each other, as long as they will provide it for each other. As soon as this ends, the proper reason for "love" will also cease, the illusion of reciprocity will vanish. For true reciprocity cannot exist if it is based only on desire or on a consumer attitude. For this attitude does not seek an expression proper to it in the shape of reciprocal love, but it seeks only satisfaction, satiation. It is basically only and exclusively egoism, whereas reciprocity must presuppose altruism in both persons. True reciprocity cannot arise from two egoisms, since only a momentary or at least periodic pretense of reciprocity can arise from them.

Hence, two conclusions follow, one with a rather theoretical and the other with a more practical meaning. The first conclusion: in light of reflections on reciprocity, it is evident how much we need to analyze love not only from the psychological but above all from the ethical angle. The second, practical conclusion: one must always "test" love thoroughly before it is declared to each other, and especially before one considers it one's vocation and starts building one's life on it. Specifically, it is necessary to test what is "in" each of the persons co-creating this love, and consequently also what is "between" them. It must be established what their reciprocity is based on, and whether it is not merely an appearance of reciprocity. For love can survive only as a unity in which the mature "we" is manifested; it will not survive as an arrangement of two egoisms in the framework of which two "I's" are manifested. Love has a structure of interpersonal community.*

---

* *"The ability to participate in the very humanity of every man constitutes the core of all participation* [emphasis original] and conditions the personalistic value of all acting and being 'together with others.'. . . This commandment [to love —Ed.] in a particularly vivid and consistent way confirms that in any acting and being 'together with others' 'neighbor' (*bliźni*) as a system of reference has a fundamental significance" (*Person and Act*, 322–323 in section 10 of chapter VII). "The 'I-thou' relation opens man directly to the other man. . . . This humanity is given in the 'I-thou' relation not as an abstract idea of man . . . but as 'thou' for 'I.' Participation in this relationship is the same as realization of the interpersonal community whose personal subjectivity 'thou' is revealed through 'I' (and in a sense also reciprocally), but above all the personal subjectivity of both is confirmed, secured, and grows in this community" (K. Wojtyła, "Osoba: podmiot i wspólnota," *Roczniki Filozoficzne* 24, fasc. 2 [1976], 36). See K. Wojtyła, "Subjectivity and the Irreducible in Man," *Analecta Husserliana* 7, 107–114.

## From sympathy to friendship

Now we must take a look at the problem of human love in yet another aspect. Although this look is already strongly associated with the psychological analysis, we will still place it within this first part of the chapter, in which we deal with the general analysis of love. The word "sympathy" is of Greek origin and consists of the prefix *syn* (together with somebody) and the stem *pathein* (to suffer).[14] Literally then, sympathy means as much as "co-passion."[15] The meaning of the word indicates two moments that are contained in sympathy, namely the moment of a certain togetherness or community expressed by the prefix, and the moment of a certain passivity ("to suffer") expressed by the stem. Therefore, sympathy signifies above all what "happens" between people in the field of their affections—that through which emotional-affective lived-experiences unite people. It must be nonetheless clearly emphasized that this "happens" to them, and not that this is their work, the fruit of acts of the will. Sympathy is a manifestation of passion rather than of action: people yield to it in a way that is sometimes incomprehensible to them, and the will is pulled into the orbit of emotions and affections, which bring two people closer to each other regardless of whether or not one of them chose the other consciously as an object of love. Sympathy is purely affective love, in which the decision of the will and the choice do not yet play a proper role. At best, the will consents to the fact of sympathy and to its direction.

Although etymologically it seems to refer to affective love "between" persons, nevertheless we often think and speak about sympathy (*sympatia*) as being "toward" some person. When some person is agreeable (*sympatyczny*) to me, then he is located in my field of awareness as an "object" that is accompanied by a positive affective overtone, and this overtone denotes at the same time a "plus" for that person. This "plus" is born together with sympathy, and it can also die together with it, for it depends precisely on the affective attitude toward the person who is the object of sympathy. Nonetheless this "plus" of the person that is based only on sympathy can turn gradually into a thorough conviction about the person's value. Within the limits of sympathy itself, the lived-experience of the value of the object seems, however, something rather indirect: X experiences (*przeżywać*) the value of Y through the mediation of his sympathy, for thanks to the sympathy, Y acquires value for X. This implies a hint of subjectivism, which, together with the passivity advanced at the beginning, contributes to a certain weakness of sympathy. The weakness of sympathy lies in the fact that sympathy takes into possession man's affection and his will, often independently from the objective value of the person to whom it turns. The value of affection replaces in some sense the value of the person (of the object of sympathy).

As it is evident, the weakness of sympathy proceeds from its inadequate objectivity. However, this goes hand in hand with a great subjective force of sympathy, which confers on human loves their subjective vividness. By itself the rational acknowledgment of the value of the other person, even if most genuine, does not yet constitute love (as it also does not constitute fondness, which we spoke of at the beginning of this chapter). Only sympathy has the power to bring people closer together in a way perceptible to them, in an experiential way. For love is experience (*doświadczenie*) and not deduction only. Sympathy places one person in the circle of the other as somebody close. Because of it, one can "feel," so to speak, the other's whole personhood, that one lives in the circle of the other, at the same time finding him at every step in one's own. Precisely for this reason sympathy is for people an experiential and perceptible manifestation of love (a manifestation between a woman and a man that is so important). Thanks to sympathy they feel their own reciprocal love, and without it they in a sense lose this love and remain in some vacuum, one they can perceive. Therefore, it seems to them that once sympathy breaks off, love ends as well.

Yet, sympathy is not in the least the whole of love, just as emotion and affection are not the whole interior life of the human person, but only one of its elements. A deeper and much more fundamental element is the will, which is a power called to form love in man and between people. This statement is important because the love between a woman and a man cannot remain on the level of sympathy alone, but it must become friendship. For in friendship—unlike in sympathy itself—the participation of the will is decisive. I want the good for you as much as I want it for myself, for my own "I." One could grasp the content and structure of friendship with this paradigm. As is evident, it contains *benevolentia*, that is, benevolence (I want the good for you), as well as a characteristic "doubling" of the subject, a doubling of the "I": my "I" and your "I" constitute a moral unity, for the will relates to both with equal favor. Thus, as a matter of fact, your "I" becomes in a sense mine; it lives in my "I" as my "I" does in itself. This explains the very word "friendship." The doubling of "I" contained in it manifests moments of the personal union that friendship brings.

This union differs from the one achieved in sympathy. There it is based exclusively on emotion and affection, and the will only consents. In friendship, however, the will commits itself. And therefore friendship really takes possession of the whole man, it is his work, it contains in itself a clear choice of the person, of the second "I" to which it turns, while all this has not yet taken place within the limits of sympathy. The objective force of friendship consists precisely in that. Friendship, however, needs to be manifested in the subject; it needs a subjective accent, as it were. And sympathy provides this. In itself sympathy is not yet friendship, although it creates conditions so that friendship between two persons can come into existence, and, once existing, can possess its subjective vividness, its climate, and its affective warmth. For the very two-sided and reciprocal "I want the good for you," even though it constitutes the core of friendship, remains nonetheless, so to speak, suspended in a vacuum once it is deprived of the affective warmth that sympathy provides. By no means can affection alone replace this "I want the good for you," which nevertheless seems cold and incommunicative when isolated from affection.

From the point of view of education of love a clear postulate emerges here: sympathy must be *transformed* into friendship, and friendship *complemented* with sympathy. This postulate, as we see, develops in two directions. Sympathy alone still lacks an act of benevolence, without which there can be no true love. So, although sympathy can already seem to be benevolence (indeed, even something more than benevolence), nonetheless this entails a certain measure of illusion. In analyzing fondness we have already paid attention to this subjectivistic feature of affection, namely to the fact that affection shows a tendency to "divert truth" from an object and to turn it as much as possible toward itself. This tendency also results in taking sympathy and affective love already for friendship, and even for something more than friendship. And therefore such facts as marriage, which objectively speaking can be based only on friendship, are often based only on sympathy. As has been stated, friendship consists in a mature commitment of the will in relation to the other person with regard to his good. Consequently, a problem exists regarding the maturation of sympathy into friendship, and under normal circumstances this process demands reflection and time. Specifically, the point is to complement the value of affection itself—as the relation to the person and to his value within the limits of sympathy alone is based above all on affection—with objective knowledge of that person's value and with conviction about that value. For the will can actively commit itself only on this basis. Affections alone can commit the will, but only in a passive and rather superficial way, with a certain measure of subjectivism. Friendship, however, demands a genuine commitment of the will with as much objective justification as possible.

On the other hand, we encounter the problem of complementing friendship with sympathy, for without sympathy friendship would remain cold and incommunicative. This latter process is possible because sympathy is not only born in man in a spontaneous way and sustained in him in an irrational manner, but despite being born in this way tends to gravitate toward friendship; it has a tendency toward becoming friendship. This is a simple consequence of the structure of man's personal interiority, in which only what possesses a full justification in conviction and in free will can acquire full value. Neither impression itself nor affection based exclusively on it will replace this justification. And therefore, the possibility or at least the modest beginning of friendship as a rule goes hand in hand with sympathy between persons (X-Y). However, sympathy often happens to be vivid from the beginning, whereas friendship is at first pale and weak. The next step is to form a reciprocal friendship while taking advantage of the affective situation that sympathy produces, thereby conferring a thorough and objective meaning on sympathy itself. A mistake often made in human love, especially concerning the love between X and Y, consists in not forming friendship consciously from it but leaving it, in a sense, on the level of sympathy. A consequence of this mistake is also a belief that once sympathy breaks off, love also ends. This belief is very dangerous for human love, and this mistake is one of the fundamental gaps in the education of love.

Love can by no means consist in "using up" sympathy or finding an "outlet" in it (which often in relations between a man and a woman is accompanied by sexual "relief"). Love, however, consists in the thorough transformation of sympathy into friendship. For by its nature it is something creative and constructive, and not merely something to consume.[16] Sympathy is always only some indication and not a definitely finished fact possessing the complete, specific weight of persons.[17] Sympathy must only, so to speak, strive after man's substratum, strive after a solid ground in friendship, as, on the other hand, friendship must be complemented with the climate and temperature of sympathy. These are two processes, which should permeate reciprocally without hindering each other. The "art" of educating love, the proper *ars amandi*, consists precisely in this.[18] This art is greatly opposed by the type of conduct in which sympathy (which is vivid especially in the man-woman relation where a strong sensual-bodily drive accompanies it) obscures the need of creating friendship and prevents it in practice. It seems that this is frequently the cause of various disasters and failures to which human love is exposed.

This whole problem contains some incoherence between *two profiles of love*: the objective profile does not coincide with the subjective profile. Sympathy, in which the subjective profile of love is vividly outlined, is not yet friendship, in which the objective profile of love finally matures. At the same time, however, love itself must be something subjective, as, after all, it must inhere in subjects, in two personal subjects, in X and Y, and must be formed and expressed in them. Nonetheless, one ought not to confuse this subjective love with subjectivism. Love is always something subjective, for it inheres in subjects, but at the same time it should be free from subjectivism. It should be something objective in the subject, in the person, have an objective profile and not merely a subjective one. Precisely for this reason, love cannot be mere sympathy but must be friendship. The maturity of friendship between X and Y can be proved, among other ways, by whether sympathy accompanies friendship, and even more by whether or not friendship is completely dependent on sympathy (on emotional moments and affective moods alone), and whether besides these it possesses its distinct objective being (*byt*) in the person and between persons. Only then may marriage and the life of two people together be built on it.

Therefore, it seems that *companionship* (*koleżeństwo*) can play an important role in the development of love between a woman and a man. Companionship differs from both sympathy and friendship. It differs from sympathy by the fact that above all it does not reach to man's emotional-affective sphere, but is based on objective foundations such as common work, common objectives, common interests. Companionship differs from friendship by the fact that this "I want the good for you as if for my own 'I'" does not yet come to light in it. Thus, what is characteristic of companionship is the moment of community caused by some objective factors. People attend the same class, work in the same scientific laboratory, serve in the same military company, or their interests lie in the same field (in philately, for instance)—and this makes them companions. Companionship may also be born between Y and X—both independently from affective sympathy and in its background. This latter combination seems to be very beneficial, for it can help pure sympathy develop into true friendship. The point is that companionship introduces between two people, a woman and a man, some objective community, whereas sympathy joins them only in a subjective way. Thus, what can emerge thanks to companionship is the objective profile of love, without which love is always something incomplete. Affections themselves are rather changeable, as experience demonstrates, and therefore they cannot durably and exclusively determine the relation between two people. It is necessary to find the means by which affections not only will find their way into the will, but—what is more—will bring about this unity of the will (*unum velle*), thanks to which two "I's" become one "we."[19] It is precisely friendship that contains this unity.

Reciprocal friendship possesses an inter-personal character expressed in this "we." In companionship this "we" is also included, although it still lacks the cohesion and depth that belong to friendship. After all, companionship can link many persons with one another, whereas friendship can do so only with a small number of them. The social feature of companionship is manifested in the fact that people linked by it usually create a certain environment. And therefore companionship can still be so very important for the formation of reciprocal love between X and Y, if their love is to mature for marriage and become the cornerstone of a new family. People who are capable of living in an environment, who are capable of creating it, are rather well prepared to confer on the community of the family the character of a cohesive environment in which a good atmosphere of shared life prevails.

## Spousal love

The general analysis of love has above all a metaphysical character, even though at every step we also refer to psychological or ethical moments. These various aspects permeate one another, so that in no way can we penetrate one of them without involving the second or the third. In the analysis thus far we have attempted to grasp what belongs to the essence of every love and is realized in a specific way in the love between a woman and a man. In an individual subject, love is formed through fondness, desire, and benevolence. However, love finds its full being not merely in an individual subject only but in an inter-subjective, inter-personal relation. Hence, we have the problem of friendship, which has been analyzed here in connection with sympathy, and the problem of reciprocity—a problem linked to friendship. The transition from "I" to "we" is for love no less essential than transcending one's "I" as expressed through fondness, love of desire, and love of benevolence. Love—especially the one that interests us in this book—is not only a striving, but still far more a meeting, a uniting of persons. Clearly, this meeting and uniting of persons occurs on the basis of fondness, love of desire, and love of benevolence as they increase in the individual subjects. The aspect of individual love does not cease to occur in the inter-personal aspect, but indeed the former conditions the latter. As a result, love is always some inter-personal synthesis and synchronization of fondness, desire, and benevolence.

Spousal love (*miłość oblubieńcza*) is something else than all the aspects or forms of love analyzed up to this point.[20] It consists in giving one's own person. The essence of spousal love is giving oneself, giving one's "I." It constitutes at once something other and something more than fondness, than desire, and even than benevolence. All these forms of going out toward the other person with regard to the good do not reach as far as spousal love. "To give oneself" means more than merely "to want the good," even if by that the other "I" became as if my own, as happens in friendship. Spousal love is something other and something more than all the forms of love analyzed so far, both from the perspective of the individual subject, from the perspective of the person who loves, and from the perspective of the inter-personal connection created by love. When spousal love enters in this inter-personal relation, then something other than friendship arises, namely the reciprocal self-giving of persons.

This problem demands a more thorough consideration. First, the question presents itself: Can a person give himself to another person? After all it was stated that every person by his essence is nontransferable—*alteri incommunicabilis*. So, he is not only his own master (*sui iuris*), but also cannot impart or give himself. The nature of the person opposes such self-giving. Indeed, in the order of nature we cannot speak of giving a person to another person, especially if we understand this giving in a physical sense. What is personal rises above any form of giving and, on the other hand, above any form of appropriation in the physical sense. The person as such cannot be somebody's possession, like a thing. Consequently, treating the person as an object of use is also excluded, which was already analyzed in more detail. However, what is not possible and correct in the order of nature or in the physical sense can be accomplished in the order of love and in the moral sense. In this sense, the person can give himself to another person, both to a human person and to God, and through this giving a particular shape of love, which we define as spousal love, is formed.* This also testifies to a particular dynamic of the person and particular laws governing his existence and development. Christ expressed this in the sentence that seems to contain a deep paradox: "Whoever wants to save his soul will lose it, and whoever loses his soul for my sake will find it" (Mt 10:39).[21]

Indeed, the problem of spousal love contains a deep paradox, not only verbal but utterly real. The words of the Gospel indicate the

---

* "In accordance with Christ's teaching, this love [spousal love—Ed.] is realized *in one way* in the exclusive self-giving to God alone, and in another way in marriage through the reciprocal self-giving of human persons. . . . At the same time, however, it is necessary to emphasize that although God as the Creator possesses the '*dominium altum*,' the supreme right in relation to all creatures and thus also in relation to man, who is a person, the total self-giving 'to God loved beyond all things' (*Lumen Gentium*, 44), which is expressed in the religious vocation, by the will of Christ himself is left to the free choice of man under the action of grace" (K. Wojtyła, "O znaczeniu miłości oblubieńczej," *Roczniki Filozoficzne* 22, fasc. 2 [1974], 171; see p. 290 in this book).

particular reality and contain the truth that is realized in the life of the person. Now, because of his nature, every person is somebody non-transferable, in-communicable. In the order of nature, the person is disposed to perfecting himself, to attaining an ever greater fullness of his being, the being which, after all, is always some concrete "I." We have already stated that this perfecting of oneself comes through love and together with love. The fullest and so to speak the most radical form of love consists precisely in the fact of giving oneself, of making one's nontransferable and incommunicable "I" someone else's possession.[22] The paradox in this case is twofold and proceeds in two directions: first, that one can go out of one's own "I" in this way, and second, that by doing so, this "I" is not in the least destroyed or devalued, but, on the contrary, is developed and enriched—of course in the supra-physical sense, in the moral sense. The Gospel emphasizes this vividly and decidedly: "will lose—will find," "to save—to lose." We evidently discover in it not only the personalistic norm itself, but also very detailed and bold instructions that develop this norm in various directions. The world of persons possesses its own laws of existence and laws of development.

Self-giving as a form of love is formed in the interiority of the person on the basis of a mature perception of values, and on the basis of the readiness of the will capable of committing itself in precisely this way. In any case, spousal love cannot be something fragmentary or fortuitous in the interior life of the person. It always constitutes some particular crystallization of the whole human "I," since by virtue of this love it is determined to govern itself precisely in this way. In giving ourselves we must find a particular proof of possessing ourselves. Concerning particular realizations of this form of love, it seems that they may be quite varied. Not to mention the self-giving of a mother to a child, can we not find self-giving, giving one's "I," in the relation of a physician to a sick person, for instance, or of a teacher who with total devotion gives himself to the task of forming his pupil, or also of a pastor who with similar devotion gives himself to the soul entrusted to his care? In a similar way great social activists or apostles can give themselves to many people—often unknown by them personally— whom they serve by serving society. It is not easy to state the extent to which the authentic love of self-giving takes place in each of the aforementioned or similar cases. For what can be at work in all these cases is simply genuine benevolence and friendship toward people. In order, for example, to realize the vocation of a physician, of a teacher, or of a pastor "with total self-giving," it is enough simply to "want the good" for whom it is performed. And even if this attitude acquires the characteristics of full self-giving and is verified in this form as love, at any rate it would be difficult to apply to it the name of spousal love.

The concept of spousal love is linked to the giving of the individual person to another chosen person. And therefore we speak of spousal love in certain cases concerning the relation between man and God, which will be discussed separately in chapter IV. There also exist the deepest reasons to speak of spousal love in connection with marriage. The love of persons, of a man and a woman, leads in marriage to reciprocal self-giving. From the perspective of the individual person, it is explicit self-giving to another person, whereas in the inter-personal relation it is reciprocal self-giving. The self-giving being discussed here ought not to be completely identified (and consequently confused) with "self-giving" in the mere psychological sense, that is, with the lived-experience of self-giving, nor even more so with "self-giving" merely in the physical sense. Concerning the former of these senses, it is only a woman, or in any case first and foremost a woman, who experiences (*przeżywać*) her share in marriage as "self-giving;" a man experiences (*przeżywać*) it differently, so that, speaking psychologically, some correlation of "self-giving" and "possessing" takes place. However, the psychological point of view is insufficient here. For when we grasp the problem objectively throughout, thus ontologically, there must also occur in this relation reciprocal self-giving on behalf of a man, which—even though differently experienced (*przeżyć*) than by a woman—must nevertheless be real self-giving to the other person. For otherwise there is a danger of treating this other person, a woman, as an object, and even as an object of use. So, if marriage is to meet the demands of the personalistic norm, reciprocal self-giving, reciprocal spousal love, must be realized in it. Two facts of self-giving, the masculine and the feminine, meet in marriage on the basis of reciprocity, and even though psychologically they have different shapes, ontologically they occur and "compose" the mature totality of reciprocal self-giving. Hence a particular task emerges for a man, who must introduce in "conquering" or "possessing" a proper attitude and content that also includes self-giving.

All the more, of course, this self-giving with regard to marriage, or even generally in the relation of X to Y, cannot possess a merely sexual meaning. Merely sexual self-giving in the reciprocal relation of persons, without being fully justified by the self-giving of the person, must lead to the forms of utilitarianism, which we attempted to analyze as thoroughly as possible in chapter I. We must pay attention to this, since a more or less clear tendency exists to understand this "self-giving" in the Y-X relation in a purely sexual or sexual-psychological way. Instead, a personalistic understanding is necessarily needed here. And therefore, the whole profile of morality in which the commandment to love plays a central role by all means agrees with reducing marriage to spousal love, or rather—taking the problem educationally—with bringing marriage forth from this form of love. Hence certain consequences emerge, to which we shall return in chapter IV where we give reasons for monogamy. The self-giving of a woman to a man the way it occurs in marriage excludes—morally speaking—the simultaneous self-giving on his or her part to other persons in the same way. The sexual moment plays a particular role in the formation of spousal love. Sexual intercourse causes it to be restricted only to one couple, although at the same time it gains a specific intensity. Only in being so restricted can this love all the more fully open toward new persons who by nature are fruits of spousal love between a man and a woman.

The concept of spousal love possesses a key meaning for establishing norms for all sexual morality. A very particular link certainly exists between *sexus* and the person in the objective order, to which corresponds in the order of consciousness a particular awareness of the right for personal possession of one's own "I." This problem will be yet analyzed separately in chapter III (in its second part: "Metaphysics of Shame"). Consequently, out of the question is a sexual self-giving that would not mean a self-giving of the person and would not enter in some way into the orbit of these demands, which we have the right to make of spousal love. These demands proceed from the personalistic norm. Although spousal love itself differs by its essence from all the forms of love previously analyzed, it nonetheless cannot be formed in separation from them. It is especially indispensable for it to be closely bound with benevolence and with friendship. Without this interrelation spousal love may find itself in a very dangerous vacuum, and the persons involved in it will feel helpless in the face of interior and exterior facts, which they improvidently permitted to come into being within and between themselves.

# Part Two

# Psychological Analysis of Love

## *Impression and emotion**

In this analysis we must begin from what constitutes, so to speak, the "elementary part" of man's psychical life, namely impression (*wrażenie*) and emotion (*wzruszenie*), which is related to it. By impression we generally mean the content of the reaction of the senses to objective stimuli. The senses are most closely linked to the constitution of the human organism, although they are not identified with it. Thus, in no way can we reduce, for instance, the sense of sight to the following relationship in man's anatomy: the external receptor—the optic nerves—and the appropriate centers in the brain. The sense of sight contains something in addition, some specific psychical property and power that is not possessed by the mentioned organs, neither by all of them together nor by each of them separately. This psychical property belongs to the sphere of cognition. By the sense of sight, just as by any other sense, we apprehend certain objects, or, better yet: we apprehend objects in a certain way. The point concerns material objects, for only these fall under the senses. Some say occasionally that the proper object of the senses are the so-called sensual qualities.

Impressions are most closely linked to the specific property and power of the senses, which is cognition.[23] The senses react to their corresponding objects with the help of impressions. The object is reflected or mirrored; the senses capture and retain its image in themselves. An impression presupposes a direct contact of the sense with the given

---

* The point below shows how the harmonious union of particular "layers" of the human being in the personal act of love takes place, and how the structures and dynamisms proper to these "layers" reveal their full sense precisely in the act of love. Hence, it constitutes an exemplification of the theory of integration of the person in the act, presented later in a systematic and full way in the study *Person and Act*, part III, 199–282.

object—the direct experience, in the proper meaning of the word, lasts as long as this contact exists. Despite the fact that this direct experience ends, the senses still retain the image of the object, except that the impression is gradually replaced with the imagination. In connection with this, we also speak of the interior senses.[24] The exterior senses are those that establish direct contact with the object when it stands before them. The interior senses are those that maintain this contact when the object is not found in the direct scope of the exterior senses.

Thus an impression always contains in itself an image of the object, and this image is concrete and particular. All characteristics of "precisely this" object are reflected in this image, of course inasmuch as the impression itself is precise. For an impression may also be imprecise; in that case we grasp in it some distinctive characteristics that help reason to classify the object in general, and we do not grasp many more individual characteristics. It is known, however, that a material object can be subjected to a more insightful observation, and then also these latter characteristics will occur and be recorded in the sensory cognition.

Man receives an enormous number of impressions. The sensory receptors work constantly so that the whole nervous system gets tired and exhausted, and for this reason it needs respite and regeneration, just like other structural parts of the human organism. Due to this great number of impressions, not all of them are recorded in the same way on the film of human consciousness. Some are recorded better and more permanently, but others not as well and more transiently. A sensory image is often linked to a certain sensation or feeling. When somebody says that some thing or person "made an impression on him," he wants to convey that, together with the image of a certain sensory content, he sensed a perceptible movement, thanks to which the impression strongly affected his consciousness. But here we cross into the sphere of emotions.

Emotions are something separate, different from impressions.[25] An emotion is also a sensory reaction to some object, although the content of this reaction differs from the content of an impression. The image of an object is reflected in the content of an impression, whereas in an emotion we experience (*przeżywać*) some value of the object. For it is necessary to take into account the fact that different objects encountered in our direct sensory experience impose on us not only their content but also their value. An impression is a reaction to the content, whereas an emotion is a reaction to the value. An emotion itself is sensory, and, moreover, it even has the body as a factor; nevertheless, the value that evokes it does not have to be at all only material.[26] It is perfectly known that emotions are at times also evoked by immaterial, spiritual values. It is another matter that such a value must be somehow "materialized" in order to evoke an emotion. Thus, one must perceive, hear, imagine, or recall this value for an emotion to arise. It then possesses a greater depth. When a material value is its object, emotion is more shallow, more superficial. However, when a supra-material, spiritual value is the object of emotion, then emotion reaches deeper into man's psyche. This is understandable: after all, the human spirit and its powers must have had—directly or indirectly—a greater share in the rise of this emotion. The force of emotion is yet something else. So, an emotion can be shallow but strong, or it can be deep in its content, but weak. The ability to feel deep and simultaneously strong emotions seems to constitute some particularly significant factor of the interior life.

When an impression is joined with an emotion, then the object of the former and of the latter so much more distinctly forces itself into man's consciousness and appears in it. For what then appears in consciousness is not only an image, but also the value of the object, and, in connection with it, cognitive consciousness acquires, so to speak, an emotional color. A more intensive lived-experience arises, thanks to which the very object becomes something more important for the subject. All this has great significance, also concerning establishing contact between persons of different sex. For instance, it is known how significant so-called first impressions are in this sphere. It is known how much content the simple sentence contains: "She made an impression on him" or "He made an impression on her." If, however, human love begins with an impression, if everything in this love must be based in some way on this impression (even its spiritual content), it is precisely because impression is accompanied by emotion, which allows one to experience (*przeżyć*) the other person as a value, or, in other words, which allows two persons, a woman and a man, to experience (*przeżywać*) each other as a value. Therefore, in our further psychological analysis of love we must constantly refer to values.

## *Analysis of sensuality*

In the direct contact of a woman and a man some sensory experience always occurs in both persons. Each of them is a "body," and therefore each falls under the senses of the other, evoking some impression. An emotion sometimes goes hand in hand with this impression. The reason is that by nature a woman represents for a man, and a man for a woman, a certain value. This value is easily associated with an impression received by the senses and whose source is the person of the other sex. This ease of associating the value with the impression, and, as a result, the ease with which emotions arise in reciprocal contact between persons of different sex, remains connected with the sexual drive as the natural property and energy of the human being.

An emotion of this type is associated with an impression received by the senses; thus it is also in some way sensory. From this, however, it does not at all follow that the value itself to which we react with this emotion is also merely sensory, that it inheres in the very body of the other person, or that it is identified with this body. It was mentioned previously that emotions constitute a wide terrain for the penetration of the spiritual life, and so it happens sometimes that we are moved by spiritual values as well. In this case, however, concerning direct contact between a woman and a man, one must take into account that the content that also falls directly under the senses will at first appear in an impression. Thus, some "exterior" image of the other person emerges. Is this image only a reflection of a "body?" No, it is some reflection of "man," of a human being of the other sex. In fact, this content of the impression is indicated by the intellectual concept that appears in the consciousness together with the impression. But it is not this concept that contributes to the vividness of the impression, and that causes this X [her] to "make an impression" on that Y [him], or vice versa, him on her. Each of these persons "makes an impression" on the other thanks to the values which, together with the cognition of the "human being of the other sex," are experienced (*przeżywać*) by the knower. Values are the object of emotion, because it is precisely they which, by being associated with the impression, contribute to its vividness in the receiving subject.

Analyzing so-called sensuality (*zmysłowość*) in this light, it must be asserted that it is something more than an ordinary reaction of the senses to an object, to a person of the other sex. Sensuality does not consist in the fact that Y sensorially perceives X or vice versa. Sensuality always consists in the lived-experience of a certain value that is linked to the sensory perception. Namely, the point concerns the sexual value linked above all to the body of the person of the other sex (at this moment we do not speak of perversions, within which this sexual value can be linked to the body of a person of the same sex, or even a non-person such as an animal or an inanimate thing). Then, it is usually stated simply as "Y acts on my senses." This action on the senses is only collaterally linked with a lived-experience of the beauty of the body, with an aesthetic experience. In fact, another moment is essential for sensuality. Here, in the movement of sensuality itself, the "body" is at times experienced (*przeżywać*) as "a possible object of use." Sensuality by itself possesses a consumer orientation. This orientation tends above all and directly in the direction of the "body" while pertaining only indirectly to the person, whom it bypasses instead. As has been said, even with the very beauty of the body, sensuality has only a collateral connection. For beauty is fundamentally the object of contemplative cognition, and the lived-experience of aesthetic values does not have the character of use but evokes joy, which St. Augustine called *frui*. Thus, properly speaking, sensuality hinders the lived-experience of beauty, even bodily, sensual beauty, for it introduces a consumer relation to the object: the "body" is then experienced (*przeżywać*) as a possible object of use.

This attitude of sensuality is spontaneous, instinctive. In this form, however, it is not, above all, something morally evil, but is above all something natural. In order to substantiate this, we must become aware of the connections that occur between the reactions of the senses and the sexual vitality of the human body. The task of a biologist, a physiologist, or a physician is to elucidate this problem more accurately. It is known that every man is born already as a being belonging to one of the sexes. However, he achieves proper sexual maturity only gradually, which happens in general in the second decade of his life. Together with sexual maturity, the whole sexual vitality of the organism is also developed. Many vegetative processes belong to it, such as, for example, the activity of certain hormones, ovulation in women, and spermato-genesis in the male organism. These processes occur in the organism and remain outside the scope of actual consciousness, which does not mean, however, that man cannot know their nature and progress with greater or lesser accuracy.[27]

Sensuality itself is not in the least identified with the sexual vitality of a woman's or a man's body, a vitality which in itself possesses a merely vegetative and not yet sensual character.[28] Therefore, we also encounter sexually colored manifestations of sensuality among children, whose organism is not yet sexually mature. Although sensuality itself differs from the sexual vitality of the human body, it nonetheless must be grasped in connection with this vitality, in connection with the whole vegetative sexual vitality. The sexual drive expresses itself in this vitality in such a way that the organism possessing masculine properties "needs" an organism possessing feminine properties in order to achieve the proper effect through being joined to it—the effect in which the sexual vitality of the body finds its natural consummation. For the sexual vital-ity is by nature disposed toward reproduction, and the other sex serves this end. This disposition in itself is not to consume, since nature does not have only use for an end. Hence, this is simply a natural disposition in which an objective need of a being comes to light.

This natural orientation, which dwells in the vegetative sexual pro-cesses themselves, is shared by the senses. Hence, sensuality possesses above all an appetitive attitude: the person of the other sex is perceived as an object of desire precisely due to the sexual value directly associated with the body itself, for in the body the senses find above all what deter-mines the distinctness, the sexual "otherness." This value reaches consciousness through an impression when this impression is accompa-nied by an emotion perceptible not only psychically but also bodily. Sensuality is linked to movements of the body, especially in its so-called erogenous zones. This is a proof of a close relation between sensuality and the interior sexual vitality of the whole organism. For a body endowed with masculine properties needs a body endowed with femi-nine properties to fulfill the objective ends that are served by the sexual drive. The disposition of sensuality would be natural and as such would completely suffice in sexual life, first, if sexual reactions in man were infallibly regulated by instinct, and, second, if the object of these reactions—who belongs to the other sex—did not demand a different relation than the one that is proper to sensuality alone.

Yet, as we know, the human person cannot be an object of use. For the body is an integral part of the person, and thus it cannot be separated from the totality of the person; both the value of the body and the value of sex expressed in the body are based on the value of the person. In this objective relationship, the reaction of sensuality, in which the body and *sexus* appear as an object of possible use, threatens to devalue the person. To experience (*przeżywać*) the body in this way means to permit the "use" of the person, and, therefore, the reaction of conscience to the movements of sensuality is something easily understandable. For the attempt is either to separate artificially the body and *sexus* from the person in order to keep them as "a possible object of use," or to valuate the person exclusively with respect to the body and *sexus* as an object of use. Both the former and the latter are fundamentally contrary to the value of the person as such. Let us add that in man "pure" sensuality, as it occurs in animals, and the infallible regulation of this reaction by instinct are out of the question. Therefore, what is completely natural in animals stands below nature in man. The very content of the reaction of sensuality, which includes the lived-experience of the body and sex as "a possible object of use," indicates that sensuality in man is not "pure," but in some way processed with regard to value. Pure, natural sensuality directed in its reactions by instinct is not disposed toward mere use in isolation from the end of sexual life, whereas in man it does possess this disposition.

Therefore, sensuality alone is not love, and can very easily become its opposite. At the same time, however, it must be admitted that in the man-woman relationship, sensuality as a natural reaction to the person of the other sex is some sort of material for conjugal love, for spousal love. Nonetheless, by itself it definitely does not fulfill this role. A disposition toward the sexual value linked to the "body" as an object of use absolutely demands integration: it must be joined in a complete and mature relation to the person, since without this it is definitely not love. Indeed, a current, as it were, of love of desire flows through sensuality. However, if it is not complemented with other, nobler elements of love (we spoke of them in the first part of this chapter) but remains desire alone, then most certainly it is not love. So, sensuality must be open to other, nobler elements of love.

For by itself sensuality is completely blind to the person and oriented only toward the sexual value linked to the "body." Therefore, it demonstrates a characteristic instability—it turns to wherever it finds this value, wherever "a possible object of use" appears. Various senses indicate its presence, each in some different way—for instance, the sense of touch in one way, the higher senses such as the senses of sight and of hearing in another. But not only the exterior senses serve sensuality; the interior senses such as imagination and memory serve it as well. Through the mediation of each of them, one can establish contact even with the "body" of a person physically absent by experiencing (*przeżywać*) the value of that body inasmuch as it constitutes "a possible object of use." This is symptomatic of sensuality. This symptomatic moment arises even when the body of the other person is not in the least treated as an object of use. For instance, it can occur when the body is an object of some research, study, or art. In that case, sensuality very often attaches itself, so to speak, "alongside": sometimes it attempts to pull into its orbit the entire relation to the body and to the person, and sometimes it only evokes in consciousness a characteristic reflex, which proves that the given relation to the body and to the person "could" have been pulled into the orbit of sensuality—sensuality that waits just behind the threshold, as it were.

All this, however, does not in the least prove that sensual excitability itself, as an innate and natural property of a concrete person, is something morally evil. Abundant excitability is merely rich—though difficult—material for his personal life. All the more and so much more maturely it must open itself to what constitutes personal love. Vehement sensual excitability (as long as it is not morbid) can then become a factor that conditions even fuller and more ardent love. This love will be, of course, a fruit of sublimation.

At this point, it is proper to mention at least in a few words so-called sex-appeal. This Anglo-Saxon word does not signify in the least the same thing as "the sexual drive." It speaks only about sensual excitability and about sensuality. This word is used in reference to the ability to evoke sensual arousal or readiness to experience (*przeżywać*) it. In sex-appeal, the function of sex is restricted to the sphere of the senses and sensuality. The point concerns the lived-experience of the sexual value linked to the "body" precisely as "a possible object of use"

—whether potential or actual. This exhausts the point of view of sex-appeal. It proclaims the value of the body and of sex to be self-reliant or self-sufficient, and thereby severs the path to integration of this value in full and mature personal love. According to this understanding, sex-appeal becomes the exponent of disintegrated love, which bears only marks of sensuality.

## *Affectivity and affective love*

Affectivity (*uczuciowość*) must be clearly distinguished from sensuality (*zmysłowość*). It has been said already that an impression usually goes hand in hand with an emotion, an emotional lived-experience. Although an impression is sensory, an emotion can turn toward the immaterial value linked to the object of the impression. Direct contact between a man and a woman always carries with itself some impression, which can be accompanied by an emotion. When this emotion has for its object the sexual value related to the "body" itself as "a possible object of use," then it is a manifestation of sensuality. However, the sexual value being the object of an emotion does not in the least have to be linked to the "body" itself as "a possible object of use." It can be linked to the whole "human being of the other sex." Then, the object of the emotional lived-experience for a woman will be the value of "masculinity," and for a man the value of "femininity." The former may be associated, for instance, with an impression of "strength," whereas the latter with an impression of "charm," but both are linked to the whole human being of the other sex and not only to his "body." So, this particular sensibility (not excitability) toward the sexual value linked to the "whole human being of the other sex," to "femininity," to "masculinity," should be called affectivity.

This sensibility is the source of affective love. It differs from sensuality not so much in its basis as in its interior content. For the basis of the former and the latter is the same sensory intuition. The content of an impression is the whole "human being of the other sex," a whole "woman," a whole "man." Within this integral content of an impression, the "body" is for sensuality immediately emphasized and contrasted, as it were, against the rest; whereas affectivity stops at the whole human being of the other sex. And so, the sexual value remains linked to the whole man and is not limited only to his "body." Accordingly, the attitude to use, which is so characteristic of sensuality, does not emerge in affectivity. Affectivity is not oriented to consume. Therefore, contemplative moments linked to beauty, to the lived-experience of aesthetic values, may come to light in it. Masculine affectivity is permeated with some deep attention and admiration in relation to "femininity," and feminine affectivity with similar deep attention and admiration in relation to "masculinity." At this point, no wish to use is heard within the boundaries of affectivity alone.

Affectivity seems to be free from desire in the sense in which sensuality is full of it. In the emotional lived-experience, however, another longing is heard and another need comes to light. This is the longing for drawing near, for closeness, and at the same time for exclusivity or intimacy, for some "one on one" while "yet together." Affective love holds both people close to each other, and even if they are physically far from each other, it commands them still to move intentionally in each other's sphere. This love encompasses memory and imagination, and it simultaneously imparts itself to the will. It does not excite it, but rather pulls the will into its orbit through a specific mood, which envelops the will by exerting a peculiar charm on it. Man moves within this mood, and in this way he remains interiorly still in the nearness of the person to whom affective love binds him. When a woman and a man bound with such love are close to each other, they then seek exterior means of expression for what binds them. These are various manifestations of tenderness, which are expressed in looks, words, gestures, reciprocal nearness, and the coming together of both individuals—at this point I am deliberately not using the phrase "the nearness of bodies," for affectivity in itself seems to both, especially to a woman, something non-bodily.[29] Indeed, it does not show the disposition toward the body as does sensuality. Therefore, affective love is so often identified with spiritual love.

Clearly, this mutual nearness as an expression of reciprocal tenderness, even though proceeding directly from affection itself, can shift very easily to the area of sensuality. It will not be at once conspicuous sensuality, one with an acutely manifested disposition toward bodily use, but sensuality that is hidden and latent in affectivity. It seems that in this respect, a characteristic difference occurs in general between a woman and a man. According to a common opinion, a woman is "by nature" more affective, whereas a man is more sensual. We have already indicated the feature that is symptomatic of sensuality (the lived-experience of the sexual value linked to the "body" as "a possible object of use"). Now, this feature is more speedily awakened in a man, more speedily crystallized in his consciousness and attitude. The very structure of the masculine psyche and personality is such that it is more speedily forced, as it were, to reveal and objectify what is hidden in love for the person of the other sex. This is linked to the rather more active role of a man in this love, and also has a bearing on his responsibility. Concerning a woman, however, sensuality is, so to speak, concealed and hidden in affectivity. And therefore she is "by nature" more inclined to consider as a manifestation of affective love what a man already clearly recognizes as an activity of sensuality and a wish to use. Hence, evidently a certain psychological divergence exists in the scope of a man's and a woman's participation in love. A woman seems more passive, although in another way she is more active. In any case, her role and responsibility will be different from the role and responsibility of a man.

Let us again return for a moment to the beginning of our reflections on affectivity and affective love. The emotional lived-experience linked to an impression has for its object the sexual value that is linked to the whole "human being of the other sex," and this lived-experience is in itself free from an attitude to use. Thanks to the fact that the whole affective relation of a man to a woman, which is centered on her "femininity," or the affective relation of a woman to a man, which is centered on his "masculinity," is free from an orientation to consume, certain characteristic processes may occur around this central value, which is the object of the affective lived-experience.[30] So, in the field of vision of the person affectively committed to another person, the value of the object of his love expands enormously, usually disproportionately to its true value. Affective love influences imagination and memory, and at the same time lives under their influence. Perhaps this explains the fact of "depositing" various values in the object of one's love—values that it does not necessarily have to possess in itself. These values are ideal, not real. They live in the consciousness of the person affectively committed, and it often happens that affective love retrieves them from hiding in the subconscious and places them in the field of consciousness. Affection is fertile inside the subject: because the subject would like these various values to be present in the person who is the object of his love, and yearns for and dreams about that, affection evokes them all and bestows them on the person to whom it turns, so that the emotional commitment will thus be all the more complete.

The phenomenon of idealizing a person who is the object of love is well known. It is characteristic especially of youthful love. The ideal in it is stronger than the real living man, and the latter often serves only as an occasion for these values which this subject clings to in the other person with his whole heart to indeed erupt in the emotional consciousness of the subject. The point is not whether these values really belong to the concrete person to whom the subject's affective love turned. For this person, as has been said, is less the object and more the occasion for affective love. Affectivity is subjective and feeds above all—and sometimes even to excess—on the values that the subject alone carries in himself, to which he clings consciously and subconsciously. This also differentiates affectivity from sensuality, for the latter is in its way objective: it feeds on the sexual value connected with the "body" of the person who is the object of desire, although, of course, this is the objectivity of desire, and not the objectivity of love.

Nevertheless, the main source of the weakness of all affective love seems to dwell in the characteristic feature of human affectivity observed a moment ago. This love demonstrates the following remarkable ambivalence: on the one hand, it seeks closeness to the beloved person, it seeks nearness and expressions of tenderness; whereas, on the other hand, it actually finds itself at a distance from the person, for it does not live on his true value, but it lives in a sense off him, on these values to which the subject himself clings as to his ideal. And therefore, affective love alone often causes disillusionments. The person—especially a woman—may be disillusioned by the fact that over time a man's affection turns out to be only, so to speak, a cover for desire or even for an explicit will to use. Both a woman and a man may be disillusioned by the fact that the values attributed to the beloved person turn out to be fiction. Because of the dissonance between the ideal and the reality, affective love is sometimes not only extinguished but even transformed into affective hatred. And the latter, so to speak, as a rule (or "by nature") does not perceive the values that are really present in the other person. Hence, it is not known whether this interior fertility of affection, together with the urge to idealize the object of love that is connected to it, is a strength or rather a weakness of affective love. However, it is known for certain that it itself—as a form of the reciprocal relation between a woman and a man—cannot suffice. It too needs integration, as does sensual desire. If "love" remains mere sensuality, mere sex-appeal, it will not be itself at all, but will be merely the using of a person by a person, or eventually the using of each other. And if it remains mere affectivity, then again love will not yet be love according to the full meaning of the word. For both persons will, after all, remain somehow separated from each other, although it may seem that they are quite close to each other since they seek nearness so much. Affection alone suffers from subjectivism, so that the mature objective profile of love must only be formed and mature on its substratum with the help of other sources—affection alone will not create this profile. Left to itself, it too may turn out to be something merely related to "consumption." We shall cover this in chapter III.

At this point, however, it is necessary to appeal to these forces that are capable of forming the objective profile of love. These are the forces of the human spirit, and thanks to them the integration of love is achieved.

## *The problem of the integration of love*

Psychologically speaking, love can be understood as a certain situation. On the one hand, it is an interior situation existing in a concrete subject, in some person, and at the same time it is a situation between two persons, between a woman and a man. In any case, both from within and from without, it is a concrete situation, at the same time unique and unrepeatable. The exterior concreteness and uniqueness of this situation we call love is most closely linked to its interior side, to what dwells in both persons as if they are actors of the drama of their own love. Love is certainly a drama in the sense that it is always a happening and at the same time an acting, which is, after all, signified by the Greek word *drao*, whence comes "drama." So, the *dramatis personae*, Y and X, find the plot of this drama in themselves; they find love always as a psycho-logical situation unique in its kind, which is a very important and absorbing affair of their interior lives. It is known that among many objects of the visible world, the person is an unusual object, endowed with a specific "interiority" and capable of interior life.

Psychology, which by its name is the science of the soul, attempts to reveal the structure and fabric of man's interior life. In its investigations it must state that the moment of truth and the moment of freedom are the most characteristic of this life. Truth is directly linked with the sphere of cognition. Human cognition does not consist only in mirror-ing or "reflecting" objects, but is most closely related to experiencing (*przeżywać*) truth or falsehood. This experiencing is exactly what con-stitutes the most interior as well as the most essential nerve of human cognition. If cognition consisted only in "reflecting" objects, one might suspect that it is of a material nature.* However, the lived-experience of truth or falsehood lies completely outside the boundaries of what mat-ter of itself can give. Truth conditions freedom, for man can retain freedom in relation to various objects that in his action present them-selves to him as good and worthy of desire, inasmuch as he is able to grasp these goods in the light of truth and in this way form his self-reliant relation to them. Without this ability, man would be doomed to determination: these goods would take possession of him and decide completely about the character of his acts and the whole direction of his activity. The ability to know truth enables man's self-determination, that is, self-reliant determination of the character and direction of his own acts—and freedom consists precisely in this.

The psychological analysis of the love between persons of different sex conducted thus far has shown that this love is born on the substra-tum of the sexual drive. This has its direct consequences in the lived-experience, which, as we have stated, in the case of each person, both the woman and the man, centers around the sexual value. This value is bound with the "human being of the other sex." When it is con-nected above all with the "body" of this man and demonstrates the characteristic orientation to use, then sensual desire dominates in the

---

* See more about consciousness and its reflexive function in *Person and Act*, 44–51 (section 4 of chapter I).

lived-experience. When, however, the sexual value as the content of the lived-experience does not relate first and foremost to the "body," then the dominant feature of the lived-experience shifts toward affectivity—desire does not move to the foreground. An enormous number of possible shapes of the lived-experience exist, depending on the prevailing relation to the sexual value. Each of these shapes is strictly individual, for it belongs to a concrete person and is formed in a concrete "interiority" as well as in concrete exterior conditions. Depending on which psychical energies come to light first and foremost, we are presented with either abundant affective commitment or passionate desire.

All this play of interior forces is mirrored in consciousness. A characteristic feature of sexual love is its great intensity, and this testifies indirectly to the force of the sexual drive and its significance in human life. This intensive concentration of vital and psychical forces strongly absorbs consciousness, so strongly in fact, that other lived-experiences in comparison with sexual love seem at times to fade and lose their specific weight. In order to be convinced of this, it is enough to observe people who are seized with this love. Platonic thought regarding the power of Eros is still confirmed. If sexual love can be understood as a certain situation inside the person, this situation is psychologically vivid and attractive. Man finds in it a concentration of such energies that, before this lived-experience, he did not even know existed in him. For him, therefore, this lived-experience is connected with pleasure, with the joy of existence, of living and acting, even if somehow pain, sadness, or despondency force themselves into it.

In this way love appears in its subjective profile, and precisely in this profile it always constitutes some concrete, unique, and unrepeatable situation of human interiority. At the same time it strives for integration both "in" the person and "between" persons. The Latin word *integer* means "whole," and therefore integration means unification, a tendency toward completeness and wholeness.[31] The process of the integration of love is based on the spiritual element in man: freedom and truth.

Freedom together with truth, and truth together with freedom determine this spiritual mark, which is impressed on various manifestations of life and of human action.[32] They enter, in a sense, the deepest recesses of human acts and human lived-experiences, and fill them with content, the traces of which we do not encounter in animal life. It is precisely to this content that the love between persons of different sex also owes its proper consistency. Although love is based on the body and the senses so firmly and explicitly, it is nevertheless not the body and the senses alone that create its proper framework and proper profile. Love is always an affair of interiority and of spirit; in fact, to the degree it ceases to be an affair of interiority and of spirit it also ceases to be love. What remains of it in the senses themselves and in the sexual vitality of the human body alone does not constitute its proper essence. The will is in a sense the last resort in the person; without its participation no lived-experience has full personal value—it does not possess the complete, specific weight of the person. This specific weight of the person is closely connected with freedom, and freedom is a property of the will. It is especially love that "needs" freedom, as the commitment of freedom constitutes, in a sense, love's psychological essence. What does not proceed from freedom, what does not carry marks of free commitment but has the mark of determination and coercion, cannot be acknowledged as love; it does not have love's essence in itself. And therefore, in the process of psychical integration, which takes place together with sexual love in the interiority of the person, the point concerns not merely the commitment of the will, but the fully-mature commitment of freedom—the point is for the will to commit itself in the fullest way, the way most proper to it.

Only by being based on truth is the truly free commitment of the will possible. The lived-experience of freedom goes hand in hand with the lived-experience of truth.* Every interior situation has its psychological veracity: sensual desire one and affective commitment another.[33] It is a subjective veracity: Y [he] truly desires X [her], for he finds in his interior life a distinct sensation with an appetitive tint, a sensation directed precisely to her and arising from the impression she made on him. Similarly, for instance, X [she] is truly affectively committed in

---

* "Freedom in the fundamental sense is the same as self-dependence. Freedom in the developed sense is independence in the intentional sphere. Turning toward various possible objects of the will is determined neither by these objects nor by their presentation. Independence in the intentional sphere, understood this way, is explained precisely by that interior relation to truth and dependence on it, which is essential for the will itself. *Precisely this dependence makes the will independent from objects and their presentation*" [emphasis original] (*Person and Act*, 145 in section 7 of chapter III).

relation to Y [him], for she finds in her interior life such emotions and such readiness for emotions, such longing for closeness and for reliance on him, born from the impression of his masculine strength, that she must acknowledge her interior situation as love. Considering the matter within the subjective profile, in both cases we are dealing with true love.

Yet, love also demands objective truth. Only thanks to it, only on its basis, can the integration of love come about. As long as we consider love only in the light of its subjective veracity, we do not yet possess its full image and cannot declare anything about its objective value. The latter is, after all, most important. In fact, we are to reach it exactly in the course of the ethical analysis of love.

# Part Three

# Ethical Analysis of Love

## Lived-experience and virtue

In contemporary ethics a characteristic tendency exists that we call situationism. In philosophy it remains closely connected to existential-ism, among other things.* According to these views, human existence consists of many situations that by themselves already constitute, so to speak, a norm of action. One must receive and experience (*przeżyć*) them in their complete content without referring to anything that is located outside this concrete situation. What is "outside the situation," by the very fact of being outside, cannot be placed in it and applied to it. Human life does not receive any general and abstract norms that are found "outside the situation"—they are too rigid and essential, whereas

---

* Reading the critique of situationism conducted by the author, one must take into consideration two points:

1) The author's intention is not to offer a comprehensive presentation of situationism, but to indicate the danger of a certain one-sided interpretation of the phenomenon of love (subjectivization of love), a one-sidedness that can be observed in the views characterized by—as the author cautiously says—a characteristic situationistic tendency. This tendency was first of all manifested in emphasizing the role of the actual character (attitude) of the agent at the expense of due consideration of the objective structure of the person who is the recipient of the action, of the structure that is fundamentally the same despite its changeable elements.

2) Situationism experienced (*przeżyć*) its evolution and attained theoretical elaboration and particular popularity—also among theologians—only in the 1960s, a few years after the publication of *Love and Responsibility*. At the same time its connection with existentialism underwent a significant relaxation, which is particularly evident in the ultra-teleological theory of argumentation for the rightness of the norms of conduct, the theory called by the name of act-utilitarianism.

This, however, does not mean that the reservations about situationism as presented in the book have lost their relevance. For at the basis of the author's critical position lies a conception of the human person (the subject and object of the moral act) that is fundamentally different from the conception implied by both of the aforementioned forms of situationism.

life is always utterly concrete and existential.[34] If we apply the above presuppositions to our problem, then love of a woman and a man, as a specific fragment of their existence (or coexistence), would consist of many situations that by themselves would determine its value. These psychological situations would be something ultimate concerning the structure of sexual love and its content. Every situation in the development of this love would be at the same time a norm outside of which nothing more and nothing deeper could possibly be sought. This position proclaims the primacy of lived-experience over virtue.

At the same time, however, the above position conceals in itself an erroneous notion of freedom. It has been said previously that freedom of the will is possible only on the basis of truth grasped in cognition. Duty is closely bound with this. For man should choose the true good. It is precisely duty that most fully reveals the freedom of the human will. The will "should" follow the true good, but this "should" indicates that it "can" also not follow it—therefore it should follow precisely because it can not follow. Situationism and existentialism, which supposedly in the name of freedom reject duty objectively substantiated, precisely by this very fact sever themselves from the really understood freedom of the will, or in any case from what most fully manifests this freedom.[35] For freedom of the human will is manifested most fully in morality through duty. And duty always arises when the will encounters some norm. Hence, one cannot seek the full integration of human love in the area of psychology alone, but must look for it in ethics.

Concerning love within the woman-man relation, it is necessary to agree to two meanings of this word: love can be understood as a certain situation in the psychological sense, but at the same time it has an ethical sense; thus it is connected with a norm. The norm in this case is the personalistic norm; the commandment to love is its expression. Situationism, which does not accept any norm, falls into ordinary psychologism in comprehending love. For love in the psychological sense must be subordinated in man to love in the ethical sense—otherwise proper integration is out of the question. As a result, then, there can be no psychological fullness of love until ethical fullness is achieved. Whether we look at love as a concrete situation or whether we understand it as a whole series of many such situations, each and all of these situations are psychologically mature and "complete" insofar as in each of them, separately and all together, love possesses its ethical value. In other words, love as lived-experience must be subordinated to love as virtue, and to such an extent that without love as virtue there can be no fullness of the lived-experience of love.

Thus, in turn, we shall look at love in the woman-man relation as at virtue. It must be emphasized at once that Christian ethics based on the Gospel knows love as a supernatural virtue, a divine virtue. Keeping this view in mind, let us attempt to analyze above all the human way this virtue is manifested and formed in the woman-man relation. For every supernatural virtue is rooted in nature and acquires some human form (*ksztalt*) thanks to man's actions, and at the same time is expressed and confirmed in his actions, both in interior and exterior acts. Thus, we can examine and analyze it as a human affair, revealing its moral value from this perspective. Precisely in this way we now intend to look at the love of a man and a woman. Let the fact that it is a virtue, and that it should be one, be embedded as thoroughly as possible in all that has already been shown by the metaphysical and psychological analyses of love. Now, we will refer to various elements of the one and the other. However, in a particular way we will try to remember that the love between a woman and a man may take the shape that was called "spousal," since it leads to marriage. Taking all this into account, we will attempt to examine in what way this love is to be realized as a virtue. It is difficult to show this in its entirety—for the virtue of love as a spiritual reality is something non-visual—thus let us grasp the elements that are most essential and at the same time appear most clearly in experience. The first and most fundamental of them seems to be affirmation of the value of the person.

## Affirmation of the value of the person

As has been said, the commandment to love is the personalistic norm. We proceed in it from the being of the person in order to acknowledge the particular value of the person. The world of beings is the world of objects: we distinguish among them persons and things. A person differs from a thing by structure and perfection. The structure of the person includes "interiority" in which we find elements of spiritual life, and this forces us to acknowledge the spiritual nature of the human soul. Therefore, the person possesses the spiritual perfection proper to him. This perfection determines his value. In no way may a person be treated on par with a thing (nor even on par with an individual animal), since he possesses spiritual perfection, since he is in a sense an (embodied) spirit, and not merely a "body," even if splendidly enlivened. An enormous distance, an impassable abyss exists between the animal psyche and man's spirituality.

The value of the person himself must be clearly distinguished from various values that inhere in the person.* These are innate or acquired values, which are linked to the whole complex structure of the human being. As we have seen, these values come to light in the love between a woman and a man; this has been indicated by the psychological analysis of love. Love of a woman and a man is based on an impression that goes hand in hand with an emotion, always having a value for its object. In the given case, the point is the sexual value, for love of a woman and a man arises on the substratum of the sexual drive. The sexual value either is bound with the "whole human being of the other sex," or turns particularly to his "body" as to "a possible object of use." The value of the person differs from the sexual value, regardless of whether the latter refers to man's sensuality or to his affectivity. The value of the person is linked with the whole being of the person, and not with sex, for sex is merely a property of a being.

---

* The "value of the person himself"—i.e., the person as person, and not, for instance, as a certain nature individualized in its own way—is the very person "read" as a quite specific and elementary value, and thus "read" independently from his various physical or psychical qualifications, from his exterior or interior "assets." The person in this sense constitutes a subject of eventual initiatives and commitments that is constitutionally "one's own," singular, and indivisible, so that he cannot be something or somebody else "even by a little bit." He can, however, without any detriment to this identity of his (as well as of the other), "host" in himself other persons and "dwell" in them as a "gift" enjoying reciprocal affirmation in the community of persons. The acts of "determining oneself"—after a given person is able to govern his nature—are not only activities but also cognitive and appetitive "attitudes" through which he contacts the world of persons and the world of things. Regardless of what displays in him this "self-determining" provenience, his very nature is qualified in a certain way, also sexually, which constitutes in him an innate and constant "interior circumstance" of moral conduct as well as a specific "instrumentarium" through which he acts and "fulfills" his fate. [*Instrumentarium*: in general, an instrumentarium denotes a group of instruments or methods used to attain a given goal. — Trans.]

Thanks to this, every person of the other sex possesses above all the value as a person, and only then does he possess some sexual value. Speaking psychologically, love of a woman and a man signifies the lived-experience that centers around the reaction to sexual value. In the field of vision of this lived-experience the person appears first and foremost as the "human being of the other sex," even if above all we do not emphasize the reaction that has for its object the "body as a possible object of use." At the same time, reason knows that this "human being of the other sex" is a person. This knowledge has an intellectual, conceptual character—the person as such is not the content of an impression, just as the being as such is not the content of an impression alone. Thus, since the "person" is not the content of an impression alone, but is only an object of conceptual knowledge, then the reaction to the value of the person cannot be something as direct as the reaction to the sexual value linked to the "body" of this concrete person or—in a broader sense—to this integral phenomenon that is the "human being of the other sex" (a woman or a man). What is directly contained in an impression acts on the emotional sphere in man differently from what the mind indirectly discovers in it. However, the truth that the "human being of the other sex" is a person, is a somebody, and is different from any thing, also inheres in the consciousness. Precisely that truth evokes the need to integrate sexual love, and demands that the whole sensual-affective reaction to the "human being of the other sex" be, so to speak, elevated to the truth that this being is a person.

So, in every situation in which we experience (*przeżywać*) the sexual value of some person, love demands integration, that is, the incorporation of this value in the value of the person—indeed, its subordination to the value of the person. This is precisely what expresses the fundamental ethical feature of love: love is the affirmation of the person, otherwise it would not be love. If it is saturated with the proper relation to the value of the person—we have called this relation here "affirmation"—love is fully itself, it is integral love. However, when "love" is not permeated with this affirmation of the value of the person, then it is a disintegrated love, and properly speaking it is not love, even though the corresponding reactions or lived-experiences can have by all means an "amorous" (erotic) character.

This refers particularly to the love between a woman and a man. In accord with the full meaning of the word, love is a virtue and not merely an affection, let alone merely an arousal of the senses. This virtue is created in the will and has at its disposal the resources of the will's spiritual potentiality, that is, it is an authentic commitment of the freedom of the person-subject, proceeding from the truth about the person-object. Love as virtue lives in the will by being disposed toward the value of the person, and so it is the source of the affirmation of the person that permeates all reactions, lived-experiences, and all conduct in general.

Love that is a virtue relates to affective love and to the love contained in sensual desire. For the point in the ethical order is not in the least to efface or bypass the sexual value, to which the senses and affection react. The point is to bind this value firmly with the value of the person, since love turns neither to the "body" alone nor even to the "human being of the other sex" himself, but precisely to the person. What is more, love is love only through this turning toward the person. It is not love through a turning toward only the "body" of the person, for here the wish to use is clearly manifested, and this wish is fundamentally contrary to love. Moreover, love is not love itself through the mere affective turning toward the human being of the other sex. It is known after all, that this affection—based so firmly on the impression and feeling of "femininity" or "masculinity"—can over time be exhausted, as it were, in the emotional consciousness of both a man and a woman if it is not firmly bound with affirmation of the person— the person to whom a man owes the lived-experience of "femininity," or to whom a woman owes the lived-experience of "masculinity."*

Sexual affectivity still moves among many such lived-experiences, among impressions received from many people. Similarly sensuality moves among many "bodies," in the presence of which an awareness of the "object of possible use" is awakened. Precisely for this reason, love may be based neither on sensuality alone nor even on affectivity alone. For both of them in some way deviate from the person and do not

---

* For this reason the confession of some Philo: "I love you madly, Laura, and all the ones like you!" could not be considered as an expression of the love that is meant here. [*The confession of some Philo: "I love you madly, Laura, and all the ones like you!"* This sentence of the editors refers to the poem "Laura i Filon" by Franciszek Karpiński, a Polish poet. —Trans.]

permit or at least do not lead to his affirmation. This happens despite the fact that affective love seems to draw someone so much near the other and to draw the other so much near this someone. But by drawing the "man" near, even affective love can easily deviate from the "person." It will be proper to return to this point both in this chapter and in chapter III. For the observation of life suggests that affective love is kindled, especially in people with a certain sort of psyche, in a sense by the phenomenon "man" itself, if it is saturated with the proper charge of "femininity" or "masculinity." However, this love by itself does not possess a mature interior cohesion of the kind demanded by the full truth about the person, who is the proper object of love.

Affirmation of the value of the person, in which the full truth about the object of love finds its reflection, must itself gain ground among the erotic lived-experiences, the most immediate subject of which is either man's sensuality or affectivity. Furthermore, affirmation of the value of the person proceeds chiefly in two directions, thus in this way marking in general the main areas of sexual morality. On the one hand, it proceeds in the direction of a certain mastery of these lived-experiences, which find their immediate source in man's sensuality and affectivity. This problem will be examined in detail in chapter III: "The Person and Chastity." The second direction, in which affirmation of the value of the person develops its activity, is the direction of choosing the fundamental vocation in life. For the person's life vocation is generally linked with another person's or other persons' participation in his life. It is clear that when a man Y chooses a woman X as the companion of his life, then by this very fact he designates the person who will take the greatest part in his life, and determines the direction of his life's vocation. This direction is most closely related to the person, for it cannot emerge without affirmation of the person's value. Again, this will be elaborated in more detail in chapter IV, especially in its second part.

## *The belonging of a person to another person*

It has been stated in the metaphysical analysis of love that the essence of love is realized most deeply in the self-giving of the loving person to the beloved person.[36] This form of love, which was called spousal, differs from its other forms and manifestations by its particular specific weight. We realize this when we understand the value of the person. The value of the person, as has been said, remains closely connected with the being of the person. By nature, that is, due to what being he is, the person is a master of himself (*sui iuris*), and cannot be imparted to the other or substituted by the other (*alteri incommunicabilis*) when the participation of his own will and the commitment of his personal freedom are required. But love, so to speak, snatches the person from this natural inviolability and incommunicability. For love makes the person want precisely to give himself to another person—to the one he loves. He wants, so to speak, to stop being his own exclusive possession and to become the possession of the other. It signifies a certain relinquishing of that *sui iuris* and of that *alteri incommunicabilis*. Love goes through such relinquishing, being guided, however, by the profound belief that this relinquishment leads not to diminishing and impoverishing the existence of the person, but on the contrary to its expansion and enrichment. This is, so to speak, the law of "ecstasy," of going out of oneself in order to exist more fully in the other. In no other form of love is this law realized so clearly as in spousal love.

The love between a woman and a man also proceeds in this direction. We have already drawn attention to its particular intensity in the psychological sense. This intensity is explained not only by the biological force of the sexual drive, but also by the nature of this form of love, which here comes to light.[37] The sensual and affective lived-experiences appearing so vividly in consciousness constitute only the exterior expression and also the exterior proof of what takes place—or in any case what by all means should take place—in the interiority of the persons. Self-giving, the giving of one's own person, can be fully-mature only when it engages the will and is the will's work. For precisely thanks to his free will, the person is a master of himself (*sui iuris*); he is somebody incommunicable and nontransferable (*alteri incommunicabilis*). Spousal love, the love of self-giving, commits the will in a particularly thorough way. It is evident that here the whole "I" must be engaged, one must "give the soul," speaking with the language of the Gospel.[38]

For contrary to the viewpoint which, grasping the whole sexual problem superficially, sees the merely bodily self-giving of a woman to a man as the last step of "love" (erotics), it is proper here to speak necessarily about the reciprocal self-giving and the reciprocal belonging (*przynależność*) of two persons. Not the mutual sexual use in which X [she] gives her body for Y [him] to possess so that both of them can experience maximum sensual delight, but precisely the reciprocal self-giving and the reciprocal belonging of the persons to each other are the complete and full grasp of the nature of spousal love, which in this case finds its completion (*dopełnienie*) in marriage. Comprehended otherwise, love is doomed to be canceled in advance for the sake of use itself (in the first and second meanings of the verb "to use"). Love cannot express itself in use alone, even though in mutual and simultaneous use. Instead, it is expressed correctly in the union of persons. The fruit of the union is the persons' reciprocal belonging, whose expression is (among other ways) full sexual intercourse—we call it conjugal relations or intercourse since, as we will see, it finds its proper place only in marriage.

From the ethical point of view, the point is above all neither to reverse the natural sequence of facts nor to omit any of them in this sequence. Thus, at first the union of persons, of a woman and a man, must be achieved by love, and then sexual intercourse between them can be an expression of this mature union. At this point, it is worth recalling what has already been said concerning the objective and subjective profiles of love. Love in the subjective profile is always some psychological situation, a lived-experience evoked by some sexual value and concentrated around it in the subject or in both subjects mutually experiencing (*przeżywać*) love. Love in the objective profile is an inter-personal fact; it is reciprocity and friendship based on a community in the good, and so it is always a union of two persons that can become their belonging to each other. The objective profile cannot be replaced by two subjective profiles or their sum—these are two completely different aspects of love.

The objective profile is decisive. It is elaborated in both subjects, of course, through the whole abundance of sensual-affective lived-experiences that belong to the subjective profile of love, although without being identified with them. Sensual lived-experiences possess their own appetitive dynamic linked to sensation and to the sexual vitality of the body. Affective lived-experiences also possess their own rhythm: they aim at creating a positive mood that facilitates a sense of closeness to the beloved person and of some spontaneous communication with him.

Love, however, aims at unifying through self-giving to each other. This fact has a profound objective, even ontological, meaning, and, therefore, it belongs to the objective profile of love. Sensual and affective lived-experiences are not identified with it, although they create a group of conditions among which this fact becomes reality. At the same time, however, there exists a different problem that is in a sense reversed: how to maintain and how to confirm (*ugruntować*) this reciprocity of persons among all these sensual-affective reactions and lived-experiences, which themselves are characterized by great mobility and changeability.

And here again we are faced with the problem elucidated previously: the sexual value, which in various shapes constitutes, so to speak, a crystallizing center of the sensual-affective erotic lived-experiences, must be firmly joined in the consciousness and the will with the relation toward the value of the person—the person who in a sense provides the content of those lived-experiences. Only then can one think about the union of persons and their belonging to each other. Without this, then, "love" has merely an erotic meaning and does not have the essential meaning—that is, a personal meaning: it leads toward a sexual union, but one that is not justified by a true union of persons. This situation has a utilitarian character, as the relation of persons to each other is determined by the realization of what is contained in the verb "to use" (considering especially the second meaning of this verb). Then, X [she] belongs to Y [him] as an object of use, and by giving Y an opportunity to be used, X herself tries to find some pleasure in it. This attitude on both sides is fundamentally contrary to love, so there can be no talk about a union of persons. On the contrary, everything is in a sense prepared for a conflict of mutual interests and only waits for an explosion. Egoism—egoism of the senses or egoism of affections—can only for a time be concealed in the recesses of the fictitious structure which, in supposedly good faith, is called "love." Over time, however, all the dishonesty of this structure must become evident. One of the greatest sufferings is when love turns out to be not what it was considered to be, but something quite contrary.

The point is to avoid such disillusionments. Spousal love, which bears in itself the interior need to give one's person to another person— a need crystallized between a woman and a man also in bodily self-giving and in full sexual intercourse—possesses its natural greatness. The measure of this greatness is the value of the person who gives himself, and not only the degree of sensual-sexual delight linked to this self-giving. It is very easy, however, to confuse here the essence of the thing with what is properly a mere collateral reflex of this essence. If one deprives this love of the depth of self-giving, of the thoroughness of personal commitment, then whatever is left will be its complete denial and contradiction. Ultimately, at the end of this path lies what is called prostitution.

Spousal love consists, on the one hand, in the giving of the person, and, on the other hand, in the reception of this giving. The "mystery" of reciprocity is intertwined in this—reception must be at once giving, and giving at once reception. Love is by its nature reciprocal: one who knows how to receive also knows how to give—of course, we mean a proficiency (*umiejętność*) that is symptomatic of love, for there is also a proficiency of receiving and a proficiency of giving that is symptomatic of egoism. So, the former proficiency of giving and receiving—the one symptomatic of love—is possessed by such a man whose relation to a woman is permeated with the thorough affirmation of the value of her person. This proficiency is also possessed by such a woman whose relation to a man is permeated with the affirmation of the value of his person. Such an attitude creates the most interior climate of giving—the personal climate of entire spousal love. Both persons need this genuine ability to affirm the value of the person, and they need this so that both the giving of one's person and the reception of this giving are fully-mature. Only that woman is capable of truly giving herself who is fully convinced about the value of her person and of the value of the person of the man to whom she gives herself. And only that man is capable of fully receiving the self-giving of a woman who is thoroughly conscious of the greatness of this gift—and he cannot possess such awareness without the affirmation of the value of the person. Being conscious of the value of the gift awakens the need of gratitude and reciprocation that would match the greatness of the gift. This also shows how thoroughly spousal love, love of reciprocal self-giving, must contain in itself the interior structure of friendship.

In any case, it is only when we move on the plane of the person, in the orbit of his essential value, that all the objective greatness of spousal love, of reciprocal self-giving and of the belonging of persons—of a woman and a man—becomes understandable and transparent. However, we cannot enter into the proper orbit of the problem as long as we reflect on this theme "from the position" of the sexual value itself and of the play of affections and passions related to it. In that case, it would be impossible to comprehend these principles of sexual morality that remain closely connected with the commandment to love, which, as has been stated, is the "personalistic norm": both it itself and all its consequences become transparent only when we move on the plane of the person, in the orbit of his essential value.

## Choice and responsibility

Perhaps nowhere else in the whole book than here does its title, which speaks of "love and responsibility," seem more relevant. There exists responsibility in love—responsibility for the person, the one who is drawn into the closest community of being and acting, who in a way is made one's possession by taking advantage of his self-giving. And therefore there exists responsibility for one's own love: is it mature and thorough enough that in its boundaries this enormous trust of the other person, the hope generated from his love—the hope that one does not lose one's "soul" by giving oneself, but, quite the contrary, finds the greater fullness of one's existence—is not going to suffer a disappointment. Responsibility for love is reduced, as is evident, to responsibility for the person, proceeding from it and also returning to it.[39] Therefore, this responsibility is enormous. However, its magnitude can be understood only by the one who has a thorough sense of the value of the person. The one who possesses only the capacity to react to sexual values connected with the person and inhering in him, without, however, seeing the very value of the person, will continue to confuse love with erotics and will complicate his own life as well as that of others, thus ruining for himself and for them the proper sense of love and its essential "flavor." For this "flavor" of love is bound with the sense of responsibility for the person. After all, this sense implies concern for the true good of the person—the quintessence of all altruism and at the same time an infallible sign of some expansion of one's "I," of one's existence, with this "other I" and with this other existence, which is for me as close as my own. The sense of responsibility for the other person is at times full of concern, but it is never in itself unpleasant or painful. For what comes to light in it is not a constriction or impoverishment of man, but precisely his enrichment and expansion. Therefore love separated from the sense of responsibility for the person is a denial of itself, and, as a rule, is always egoism. The more the sense of responsibility for the person, the more true love there is.

This truth sheds great light on the problem of the choice of a person. For we still take into account that love between a woman and a man tends naturally to reciprocal self-giving and belonging of persons. On the way to what constitutes the ultimate form of love there must be present on both sides, namely in a man and a woman, the choice of the person—the person to whom spousal love and self-giving will turn. The choice possesses the same specific weight as that to which it leads. Indeed, one chooses a person and together with him the spousal form of love—reciprocal self-giving. By choosing another person one chooses in him, in a sense, another "I," as though one were choosing oneself in the other and the other in oneself. Therefore, precisely on both sides the choice must have not only a truly personal character but also a genuine personal mark. Only such persons (Y and X) can belong to each other for whom it is objectively good to be with each other. For man is always, above all, himself (a "person"), so in order that he can not only be with the other but, what is more, live by and for the other, he must in some way constantly find himself in the other and the other in himself.[40] Love is impossible for beings that are impenetrable to each other; only spirituality, together with the persons' "inwardness" (*wewnętrzność*) linked to it, creates conditions of reciprocal permeation so that the persons can live in and by each other.

At this point, a very interesting and very rich collateral problem emerges, which could be called the problem of the "psychology of choice." What moments, what psycho-physiological factors make two people suitable for each other, so that it is good for them to be together and belong to each other? In all this are there some general rules and principles drawn from the psycho-physiological structure of man? What do somatic and constitutional factors, as well as temperament and character, contribute here? These are fascinating questions, although it seems that despite various attempts to provide an answer of some wider scope in this matter, it ultimately remains a mystery of human individualities. There are no rigid rules, and philosophy and ethics owe their authority as teachers of life's wisdom precisely to their attempts of explaining these problems as much as they can be explained. Particular sciences, such as physiology, sexology, or medicine, will do well if they adopt the same principle, at the same time helping philosophy and ethics to fulfill their practical task.

According to the presuppositions of healthy empiricism, one must acknowledge that the choice of a person of the other sex—a person who is to be the recipient of spousal love and at the same time who is to co-create this love thanks to his reciprocity—must be based to some degree on sexual value. After all, this love is to have its sexual overtone, which is to constitute the basis of the whole interaction between persons of different sex. This is in no way conceivable without the mutual lived-experience of the sexual value. As it is known, the sexual value is connected not only with the impression of the "body as a possible object of use," but also with the complete impression provided by the "human being of the other sex:" a woman by her "femininity" and a man by his "masculinity." This latter impression is more important and appears chronologically earlier: the incorrupt, naturally healthy youth refer first lived-experiences linked with the sexual value to the "human being of the other sex," and not first and foremost to the "body as a possible object of use." If the former makes itself heard earlier and above all, we are already presented with some effect of corruption—this lack of the natural order in the reaction to the sexual value will impede love; it will impede above all the process of choosing a person.

For the choice of a person is a process in which the sexual value cannot play a role of the only motive or even—in the ultimate analysis of this act of the will—the primary motive. This would contradict the very notion of the "choice of a person." If the only, or at least, the primary motive of this choice were the sexual value itself, then we would not be able to speak of choosing a person, but only of choosing the other sex connected with some "man" or even with some "body that is a possible object of use." It is clear that if we are to speak of choosing a person, the primary motive must be the very value of the person. The primary motive, however, does not mean the only motive. Otherwise, the position would lack the characteristics of healthy empiricism and would be burdened with the mark of apriorism that characterizes Kant's ethics with its formalistic personalism. The point is to choose a person truly and not to choose only the values linked to the person without considering the person himself as the fundamental value. Such would be the case with this Y [him] choosing some X [her] in regard to the sexual values he finds in her. Such a choice from the start possesses explicit utilitarian tendencies, and thereby stands below the love of the person. The sexual values Y [he] finds in X [her]—or which she finds in him—certainly motivate the choice, but the person who chooses must be simultaneously fully conscious that he chooses a person. Even though the sexual values in the object of choice may disappear, undergo change, and so forth, the fundamental value—the value of the person—will nevertheless remain. The choice is then a true choice of a person when it takes into account this value as most important and decisive. So, when we observe the entire process of choosing a woman by a man or a man by a woman, we must state that it is formed through the sexual values somehow sensed and somehow experienced (*przeżyć*), although ultimately each of them chooses not so much the person with respect to the values but the values with respect to the person.

And only then, when each of them has chosen in this way, is the act of choice interiorly mature and complete. For only then is the proper integration of the object accomplished in it: the object of choice—the person—was grasped in his whole truth. The truth about the person as the object of choice is crystallized precisely in the fact that the very value of the person is, for the one who chooses, the value to which he subordinates all others. Sexual values, which act on the senses and affections, are grasped properly. If they constituted the only or the primary motive of choosing a person, this choice would be in itself incomplete and untrue, for it would deviate from the full truth about its object, about the person. Such a choice would have to constitute the point of departure for love that is disintegrated, hence also incomplete and untrue.

True love, love that is interiorly full, is one in which we choose a person for his own sake; thus in it a man chooses a woman and a woman a man not merely as a "partner" for sexual life, but as a person to whom he or she wants to give his or her life. The sexual values, so vibrant in sensual and affective lived-experiences, accompany this decision and contribute to its psychological vividness, but they do not determine its depth. The very "core" of choosing a person must be personal, not merely sexual. Life will test the value of the choice and the true greatness of love.

It is most fully put to the test when the sensual-affective lived-experience itself diminishes and the sexual values themselves cease, in a sense, to act. Then, only the value of the person will remain, and the interior truth of love will become evident. If this love was true self-giving and a belonging of persons, then it will not only survive but even be strengthened and confirmed. However, if it was but some synchronization of sensuality and emotion, then it will lose its *raison d'être*, and the persons involved in it will suddenly stand in a vacuum. It is necessary to take seriously into account that every human love must undergo some test, and only then will its true value manifest itself.

When the choice of a person is interiorly mature, when love together with this is properly integrated in the interior life of the person, then love acquires a new character both in its psychological respect and, above all, in its affective one. For if not only sensuality but also affectivity itself manifests a certain mobility and changeability—which in turn always evokes a certain anxiety, even if subconscious—then interiorly mature love frees itself from this anxiety by the choice of a person. Affection becomes peaceful and certain, for it stops revolving around and following itself, and instead follows its object, the person. The purely subjective truth of affection yielded its place to the objective truth of the person, who is the object of the choice and of love.[41] Thus, thanks to this, affection alone acquires new properties, as it were. It becomes simple and, in a sense, sober. So, if this idealization (which we spoke of in the psychological analysis) is characteristic of purely affective love—affectivity, in a sense, itself creates various values and bestows them on the person to whom it turns—then this love of the person, a love that is mature with the interior act of choice and focused on the value of the person himself, makes us affectively love the person as he truly is—not our image of him but the real person. We love him along with his virtues and vices, in a sense independently of the virtues and despite the vices. The greatness of this love is manifested the most when this person falls, when his weaknesses or even sins come to light. One who truly loves does not then refuse his love, but in a sense loves even more—he loves while being conscious of deficiencies and vices without, however, approving of them. For the person himself never loses his essential value. Affection, which follows the value of the person, is faithful to man.

## *The commitment of freedom*

Only the truth about a person makes a real commitment of freedom in relation to this person possible. Love consists in a commitment of freedom because, after all, love is self-giving, and to give oneself means precisely to limit one's freedom on account of the other person. The limitation of one's own freedom would be something negative and unpleasant, but love makes it something positive, joyful, and creative. Freedom is for love. Freedom that is unused, not employed by love, becomes precisely something negative—it gives man a sense of emptiness and unfulfillment. Love engages freedom and fills it with what the will clings to by nature: it fills freedom with the good. The will tends to the good, and freedom belongs to the will, and therefore freedom is for love, for through love man most fully participates in the good. This is the essential basis for the primacy of love in the moral order, in the hierarchy of virtues, and in the hierarchy of the healthy longings and desires of man.[42] Man longs for love more than for freedom—freedom is the means, whereas love is the end. Man, however, longs for true love, because the authentic commitment of freedom is possible only when it is based on truth. The will is free, but at the same time it "must" seek the good, which will correspond to its nature; it is free in seeking and choosing, but it is not free from the very need to seek and to choose.

However, the will does not bear having an object (as a good) imposed on it. It wants to choose by itself and affirm by itself, for a choice is always an affirmation of the value of the chosen object. So, a man by choosing a woman affirms her value—the point is that he is to affirm the value of the person as such and not merely the person's "sexual" value. After all, the sexual value somewhat imposes itself, whereas the value of the person awaits affirmation and choice. And therefore in the will of the man who has not yet yielded to passions themselves, but who retains an interior freshness, some battle is usually being waged between the drive and freedom. The drive attempts to impose its object and its end; it attempts to create in man an interior *fait accompli*.[43] We use the word "drive" here not in its proper and full meaning, which has been interpreted in the previous chapter, but in a partial meaning—the point here concerns only certain manifestations of the sexual drive, thanks to which the sexual value takes possession of man's sensuality and affectivity, and by this in a sense "besets" the will. When the will yields to the sensual drive, then it begins to desire a given person. Affection deprives desire of its bodily and also consumption-oriented character, and makes it more of a longing for a "human being of the other sex." Nonetheless, as long as the will yields to what the senses follow and what affection clings to, the will's own creative contribution in love does not come to light.

The will loves only when man consciously commits his freedom toward another human being as the person whose value he fully acknowledges and affirms. This commitment does not consist above all in desiring that person. The will is a creative power capable of giving the good from within itself, and not only of assimilating the good that already exists. The love of the will is expressed above all in desiring the good for the beloved person. To long for a person for one's own sake does not yet reveal the creative potentiality of the will, and it also does not yet constitute love in the complete positive meaning of the word. The will by nature wants the good—the good without limits, that is, happiness. In striving for it, the will seeks a person and longs for him for itself as this concrete good, which may bring that happiness. This way X longs for Y, and Y longs for X—and love of desire consists in this. The senses and affections help this love. But love that is helped by the senses and affection constitutes, so to speak, the nearest opportunity for the will, which by nature tends to the good without limits, i.e., happiness, to begin to want this good not only for its own subject, but also for the other person, for the person who is the object of desire, based on the senses and affection. And precisely here the tension between the dynamic of the drive and the will's own dynamic appears. The drive makes the will desire and long for the person because of his sexual value, but the will is not satisfied with this. The will is free, that is, it is able to long for everything in relation to the absolute good, the good without limits—happiness. And it engages precisely this ability, this natural and noble potentiality of its own, in relation to the other person. It longs for the absolute good, the good without limits, happiness, for the other person—and in this way, so to speak, counterbalances or interiorly compensates for the fact that it longs for that very person, the person "of the other sex," for its own sake.* Of course, we have in mind here only a partial meaning of the word "drive." For the will not only struggles with the drive, but at the same time takes up within spousal love what constitutes the natural end of this drive. For the drive is turned toward the existence of mankind, which concretely always signifies the existence of a new person, a child, as a fruit of the love between a man and a woman in marriage. The will turns toward this end, and through the conscious realization of this end it attempts to expand further the creative tendency proper to it.

In this way true love, taking advantage of the natural dynamic of the will, attempts to introduce a feature of thorough disinterestedness in the relation between a woman and a man, in order to free this love from the attitude to use (in the first and the second meanings of the verb "to use"). And in this consists what we have called here the struggle between love and the drive. The drive wants above all to take, to make use of the other person, whereas love wants to give, to create the good, to make happy. Again, it is evident how greatly spousal love should be permeated with what constitutes the essence of friendship. The longing for the good "without limits" for the other "I" contains in the bud, as it were, the whole creative urge of true love, the urge to endow beloved persons with the good, to make them happy.†

This is a "divine" feature of love. Indeed, when Y [he] wants the good "without limits" for X [her], then properly speaking he wants God

---

* The expression "counterbalances" or "compensates" means here: subordinates the longing for possessing a person to the longing for his absolute good (happiness). This "equilibrium" would be upset if the former longing dominated. We would then deal with egoism: with longing for the other person at the expense of that person's good. Love, which by definition is an act of affirmation of the person for his own sake, does not in the least, however, exclude the longing for the closest possible bond with somebody who is affirmed in this way.

† In this way love as an attitude of benevolence (the intention of love), i.e., the "*good will*" (*bene-volentia*), finds its objectivized expression and accreditation in a good act with respect to the beloved person, i.e., in "willing the *good*" that effectively serves his existence and development (*bene-ficentia*).

for her: God alone is the objective fullness of the good, and only he can satisfy every man with this fullness. Man's love through its relation to happiness, that is, to the fullness of the good, in a sense passes as close to God as possible. It is another matter that this "fullness of the good," as well as "happiness," is not often understood clearly in this way. "I want happiness for you" means: I want what will make you happy, but I do not (for the time being) specify what that is. Only people of deep faith say to themselves quite clearly: it is God. Others do not complete this thought, as if they left this "position" to be filled in by the beloved person: it is what you yourself want, in which you see the fullness of the good for yourself. Consequently, the whole energy of love focuses above all on the fact that "I" truly want this for you.*

The great moral power of true love lies precisely in this longing for the happiness of the other person, that is, for his true good. Thanks to this, love is able to regenerate man—it gives him a sense of interior richness, of interior fertility and creativity: I am capable of wanting the good for the other person, so I am in general capable of wanting the good. True love forces me to believe in my own spiritual powers. Even when I am "bad," true love—if it is awakened in me—commands me to seek the true good for the sake of the person, to whom it turns.[44] In this way the affirmation of the value of the other person finds a deep resonance in the affirmation of the value of my own person, because in fact the need to long for the happiness of the other "I" is awakened in a given subject precisely due to the sexual value itself. When love achieves its full dimensions, then it contributes not only that genuine personal

---

\* In love between two persons one can notice a characteristic incongruity between the magnitude of the good desired for the beloved person and the possibility of its realization. The lover [he] is not able to bestow immortal life on the beloved person [her], although while loving her he desires it for her and undoubtedly would bestow it on her if he were almighty. [*The lover (he) is not able to bestow immortal life on the beloved person (her), although while loving her he desires it for her and undoubtedly would bestow it on her if he were almighty.* The sentence is structured in Polish in such a way that the lover and the beloved could be a man-woman or woman-man pair. I kept the man-woman arrangement to avoid inaccurate readings. — Trans.] This is also a reason why "he in fact wants God for her." The experientially imposed connection between love and the affirmation of life (of existence) demands—as a result of the metaphysical interpretation—an acknowledgment that the death of personal beings in the perspective of the Creative Love can only be a transition to a higher form of life. *Morte fortius caritas.* [*Morte fortius caritas*: Charity (is) stronger than death. — Trans.]

"climate," but also some sense of the "absolute," the encounter with what is absolute and ultimate.[45] Indeed, love is the highest moral value. In addition, the point concerns the proficiency of transferring the dimensions of love into the ordinary matters of daily life. Precisely here the problem of educating love is born.

## *The problem of the education of love*

What does "the education of love" mean? Can love be educated at all? Is it not something at once ready-made, something given to man or to two people as a certain kind of adventure of the heart? This is what young people in particular very often think, and a consequence of this view must be at least a partial canceling of what we have called here the integration of love. In that case love remains only a psychological situation, which is (as if against its nature) subordinated to the demands of objective morality.[46] However, quite the contrary, love is guided by a norm, i.e., by a principle, from which the fullest value of each psychological situation ought to be drawn; only then will the situation itself achieve its proper fullness, become an expression of the mature commitment of the person.[47] For love is never something ready-made, something merely "given" (*dany*) to a woman and a man, but at once it is always something "entrusted" (*zadany*). It is necessary to look at it this way: love in a sense never "is," but only constantly "becomes," depending on the contribution of each person, on their thorough commitment. This commitment is based on what is "given," and therefore the lived-experiences that have their basis in the sensuality and natural affectivity of either a woman or a man constitute only the "material" of love. A tendency exists to consider them as a ready-made form of love. This is an erroneous tendency—it conceals the consumption-oriented and utilitarian attitude, which—as is known—is contrary to the nature of love itself.

Man is a being, so to speak, doomed to creativity. This creativity also obliges in the sphere of love. How often we witness that from the promising "material" of affections and longings not true love is formed, but in fact something contrary; whereas at times truly great love is formed from modest "material." But this great love can only be a work of persons and—let us add at this point for the sake of completing the picture—a work of grace. In this book we would like to take a look at this work. Hence, we shall look at love above all as a work of man; we will try to analyze the main ways of his own actions in this direction. But the operation of grace is hidden in these actions as a contribution of the invisible Creator, who being love himself has the power to form any love, including love which in its natural development is based on the value of sex and the body, if only people want consciously to co-create it with him. There is no need to be discouraged that this happens sometimes in intricate and convoluted ways. Grace has the power to make straight the ways of human love.

So, in order to answer the questions posited at the beginning, perhaps we must simply turn once more to all the reflections contained in this chapter. We must deepen them further in the light of the Gospel that is read and understood more wholly than here. But even here it is already evident that the education of love consists of many actions that are interior to the greatest extent, although having their exterior expression, and in any case are deeply personal. These actions aim at what was called here the integration of love "in" the person and "between" persons. The reflections on love in the man-woman relation, however, often made us conscious of the possibility of disintegration creeping into their reciprocal relations. And therefore, these reflections must be necessarily supplemented so that it will become clear in which way the love of a man and a woman defends itself against disintegration. The reflection on chastity is to serve this precise purpose.

# CHAPTER III

# The Person and Chastity

Part One

# Rehabilitation of Chastity

## *Chastity and resentment*

The title of this paragraph is borrowed from Max Scheler, who published the study *Rehabilitation of Virtue* (*Rehabilitierung der Tugend*). This title may seem like a provocation. For when we speak of rehabilitation, we think of somebody (or something) that has lost his (or its) good name and the right to be esteemed among people. Rehabilitation restores his good name and the right to be esteemed. Has virtue lost its good name? Has the virtue of chastity lost its good name? Is it that people do not regard chastity as a virtue? However, not only a good name is at stake here. The mere name of the virtue and a nominal esteem do not solve the problem, for the point is the right of citizenship in the human soul, in the human will—this is the proper place of virtue and the ground without which it ceases to exist as a real being.[1] Mere esteem for the words "virtue" and "chastity" would thus lack deeper significance. Scheler saw a need for the rehabilitation of virtue because he perceived in contemporary man a characteristic spiritual attitude unfavorable to a genuine esteem for virtue. He defined this attitude as "resentment."[2]

Resentment consists in an erroneous, distorted relation to value. It is a lack of objectivity in assessment and valuation (*ocena i wartościowanie*), a lack whose sources lie in the weakness of the will. The point is that a higher value demands a greater effort of the will if we want to attain or realize it. So, in order to be subjectively excused from this effort, in order to justify to ourselves our lack of this value, we diminish its meaning; we deprive it of what is in reality due to it, we see in it almost some evil, even though objectivity obliges us to acknowledge the good. As is evident, resentment possesses typical characteristics of the cardinal vice of sloth (*lenistwo*).[3] St. Thomas defines sloth (*acedia*) as "sorrow proceeding from the fact that the good is difficult."[4] Sorrow itself does not falsify the good, and even indirectly sustains in the soul an esteem for its value. However, resentment goes further: not only does it falsify the image of the good, but also depreciates what should merit the esteem, so that man does not have to take pains to measure up to the true good, but can "safely" acknowledge as the good only what suits him, what is convenient for him. Resentment is contained in the subjectivistic mentality: here pleasure replaces a superior value.

It seems that of all virtues, chastity above all has been deprived by resentment of many rights in the human soul, in the will and the heart of man. A complete case against it has been created in order to demonstrate that it is not beneficial for man but detrimental. It is enough to recall here at least in a cursory way the various reservations of an allegedly hygienic and medical nature directed against chastity and sexual self-control. The argument still circulates that "excessive chastity (NB: it is difficult to determine what that means) is detrimental to health, and that a young person should have a sexual outlet." Above all, however, chastity and sexual abstinence are seen as dangerous opponents of human love, and therefore they are denied the right of citizenship in the human soul. According to these views, chastity has its *raison d'être* outside of the love between a man and a woman, so it must yield to love. Resentment increases primarily due to such views. In fact, resentment is not a particular property of our age since the inclinations to it are latent in the soul of every man. Christianity considers them as one of the effects of original sin. So, if we are to free ourselves from resentment, and in particular from its consequences in regard to this important problem, we must bring about a certain rehabilitation of chastity. For this purpose, we must above all remove the enormous buildup of subjectivism in our understanding of love and of the happiness that love can provide to a man and a woman.

For it is known that love demands integrity in each of the loving persons and also between them. This has been demonstrated in the analysis conducted in the previous chapter. By analyzing love under three different aspects (the metaphysical, psychological, and ethical), we managed to distinguish many of its elements. The point is to integrate the elements correctly, both in every person and between them, between a woman and a man, so that they form a proper personal and inter-personal whole. That is why the function of integration is so important. Love cannot remain merely a subjective "situation" in which the energies of sensuality and of affectivity that are awakened by the drive come to light. For then it does not measure up to the person nor does it unite persons. Love must be firmly based on affirmation of the value of the person so that it can attain full personal value and unite properly a man and a woman. Taking this affirmation as a departure point, one can easily proceed to thoroughly desiring the good for the beloved person—the good worthy of the person—which confers on love a "beatifying" (*szczęściodajny*) character. People, a woman and a man, long for love, because they count on the happiness that it will bring into their life.

Longing for the true happiness for the other person and genuine self-giving for his good impress on love the invaluable mark of altruism. All this, however, may not mature and crystallize in the love between a man and a woman if what prevails is the concupiscible attitude, love of desire, or especially desire born from the reactions of sensuality, even if placed against the background of rich affective lived-experiences. These lived-experiences give love a "flavor," but do not always contain its objective essence, which is most closely connected with reciprocal affirmation of the value of the person. From the mere richness of affections one cannot pass judgment on the value of the reciprocal relation of persons. The very abundance of emotional lived-experiences born on the ground of sensuality can conceal in itself a lack of true love, and even downright egoism. For love is something different from amorous lived-experiences. Love is formed on the basis of a thorough and fully responsible relation of a person to another person, whereas amorous lived-experiences are born spontaneously in reactions of sensuality and affectivity. A very abundant development of these lived-experiences may conceal in itself an underdevelopment of love. Therefore, in our analysis of love, we drew attention to the necessity of distinguishing between these two profiles: the objective and the subjective.

And therefore, we must consider very seriously the possibility of a *disintegration* of love. This refers to a lived-experience or even a number of amorous lived-experiences that find their source and basis in the senses and affections, while themselves being still personally immature.

The disintegration means above all an underdevelopment of the ethical essence of love.* The manifestations of sensuality or affectivity in relation to the person of the other sex, manifestations that are born earlier and developed faster than virtue, are not yet love. However, they are usually taken for love and called by the name of love—and so chastity as a hindering factor is posited against "love" thus understood.

Thus, the main argument against chastity, namely that "chastity hinders love," does not sufficiently consider the integration of love nor, on the other hand, the possibility of its disintegration.

Only the correct concentration of the particular sensual-affective elements around the very value of the person allows us to speak of love. Hence one may not call love what is merely its element or "part," since an improper concentration of these "parts" or elements can result not in love, but rather in the denial of love. Furthermore, there is a fundamental postulate from the viewpoint of ethics: for the good of love, for the sake of realizing love's true essence both in every person and between persons, it is necessary to be freed from all those "amorous" lived-experiences that do not find justification in true love, that is, in the reciprocal relation between a man and a woman based on a mature affirmation of the value of the person. This postulate hits the crux of the matter concerning chastity. The word "chastity" (*czystość*) speaks of being free from all that "makes dirty."[5] Love must be in a sense transparent: through all lived-experiences, through all deeds that find their source in it, it must always be apparent that this relation to the person of the other sex proceeds from a genuine affirmation of his value. Since the lived-experiences and deeds that deprive love of this transparency spring from the substratum of the senses and the affections connected to them, a separate

---

* Man as a composite, "multilayered" being is manifested in a multitude of dynamisms having their specific interior ends.

The bodily, psychical, and also personal "layers" take part in the lived-experience of love. The integration of these three kinds of dynamism takes place in the human act, that is, in this case, in the act of love. They become then a part of the human act, which means that its totality is manifested in them as in proper parts, in the way appropriate for each part. This integration is not something arbitrary, but constitutes the program of "unifying oneself," of fulfilling oneself, that is proper to man. Therefore, the lack of integration of these factors in the act is not only a lack but also a counter-integration. And the "*disintegration means some*—more or less profound—*inability to possess oneself and govern oneself through self-determination*" [emphasis original] (*Person and Act*, 205 in section 2 of chapter V).

virtue is needed in order to protect from this side the true character and objective profile of love. This virtue is chastity, which is allied most closely with the love of persons Y and X. Let us attempt to demonstrate this by a more thorough analysis, applying the results of the analysis of love itself conducted in the previous chapter. It will then become more obvious that opposing love and chastity, which one hears about so often, is a fruit of resentment.

## *The concupiscence of the flesh*

At the outset of this analysis, it is worth recalling the fundamental fact already mentioned at the beginning of the book. The interaction and especially relations between persons of different sex consist of many "deeds" whose subject is a person of one sex and whose object is a person of the other sex. Love itself blurs this relation, so that the relation of the subject to the object yields to the union of persons, in which a man and a woman have the sense that they constitute, in a sense, one common subject of action. A subjective state of their consciousness, which, by the way, constitutes a reflection of the objective union, is expressed in that sense—their wills unite through the fact that they want one good as an end, while their affections unite through the fact that they together experience (*przeżywać*) the same values. The deeper and more mature the union is, the more a man and a woman have the sense that they constitute, in a sense, one subject of action. This sense, however, does not in the least abolish the objective fact that they are two really different beings and two different subjects of action; indeed, each of the two persons is the subject of numerous "deeds" whose object is the other person.

By "deeds" or simply "acts" we understand not only exterior deeds (*actus externi*), i.e., which can be perceived and defined from without by means of observation, but also interior deeds (*actus interni*), which are known only to the person performing them, as only he can grasp and define them by way of introspection. In this case we use the word "deeds," although this word is generally used only in relation to exterior acts. The Latin word *actus* is more universal, and is at times rendered in Polish as "*akt.*" However, only those who are familiar with Latin know that the word "*akt*" can also mean "*czyn*" (act) or "*uczynek*" (deed), for in general it has a different application in the Polish language.[6]

The field that interests us in this book, and especially in this chapter, provides an incentive to reflect on both exterior and interior deeds. In the sixth commandment ("You shall not commit adultery") and the ninth commandment ("You shall not covet your neighbor's wife"), the Decalogue already pays very explicit attention to these two groups of deeds. This point concerns deeds that have for their object a person of the other sex—not sex, but the person, and the distinctness of sex is what generates a particular moral problem. For the person, being a person, should be an object of love. Sex, however, which is above all manifested in the body, and which as a property of the body falls under the senses, creates a possibility of concupiscence. The concupiscence of the flesh is most closely linked to sensuality. The analysis of sensuality conducted in the previous chapter indicated that it characteristically reacts to "the body as a possible object of use." Sensuality reacts to the sexual values connected precisely with the body, and this reaction possesses a directional character.[7] A directional reaction is not yet identified with desire. It is only a direction of the whole psyche toward the aforementioned value, in a sense an "interest" or "absorption" in it. From this first stage of the reaction of sensuality it is very easy to transition to the next one, which is desire. Desire differs from the interest or absorption of sensuality in the sexual value connected with the body—in that case we find out that this value "reaches" the subject, whereas in the case of desire, the subject clearly turns toward the value. Something in the subject starts to gravitate toward and cling to it, and moreover, some vehement, spontaneous process starts in the subject (in man) and proceeds in the direction of ultimately willing this value. Sensual desire itself is not yet willing, but clearly tries to become it. This well-perceptible ease of transitioning from one stage to another—from interest to desire, from desire to willing—is a source of great tensions in the interior life of the person; these tensions are linked to the virtue of temperance. The structure of this virtue, which we will separately describe in this chapter, remains closely correlated to what we have delineated here as the structure of the concupiscence of the flesh.

The expression "the concupiscence of the flesh" is justified because this concupiscence, as it is linked to the reactions of sensuality, has the body and *sexus* for its object, and also because in the subject it proceeds from the body and seeks an outlet in "bodily love."[8] Perhaps it is worthwhile to mention here that a difference exists between "bodily love" and the "love of the body," for the body as a component of the person can also be an object of love, not only of concupiscence.

The fact that the first reaction of sensuality, i.e., interest in the sexual value "linked with the body" so easily changes into another, i.e., into bodily desire, proves that a power of sensual desire exists, and it is precisely this power that hides behind sensuality, so quickly conferring on its reactions the concupiscible direction. That is how St. Thomas Aquinas grasped this problem as he clearly distinguished the concupiscible power (*appetitus concupiscibilis)* from the irascible power (*appetitus irascibilis*).[9] According to him, these are the two principal powers of the sensitive soul (*anima sensitiva*) most closely linked to sensory cognition.[10] These powers also concentrate around themselves a whole group of affections (that St. Thomas called *passiones animae*).[11] Hence, certain human affections have a more concupiscible character, such as thirst, while others have a more irascible character, such as anger. By affections we understand here both the first emotions and also certain more permanent emotional states of the human psyche, within which we can again observe various degrees of intensity (from moods to passions, e.g., a mild affection of love and a vehement amorous passion, or a light irritation—a movement of anger—and an uncontrolled outburst of fury).

The reactions of sensuality possess a directional character not merely from the side of the object, where the concupiscence of the flesh is not limited to the sensitive concupiscible power (*appetitus concupiscibilis*) but imparts itself to the will and attempts to impose on the will its own proper relation to the object. Here again, the reaction of sensuality has a distinct directional character: the direction of the reaction first of all points to the "body and sex," and secondly to "use." It is sensual desire that tends toward this together with "bodily love," which seeks satisfaction in the "body and sex" through use. Once this "love" is satisfied, the entire relation to the object ceases; interest in it disappears until the moment when desire re-awakens. Sensuality finds its "outlet" in desire. This word does belong here. The concupiscence of the flesh goes in the direction of finding "an outlet," and after having found it, the entire relation to the object of desire breaks off. In the animal world, where sexual life is regulated by the reproductive instinct correctly aligned with the need to preserve the species, such a closing of the concupiscible reaction is completely sufficient. In the world of persons, however, a serious danger of a moral nature emerges at this point.

This danger is closely connected with the problem of love, and thus with the relation to the person. "Bodily love," which grows from the very concupiscence of the flesh, does not contain in itself the value that love of the person should possess. For the concupiscence of the flesh replaces the object of love, which is the person, with another, namely the "body and sex" linked to some person. As is known, the reaction of sensuality is not related to the person as person, but only to the "body and sex" of a concrete person, precisely "as a possible object of use." Thus, as a matter of fact, in the field of vision of desire proceeding from the concupiscence of the flesh, the person of the other sex is present not as person but as the "body and sex." The place of the personal value that is essential to love is taken by the sexual value itself, which in turn becomes the center for crystallizing the whole lived-experience. Because this lived-experience is accompanied by the sensual affection of love, desire acquires the character of an amorous lived-experience—one that is strong and intense, because it is firmly based on the sexual reactions of the body and on the senses. When speaking of the "sensual affection of love" we do not mean the reaction of affectivity alone, which itself does not react to the "body and sex," but to the "human being of the other sex"—the "femininity" or "masculinity," as the analysis in chapter II revealed. "Affection" in this case signifies a sensual state evoked first of all by the desire of the "body and sex" as that which corresponds to sensuality alone, and then by the satisfaction of this desire through "bodily love."

We can see now what constitutes the *moral danger* linked to the concupiscence of the flesh. This concupiscence leads to "love" that is not love, for it evokes amorous lived-experiences on the basis of sensual desire alone and its satisfaction. These lived-experiences have the person of the other sex for their object, and at the same time they do not measure up to the person, for they stop merely on the level of the "body and sex" as their proper and only content. From here the disintegration of love proceeds. With great force, the concupiscence of the flesh pushes toward bodily intimacy, toward sexual intercourse. However, this intimacy and intercourse grown out of the concupiscence of the flesh alone do not unite a man and a woman as persons, do not have the value of a personal union, and are not love in its proper (i.e., ethical) meaning. On the contrary, this sexual intimacy and intercourse that grow out of the concupiscence of the flesh alone are a denial of the love of persons, for at their basis lies the directional reaction to "use"—the reaction characteristic of pure sensuality. This reaction must be incorporated in a correct and honorable relation to the person, and this we call integration. When left to its own devices, the concupiscence of the flesh is not a source of the person's love, even though it evokes amorous (erotic) lived-experiences charged with a large dose of sensual affections.

A serious possibility exists here not only of deforming love, but also of wasting its natural material. For sensuality provides material for love, but an appropriate creativity of the will is necessarily needed in relation to this material. Without this creativity love cannot exist, what is left is only the material that the concupiscence of the flesh merely uses up, finding an "outlet" in it. Then, interior or exterior deeds are born that have for their object merely the sexual value linked to the person. These deeds remain within the aim of the directional reaction characteristic of sensuality itself: oriented to the "body as a possible object of use." Thus, they relate to the person in a utilitarian, consumption-oriented way. Whether the deeds are exterior or only interior depends to a large extent on the structure of sensuality itself in a given person.[12]

Affectivity is, so to speak, a natural protection against the concupiscence of the flesh. It is known from the analysis conducted in the previous chapter that in a given case affectivity is the ability to react to a sexual value, to the one, however, that is tied with the whole "human being of the other sex," and not with the "body as a possible object of use." Thus, in this sense it is the ability to react to "femininity" or "masculinity." The reactions of affectivity also possess a directional character, although their direction differs from that of the reactions of sensuality. Affectivity does not tend toward the using that has for its object the "body and *sexus*" and seeks an outlet in "bodily love" alone. If we sometimes speak of the need for an affective outlet, it is not in the same sense as when one speaks of a sensory-sexual outlet. Concerning the former, the point is rather a satisfaction of the need for affective lived-experiences themselves, the need to "be in love" with somebody or to suffer someone's affection ("to be loved"). Affectivity has its separate world of interior and inter-personal facts, which by themselves stay away from the concupiscence of the flesh. Affective love seems to be pure to the extent that any comparison of it to sensual passion amounts to a debasement and brutalization.

However, it does not constitute a positive and full solution to the problem of the concupiscence of the flesh. At most, affective love moves this problem away from the field of consciousness, even bringing into the relation of a woman to a man (or vice versa) that idealization we spoke about in the preceding chapter. But to move a problem away does not mean to solve it or even to come out and face it. Experience teaches that a one-sidedly "idealistic" approach to love sometimes later becomes a source of bitter disillusion, or generates an explicit lack of consistency in conduct, especially in conjugal life. What affectivity brings into the reciprocal relation between a woman and a man is still only the "material" of love. Fully-mature protection against the concupiscence of the flesh is found only in the deep *realism of virtue*, and the point here is precisely the virtue of chastity. Affectivity, however, and this "idealization" that is born on its substratum in the relation X-Y and Y-X, can be very helpful in forming the virtue of chastity. Nevertheless, even the most delicate natural reactions that arise on the ground of affectivity with respect to "femininity" or "masculinity" do not by themselves create an adequately deep basis for the love of the person to crystallize.

In fact, a certain danger exists that the concupiscence of the flesh will absorb these reactions, that it will assimilate them as a kind of "accompaniment" that will obscure its proper relation to the human being of the other sex. In that case, "love" will be, above all, a bodily affair and a domain of concupiscence, although a certain measure of "lyricism" proceeding from affectivity will be attached to it. It must be added that when affectivity is not strengthened with virtue but left to its own devices, and in this way made to face the powerful concupiscence of the flesh, it is most often reduced to that role. Indeed, it then adds from itself a certain new moment; it makes of love something of a subjective "taboo," in which affection is everything and decides everything.

## Subjectivism and egoism

The problem of subjectivism appears right here, for it is affection more than anything else that introduces a subjective moment into human love. Affection (*uczucie*) must be distinguished from affectivity (*uczuciowość*). By affectivity we understand the ability to react to certain values connected with the "human being of the other sex" ("femininity"–"masculinity," "charm"–"strength"). Affection, however, is a subjective psychical fact bound with the reaction to various values, and therefore it is bound with deeds that are formed in the orbit of that reaction, in its extension, so to speak. So, sensual-bodily affections are joined with the reaction of sensuality and with the exterior or interior deeds that have their source in the concupiscence of the flesh. Affections are also joined with the reactions of affectivity and with deeds to which these reactions create a stimulus. When we speak of the need for integration, that is, for the correct incorporation of all that proceeds from sensuality and affectivity into an ethically and fully-mature relation of one person to another, then we take fully into account the plasticity of human affection. Affection can develop and adjust to what man consciously forms with his will. The integration of love demands that man consciously forms with his will all that the senses provide him with in the reactions of sensuality and affectivity, so that by thoroughly affirming the value of the person he places all this on the level of a relation between persons and keeps it within the boundaries of a true union of persons.

*Subjectivism* differs fundamentally from *subjectivity*, from the subjective profile of every love. Subjectivity belongs to the nature of love which concerns two subjects (a subject—*subiectum*), Y and X. Subjectivism, on the other hand, is a distortion of the essence of love—it is such an overgrowth of the subjective moment that the objective value of love becomes partially or completely absorbed and lost in it. The first form of subjectivism can be defined as *subjectivism of affection*. Affections play an enormous role in the formation of the subjective side of love; one cannot imagine the subjective profile of love without affection, hence it would be absurd to demand, as the stoics or Kant did, that love be "affectionless." On the other hand, we cannot ignore the possibility of subjectivism of affection, so that one can speak even of a certain "danger of affection," i.e., a danger that threatens love from the side of affections. Already in the analysis of fondness (in the second section of chapter II) we drew attention to the fact that affection in a sense changes the direction of experiencing (*przeżywać*) truth. Man—a rational being—possesses a natural need to know truth and to be guided by it; the point is the objective truth of action, the truth containing the very core of human morality. Now, affection in a sense averts the "gaze of truth" from what is objective in action, from the object of the act and from the act itself, and turns it toward what is subjective in action, toward the lived-experience alone. Affection makes human consciousness, above all, absorbed in the subjective "veracity" of lived-experience. And the lived-experience is true, that is, "authentic," inasmuch as it is saturated with true (sincere) affection.*

This fact has two consequences: (1) Some "disintegration" takes place: the actual lived-experience rises above all the remaining objective facts and especially the principles to which they are subjected—it breaks away from their totality; (2) In place of these objective principles, which constitute a test of the value of a given deed, the value of affection itself is introduced, and it starts to determine the value of the act: an act is good because it is "authentic," i.e., it is saturated with "true" affection. However, by itself affection possesses only a subjective veracity: true affection can also infuse an act that objectively is not good. Therefore, subjectivism of affection constitutes a wide gate through which various interior or exterior deeds can enter the love of a woman and a man, deeds incompatible with the objective essence of love, even though as lived-experiences they have an "amorous" (erotic) character. The legitimation of these lived-experiences and deeds will be precisely their

---

* It is not the strength, the power of conviction, or the authenticity of belief with which the given subject passes a judgment that determines the veracity of the judgment, but its conformity with that to which or to whom the given judgment pertains. The subject is the exclusive author of the judgment, but is not, however, the author of its truth. This distinction is often forgotten, especially when the pertinent judgments or assessments are accompanied by strong affective reactions. For this reason, it is recommended to treat the "testimony of one's affection" with a certain measure of mistrust. Also, the role of testimony, which in this case even the spouses themselves are sometimes ready to give, should not be overestimated. In the name of realism, we cannot forget that "eternally faithful love" is declared at the beginning always sincerely even by those who afterward—again in the name of the "truth of affections"—change, sometimes often, the object of their love. The "truth of affection" does not hinder them in that at all. See supra (the chapter II sections "Love as fondness" in part 1 and "Choice and responsibility" in part 3).

"authenticity" in the sense described above. It is known, however, that the affections which accompany the very concupiscence of the flesh or its satisfaction are also "true" affections; they possess their subjective veracity, just like any other affection.

From this shape of subjectivism, from subjectivism of affections, a straight and easy path leads to *subjectivism of value*, so easy that there simply seems to be no way and reason for not following it once one has already entered the sloping plane of subjectivism. Love itself is disposed toward the objective value. Such, above all, is the value of the person, which is mutually affirmed in love; the union of persons, to which love leads, possesses this value. Those values that sensuality and affectivity turn to in their natural reactions are also objective—the value of the "body as a possible object of use," and the value of the "human being of the other sex" linked to his "femininity" or "masculinity." Subjectivism of value consists in this: all these objective values, either the person, the "body and sex," or "femininity/masculinity," are treated only and exclusively as an opportunity to evoke pleasure or various degrees of delight. Pleasure becomes the only value and the complete basis of valuation. What follows is a confusion of the directions of experiencing (*przeżywać*) and acting ("deeds"), which ultimately ruins completely not only the very essence of love, but also the truly amorous character of lived-experiences.* For not only must love be clearly directed toward the person, but even sensuality and affectivity, which in a given case provide it with the "material," react in a natural way to the appropriate values

---

* The author analyzes here the phenomenon of "separating lived-experience from act" that occurs in practice. Also in theory, cases of this type of fission can occasionally constitute an incentive for attempts to absolutize lived-experiences, emotions, etc. The author took an interest in this problem particularly in his treatise *Ocena możliwości zbudowania etyki chrześcijańskiej przy założeniach systemu Maxa Schelera* (*An Assessment Concerning the Possibility of Building Christian Ethics on the Suppositions of Max Scheler's System* [Lublin, 1959]). See K. Wojtyła, "Problem oderwania przeżycia od aktu w etyce na tle poglądów Kanta i Schelera" (The Problem of Separating Lived-Experience from Act in Ethics in Relation to the Views of Kant and Scheler), *Roczniki Filozoficzne* 5, fasc. 3 (1955–57), 113–140; "*W poszukiwaniu podstaw perfekcjoryzmu w etyce*" (In Search for the Basis of Perfectiorism in Ethics), ibid., fasc. 4: 303–317; "O kierowniczej lub służebnej roli rozumu w etyce. Na tle poglądów Tomasza z Akwinu, Hume'a i Kanta" (On the Governing or Subservient Role of Reason in Ethics: Based on the Views of Thomas Aquinas, Hume, and Kant), ibid. 6, fasc. 2 (1958), 13–31.

connected with the person. Subjectivism of value, however, signifies a disposition toward pleasure alone: pleasure is the end, and everything else a means to it—including the person and his body, together with the "femininity" or "masculinity" that is linked to them.

This form of subjectivism, then, ruins the very essence of love and sees the complete value of amorous lived-experiences (as well as of "love" itself) in pleasure. The amorous (erotic) lived-experiences provide a woman and a man with a strongly perceptible pleasure, a delight in various degrees. Precisely this pleasure-delight becomes the complete and exclusive *raison d'être* for both individual lived-experiences and, indirectly, love itself between a woman and a man. The hedonization of love in theory and practice is the last fruit of subjectivism. Here, what rises above the body of facts, and especially the principles determining true love, is not simply the individual, actual lived-experiences, but pleasure alone, which accompanies these lived-experiences. Pleasure becomes the complete and absolute value to which everything should be subordinated, for here it is the interior measure of all human acts. This resembles the program of utilitarianism, critiqued in chapter I. At this point, the "danger of affections" is manifested even more strongly, for affections by nature gravitate toward pleasure—pleasure is a good for affections, whereas pain is an evil they avoid. Inasmuch as affections directly attempt to manifest themselves as the exclusive and proper content of love (subjectivism of affection), when left to themselves they indirectly steer one toward seeking pleasure and delight. As a result, love itself is assessed and valuated according to whether it provides this pleasure.

Subjectivism in both its forms, and especially in the latter, is the ground upon which *egoism* develops. Both subjectivism and egoism in some way contradict love, for, firstly, love's disposition is objective: toward the person and his good, and, secondly, its disposition is altruistic: toward another human being. Subjectivism replaces that with the subject and his lived-experience; it looks after the "authenticity" of this lived-experience, after the subjective verification of love in affection itself. Egoism is disposed exclusively toward its own "I," toward ego, and it seeks the good of this "I" without taking other people into account. Egoism excludes love, for it excludes the common good; it also excludes the possibility of reciprocity, which is always based on a striving for the common good. Putting its own "I" forward and fixating on its good in an exclusive, narrow way—which is characteristic of egoism—always presupposes some exaggerated preoccupation with the subject (*subiectum*).

One's own "I," grasped above all as a subject, becomes egoistic once we stop seeing correctly its objective position among other beings, and the relations and dependencies that link this "I" with them. Especially the second form of subjectivism, subjectivism of value, cannot be *de facto* anything else but egoism. Since pleasure is the only value of interest in the relation of Y to X and X to Y, then both reciprocity and the union of persons are out of the question. Orientation toward pleasure as the end confines each of them exclusively within his own "I." Consequently, one cannot speak of reciprocity but only of "two-sidedness"; a sum of pleasure exists that proceeds from the interaction between two persons of different sex, and that must be skillfully divided between the persons so that each of them obtains as much as possible. Egoism excludes love, but allows a certain calculation and compromise: where there is no love, however, a bilateral arrangement between egoisms may exist.

However, this state of affairs excludes a "common 'I,'" which is created when one of the persons wills the good of the other as much as his own, and in that good finds his own good.* [13] Precisely in this way pleasure alone cannot be willed because it is a purely subjective good, neither trans-subjective nor even inter-subjective. Thus, at most one can want the other's pleasure "next" to his own pleasure, but always only "on condition" of one's own pleasure. Therefore, subjectivism of value, that is, the orientation toward pleasure alone as the exclusive end of the interaction and relations between a woman and a man, is, as a rule,

---

* Love is the realization of a certain kind of community based on the common good. The problem of community has two aspects: objective and subjective. Objectively, community is described in view of the goal of common pursuit. This is a less perfect description of community. Community is more strictly defined by the subjective aspect—participation (*uczestnictwo*), when "man chooses what others choose, or even he chooses because others choose—and at the same time he chooses this as his own good and the end of his own pursuit. What he then chooses is his own good in the sense that man as person fulfills himself in it" (*Person and Act*, 306 in section 5 of chapter VII). See K. Wojtyła, "Osoba: podmiot i wspólnota," *Roczniki Filozoficzne* 24, fasc. 2 (1976), 6–39.

egoism. This follows from the nature of pleasure. However, the point is not in the least to see pleasure itself as evil—in itself pleasure is a specific good—but to indicate the moral evil that is here contained in the disposition of the will toward pleasure alone. For this disposition is not only subjective, but also egoistic.*

One can sometimes hear about *egoism of the senses* and *egoism of affection*. This distinction is based on distinguishing sensuality from affectivity—the two different centers of reaction to sexual value. Nonetheless, affection lies at the basis of each of these egoisms: in the first case the sensual-bodily affection, which is linked with satisfying sensuality, and in the second case the more subtle "psychical" affection, which accompanies reactions of affectivity. Affection as a "strong" lived-experience, or as an emotional state that fills consciousness more permanently, facilitates concentration on one's own "I," and here appears pleasure as a good of this "I," a good connected with affection.

Sensual egoism is associated more with subjectivism of value. The subject strives directly for pleasure, which can be provided by erotic lived-experiences linked with the "body and sex"—at that point the person is treated quite explicitly as an "object." This form of egoism is

---

* Pleasure in conjugal love can be and is at times a *fruit* of striving to affirm the other person. It should not be, however, the fundamental *end* of this striving, as raising this fruit to the position of the primary end is precisely an act of egoism. However, this egoism not only injures the person-object of love by reducing him to the role of a means to an end, but also impedes the attainment of the fullness of happiness for the subject of action. For man attains happiness through self-giving proper to the person, self-giving in love up to the point of losing oneself (see the evangelical "Unless a grain of wheat dies, it remains just a grain of wheat; but if it dies, it produces much fruit"). [*Unless a grain of wheat dies* . . . : See Jn 12:24. — Trans.] For this reason, it is morally reprehensible not only to subordinate other people to one's striving for pleasure, but also to seek a good for another person that does not take into account the dignity of the person.

It is worthwhile to remember that the essential good of man not only is not identified with the pleasure he feels, but also is difficult to calculate. For even in the non-eudaemonistic interpretation of utilitarianism (see footnote, p. 18) a danger exists of preferring "calculable" goods over those whose realization sometimes demands a very long time and considerable dedication, goods that themselves are incommensurable. The latter goods certainly include the full self-realization of the person attainable through reciprocal conjugal love. This love is honorable and praiseworthy precisely when its end is the thorough happiness of the other person, and not simply multiplication of pleasure and avoidance of pain.

rather clear. Egoism of affections does not possess this clarity, and therefore it is easier to become entangled in it. For it is associated above all with subjectivism of affection, where pleasure does not yet move to the foreground, but which merely concerns affection itself, because affection constitutes the condition for the authenticity of lived-experience. And so, in egoism of affection there is more seeking one's own "I" than seeking pleasure. However, even here pleasure is an end, and the orientation toward it ultimately determines egoism. For the point is pleasure that is contained in the very lived-experience of affection or the sensation of it. When affection becomes the end only because of the pleasure contained in its lived-experience or sensation, then the person to whom the affection turns or from whom it originates is again but an "object" that provides an occasion to satisfy the emotional needs of one's own "I." Egoism of affection, which often borders on a certain sort of game ("playing with someone else's feelings"), is a no less deep distortion of love than egoism of the senses—the only difference being that the latter is manifested more clearly as egoism, whereas the former can be concealed more easily in the appearances of love. Let us add that egoism of affections can contribute—not less clearly, although in a different way than egoism of the senses—to unchastity in the mutual relations of the persons Y and X.

At the beginning of these reflections, subjectivism was distinguished from subjectivity. Love is always some subjective and inter-subjective fact, that is, it possesses a subjectivity proper to itself. At the same time, however, it must be protected from subjectivistic distortion, through which the disintegration of love creeps in and egoism of various shapes germinates. Therefore, each of the persons committed in love, while working toward full subjectivity, the full subjective profile of their love, should at the same time endeavor to achieve objectivity. Joining one with the other demands a particular effort, but this effort is indispensable to secure love's own being.*

---

* Man "unifies himself," "fulfills himself" always and only when he loves, i.e., when he affirms the dignity of the recipient of the act in his whole truth, which is objectively given and entrusted to the subject to be affirmed. See *Person and Act*, 182–189.

## *The structure of sin*

The analysis of the problem of the concupiscence of the flesh, and perhaps even more of the problems of subjectivism and egoism, will enable us to grasp the concept of "sinful love." This expression is encountered frequently and is generally understood quite accurately. However, it conceals a deep paradox, since love is a synonym of the good, whereas sin signifies moral evil. Yet, there can be "love" that besides being morally not good, is on the contrary "sinful"; it contains in itself the elements (*pierwiastki*) of moral evil. How then can it be love? We have stated that sensuality and affectivity provide, so to speak, the "material for love," i.e., they create the facts "inside" the person and the situations "between" persons in which love can be realized. Nonetheless, these "situations" by themselves are not yet love. They become love only if they are integrated, that is, through lifting them up to the personal level, through the reciprocal affirmation of the value of the person. Without this, these psychological facts born in sensuality alone (or even in affectivity alone) may easily become the "material" for sin. We must thoroughly realize the way in which sin may be formed from this material. Hence we offer this reflection on the structure of sin.

As we have stated previously, the concupiscence of the flesh does not merely signify the natural capacity for bodily desire, i.e., for directing oneself toward the values that the senses present in the sexual sphere. The concupiscence of the flesh is a constant inclination to see the person of the other sex through the values of *sexus* alone as an "object of possible use." So, the concupiscence of the flesh means a latent readiness in man to overturn the objective order of values. For the correct vision and desire of the person is a vision and "desire" through the values of the person. In this vision and desire the point is not some "a-sexuality," some blindness to the value of the "body and sex," but instead the point is so that this value is incorporated correctly into the love of the person—love in the proper and full meaning of the word. Yet, the concupiscence of the flesh relates to the person as a "possible object of use" precisely on account of this value of the "body and sex," (whereas the body itself as a component of the person also should be the object of love on account of the value of the person)—hence the distinction between the "love of the body" and "bodily love."

So, the concupiscence of the flesh is in every man the terrain on which two approaches toward the human being of the other sex clash and struggle with each other. The object of the struggle is the "body," which, because of its sexual value (the "body and sex"), awakens a desire to use, whereas it should awaken love because of the value of the person—since in fact it is the body of the person. The very concupiscence of the flesh means a constant inclination only to "use," whereas one should "love." Therefore, we need an appropriate qualification in presenting the view formulated in the analysis of love, namely that sensuality and affectivity provide the "material" for love. This happens insofar as the reactions of sensuality and of affectivity are not absorbed by the concupiscence of the flesh alone, but are allowed to be drawn into the true love of the person. This is difficult especially with respect to the reactions of sensuality, for we have stated that they are spontaneous, directional reactions, and that their direction is the same as that of the concupiscence of the flesh, so much so that the concupiscence of the flesh is evoked in a sense by the reactions of sensuality. Sensuality is the ability to react to the sexual value connected with the body as a "possible object of use," whereas the concupiscence of the flesh is the constant inclination toward the desire evoked by the reaction of sensuality.

From the viewpoint of the structure of sin (within the analysis of "sinful love") we must emphasize that *neither* sensuality alone *nor* the very concupiscence of the flesh *is yet a sin*. Catholic theology sees in the concupiscence of the flesh only the "hotbed of sin" (*zarzewie grzechu*). It is difficult not to acknowledge that the hotbed of sin is the constant inclination to desire the body of the person of the other sex as an "object of use," whereas we should relate to the person in a supra-utilitarian way (for this is contained in the concept "to love"). Therefore, grounding itself in Revelation, theology sees in the concupiscence of the flesh an effect of original sin. This constant inclination to relate improperly and incorrectly to the person on account of the sexual value connected with his body must have a cause. A lack of cause would become a reason for pessimism, unintelligible just like every evil. The truth about original sin explains this elementary and at the same time prevailing evil, namely, that when encountering a person of the other sex, man does not know how to "love" simply and spontaneously, but his whole approach to this person becomes interiorly disturbed by the desire to "use," which at times rises above "loving" and deprives love of its proper essence while often keeping up only its appearances. Thus, man cannot quite safely trust the reactions of sensuality (or even of affectivity, since affectivity in the psychical life is joined with sensuality by, in a sense, a common source), he still cannot acknowledge them as love, but only must bring love out of them. A certain pain accompanies this, for man would simply like to follow what is spontaneous; he would like to find love ready-made in all reactions that have the other human being as their object.

Neither sensuality nor even the concupiscence of the flesh is by itself a sin, for a sin can only be what proceeds from the will—an act characterized by appropriate consciousness and voluntariness (*voluntarium*). The act (*czyn*) as an act (*akt*) of the will is always interior, whereas sin can dwell both in interior and exterior deeds, for the will initiates them and is a mainstay to both. Therefore, the reaction of sensuality alone and the "movement" of the concupiscence of the flesh, which is born of that reaction and occurs in man "next to" the will and outside of the will, cannot be sins by themselves. One must take seriously into account the fact that the concupiscence of the flesh possesses in every normal man its own dynamic, which is also manifested by the reactions of sensuality themselves. We have already paid attention to their directional character. The sexual values connected with the body of the person become not only an object of interest, but also—quite easily—an object of sensual desire. The source of this actual desire is the concupiscible power (*appetitus concupiscibilis* according to St. Thomas), not the will. However, what is manifested in sensual desire is the tendency to become the willing—an act of the will.* The boundary between the one and the other, i.e., between the actual sensual desire and the willing, is nonetheless distinct. The concupiscence of the flesh does not

---

* In the terminology adopted by the author "wanting" is an act of the will. This elicits two remarks.

1) Whenever we say, e.g., "I am in want of" something (*chce mi się czegoś*) or "I feel like" something (*zachciewa mi się czegoś*), we refer this not to the person himself but to concupiscence and its "own dynamic." [*I am in want of something*: The constructs in Polish used in this sentence express a situation, in which the wanting is not initiated by man's will, but in a sense discovered by him in his person. — Trans.]

2) Although the very existence and manifestation of this dynamic in us is necessitated, man is responsible to a certain degree for its vehemence and disorder.

at first aim for the will to want fully and actively what the actual sensual desire is directed to—merely the consent of the will suffices.

The threshold of sin lies precisely here—and therefore the concupiscence of the flesh, which constantly, habitually attempts to persuade the will to cross it, was rightly called the "hotbed of sin." From the moment it consents, the will begins to want what is "happening" in sensuality itself and sensual desire. Henceforth, all this not only does "happen" in man, but also he himself starts to "do" it somehow—only interiorly at first, for the will directly is the source of interior acts ("deeds"). These deeds possess a moral value, they are good or evil; and if they are evil, we call them sins.

In practice, sometimes the problem of the boundary of sin arises here, a problem that is quite difficult for some persons. Objectively, this boundary runs together with the act of the will, with the conscious and voluntary consent of the will. There are, however, people who have difficulties with grasping this boundary. And because it is known that the concupiscence of the flesh in man possesses its own dynamic, by virtue of which it strives to become a willing—an act of the will— then, due to a lack of discernment, someone can easily take as an act of the will what is still only a movement of sensuality and of the concupiscence of the flesh.* The reaction of sensuality develops in its own direction by virtue of the dynamic that dwells in the concupiscence of

---

* The act of the will (the "wanting" or "not wanting" something) implies intellectual cognition of this something, thus a judgment of reason. Hence, the behavior of a man who experiences "morally suspect" affections in the situation that allows only for "imagined judgments" that are not really passed—regardless what kind of behavior it was—cannot be the object of moral assessment. Only on the basis of intellectual consciousness, and not purely imaginational consciousness, can there be born a judgment of moral duty (to imagine that one is obligated to do something is not enough to be actually obligated; similarly to imagine to want something, e.g., on the theatrical stage, and to want something actually are two different things).

Directing one's own action in accordance with the "truth about the moral good" can be, in a sense, "subconscious," but only in the sense that the reasons previously received and secured in specific functional dispositions rationalize a given action that is outside the field of actual attention. Moral value of human actions—with high frequency of changes occurring in regard to their object and circumstances—cannot be ceaselessly controlled and verified within the field of attention, which also must encompass other kinds of assessments. Therefore "a man of good will" rightly trusts—as in any case he must trust—this "acquired spontaneity," which he owes to his morally valuable dispositions (as is the case in a self-respecting society where the citizens—or, e.g., passers-by in the street—are considered unsuspected *donec contrarium probetur*). [*Donec contrarium probetur*: Until the contrary is proven. —Trans.]

the flesh, not only when the reaction fails to find the consent, but also when it is explicitly opposed by the will. The act of the will directed against the sensual movement in general does not evoke an immediate effect. The reaction of sensuality in its (i.e., sensual) sphere of psyche usually, so to speak, reverberates until the end, even if in the sphere of the will it encounters explicit opposition. And nobody can demand from himself both that the reactions of sensuality do not arise in him and that they recede immediately, as soon as the will does not consent or explicitly declares itself "against." This is important for practicing the virtue of self-mastery (*continentia*). There is a difference between "not willing" and "not feeling," "not suffering."[14]

Therefore, when analyzing the structure of sin, one must not exaggerate the significance of sensuality itself and of the very concupiscence of the flesh. The mere spontaneous reaction of sensuality, the mere reflex of the concupiscence of the flesh, is not yet a sin and will not become one if the will does not lead to that. And the will leads to sin inasmuch as it is badly disposed, inasmuch as it is guided by a misconception of love. The *temptation* that opens the way to "sinful love" consists precisely in this. Temptation is not only "erroneous thinking," for a nonculpable error does not bring sin. If I judge that "A is good" and do A, then I act well, even if A in reality were evil.* Temptation, however, presupposes

---

* In connection with the above, a significant distinction remains between the morally good (*dobry*) and the morally right (*słuszny*) act, and the twofold function of conscience as the informer in relation to both aforementioned aspects of the act. For my judgment "I should perform the act A in relation to the person P" possesses two dimensions that are structurally different, although closely joined with each other. The first dimension is expressed by the judgment "I should affirm P (and any other in his place)." This dimension can be called the dimension of pre-conscience. The second dimension is expressed by the judgment "A is an appropriate (or even the only) way to affirm the person P." Only in its first dimension is this judgment a reliable informer. Thus, while choosing (attitude, intention) an action in conformity with conscience, the subject is certain only that he *wanted* to affirm P, but he is not sure whether he chose an act that is *really suitable* for the role of affirming P. In other words, it is possible to act to the detriment of the person P while acting in accordance with conscience (having a good intention). We say then that the act is morally positive only in the aspect of attitude or intention, i.e., *morally good*, but it is not morally positive in its objective impact on the recipient of action. In other words, it is *morally wrong (niesłuszny)*. [*We say then that … it is morally wrong (niesłuszny)*: This statement of the Polish editors seems a bit confusing and impractical. It is better to hold fast to the teaching of St. Thomas on the integrity of the moral act. In discussing the good and evil of human acts, St. Thomas applies the Dionysian formula: *Quilibet singularis*

the consciousness that "A is evil," which is in some way falsified in order to create a suggestion that "After all, A is good." Subjectivism of all sorts contributes to such falsification in the reciprocal relation between persons of different sex.

Subjectivism of affection promotes the suggestion that whatever is linked with "true" affection, whatever must be acknowledged as "authentic" from the side of affection, is good. A temptation arises of reducing love to subjective, emotional states alone. In that case, "love" follows affection as its only content and its only criterion. The affirmation of the value of the person, the striving for his true good, for union in the true common good—all this does not enter the field of vision of the will disposed subjectivistically toward affection alone. Sin is then born from the fact that man does not want to subordinate affection to the person and love, but on the contrary, he subordinates the person and love to affection. "Sinful love" is often very affective; it is saturated with affection, which supplants everything else in that love. Of course, its sinfulness does not lie in the fact of being saturated with affection; it does not lie in affection itself, but in the fact that the will places affection before the person, and this cancels all objective laws and principles that must govern the union of persons, of a woman and a man. The "authenticity" of the lived-experience sometimes becomes the enemy of truth in conduct.[*]

Subjectivism of values proposes a different type of suggestion: that what is pleasant, is good. The temptation of pleasure, of delight, often

---

*defectus causat malum, bonum autem causatur ex integra causa,* i.e., "Evil results from any single defect, but good from the complete cause." This means that a morally good act requires the goodness of all its sources together, namely of the object, of the end, and of the circumstances, including the consequences (cf. *Catechism of the Catholic Church,* 1755); see *Summa Theologiae* I–II 18.4; herein after cited as STh.—Trans.]. Action in conformity with conscience is thus always morally good, but it is not at the same time always morally right. However, conscience, even if being erroneous, always obliges to action in conformity with it, because the one who errs does not know *ex definitione* about his error. [*Ex definitione*: By definition.—Trans.] The possibility of making a mistake in such an essential issue inclines one toward particular care for the accuracy of one's moral recognitions. The only way to guarantee this accuracy is to strive for ever deeper knowledge of who man is in his objective structure. To present precisely this structure of man, of a man and a woman, within the totality of their vocation to reciprocal love, is the main task of this book.

[*] See footnote, p. 136.

replaces the vision of true happiness. It happens when the will is disposed toward seeking pleasure alone. Once again, temptation is not
merely an "error of thinking" ("I thought that this was permanent happiness, but it turned out to be only fleeting pleasure"), but it results
from an attitude of the will wanting in an inordinate way the pleasure
desired by the senses. Precisely then, love is reduced most easily to
satisfying the concupiscence of the flesh. The very concupiscence of
the flesh or its spontaneous "movements" are not yet sins. However, sin
is a conscious commitment of the will to what the concupiscence of
the flesh incites against the objective truth. Of course, the will can
temporarily yield to this concupiscence—sometimes we call it the sin
of weakness. It yields to this concupiscence, however, inasmuch as it
sees the good in pleasure alone, and to such an extent that pleasure
obscures everything else: both the value of the person and the value of
the true union of persons in love.

Once it becomes the complete principle of the will's operation, the
suggestion "That which is pleasant, is good" leads to a thorough distortion of the will. This means a habitual inability to "love" a person—the
will lacks love.[15] Love as virtue has been ousted from the will and
replaced by a disposition toward sensory-sexual use alone. The will has
no contact with the value of the person; actually it lives by the negation
of love, offering no resistance to the concupiscence of the flesh.

With this attitude of the will, the concupiscence of the flesh, the
"hotbed of sin," burns completely freely, for it does not find in the will
any counterbalance in affirmation of the person's value and in striving
for the person's true good. "Sinful love" takes place when instead of
affirming the person's value and instead of striving for the person's true
good—which constitute the core of true "loving"—seeking pleasure
alone and the delight connected with the sensory-sexual lived-experiences forces itself into the relation toward the person of the other sex,
into the reciprocal relation of the persons Y and X. Then, "using" ousts
"loving." As is known, the moral evil contained in sin lies in the fact that
the person is treated as an "object of use" or that both persons, Y and X,
treat each other in this way.

However, erotic lived-experiences themselves do not—at least for
the time being—reveal this attitude "to use." With all their might they
attempt to retain the "flavor of love." This leads to the flight from

reflection, for reflection carries with itself some inherent necessity of objectivization—so that the sinfulness of this love would then have to come to light. Precisely here, the evil of subjectivism as an attitude of the will is manifested: subjectivism is not merely an error of thinking, but a distortion of the whole direction of action. When Y or X or, above all, when both of them together undertake to be objective, then they must truly define what exists between them. However, the subjectivistic attitude of the will not only prevents the realization of true love due to an excessive orientation toward the subject, but also suggests that the subjective state in which the subject is satiated by an appropriate affection is already a fully-mature love, that this is "all" there is in love. Hand in hand with an orientation toward the subject goes an orientation toward one's own "I"—subjectivism is often the source of egoism. However, this egoism (egoism of the senses) is frequently experienced (*przeżywać*) as "love" and called so, as if what is only a certain form of "using" were "loving."

A particular danger of "sinful love" consists *in a fiction*, namely, that actually and before reflection "sinful love" is not usually experienced (*przeżywać*) as "sinful" but above all as "love." Although this circumstance in fact directly diminishes the gravity of sin, it indirectly increases the danger of it. The fact that so many "deeds" in the interaction and relations between persons—women and men—occur spontaneously, "in passion" or "out of passion," does not, after all, change the fact that the personalistic norm exists and is binding in the relations between persons. Only on the basis of the principle contained in it can one speak of the union of persons in love, and also in conjugal love, where the union of a woman and a man is complemented by sexual intercourse.

Sin is always a transgression of this principle, including when its actual source is constituted by amorous affection (*amor sensitivus*) that develops around the lived-experiences provided to man by sensuality or affectivity (if affectivity has yielded to sensuality and is subordinated to it). Sin is a violation of the true good. For the true good, which is the concern of love between a man and a woman, is above all the person, and is neither affection for its own sake nor, much less, pleasure for its own sake. After all, these are secondary goods and from them alone it is impossible to build love, that is, the durable union of persons, even though these goods are so strongly manifested in love's subjective, psychological profile. A person may never be sacrificed for them, however, for that would introduce an element (*pierwiastek*) of sin into love.

"Sinful love" is nothing else but precisely a system of reference between two persons Y and X in which affection alone, and even more so pleasure alone, assumes the dimension of the self-reliant good and determines everything, ignoring the objective value of the person and the objective laws and principles of interaction and relations between persons of different sex.

Sin which is contained in "sinful love" dwells by its very essence in free will. The concupiscence of the flesh is merely its "hotbed." For the will can and should prevent the "dis-integration" of love; it should prevent pleasure or even affection alone from assuming the dimension of the self-reliant good, to which everything else is subordinated in the relation toward the person of the other sex or within the reciprocal interaction and relations between persons. The will can and should be guided by objective truth. It can, and so it should, demand that reason give it the true vision of love and of the happiness that love can bring to a woman and a man (so much evil proceeds here from a false, purely subjectivistic vision of happiness in which the "fullness of good" was replaced by a mere "sum of pleasures"). It is known that in man there are irrational forces that facilitate the whole process of "subjectivization" not only of the theoretical view of happiness, but above all of its practical pursuit—thereby paving the way for egoisms that dissolve human love and destroy it ("dis-integration"). The task of the will, for which true love should be particularly attractive because it enables the will's real deepening in the good, is to protect itself from the destructive action of these forces, to protect the person from "evil love." Not only one's own person is to be protected: since love always joins two persons, when protecting one's own person, the other is also protected.[16]

## *The full sense of chastity*

Now we move on to fully presenting the problem of chastity. We have been prepared for this by the analysis of the problems concerning the concupiscence of the flesh, subjectivism, and egoism, and especially by the last analysis of the structure of sin, that is, "sinful love." The negative attitude toward the virtue of chastity, which we spoke of at the beginning of this chapter, is essentially a fruit of resentment. Man does not want to acknowledge the enormous value that chastity possesses for human love when he does not want to acknowledge the full and objective truth about the love of a woman and a man, substituting a subjectivistic fiction in its stead. However, when he fully receives the objective truth about love, then chastity too will manifest its own full value; it will turn out to be a great positive factor of human life, a fundamental manifestation of the "culture of the person," which constitutes the essential core of all human culture.[*]

The full sense of the virtue of chastity cannot be fully comprehended without understanding love as the function of relating one person to another, the function disposed toward the union of persons. Precisely for this reason, reflections on the psychology of love had to be separated from reflections on the virtue of love. Therefore, it was necessary to underscore firmly the principle of integration: love in the world of persons must possess its ethical completeness and fullness (*integritas*); its psychological manifestations alone will not suffice—indeed, love is mature, also psychologically mature, only when it possesses an ethical value, when it is the virtue of love. Only in the virtue of love are the objective demands of the personalistic norm realized, the norm that commands "loving" the person and rejects any "use" of him. Within the manifestations that psychology itself describes as manifestations of love between a woman and a man, this principle is not always fulfilled; what is at times called the "manifestation of love" or even "love" does not, after a thorough critical examination, display the very ethical essence of "loving," but despite all appearances is only a form of "using" the person. What results, hence, is a great problem of responsibility—at the same time it is responsibility for both love and the person.

---

[*] Although every culture is distinguished from nature (*przyroda*) precisely in that it is the work of persons, the cultivation of interior life—which the author calls here the "culture of the person"—determines in every society both the "departure points" and the "arrival points" of any culture-creating actions, including also their historical and universal significance.

What is the full sense of chastity? According to Aristotle, by observing the moral life of people one can perceive in it various virtues, which in turn can be classified and organized in a certain system. The same thought was taken up by St. Thomas Aquinas, who created a very extensive and, at the same time, insightful and detailed treatise about virtues in his *Summa Theologiae* (II–II). In the system of virtues there are certain principal virtues that in a particular way improve the principal powers of the human soul, both the intellectual powers, reason and the will, as well as the sensual ones, i.e., the irascible power (*appetitus irascibilis*) and the concupiscible power (*appetitus concupiscibilis*), which were already mentioned in this chapter. These principal virtues, also called "cardinal" (from the Latin word *cardo*—a hinge, and thus being, so to speak, the hinges of the whole moral life), constitute the basis for many other virtues, each of which either bears in itself something of the cardinal virtue, some characteristic feature of it, or is needed by the cardinal virtue in the sense that the latter would not be a fully-mature virtue without it.

According to St. Thomas' classification, chastity has been linked with the cardinal virtue of temperance (*temperantia*) and subordinated to it. The virtue of temperance (*umiarkowanie*)—whose direct subject in man is, according to St. Thomas, the concupiscible power (*appetitus concupiscibilis*)—dwells in this power in order to restrain the concupiscible impulses which are born with respect to various material, bodily goods imposing themselves on the senses. It is necessary for the sensual movements (*erga bonum sensibile*, in relation to the good perceivable sensorially) to be subordinated to reason: this is the precise task of the virtue of temperance. If man lacked it, the will could easily yield to the senses and would choose as the good only what the senses perceived and desired as the good. The task of the virtue of temperance is to defend the rational being against such a "degeneration" (*wynaturzenie*). For to long for and pursue what reason acknowledges as good is natural (i.e., in conformity with nature) for a rational being such as man. Only in such a pursuit, in such a relation toward goods, is the true perfection of a rational being, of a person, expressed and realized. The virtue of temperance contributes to this by helping rational beings to live in a rational way, and thus to achieve the perfection proper to their nature. The viewpoint of Aristotle's and St. Thomas' entire ethics is fundamentally perfectioristic, which, after all, agrees with the fundamental orientation of the Gospel expressed in the well-known words: "Be perfect . . ." (Mt 5:48).* [17]

However, in this case we are concerned with a more particular problem, namely with the subordination of the virtue of chastity to the cardinal virtue of temperance. That virtue assists the will, and above all the concupiscible power itself (*appetitus concupiscibilis*), in mastering sensual movements. These also include the concupiscible movements that arise in man together with the reaction of sensuality (or in a different sense, together with the reaction of affectivity—with the variously colored and variously oriented reactions to the value of *sexus*).[18] According to the above understanding, the virtue of chastity is simply the habit of mastering concupiscent movements connected with the aforementioned reactions. "Habit" (*sprawność*) means more than "ability" (*zdolność*), and virtue is a habit—and a "constant" habit at that. For if a habit were merely provisional, it would not be a habit properly speaking; it would be possible to say that the given man "managed" to master a movement, whereas a virtue should give the assurance that this man will master it for certain. The proficiency of mastering merely provisionally the concupiscent movements that originate from sensuality is not yet a fully-mature virtue; it is not chastity in the full meaning of the word, even if one happens to manage it almost every time. The fully-mature virtue is a habit that consists in keeping constantly in balance the concupiscent power by the habitual relation to the true good (*bonum honestum*), which is defined by reason.† [19] Hence, "temperance" (*umiarkowanie*), according to the first and less full meaning, is a habit of provisionally "moderating" (*miarkowanie*) concupiscent movements,

---

* The author wrote about perfectiorism in more detail in the article titled "W poszukiwaniu podstaw perfekcjoryzmu w etyce" (In Search for the Basis of Perfectiorism in Ethics), *Roczniki Filozoficzne* 5, fasc. 4 (1955–57), 303–317.

† Reason defines the true good in the sense of being the authority passing appropriate value or duty judgments. However, being a creator of these judgments, it does not create their truth, but only reads this truth. So, only presuming the conformity of a judgment being passed with what this judgment regards, reason is ready to pass the given judgment, and actually passes it. Hence, "the lived-experience of duty is most closely joined with the lived-experience of veracity" (*Person and Act*, 172 in section 4 of chapter IV). "The fact of conscience is not so subjective as not to be in a certain measure intersubjective. In conscience ( . . . ) there takes place this particular *coupling of veracity with duty, which is manifested as the normative power of truth*" [emphasis original] (ibid., 161 in section 3 of chapter IV).

even if managed so every time. According to the second and fuller meaning, "temperance" is a habit ensuring constant moderation (*umiar*) and, together with it, the rational equilibrium of the sensual-concupiscent power.

It is difficult not to acknowledge that this theory of virtue is deeply realistic. However, the derivation of the full essence of chastity from temperance awakens certain reflections. Namely, a question arises whether this is the way of emphasizing most properly its essential value and meaning in human life. In fact, considering all the preceding reflections and analyses, it seems necessary to explicate and emphasize much more strongly the kinship of chastity with love.

There is no way to comprehend chastity without the virtue of love. Its task is to liberate love from the attitude to use. As follows from the analyses previously conducted in this chapter, this attitude proceeds not merely (and not so much) from sensuality alone or from the concupiscence of the flesh, but from subjectivism of affections, and especially from subjectivism of values, which implants its roots in the will and directly creates the conditions favorable to various egoisms (egoism of affections, egoism of the senses). These are the closest dispositions for "sinful love," which contains the attitude "to use" that is concealed by the appearances of love. The virtue of chastity, whose task is to liberate love from the attitude to use, must grasp not only sensuality and the concupiscence of the flesh themselves, but, in a sense even more so, those interior centers in man from which the attitude to use emerges and spreads. There can be no chastity without overcoming the aforementioned forms of subjectivism in the will and the egoisms concealed underneath them: the attitude to use is the more dangerous the more it is disguised in the will. "Sinful love" most often is not called "sinful," but simply "love," thereby trying to impose (on oneself and others) the conviction that it is precisely so and cannot be otherwise. To be chaste (*czysty*) means to have a "transparent" relation to the person of the other sex—chastity is the same as the "transparency" of interiority, without which love is not itself, for it is not itself as long as the wish to "use" is not subordinated to the readiness to "love" in every situation.

This "transparency" of relation to persons of the other sex cannot consist in some artificial pushing of the values of the body (or in particular the values of *sexus*) down to the subconscious, in creating the appearance as if they did not exist or act. Very frequently chastity is understood as a somewhat "blind" inhibition of sensuality and of the movements of the body when the values of the body and the values of *sexus* are pushed down to the subconscious, where they await an opportunity to explode. This is of course a false understanding of the virtue of chastity, which indeed creates a danger of such "explosions" if it is practiced in that way. Because of this erroneous view of the essence of chastity, a purely negative character of this virtue is suggested: chastity is only a "no." However, chastity is first and foremost a "yes," from which a "no" then proceeds. The underdevelopment of the virtue of chastity occurs when someone "does not keep up" with the affirmation of the value of the person, when he allows himself to be overpowered by the values of *sexus* themselves which, upon seizing the will, form badly the whole relation to the person of the other sex. The essence of chastity lies precisely in "keeping up" with the value of the person in every situation and in "pulling up" to this value every reaction to the value of the "body and sex." This particular effort is interior, spiritual, because the affirmation of the value of the person can only be a fruit of the spirit. However, this effort is above all positive, creative "from within," and not above all negative and destructive. The point is not a provisional "destruction" of the value of the "body and sex" in consciousness by pushing the lived-experience of the value down to the subconscious, but a durable and long-term integration: the value of the "body and sex" must be embedded and confirmed in the value of the person.

Thus, the charge that the virtue of chastity has a negative character is unjustified. Chastity does not possess such a character at least because it is linked to the virtue of temperance (*temperantia*). For "moderating" lived-experiences and deeds connected with the sexual value serves the value of the person and love. Furthermore, true chastity leads neither to contempt of the body nor to a deterioration of marriage and sexual life. What leads to that is "chastity" that is falsified to some degree, chastity with a certain influence of pharisaism, and, even more so, unchastity. Perhaps this is surprising and strange, but it cannot be otherwise. The condition of acknowledging and experiencing (*przeżywać*) the full value of the human "body and sex" is precisely the "appreciation" (*do-wartościowywanie*): elevating it to the value of the person, which is symptomatic of and essential precisely to chastity. Therefore, only a chaste woman and a chaste man are capable of true love.* For chastity frees their reciprocal interaction, including their conjugal intercourse, from the attitude of using the person, the attitude which in its objective essence contradicts "loving," thereby introducing in this interaction and intercourse a particular disposition to "love." The link between chastity and love proceeds from the personalistic norm, which—as has been stated in chapter I—contains a twofold content: the positive ("love") and the negative ("do not use"). It is another matter that all people—both men and women, although in slightly different ways—still must rise interiorly and exteriorly to this chaste "loving." They must mature to "savor" it, for every man by nature is burdened with concupiscences of the flesh and is inclined to locate the "flavor" of love above all in satisfying that love. For this reason, chastity is a difficult and long-term affair: one must wait for its fruits, for the joy of loving that it should bring. At the same time, however, chastity is a reliable way toward that.

Chastity does not lead to contempt of the body, but contains in itself a certain humility of the body.† Humility (*pokora*) is the proper attitude toward every true greatness, including one's own, but above all toward the one which I am not, and which resides outside of me. The human body should be "humble" toward the greatness that is the person: this is the true and definitive greatness of man. Moreover, the

---

* On the other hand, it is only through love, i.e., through the affirmation of the person, that chastity becomes a virtue, a moral habit, in accord with St. Augustine's expression: *caritas est forma virtutum*. [*Caritas est forma virtutum*: Charity is the form of virtues. In his *Summa Theologiae* (II–II 23.8), St. Thomas attributes this saying to St. Ambrose. —Trans.]

† Often in ethical discussions, and particularly in those that were carried on after the publication of the encyclical *Humanae Vitae*, striving for chastity—or, speaking more broadly, for conforming love to the demands of the natural law in this sphere—was portrayed as a manifestation of contempt or turning away from what is bodily (*contemptus mundi*), or even as a manifestation of Manichaeanism. [*Contemptus mundi*: The contempt of the world. —Trans.] Here the demand for chastity is understood precisely as respect for the body and human somatic dynamism. At the same time it is underscored that this dynamism acquires the fullness of human expression through its integration with the whole human dynamism by "elevating" it to the personal plane. For the dynamisms of the body are not a self-subsisting and self-reliant manifestation, but in a natural way are directed to serving the integral good of the human person.

human body should be "humble" toward the greatness which is love—humble, i.e., also subordinated to it. Chastity contributes precisely to that. When chastity is missing, the "body" is not subordinated to true love but, on the contrary, attempts to impose its own "laws" and to subject love to itself: the bodily use alone based on the intensive co-experience (*współprzeżywanie*) of the value of *sexus* then takes over the essential, personal role of love and precisely in this way annihilates love. Therefore, humility of the body is needed.

The body should also be humble toward the great affair of human happiness. How often does the "body" insinuate that by itself it possesses the key to the mystery of happiness. "Happiness" would then be identified with delight alone, with the sum of pleasures provided by the "body and *sexus*" in the relationship between a woman and a man. This superficial vision of happiness obscures even the truth that a woman and a man can and should seek their temporal, earthly happiness in a durable union, which has a personal character because in both of them it is based on the thorough affirmation of the value of the person. All the more, the "body" can—insofar as it is not "humble," not subordinated to the full truth about man's happiness—obscure the ultimate vision of the happiness of the human person in union with the personal God. In this sense we must understand what Christ said in the Sermon on the Mount: "Blessed are the pure of heart, for they see God" (Mt 5:8).[20] It must be added that it is precisely the truth about the union of the human person with the personal God, which in its fullness is to be accomplished in the dimension of eternity, that elucidates and explains all the more fully the value of human love, the value of the union of a man and a woman as two persons. Not without a significance is the fact that the Old and New Testaments speak about the "marriage" of God with mankind (in the chosen people, in the Church), and the writings of the mystics about the "conjugal" union of the human soul with God.

Let us now move on to reflect on the two elements of the virtue of chastity: shame (*wstyd*) and continence (*powściągliwość*).

Part Two

# Metaphysics of Shame

*The phenomenon of sexual shame*
*and its interpretation*

In recent times, the phenomenologists (Max Scheler, Franciszek Sawicki) dealt with the phenomenon of shame, and of sexual shame in particular.[21] This is a theme that opens broad perspectives and is suitable for a thorough analysis. Taking the phenomenon of shame superficially, we can say that we always perceive in it some striving for concealment. The point may be to conceal certain exterior facts as well as certain interior states or lived-experiences. The issue cannot be oversimplified by maintaining that one strives to conceal only what is considered evil, for we often feel shame for the good, e.g., for a good deed.[22] Perhaps in the latter case the shame pertains not so much to the good itself, but rather is concentrated merely on the fact of exteriorization of the good which, in the opinion of the agent, should remain hidden, for the very exteriorization is then felt to be something evil. It can be therefore said that the phenomenon of shame occurs when that which by reason of its essence or its purpose should be interior leaves the sphere of the interiority of the person and becomes in some way exterior.

In all this we observe a distinct connection between shame and the person. At this point, it is difficult to discuss whether this phenomenon also occurs in the animal world. It seems that there we deal only with various forms of fear. Fear (*lęk*) is a negative affection evoked always by some evil that threatens the subject. This evil first of all must be perceived or imagined, which is then followed by the affection of fear. Shame differs from fear, even though taken exteriorly it seems to lie close to fear. If man feels shame for something, this is also accompanied by the fear of bringing to light that which in his opinion should be hidden. Thus, although it is linked to shame, fear is then something merely indirect and collateral. The very essence of shame reaches beyond this fear. In no way can the essence of shame be comprehended without firmly emphasizing the truth that the person is an "interior" being, i.e., that he possesses interiority proper only to him, whence is born the need for concealing (that is, for keeping inside) certain contents or certain values, or for retreating inside with them. Fear does not display this inwardness, as it is a simple reaction to a perceived, imagined, or realized (*uświadomiony*) evil. This reaction does not need "interiority," which is indispensable for comprehending shame. The need to conceal, which is characteristic of shame, is born in man due to a terrain, as it were, residing in him that is suitable for concealing some contents or values—the interior life. This is something different from the concealment of the anxiety reaction itself, since this reaction can hide in the psyche—a situation perhaps also possible in animals. Shame, on the other hand, is linked with the person, and its development goes hand in hand with the development of personhood.

Our particular point concerns sexual shame. Its exterior manifestations are bound up with the body—in a certain measure it is simply the *shame of the body*. In a particular way the object of shame is the parts and organs of the body that determine its sexual distinctness. Among people an almost general tendency exists to conceal them from the sight of others, especially from the sight of persons of the other sex. This explains to a large extent the need to avoid the nakedness of the body. Of course, other considerations are also taken into account here, especially the need to protect the organism against cold, which is most closely related to climate. This also explains the partial or even complete nakedness of primitive peoples living in subtropical areas. Many facts from their life indicate that the nakedness of the body is not identified in a simple and unequivocal way with shamelessness. So, for example, what constitutes a manifestation of shamelessness for some primitive peoples is—on the contrary—the covering of the parts of the body that are uncovered in others. Certainly, what is at work here is also a custom, a collective wont, created against the background of the predominant climate conditions. To uncover the body is then above all a simple function of adjusting the organism to these conditions, so that directly no other intention is perceived in it. However, such an intention may be easily associated with concealing the parts of the body that determine the sexual distinctness of a woman and a man. It turns out that dress can serve not only to hide them, but also in some way to emphasize them. So, sexual shame is not identified in a simple way with the very usage of dress, just like shamelessness is not identified with the lack of dress and with the complete or partial nakedness of the body. That is a collateral and conditional factor. At the most, it can be stated that the tendency to cover the body and those of its parts that determine the sexual distinctness of a woman and a man goes hand in hand with sexual shame without constituting its essence.

However, what is essential in this shame is the tendency to conceal the sexual values themselves, first and foremost inasmuch as they constitute in the consciousness of the given person "a possible object of use" for persons of the other sex. Therefore we do not encounter the phenomenon of sexual shame in children, for whom the sphere of sexual values does not yet exist; their consciousness has not yet opened to these values. As they become conscious or as they are made conscious of the existence of this sphere of values, they start to experience (*przeżywać*) sexual shame, indeed not as something imposed from without, from the side of the environment in which they live, but as an interior need of their own personhood that is being created. The development of the sense of shame (*wstydliwość*)—this is what we shall call the constant ability and readiness to feel shame—follows a somewhat different path in girls and women as compared to boys and men.[23] This is related to the somewhat different arrangement of psychical forces, to the different relation of sensuality to affectivity, all of which was already emphasized in the psychological analysis of love. For whereas in men sensuality with its disposition toward the body as a possible object of "use" is in general stronger and more imposing, the sense of shame and shame as the tendency to conceal sexual values connected precisely with the body should be more manifest in girls and women. At the same time, however, they are less conscious of sensuality and its natural orientation in men, insofar as in girls and women themselves affectivity gets the upper hand of sensuality, and the latter is rather hidden in affectivity. For this reason it is sometimes stated that a woman is by nature "more chaste" than a man, which by no means says anything yet about the virtue of chastity. She is "more chaste" inasmuch as she experiences (*przeżywać*) more strongly the value of "the human being of the other sex," the value of a certain kind of psychical "masculinity," which after all is also strongly influenced by physical masculinity—although in a woman the very lived-experience of the one and the other is more psychical. But precisely this feature of her psyche at the same time may in a sense impede the sense of shame. A woman does not find in herself such sensuality that in general a man must discover in himself; she does not feel so great a need as to conceal the "body as a possible object of use." What is needed in order to fashion the feminine sense of shame is empathy with the masculine psyche.

The natural development of the sense of shame in a boy and a man generally follows a different path. A man does not have to fear feminine sensuality as much as a woman must fear the masculine one. However, he strongly experiences (*przeżywać*) his own sensuality, and this for him is a source of shame. Sexual values are for him linked more to the "body and sex as a possible object of use," and in this way he experiences (*przeżywać*) them—and experienced (*przeżywać*) in this way they constitute for him a cause for shame. So, he feels shame above all for his way of experiencing (*przeżywać*) the sexual values of persons of the other sex. He also feels shame for sexual values linked to his own "body"; perhaps this is a consequence of the former shame: he feels shame for the body because he feels shame for this experiencing (*przeżywać*) of the values of the "body," which he encounters inside himself. Of course, regardless of that, he also feels shame for his body and for the sexual values linked to it in a way that is, so to speak, immanent, whereas the previous way we would call relative. Shame is not only a response to someone's sensory-sexual reaction directed toward the "body as an object of use"—a reaction to a reaction—but is also, and above all, an interior need to avoid those reactions to the body that remain in conflict with the value of the person. This is precisely whence the sense of shame, that is, the constant readiness to avoid what is shameless, is formed.

What is manifested here is that deep connection between the phenomenon of shame and the nature of the person. The person is his own master (*sui iuris*); no one else but God the Creator has or can have any right of ownership in relation to the person. The person owns himself, he has the power of self-determination, and no one can violate his subsistence (*samoistność*). Furthermore, no one can make the person his own possession, unless the person himself permits this by giving himself to the other out of love. In fact, this objective incommunicability (*alteri incommunicabilitas*) and inviolability of the person come to light precisely in the lived-experience of sexual shame. The lived-experience of shame is a natural resonance of what the person simply is. As, on the one hand, the lived-experience of shame needs the interior life of the person as the only area where it can appear, when we reach even deeper, however, we see that this lived-experience needs the very being of the person as its natural basis. Only the person can feel shame, because only the person by his nature may not be an object of use (in the first and the second meanings of the verb "to use"). Sexual shame is in a sense a revelation of the supra-utilitarian character of the person, both when the person (e.g., X) feels shame for the sexual values linked to his body, and when he (e.g., Y) feels shame for his relation to these values in persons of the other sex, for his attitude only to use them. In the first case, by experiencing (*przeżywać*) shame X [she] realizes that, on account of the sexual values linked to her, her person should not be an object of use not only in reality but even in intention, whereas in the second case, by experiencing (*przeżywać*) shame Y [he] realizes that the person of the other sex should not be treated (even if only in an interior attitude) as an object of use.

Hence, it is evident that sexual shame in a certain measure charts the direction of all sexual morality. However, a mere description of the phenomenon does not suffice, even if it was as insightful as when given by phenomenologists, but a metaphysical interpretation of it is needed. In this way sexual ethics can find an experiential point of departure from the lived-experience of shame. All that has constituted the object of our inquiry, especially in chapter I, can be obtained from the lived-experience of sexual shame as a simple experiential fact. In interpreting this fact we take into consideration the whole truth about the person, i.e., we attempt to define what kind of being he is—as we have done at the beginning of chapter I. Only in this way is the lived-experience of sexual shame fully explained to us. The person is in the center of this lived-experience, and at the same time he constitutes its foundation. Although the direct object of shame, the direct content of the lived-experience of feeling shame, is the sexual values, the indirect object nonetheless is the person and the relation toward the person, and also the one originating from the person. Specifically, the point is to exclude—passively (more properly in a woman) and actively (more properly in a man)—the relation toward the person that fails to correspond to the person's supra-utilitarian character, the relation that fails to correspond to the very "personhood" of his being. Since the danger exists of such a relation precisely because of the sexual values that dwell in the person, sexual shame is thus manifested as a tendency to conceal them. This is a natural and spontaneous tendency; it is evident here how the moral order is linked with the order of being, with the order of nature. Sexual ethics is rooted in the law of nature.* [24]

This spontaneous urge encountered in a woman and a man to conceal the sexual values and the sexual character of lived-experiences has, however, a still deeper sense. The point is not only in a sense to flee with all that is sexual from the reaction of the person of the other sex, and also not only to "flee" interiorly from the reaction to the person of the other sex. For hand in hand with this flight from the reaction to the sexual values themselves goes the longing for evoking love, that is, some "reaction" to the value of the person, and the longing for experiencing (*przeżywać*) love in the same sense—the former is stronger in a woman, whereas the latter in a man, although there is no need to understand this too unilaterally. A woman rather wants to suffer love so that she can love. A man rather wants to love so that he can suffer love.[25] In either case sexual shame is not a flight from love, but quite the contrary, it is some opening of a way toward it. The spontaneous need to conceal the sexual values themselves linked to the person is a natural way to unveil the value of the person himself. The value of the person is closely connected with his inviolability, with his position, which is "above an object of use." Sexual shame defends this position in a sense instinctively, and

---

* "These two norms—the first one, obtained from the nature of the sexual drive and demanding respect for its finality, and the second one, obtained from the dignity of the person, due to which love is owed to the person—contain and condition each other in every interpersonal relation connected with the factor of sex. ( . . . ) The norm of the order of nature demanding respect for the finality of the drive is more elementary and fundamental. The norm demanding the proper relation to the person within the sexual relation is superior and plays a perfective role—especially in its evangelical concretization. Fulfilling the personalistic norm, especially in its Christian, evangelical concretization, is out of the question without respecting the finality of the drive in relation to the person of the other sex" (K. Wojtyła, "Zagadnienie katolickiej etyki seksualnej," *Roczniki Filozoficzne* 13, fasc. 2 [1965], 14).

so it also defends the value of the person. But the point is not only to defend it. The point is in a sense to reveal this value, and to reveal it precisely in connection with the sexual values joined with it in the given person. Shame does not manifest the value of the person in some abstract way, as a theoretical magnitude accessible only to reason, but manifests it in a living and concrete way, the way it is joined with the values of *sexus* but nonetheless being superior to them. Hence we have that lived-experience of inviolability (X [she]: "You must not touch me even with the interior desire itself"—Y [he]: "I must not touch her even with the interior will to use; she may not be an object of use"). This "fear of contact," which is characteristic of persons who truly love each other, is an indirect expression of affirming the value of the person as such, and it is known that this is a constitutive moment of love in the proper, i.e., ethical, meaning of the word.

There also exists a certain natural shame of experiencing (*przeżywać*) love as an affair of the body. We rightly speak of the *intimacy* of these lived-experiences. A woman and a man then flee from the gaze and presence of other people, and every morally healthy person will consider another way of conduct as remarkably indecent. What is taking place here is, so to speak, a divergence between the objective greatness of this act, the matter already discussed in chapter I, and this shame that surrounds it in the consciousness of people. The shame has nothing in common with prudery, that is, with false shame. This shame is right, for profound reasons exist to conceal the manifestations of love between a woman and a man, and especially their conjugal intercourse, from the eyes of other people. Love is a union of persons that is complemented in a given case by bodily intimacy and intercourse. The latter consists in some co-experience (*współprzeżywać*) of the sexual values, which determines the shared sexual use of a woman and a man. This co-experiencing (*współprzeżywać*) of the values of *sexus* can be thoroughly joined with love; it can find in love its objective justification and substantiation (this is precisely the way to overcome shame in the very persons who take part in the sexual act; we will speak of this later).

However, only they are conscious of this justification and substantiation; only for them is love some affair of "interiority," an affair of the soul, and not merely of the body. But every man from outside would perceive only exterior manifestations, and so merely this co-experience (*współprzeżywać*) of the values of *sexus*, whereas the very union of persons, the objective essence of love would remain inaccessible from without. It is understandable that shame, which strives to conceal the sexual values in order to protect the value of the person, also strives to conceal the very co-experience (*współprzeżywać*) of the sexual values in order to protect the value of love itself, above all for the two persons who experience (*przeżywać*) it together. And so, this shame is not only relative, but also immanent.

The very co-experience (*współprzeżywać*) of the values of *sexus* is linked to the facts that always demand some concealment. As a rule, man feels shame for what merely "happens" in him and what is not a conscious act of his will. Thus, for example, he feels shame for outbursts of passions, such as anger or fear, and even more so he feels shame for certain physiological processes that occur under certain conditions independently of his will; the action of the will is limited to evoking these conditions or to permitting them. We find in this a confirmation of the spirituality and "inwardness" of the human person, who perceives certain "evil" in all that is not sufficiently interior, i.e., spiritual, but merely exterior, bodily, irrational. Therefore, because all this comes to light and is manifested very strongly in the co-experience (*współprzeżywać*) of the sexual values by a woman and a man, while their personal union itself is, in a sense, hidden inside each of these persons and accessible to no one from outside, the need arises to conceal the whole of love as an affair of the "body and sex."

## The law of absorption of shame by love

Insofar as love as an affair of the body is joined with shame in a natural way externally (i.e., in relation to any other person apart from this woman and this man who experience (*przeżywać*) love together, it is within, that is, between them, that a characteristic phenomenon takes place, defined here as the "absorption of shame by love." Shame becomes in a sense absorbed by love, melted in it, so that both a woman and a man cease to feel shame for co-experiencing (*współprzeżywać*) the values of *sexus*. This process has an enormous significance for sexual morality; it includes some profound piece of advice, which should be taken advantage of in ethics. For this is a natural process that can be by no means understood without grasping the proper proportion between the value of the person and the sexual values in man and in the love of a man and a woman.

While analyzing the phenomenon of sexual shame, we arrived at the conviction that it concerns a fact possessing a profound personal meaning, and, therefore, sexual shame has its *raison d'être* only in the world of persons. By the way, this fact has a twofold meaning: on the one hand, a flight—a tendency to conceal the sexual values so that they do not obscure the value of the person as such; on the other hand—the longing for love, for evoking or experiencing (*przeżyć*) it (love between a woman and a man is formed, as is known, on the basis of the values of *sexus*, but ultimately it is determined by the reciprocal relation to the value of the person, since love is a personal union of persons). Therefore, even from the very analysis of sexual shame it is evident that this shame, so to speak, paves the way to love.

When we speak of the "absorption" of shame by love, we do not mean that love abolishes or destroys sexual shame. On the contrary: all the more does love sharpen the sense of this shame in a man and a woman, for it is realized in full while most fully preserving this shame. The word "absorption" means merely that for its own sake love thoroughly takes advantage of the data that dwell in the phenomenon of sexual shame. Namely, it takes advantage of the proportion between the value of the person and the values of *sexus* that shame introduces into the reciprocal relation of a woman and a man as something natural that is experienced (*przeżywać*) spontaneously, and which, however—if not properly cultivated—may undergo destruction to the detriment of persons and their reciprocal love.

So, in what does this absorption of shame by love consist, and what explains it? Now, shame constitutes in a sense a natural self-defense of the person against descending or being pushed into the position of an object of sexual use. This position—as has been frequently stated—is contrary to the very nature of the person. The person himself may not (should not) descend to the position of an object of use for the other person or other persons; so, for example, X may not descend to this position in relation to Y. Furthermore, the person cannot push any person of the other sex to the position of an object of use, so Y cannot act this way in relation to any X. In both cases, this is opposed by sexual shame—both of the body and of the lived-experience. But love, as we have stated at the beginning of this book, is the relation of one person to another (Y to X, and X to Y) which from its very foundations excludes treating the person as an object of use; it definitely does not permit the person to descend to the position of an object of use, nor does it allow the person to be pushed to that position. Precisely for this reason, in such a natural way shame opens to love.

What is essential for love is above all the affirmation of the value of the person; by being based on it, the will of the loving subject tends to the true good of the beloved person, the good that is full and complete, the good "in every respect"—this good is identified with happiness. This attitude of the will in the loving person is completely contrary to any attitude of the will to use. Love and the relation to the person as an object of use are mutually exclusive. Thus, faced with this, shame as a natural form of fleeing from that relation recedes, for it loses its objective *raison d'être*. However, it recedes insofar as the person loved in this way, e.g., X, also responds with love to the loving person (Y), and— what is most important—with love that is ready to give himself. At this point we should recall what the analysis of spousal love has explicated. In any case, the law of absorption of shame by love explains to us on the psychological plane the whole problem of chastity, or rather of the conjugal sense of shame. After all, the fact is that sexual intercourse between spouses does not constitute merely some form of shamelessness legalized from outside, but interiorly conforms with the demands of shame (unless the spouses themselves will make it shameless by the very way they perform it).

Taking the matter integrally (for which we have already been prepared in the previous chapter by the integral analysis of love), it must be stated that only true love, hence love possessing in full its ethical essence, is capable of absorbing shame. This is understandable in view of the fact that shame constitutes a tendency to conceal the sexual values in order not to obscure the value of the person with them, but on the contrary— in order to manifest it all the more. True love is a love in which the sexual values are subordinated to the value of the person. It dominates, and the affirmation of the value of the person permeates all the lived-experiences that are born from man's natural sensuality or affectivity themselves. It is known that these lived-experiences are in a natural way connected to the sexual values (sensuality with the value of the "body and sex" and affectivity with the value of "femininity" or "masculinity" in the human being of the other sex). Now, true love makes these lived-experiences to be permeated with the affirmation of the value of the person to such an extent that the relation of the will to another person as an object of use is excluded. It is in this, in practice, that the essential power of love consists, whereas the theoretical affirmation of the value of the person alone does not yet constitute it.

With such an attitude, then, there is no reason for shame, that is, for concealing the values of *sexus* as the ones that obscure the value of the person, which strike at the person's incommunicability (*alteri incommunicabilitas*) and inviolability by reducing him to the position of an object of use. Then, there is no reason for the shame of the body (on the part of X, for instance), because the positive tendency contained in that shame, the tendency to evoke love, has met with an adequate response. There is also no reason for the shame of lived-experience (on the part of Y, for instance), because the relation to the person (X) as to an object of use does not take place. Even if sensuality itself in its proper way reacts to the "body" as a "possible object of use," the will, nonetheless, is oriented by love toward the true good of the person, and not toward using him, and this by no means excludes the fact that (in marriage) it is the very person, this X, that is joined to the given Y by bodily intercourse, and thus also by shared sexual use. The need for shame has been interiorly absorbed by the very fact of mature love for a person: Y does not have to conceal interiorly (as well as exteriorly) his disposition to use that is directed toward X, since this disposition has been absorbed by the true love of the will. The affirmation of the person permeates all sensual-affective reactions linked to the sexual values to the extent that the will is not threatened by the attitude to use, which is incompatible with the relation to the person. In fact, this affirmation is imparted to affectivity, so that the value of the person is not only understood abstractly, but also deeply felt. This then is also a psychological fullness of love in which the correct absorption of sexual shame is thoroughly accomplished. A woman and a man can constitute "one flesh"—in accord with the well-known words of Genesis (2:24), by which the Creator defined the essence of marriage—and this unity will not be any form of shamelessness, but only a full realization of the union of persons that proceeds from reciprocal spousal love. This is most closely linked with the problem of relating to parenthood, but this issue will be discussed separately in chapter IV.

In connection with this remarkable phenomenon of "absorption" of sexual shame by love, it is necessary to indicate a certain danger. Shame has its roots deep in the very being of the person, and therefore it is precisely the metaphysics of the person that was necessary for a full understanding of his essence. However, a danger exists of an overly superficial treatment of both shame and its absorption that is correctly accomplished by love. It is known that subjectively speaking shame is a certain affection of a negative character, somewhat similar to the affection of fear. The affection of fear is linked in consciousness with the sphere of sexual values, and recedes together with the conviction that these values are not the stimulus evoking only "sexual desire." However, this affection also recedes inasmuch as the affection of love is born, as, for instance, in X in relation to Y. Similarly, the affection of shame evoked in Y by the lived-experience of sexual desire directed toward X becomes, in a sense, effaced in consciousness, inasmuch as an affective relation to the given X is joined to it. Evidently then, the affection of love has the power of absorbing the affection of shame, the power of liberating consciousness—both the consciousness of Y and that of X—from the feeling of shame. This emotional-affective process explains that view, so frequently stated and suggested, according to which the mere "affection (of love) gives the right to bodily intimacy and to sexual intercourse of a man and a woman."

This is an erroneous view, for the very lived-experience of amorous affection, even if mutual (i.e., simultaneous on the part of Y and X), is not yet by any means equivalent to the mature love of the will. For this love presupposes a reciprocal choice of persons (X by Y, and Y by X) that is based on the thorough affirmation of their values, and that aims at their durable union in marriage, while the relation toward parenthood is clearly established. The love of persons possesses—and should possess—its distinct objective profile. Love as an emotional-affective lived-experience often possesses only a purely subjective character and lacks appropriate maturity in an ethical respect. It has been said many times that one must not confuse the very using up of the "material" with creativity in this sphere, nor identify an ephemeral amorous lived-experience with love.

Therefore, this "absorption of shame by love" must have a deeper meaning than merely an emotional-affective one. The mere removal of the "lived-experience of shame" by any "amorous lived-experience" does not suffice, for precisely this contradicts the thoroughly understood essence of sexual shame and in fact conceals some form of shamelessness. (Shamelessness is granted its "rights" thanks to the ephemeral lived-experiences alone.) The ease with which the affection of shame recedes before just any emotional-affective lived-experience is precisely a denial of shame and the sense of shame. True shame recedes with difficulty (and thanks to that, it does not leave the person in an ultimately shameless situation). True shame can be absorbed only by true love—love which, while affirming the value of the person, seeks his fullest good with all its might. Such shame is a genuine moral strength of the person. However, because a real danger exists of making it shallow due to various interior causes (there are people who are, so to speak, shyer "by nature") or exterior ones (diverse views, lifestyles, and styles of conduct of men and women with respect to one another in various environments and epochs), a need also exists to educate sexual shame. This need is most closely joined with the education of love, precisely because only true, genuine shame demands true, fully-mature love in accord with the "law of absorption" discussed here.

## *The problem of shamelessness*

In light of what has been said above concerning sexual shame and the absorption of shame by love, let us now look at the problem of shamelessness. The very word "shamelessness" (*bezwstyd*) simply speaks of a lack of shame or of its denial. Actually, in practice this turns out to be the same. We encounter various facts, various ways of being and of conduct in persons of both sexes, various situations between them that we call shameless, by which we state that there is nothing in them that is required by shame, that they remain in conflict with the demands of the sense of shame. A certain relativity exists in defining what is shameless. This relativity is explained by various interior dispositions of particular persons, so, e.g., by greater or lesser sensual excitability, by the given individual's greater or lesser moral culture, or even by this or that worldview. It is also explained by diverse exterior conditionings, for instance by climate, which has already been mentioned, and in addition by dominant customs, collective wonts, and so forth.

However, this relativity in regarding particular symptoms of life and interaction between persons of different sex as shameless by no means proves that shamelessness itself is something relative, that in people's conduct and way of being no factors or moments exist that constantly determine it, even despite the fact that these diverse conditionings from within and from without command various people or those in various environments to regard different things as shameless (of course, different things are regarded as modest, i.e., in conformity with the demands of sexual shame). The point here is not the latter, i.e., the arrangement of various views on what is shameless and what is modest, but the former, namely, the grasp of the common moment. After all, the preceding stages of the analysis, which fit within the framework of the "metaphysics of shame," have led us to that.

Shame is this extremely characteristic tendency of the human person to conceal the sexual values connected with him so that they do not obscure the very value of the person. The aim of this tendency is a specific self-defense of the person, who does not want to be an object of use either in deed or even in intention, but wants to be an object of love. Because the person can become an object of use precisely on account of the sexual values, a tendency arises to conceal them, but only to the extent that together with the value of the person they can constitute at the same time, so to speak, an anchor point for love. Hand in hand with this form of shame, which can be called the "shame of the body" since the sexual values are exteriorly connected first and foremost with the bodies of men and women, goes another form, which we called the "shame of lived-experience," which is the tendency to conceal the reactions and lived-experiences that manifest the relation to the "body and sex" as an object of use precisely due to the fact that the body and sex are a property of the human person, who may not be an object of use. Both the former and the latter form of shame can be correctly absorbed only through love.

Shamelessness destroys this whole order. Analogically to the distinction between the shame of the body and the shame of lived-experiences we can also speak of the shamelessness of the body and that of lived-experiences. What we shall call the shamelessness of the body is the way of being or of conduct of some concrete person, in which he moves the very value of *sexus* so much to the foreground that it obscures the essential value of the person. Consequently, the person places himself in a sense on the level of an object of use, on the level of a being to which one can relate only by using it (especially in the second meaning of the verb "to use") and not loving it. The shamelessness of lived-experience consists in rejecting the healthy tendency to feel shame for the reactions and the lived-experiences in which the other person appears as a mere object of use on account of the sexual values that belong to him. Thus, for example, some concrete Y [he] is shameless in his lived-experiences toward X [her] when he is not interiorly ashamed of the attitude to use in the sensory-sexual manner, when he posits this attitude as the only form of relation to X, while not endeavoring to subordinate this attitude to true love of the person and not to incorporate it correctly into this love.[26]

This interior "shame of lived-experience" has nothing in common with prudery. For *prudery* consists in concealing proper intentions in relation to persons of the other sex or in general to the whole sexual sphere. Someone who yields to prudery, and who is guided by the intention to use, attempts to create appearances that his point is not to use—he is even ready to condemn any manifestations of sex and of what is sexual, even most natural. In fact, very often we do not deal here with prudery, which is a certain form of mendacity, of falsifying the intention, but only with some prejudice or conviction that whatever is sexual can only be an object of use, that sex merely gives the occasion for sexual outlet and in no way paves the paths for love among people. This view has a flavor of Manichaeanism and clashes with the relation to the affairs of the body and sex that is characteristic of both the Book of Genesis and—above all—the Gospel. Therefore, the true shame of lived-experience is by no means identified with an act of prudery. The shame of lived-experience is a healthy reaction within a person (e.g., Y) to the relation toward another person (X) that bypasses that person's essential value and reduces him to the position of an object of sexual use. In the well known and previously quoted words (Mt 5:28: "Whoever looks at a woman in order to desire her . . .") Christ protested against such a relation to the person (to a "woman"). Evidently, the point was the interior act. Prudery is often, and even as a rule, linked to the shamelessness of intention. This is something different than the shamelessness of lived-experience. We have already mentioned relativity in considering some fact—especially an exterior fact, some exterior way of being or conduct—as shameless. A separate problem arises in the case of considering some interior fact—a way of thinking about or sensing the values of *sexus*, a way of reacting to them—as shameless. With respect to this, no close correlation occurs among particular people who live even in the same epoch and in the same society. It does not occur especially between women and men. Very often a concrete X [she] does not consider, for instance, a certain way of dressing as shameless (the point is the "shamelessness of the body"), the way which a man or even many different men will judge as shameless. Conversely, some Y [he] can experience (*przeżywać*) shamelessly his relation to a woman or various women (the point is the shamelessness of lived-experience), even though none of them gave a reason for it by a shameless way of being or conduct, e.g., by indecent dress or dance.

Generally speaking a certain correlation exists here: the shame of the body is needed because a possibility exists of the shamelessness of lived-experiences, especially, as it seems, in the direction from X to Y. And vice versa: the shame of lived-experiences is needed because a possibility exists of the shamelessness of the body (this occurs rather in the direction from Y to X). However, it is difficult to grasp this correlation in all particular cases. But precisely for this reason, one must rather accept certain presuppositions broadening the possibility of shamelessness on the one as well as the other side. In this consists the formation of healthy customs in the sphere of relationships between persons of different sex, or rather in various spheres of their relationship. However, this cannot have anything in common with puritanism in the sexual sphere. For exaggeration easily evokes prudery.

We have already mentioned in passing the issue of *dress* or clothing. This is one of the particular issues regarding which the problem of shame and shamelessness most often arises. Again, it is difficult to go into details concerning all the specifics of this problem, the nuances of feminine or masculine fashion. The problem of shame and shamelessness is certainly connected with this issue although perhaps not in the way that is generally presumed. It is known that dress can in different ways contribute to manifesting the values of *sexus*—let us also add: in different ways and on different occasions, even if we disregard innate or acquired dispositions in a given individual. The manifestation of the values of *sexus* by dress is actually unavoidable and does not in the least have to clash with shame. What is shameless in dress is that which clearly contributes to a deliberate obscuring of the most essential value of the person by the sexual values, and which "has to" awaken such a reaction as if that person was merely a "possible way to use" on account of *sexus*, and not a "possible" object of love on account of his personal value.

The principle is simple and obvious, but its application in concrete cases, however, belongs to particular individuals and to entire environments and societies. The issue of dress is always a social affair, thus it is a function of a healthy (or unhealthy) custom. It is furthermore necessary to underscore that although considerations of an aesthetic nature seem to be decisive here, they are not and cannot be exclusive: beside them and together with them considerations of an ethical nature also exist. Unfortunately, man is not such a perfect being so that the sight of the body of a person, especially of a person of the other sex, awakens in him only a disinterested fondness that is followed by simple love for that person. Actually, what it also awakens is "desire," i.e., a wish to use that is concentrated on the values of *sexus* while disregarding the essential value of the person. And this must be taken into account.

However, this does not mean in the least that the shamelessness of the body is to be identified simply and exclusively with the body's complete or partial nakedness. There are circumstances in which nakedness is not shameless. If somebody uses it as an occasion to treat a person as an object of use (even in interior acts), it is only that somebody who engages in shamelessness (of lived-experience), not the other person. The very nakedness of the body is not yet equivalent to the shamelessness of the body. This shamelessness occurs only when nakedness performs a negative function in relation to the value of the person, when the end of nakedness is to awaken the concupiscence of the flesh, thereby placing the person in the position of an object of use. What happens then is in a sense depersonalization by sexualization. This, however, does not have to take place at all. Even then, when nakedness is joined to the shared sexual use of a man and a woman, regard for the dignity of the person can be fully preserved. This is precisely how it should be in marriage, where objective conditions exist for the true absorption of shame by love to be accomplished. We shall return to this issue in the next chapter. In any case, without this view on the role of the body in the love of persons, it is impossible to think and speak about the sense of shame and chastity of conjugal intercourse, which after all constitute a constant theme of Catholic teaching.

Although the shamelessness of the body is not identified in a simple way with the very nakedness of the body, nonetheless a very thorough interior effort is needed in order not to relate to the naked body in a shameless way. It must be added, however, that the shamelessness of lived-experience is not identified with the unprompted reaction of sensuality, which relates spontaneously to the body and sex as to a "possible object of use."[27] Just as the human body is not in itself shameless, so too the reaction of sensuality or human sensuality in general is not shameless in itself. Shamelessness (just as shame and the sense of shame) is a function of the interiority of the person, and in it a function of the will, the will which simplistically receives the reaction of sensuality and reduces the other person through the "body and sex" to the role of an object of use.

Since we are speaking about dress in connection with the problem of shamelessness and the sense of shame, perhaps it is worthwhile to call our attention to a certain functionality of various clothing. In fact, just as certain objective situations exist in which even complete nakedness of the body is not shameless, because the proper function of this nakedness is not to evoke the relation to the person as an object of use, there certainly also exist different functions of various clothing, various ways of dressing, that include a partial uncovering of the body, for instance, during physical labor in hot weather, while bathing, or at the doctor's. So, if the point is a moral qualification of these various ways of dressing, it is necessary to proceed from the various functions they are to perform. When a person uses dress like that within the framework of its objective function, then we cannot see shamelessness in this, even though the dress is connected with a partial uncovering of the body.

However, the use of such dress outside of its proper function will be shameless, and it must be felt that way. For example: it is not shameless to use a bathing suit while bathing, but to use it in the street or even on a walk will clash with the demands of shame.

It is difficult not to mention, at least cursorily, another particular problem, namely the problem of *pornography* (i.e., shamelessness) in art.[28] The problem is extensive and very complicated in details due to the very diverse specificity of various branches of art. The point now is to grasp the essence of the problem. By art we understand man's entire production (*wytwórczość*), and in particular the artistic one, e.g., literary or sculptural. Although an artist communicates in his work his own thoughts, affections, and attitudes, the work does not serve only this purpose. It serves the truth, for it is to grasp and convey in a beautiful way some fragment of reality. Artistic beauty is the most characteristic property of a work of art. The fragment of reality that artists very often attempt to capture is precisely the love of a woman and a man, and in fine arts the human body. This proves indirectly how important and attractive this theme is in the totality of human life. In the name of realism, art has the right and obligation to reproduce the human body. Art also has the right to reproduce the love of a man and a woman as it is in reality and speak the whole truth about it. The human body is an authentic part of the truth about man, just as the sensory-sexual moment is an authentic part of the truth about human love. A mistake will occur if this part obscures the whole. And precisely this sometimes happens in art.

However, the essence of what we call pornography in art lies even deeper. Pornography is an explicit tendency to emphasize in a work of art the moment of *sexus* in the reproduction of the human body or in the reproduction of love and persons who experience (*przeżywać*) it. This tendency aims at evoking in the recipient of this work, a reader or a viewer, a conviction that the sexual value is the only essential value of the person, and that love is nothing else but experiencing (*przeżywać*) or co-experiencing (*współprzeżywać*) this value. This is a harmful tendency, because it destroys the complete image of this important fragment of human reality that consists in the love of a woman and a man. For the truth about human love always lies in the reproduction of the reciprocal relation of persons regardless of how much the values of *sexus* would dominate in this relation. It is the same as with the truth that man is a person regardless of how much the sexual values are manifested in his body.

A work of art should bring out this truth regardless of the extent to which it happens to touch the sphere of *sexus*, and if it contains a tendency to distort this truth, it deforms the image of reality.[29] But pornography is not merely a mistake or an error—it is a tendency. Once the deformed image becomes equipped with the prerogatives of artistic beauty, a greater possibility exists that it will be accepted and engrafted in the consciousness and the will of the recipients. For concerning this point the human will very often displays a great susceptibility to accepting a deformed image of reality.[30]

# Part Three

# Problems of Abstinence

## *Self-mastery and objectivization*

In the first part of this chapter we have indicated that practicing the virtue of chastity is very closely linked to the cardinal virtue which—following Aristotle—St. Thomas Aquinas called *temperantia*. This virtue's task is to moderate (*miarkować*) the movements of the concupiscence of the flesh, whence originates its name in the Polish language: "*umiarkowanie*" [i.e., temperance]. In the sexual sphere, particular attention must be paid to that disposition toward the virtue of temperance, namely self-mastery (*opanowanie*). The chaste man is precisely the "self-possessed" (*opanowany*) man. Aristotle and Thomas Aquinas knew the concept of self-mastery (*continentia*). Man should master the concupiscence of the flesh; he should master it when it makes itself heard and demands to be satisfied against reason, against what reason acknowledges as right, as truly good, for we agree that reason knows the objective order of nature, or in any case can and should know it. In this way conformity with reason is at the same time a condition of realizing this order and a condition of honorableness of action. The "honorable" (*godziwe*) is precisely what is in accord with reason, thus what is worthy of a rational being, of a person.\* The principle of honorableness in action constitutes the substantive opposite of the principle of utility advocated by the utilitarians. Thus, mastering the concupiscence of the flesh is

---

\* "Honorableness" *(godziwość)* can be understood in two ways:

1) In a broader sense—just as in precisely this case—the point is nonutilitarian rationality of action, i.e., *full rationality*, which takes into consideration accounts that are not only nor first of all utilitarian.

2) In the strictly personalistic understanding, the ethical qualification called "honorableness" speaks about conformity of the given moral act with the quite specific value that is immutable and inalienable and that is represented by every person through the very fact that he is a person and not a thing ("somebody to somebody" and not "something for something").

worthy (*godny*) of the person. If a person does not do this, he jeopardizes his natural perfection; he allows what is inferior to and dependent on him to act in him, and even more—he subjects himself to it.[31]

Positing the issue of self-mastery this way is above all a result of perfectioristic tendencies in ethics. They do not clash with the totality of our reflections, although the main accent here is placed on love of the person, and the entire analysis of chastity and its "rehabilitation" does proceed in this direction. Therefore, mastery of the concupiscence of the flesh aims not only at the perfection of the person, who pursues it, but also at the realization of love in the world of persons and above all in the reciprocal relations between persons of different sex. By mastering the concupiscence of the flesh, man must restrain the movements of the sensitive concupiscible power (*appetitus concupiscibilis*) and at the same time moderate diverse sensations or affections that are linked to these movements, because they accompany the reactions of sensuality. It is known in fact that what originates from here are the deeds, the interior or exterior acts, which can easily collide with the principle of loving the person by being merely a use of him, due to being based on the sexual value itself.

Concerning sensuality and the natural dynamic of sensations and of sensual affections (St. Thomas' *passiones animae*) that is connected with it, Aristotle observed extremely accurately that in this sphere differences exist between individual people that require us to speak, on the one hand, of sensual overexcitability (*hyper-sensibilitas*) and, on the other hand, of the inadequate, unnaturally low excitability (*hypo-sensibilitas*). Because we have distinguished sensuality from affectivity, which is the capacity for reactions of a different content-related tint and also of a different directional character, we therefore can speak in a parallel way of affective oversensibility and of inadequate, unnaturally low sensibility.[32]

What still remains to be discussed is the problem of moderation (*umiar*), which is suggested by the very word "temperance" (*umiarkowanie*). Presupposing the realistic notion of man, we agree that both sensual excitability and affective sensibility are something natural in him, that is, fundamentally in conformity with nature, thus this way also fundamentally not opposed to the realization of love in the world of persons, especially the love that joins a woman and a man. In light of this position it is proper to solve the problem of moderation, without which the virtue of chastity cannot exist in the reciprocal relation of persons. By moderation we mean the ability to find such a "measure" in mastering sensual excitability and affective sensibility, which in every concrete case, in every inter-personal configuration or situation, helps the most in realization of love, avoiding at the same time the danger of the exclusive attitude to use, which—as is known—very easily attaches itself not only to the reaction of sensuality, but even to that of affectivity.

This moderation, however, is not in the least identified with some "mediocre" excitability or "mediocre" affective sensibility. According to such a supposition, the people who exhibit inadequate excitability or sensibility, the "hypo-sensitive," would already be temperate. However, temperance is not mediocrity, but the ability to maintain equilibrium among the movements of the concupiscence of the flesh. The task of this equilibrium is to create in the sensual-affective sphere the constant interior "measure," the measure of acts, and in a sense also the measure of lived-experiences. Virtue is most closely connected with this measure, is manifested in it, and is in some sense a constant function of moderation—moderation that we do not understand in a rigid way, for it is formed in different persons differently in accordance with natural dispositions in this sphere. The very essence of moderation is something unequivocal: whoever has not attained it is not self-possessed and temperate—is not chaste. Furthermore, the forms realizing this moderation will be different in accordance with diverse interior dispositions, exterior conditions, the state or direction of life's vocation, etc.

It is difficult to speak of the diverse forms of self-mastery in the sexual sphere—self-mastery without which it is impossible to be chaste. However, we can attempt to describe the principal methods of realizing it. Often at this point one can hear the word "abstinence" (*wstrzemięźliwość*), which suggests that the basic method that defines this word has something in common with the activity of restraining.[33] What illustrates this perfectly to us is the well-known interior situations in which a person experiences (*przeżywać*) something like an invasion that finds its principal control centers in sensuality, in the concupiscence of the flesh, or (indirectly) in natural affectivity. What follows then is a need for defense that is born in the very rational essence of the person. The person defends himself against the "invasion" that comes from the side of sensuality and the concupiscence of the flesh, and he defends himself against it because first and foremost it threatens his natural power of self-determination. For the person himself must "will" and should not permit anything that is not good to "happen" to him. A further reason for this natural defense of the person lies already in the order of values, precisely on which self-mastery is based. Self-mastery is firmly connected with the natural need of the person to govern himself.

However, we have previously indicated that the full meaning of virtue does not consist in merely inhibiting the movements of the concupiscence of the flesh or the reactions of sensuality by pushing the contents brought with them down to the subconscious. Chastity does not consist in a methodical depreciation of the value of the "body and sex," nor, on the other hand, is it identified with some unhealthy fear that can be even instinctively awakened by them. These are not symptoms of interior strength, but rather of weakness. Virtue, however, must be the strength of the human spirit.* Ultimately this strength proceeds from reason, which "sees" the essential truth about values and places the value of the person and love above the values of *sexus* and above the use connected with them. But precisely for this reason chastity cannot consist in "blind" continence. Continence (*powściągliwość*), the habit of restraining the concupiscence of the flesh by the will, the ability to moderate effectively the sensations connected with the reactions of sensuality and even of affectivity, is an indispensable method of self-mastery, although it does not yet determine the full realization of virtue. Above all, continence cannot be an end in itself. At the very least this follows from a general analysis of values and the relation of man to them.

---

* The concept of virtue in this context is closely related to the concept of transcendence, that is, the "superiority of the person with regard to himself" and with regard to his dynamism. The person is "above" his action and "above" the object of his action. This enables self-possession and self-governance of the person, which are necessary conditions for virtue—the habit of action—to exist. Transcendence understood this way is an expression of man's spirituality, and at the same time points out that spirituality. See part II of *Person and Act*: "Transcendence of the Person in the Act."

By a value in the objective sense we mean all that to which man opens himself by his interior life, for which he strives in his action.* 34 Thus, a mere severance from some values, e.g., those to which sensuality or affectivity turns by nature, does not develop the person, unless it proceeds from an acknowledgment of the objective order connected with the lived-experience of truth about values. What is necessary is at least that acknowledgment, if not indeed the "lived-experience of truth" in relation to values. This is precisely what constitutes the method of objectivization. "Blind" continence alone is not enough. There is no mature abstinence without acknowledging the objective order of values: the value of the person stands above the values of *sexus*. The point here is a practical acknowledgment, i.e., one that influences action. The fundamental condition of self-mastery in the sexual sphere is that the acknowledgment of the superiority of the person over *sexus* can come to light when sensuality and (indirectly) affectivity react above all to the sexual values. One could speak here of some implantation of the value of the person amid the lived-experience, which intensively occupies the whole consciousness with the values of *sexus*. This is the first step on the path to realize chastity: continence, which is subordinated to objectivization understood in this way, is needed so that among the values that the senses opt for, the value of the person that reason opts for can reach consciousness.

In turn, the point is that the value of the person in a sense "takes the lead" in the whole lived-experience. Then, continence is not "blind" any more. The inhibition and severance are not the end, but together with them there also ensues a certain new "opening" in consciousness and the will—the opening toward the value which is at the same time true and higher. Therefore, objectivization is closely connected with sublimation.

---

* Certain kinds of values (including moral values) are values not because somebody strives for them, but vice versa: we strive for them (and even feel the obligation to strive for them) because they are values. The origin of conventional values, for example (as in a collecting hobby), is fundamentally different. Therefore every value—in itself—is not the same as the object that represents it, since a value constitutes only a specific relation (subjective-objective or objective-subjective with regard to its genesis)—a relation of this or that correspondence (of somebody to somebody, of something to somebody, or of something to something because of somebody). However, just as in this case, what we call "a value" (through metonymy) is an object that represents it.

What is the relation between the method of objectivization and the necessity of restraining the sensual or sensual-affective movements? Objectivization does not dispense from this necessity: if somebody merely "objectivized," i.e., if he objectively and accurately grasped the value of the person in relation to the values of *sexus*, but without at the same time restraining the movements of the concupiscence of the flesh, by no means could he be called self-possessed or chaste. This would be only theory without practice. Mere objectivization without continence does not yet constitute virtue, whereas it is only thanks to objectivization that continence acquires the meaning of a fully-mature virtue. For man is a being so constructed interiorly that the movements of the concupiscence of the flesh do not recede from him completely once the power of the will restrains them—they recede then only somehow superficially; in order for them to disappear completely, man must know "why" he restrains them. It is possible to replace this "why" with a mere prohibition—"because I must not"—but this does not solve the issue thoroughly enough, and hence does not yet constitute true objectivization.* We can speak of objectivization only when the will is faced with the value that fully explains the necessity of restraining what has been awakened in the concupiscence of the flesh and in sensuality.† As this value seizes consciousness and the will, the will calms down and is liberated from a characteristic sense of "loss." For it is a fact known from

---

* The author here expresses a position according to which the unconditionality that is specific for moral duty is explained neither by the very fact of command (moral positivism, decretalism), nor the fact of exterior authority in relation to the agent (heteronomic positivism), nor the fact of interior authority in relation to the agent, e.g., by the imperative of "practical reason," whose function was identified with the function of the will (Kant's autonomic positivism). For then moral duty is identified with exterior or interior pressure depriving the agent of moral subjectivity. The inalienable right to posit the question "why?" to moral duty belongs to the essence of this subjectivity. The reason directly founding the fact of moral duty is the dignity of the person.

† Objectivization of the moral order in man happens through the grasp of truth ("truth about the good," "axiological truth"). This truth is grasped through cognition, in intellective experience. The statement that something is really good and right evokes duty in man and prompts the action realizing this good. Thanks to the grasped and accepted truth, the superiority (transcendence) of the person with regard to his own dynamisms and objects of his pursuit causes the realization of the good, and thereby the "fulfillment of the person." See chapter I ("The Person and the Act in the Aspect of Consciousness") and chapter IV ("Self-determination and Fulfillment") of *Person and Act*.

interior experience that the practice of self-mastery and of the virtue of chastity is accompanied—especially during the earlier phases of their development—by a sense of some loss, of relinquishing value. This sense is a natural phenomenon; it indicates how strongly the reflex of the concupiscence of the flesh acts in consciousness and the will. As true love of the person develops in them, this reflex grows weaker, for values return to their proper place. So, the virtue of chastity and the love of the person mutually condition each other.

The issue of the sublimation of affections plays an important role in this whole process—as has been said a moment ago, objectivization is closely connected with sublimation. A certain possibility of the sublimation of affections already exists thanks to the fact that the reaction to the person of the other sex is born not only on the basis of sensuality but also affectivity. In connection with this, sensual passion may yield to another form of emotional commitment that does not include the preoccupation with the "object of use" that is characteristic of sensuality. However, is affectivity alone able to oust sensuality and form the relation to another human being within the orbit of its reactions and its attitude? We already know that this attitude differs from the one dominating in sensuality. A longing in that case does not relate to sensual-bodily use itself, but it is much more a longing for closeness to the human being of the other sex. If, however, we leave everything to the course of unprompted reactions, we ought to take into account a danger of sliding (if only secondary) from the plane of affection to that of sensuality. It is difficult to think of the sublimation of affections without the contribution of reflection and virtue.

Affectivity, however, can play a very important auxiliary role in this whole process of sublimation. For the value of the person should not be only "coldly" understood, but also felt. The mere abstract concept of the person does not yet generate the feeling of the value of the person. In general, the feeling of the value of the person in its full metaphysical meaning seems to rise above the upper limit of our emotional life, but it is developed hand in hand with the spiritualization of interior life. In fact, on the path to this feeling one can take advantage of what dwells precisely in affectivity. The ability to react spontaneously to the value of the "human being of the other sex," to "femininity" or "masculinity," joined with the tendency to idealize involving these values, can be fairly easily coupled in lived-experience with the concept of the person, so that the whole process of emotional idealization, which for affectivity is unprompted, will develop not simply around the value "femininity"—"masculinity," but precisely around the value of the person maturing at the same time in the mind by way of reflection. In this way the virtue of chastity also gains for itself a certain basis in the emotional sphere.

After all, this is the point in the rightly understood practice of that virtue, as already Aristotle and Thomas Aquinas indicated. They both emphasized that in relation to the sensual-affective sphere of man's interior life, an appropriate tactic or even some diplomacy (*principatus politicus*) must be applied.[35] The way of command alone is of little use here; it can even produce effects quite opposite to what has been intended. Placing the issue in this light is a proof of great experience and practical wisdom. Indeed, every man in himself must appropriately manage the energies that are latent in his sensuality and affectivity so that they become allies in pursuing true love, for they can also be, as is well known, its enemies. This proficiency for making allies of potential enemies is perhaps even more characteristic of the essence of self-mastery and the virtue of chastity than "pure" continence itself. This includes the first part of the specific sphere of problems which here, in accord with the most frequent way of expression, we have called the problems of abstinence in the analysis of conjugal morality (the next chapter contains a further discussion of them). The second part concerns the reciprocal relation between tenderness and sensuality—it runs parallel to the first one without being identified with it, even though at times the two of them seem to meet. Let us in turn discuss it.

## Tenderness and sensuality

At this point, it is still necessary to reflect on the problem of tenderness, for tenderness (*czułość*) also grows from affectivity and is formed on the substratum of those concupiscible affections already considered several times in this book. Tenderness, however, possesses a very specific meaning and performs a specific function in human life, especially in the interaction between a man and a woman—the sublimation of their reciprocal relation is to a large extent based on tenderness. Therefore, we must now explain its role.

We experience (*przeżywać*) tenderness for some person (or even for some irrational being, e.g., an animal or a plant) when we become conscious in a certain way of his link with us. The consciousness of community in being and acting, in joy or suffering, requires us to think with tenderness not only about other people but also, e.g., about animals, which share our lot. We are filled with tenderness for the various beings with which we feel joined in such a way that we can, in a sense, empathize with their inner state and experience (*przeżyć*) the same state on the ground of our own interior "I." Tenderness borders very closely on co-feeling (*współ-odczuwanie*) (not on compassion [*współczucie*], which rather can be considered as a consequence of tenderness, even though sometimes compassion is born in man independently from it). At times, this empathizing with the inner state of another being is at least partly fictional, e.g., when we ascribe to an animal the "interior" lived-experiences that are only our "human" lot, or when we think about the "injury" of trampled or broken plants. Man rightly perceives his connection and union with the whole of nature (*przyroda*), although what is closest to man by nature is the connection and union with other people—and therefore a particular basis for tenderness dwells in him.[36] In relation of one human being to another a particular possibility and, at the same time, a need occurs to empathize with the lived-experiences and interior states of the other, with the whole life of his soul, and furthermore a possibility and a need to communicate this to him. These in particular are the functions of tenderness.

Tenderness is not only an interior ability to co-feel, a sensitiveness to the other's lived-experiences and the states of the other person's soul. Tenderness contains all that, although that does not yet constitute its essence, which expresses the tendency to embrace the other's lived-experiences and the states of the other person's soul with one's own affection. This tendency is expressed outside, for there is a need to communicate to the other "I" my concern for his lived-experiences or interior states so that the other man feels that I share all that, that I also experience (*przeżywać*) it. It is thus evident that tenderness grows from feeling the interior situation of the other person (and indirectly also the exterior situation, for the interior one is formed amidst it) and tends to communicate actively one's own closeness regarding the other person and his situation. This closeness proceeds from affective commitment. The analysis of affectivity conducted in the previous chapter indicated that affectivity enables the lived-experience of closeness toward the other "I": affection by nature draws people together. The need to communicate actively this closeness is born in this context, and, therefore, tenderness expresses itself in certain exterior deeds which by their own character reflect this interior drawing near to the other "I." These deeds may be quite varied in their exterior look, although they all regard one thing: they have a common interior meaning. Hence, on the outside this is expressed, e.g., in holding the other person, in embracing or supporting him by the arm (which after all may be only a form of helping the other; the so-called walking hand in hand is a different matter), and also in some forms of kissing. These are active manifestations of tenderness. A readiness for receiving them does not yet fully prove the reciprocity of affection, but only proves that no affective opposition exists toward that person who in this exterior way shows an expression of his tenderness. Tenderness lies in the interior affective relation and not in mere exterior manifestations, for the latter may be something purely conventional and public. But tenderness is always something personal, interior, one's own—at least in a certain measure it escapes the gaze of others; it is shy. It can be freely revealed only to those who properly understand and feel it.

It is necessary to draw a very distinct boundary line between tenderness, with its various exterior forms, and various forms of satisfying sensuality. The sources from which the former and the latter proceed are completely different, and they concern different things. By nature sensuality is disposed toward the "body as a possible object of sexual use" and naturally tends to satisfy this need to use, and this is when we speak about having a sexual outlet. Tenderness, on the other hand, proceeds from affectivity and its characteristic reaction, the reaction to the "human being of the other sex." What is expressed in it is not desire, but rather benevolence and devotion to the other. Of course, a need to satisfy affectivity is also present in it, but this need has a fundamentally different character from the need to satisfy sensuality. Affectivity is more concentrated on "man," not on the "body and sex"; its immediate point is not the "use" but the "lived-experience of closeness."

All this highly deserves to be emphasized. Tenderness, both in its interior orientation and in the exterior manifestations, differs from sensuality and from sensual use, so that neither one can be reduced to the other, nor identified with it. Both exterior and interior deeds that find their source in tenderness demand a completely different ethical qualification than those whose source is sensuality and the will for sexual use. As distinguished from them, tenderness can be completely disinterested when it is above all marked by a regard for the other, for his interior situation. This disinterestedness recedes as various manifestations of tenderness serve first and foremost the need to satisfy one's affectivity. However, even that may still be valuable insofar as it brings a lived-experience of the closeness between two people, especially when both of them need this closeness. Certain "self-interest" does belong to human love, although without canceling at all its proper character, as has been demonstrated by its metaphysical analysis. Every man is a limited good, thus capable only of limited disinterestedness.*

Thus, there exists a problem of educating tenderness, and this is a part of the problem of educating love "in" a man and a woman, and consequently "between" them. This problem falls within the problems of abstinence. For tenderness demands some vigilance, so that its diverse manifestations do not acquire a different meaning, so that they do not become merely forms of satisfying sensuality and of a sexual outlet. Therefore, tenderness cannot do without a cultivated interior self-mastery, which in this context becomes an exponent of interior subtlety and delicacy with regard to the person of the other sex. Whereas sensuality alone pushes toward the use, so that the man who is wholly seized by it does not even see that there can be another sense and another "style" of the interaction between a man and a woman, tenderness, so to speak, reveals this sense and enables the "style" of reciprocal interaction, consequently taking care not to lose it.

---

* An act of love, as an act of affirming the person of the recipient of an action because of his dignity, is by its essence a disinterested act. At the same time, next to its transitive effects (it is precisely an act of beneficence, *actus bene-ficentiae*) it possesses intransitive effects. It is *sui generis* "beneficence for the subject of action," who by performing an act of love fulfills himself through this act most thoroughly. See K. Wojtyła, "Il problema del costituirsi della cultura attraverso la praxis umana" (The problem of the formation of culture through human praxis), *Rivista di filosofia neo-scolastica* 69, vol. 3 [1977], 513–524.

Can we speak of a "*right to tenderness*"? This expression must be understood, on the one hand, as the right to receive tenderness, and, on the other hand, as the right to show it. Customarily and in the latter case we speak of a "right," and not of an obligation, even though there is no doubt that sometimes some kind of obligation exists to show tenderness to the other. And so, the right to tenderness belongs to all people who particularly need tenderness, e.g., the weak, the sick, the suffering in any way (also morally). It seems that a particular right to tenderness belongs to children, for whom (and in any case not only for them) tenderness is a natural way of manifesting love. Therefore, in these manifestations of tenderness, especially the exterior, one and only one measure must be introduced, namely the measure of love of the person. For a danger also exists of fueling egoism in this way. Exaggerated tenderness may lead to that. Such tenderness is used by the person who shows it to satisfy his affectivity above all, without taking into account the objective need and the good of the other. Therefore, true human love, love "for" a person and love "between" persons, must join in itself two moments: of tenderness and of a certain firmness. Otherwise, it will lose its healthy and firm interior profile; it will change into fruitless sentimentality and softness. We must not forget that man's love must also contain certain elements of struggle—struggle for precisely that man, for his true good.

Indeed, tenderness itself gains in value through being joined with a certain firmness and "resoluteness" in the attitude of the will. Tenderness that is too easy, especially so-called mawkishness (*czułostkowość*), does not induce deep trust; quite the contrary, it arouses a suspicion that the man who is affectionate in this way seeks in the manifestations of tenderness only to satisfy his affectivity, or perhaps even sensuality and the will to use. And therefore, only the forms of tenderness that find full, mature justification in the love of the person, in what truly binds two people, have their moral substantiation. This is understandable since tenderness has its sole *raison d'être* in love. Outside of love we do not have the "right" to show or receive tenderness; its exterior manifestations are then suspended in the void.

These remarks apply particularly to the reciprocal relation between a woman and a man. Here in particular it must be demanded that various forms of tenderness have a thorough justification in the true love of the person. For we must take into account that the love of a woman and a man is formed to an enormous extent from the potential hidden in sensuality and affectivity, which themselves demand to be satisfied, to be satiated. Hence various forms of tenderness may easily diverge from love of the person, and approach egoism of the senses or even egoism of affection. In addition, exterior manifestations of tenderness may create an appearance of love, love that truly does not exist. A man-seducer as a rule uses various methods of tenderness, similarly to a woman-flirt, who tries to play on the senses, although in the former and the latter case, love of the person is missing. However, disregarding the facts pertaining to some "game of love," which can be called different names (flirting, romance, etc.), we must pay attention to the fact that all love between a woman and a man, including the one that both intend to be true and honest, in general develops in such a way that its subjective profile grows faster than its objective one. Various elements of its psychological structure, so to speak, germinate earlier, whereas its ethical essence itself must mature slowly and gradually. Much here also depends on age and temperament. In young people the divergence of these two interior processes is generally greater than in older and generally more mature people. In people endowed with a lively and fiery temperament (e.g., in persons of sanguine disposition) love as lived-experience, as affection, erupts violently and with might, whereas virtue must be all the more educated and formed with interior effort.

Accordingly, it is necessary to call for even greater responsibility in granting a woman and a man the "right to tenderness," both with regard to receiving as well as showing it. A tendency certainly exists—especially in some people—to widen these rights, to take premature advantage of them, while we are presented in both persons merely with the arousal of affectivity and sensuality with it, yet the objective profile of love and the union of persons are still missing. This premature tenderness in the interaction between X and Y at times even destroys love or at least does not allow it to be developed in full, in all its interior as well as objective truth.

At this point we do not think about various forms of familiarity (*poufałość*), which belong to still another series of facts pertaining to the interaction between a man and a woman. Excessive familiarity is a form of irresponsible sexual use, and, furthermore, can also be a manifestation of boorishness or simply indiscretion. What is solely at stake, however, is tenderness. Without the virtue of temperance, without chastity and self-mastery, it is impossible to educate and develop tenderness in man, so that it does not hinder love but serves it. For a serious danger occurs of some shallow, superficial lived-experience of love and at the same time its "consumption" (i.e., using up the "material" from which love is formed in a woman and a man). Within limits of such lived-experience both persons will fail in the effort to reach love's objective profile and the proper good, but will remain with purely subjective manifestations, deriving from them merely ephemeral pleasure. Then love, instead of constantly beginning anew and constantly growing between them, quite the contrary, constantly, so to speak, ends and breaks off. Let us add that among other things a great deal depends here on the correct education of tenderness, on the responsibility for its manifestations.

For it is necessary to emphasize again that tenderness is an important factor of love. It is impossible to question the truth that the love of a man and a woman is to an enormous extent based on affection, which is the material that natural affectivity should constantly provide in order to join thoroughly the objective profile of love with the subjective one. The point is not so much the "first" raptures of affectivity, which in a certain sense "artificially" amplify the value of the beloved person by referring to the lived-experience of "femininity" or "masculinity." But even more so, the point is a constant contribution of affection, its constant commitment in love, for affection makes a woman and a man close to each other; it creates the interior atmosphere of communicativeness and reciprocal understanding. On this substratum tenderness is something natural and true, something authentic. A great deal of such tenderness is needed in marriage, in the entire life together where, after all, not only a "body" needs a "body," but above all a human being needs another human being. Tenderness has an enormous role to fulfill here. When thoroughly joined with true love of the person, and being disinterested, it is capable of leading love out of various dangers of egoism of the senses, out of the dangers of the attitude to use. Tenderness is the ability to feel the whole man, the whole person, in all, even the most hidden movements of his soul, but always bearing in mind the true good of that person.

A woman expects this tenderness from a man; she has a particular right to it in marriage, in which she gives herself to a man, where she experiences (*przeżywać*) moments and periods that are tremendously important and difficult for her, such as pregnancy, childbirth, and all that is connected with them. Her affective life is at the same time in general more abundant, and hence comes a greater need for tenderness. A man also needs it, although in a different measure and in a different shape. Both in a woman and in a man tenderness evokes the conviction that one is not alone, that all by which one lives is also the content of the life of the other, closest person. This conviction helps enormously and sustains the consciousness of union.

Nonetheless, it may seem strange that the reflections on tenderness are located in this part of the chapter, which speaks of the "problem of abstinence." However, there is a close connection and the reflections here are in their proper place. There can be no true tenderness without mature continence, which has its source in the will that is always ready to love, thus consistently overcoming the attitude to use imposed by sensuality and the concupiscence of the flesh. Without this continence the natural energies of sensuality and the energies of affectivity absorbed in their orbit will become mere "material" for egoism of the senses, and eventually for egoism of affection. This must be clearly and explicitly stated. Life teaches this at every step. The faithful know that behind this lies the mystery of original sin, whose consequences weigh in some particular way on the sphere of *sexus* and threaten the person, the greatest good among those of the created universe. This danger in a sense borders on love: what can be developed on the basis of the same material is true love, a union of persons, as well as ostensible "love," which merely provides a cover for the interior attitude to use, for egoism that contradicts love. How enormous and in effect how positive a role abstinence fulfills here, for it liberates from that attitude and from egoism, and thereby indirectly forms love. The love of a woman and a man cannot be built otherwise than through a certain sacrifice and denial of oneself. We find the formula for this denial in the Gospel, in the words of Christ: "Whoever wishes to come after me, let him deny himself (. . .)."[37] The Gospel teaches abstinence as a way of loving.

# Chapter IV

# Justice with Respect to the Creator

# Part One

# Marriage

## Monogamy and indissolubility

The entire course of reflections contained in the previous chapters leads with a strict interior necessity to acknowledging the principle of monogamy and the indissolubility of the marital union. The personalistic norm formulated and explained in chapter I is at once the ultimate foundation and the first source of this principle. If the person X may not by any means be an object of use for the person Y, but only an object (or rather a co-subject) of love, an appropriate framework is needed for the union of a man and a woman in which full sexual intercourse is realized in such a way that at the same time the durable union of persons composing this union is secured. It is known that such a union is called marriage. Attempts to solve the problem of marriage in a different way—outside strict monogamy (which already implicates indissolubility)—are incompatible with the personalistic norm; they do not meet its strict requirements. A person is then placed in the situation of being an object of use for another person, and it is especially a woman (X) in relation to a man (Y) that is placed in this situation. This happens in the case of polygyny, of which we usually think when speaking about polygamy (*poly-gynia*: a union of one man with many women; *poly-gamia*: plural marriage). It is known, however, that in the history of mankind we also meet with cases of polyandry (*poly-andria*: a union of one woman with many men); plural marriage then goes in the opposite direction.

We consider here the problem of marriage first of all with respect to the *principle of loving the person* ("the personalistic norm"), i.e., treating the person in a way corresponding to the being he is. This principle is fully compatible only with monogamy and the indissolubility of marriage, and fundamentally opposes all forms of polygamy, i.e., both polygyny and polyandry, as well as the principle of dissolubility of marriage. For, essentially, in all these cases the person is posited as an object of use for another person. Accordingly, marriage itself is only (or in any case, above all) an institution within which the sexual use of a man and a woman is realized, and a durable union of persons based on reciprocal affirmation of the person is not realized. For such a union must be durable; it must endure as long as one person endures in the relation to the other one. The point here is not the person's spiritual enduring, for that is supra-temporal, but the enduring in the body that ends with death.

But why is this abiding at stake? Because marriage is not only a spiritual union of persons, but also a bodily and earthly one.* In accordance with the answer Christ gave to the Sadducees (Mt 19:3–9) who asked about the fate of marriage after the resurrection of bodies—which of course is a tenet of faith—people then living again in (glorified) bodies will "neither marry nor be given in marriage." Marriage is closely linked to the bodily and earthly existence of man. This explains its natural dissolution by the death of one of the spouses. The other spouse is then free and can enter into marriage with another person. In the law this is called *bigamia succesiva* (second marriage), which must be categorically distinguished from *bigamia simultanea*, which in colloquial language is simply called bigamy, and which is a marital union with a new person while the marriage with some other person wedded earlier still exists. Although a second marriage after the death of a spouse is justified and permitted, it is nevertheless by all means praiseworthy to remain in the state of widowhood, for in this way the union with the person who passed away is, among other things, better expressed.[1] After all, the very value of the person does not pass away and the spiritual union with him can and should continue, even when the bodily union has ceased. In the Gospel, and especially in St. Paul's epistles, at times we read about the praise of widowhood and of absolute monogamy.[2]

In general, in the teaching of Jesus Christ the issue of monogamy and indissolubility of marriage was posited definitely and decisively. Christ had before his eyes the fact of the original institution of marriage by the Creator, marriage of a closely monogamous (Gen 1:27, 2:24) and

---

* See K. Wojtyła, "Myśli o małżeństwie" (Thoughts about marriage), *Znak* 7 (1957), 595–604.

indissoluble character ("What God has joined together, let no man put asunder"), to which he appealed constantly.[3] For in the traditions of his immediate listeners, the Israelites, lived the memory of the polygamy of the patriarchs and the great leaders and kings of the nation (e.g., David, Solomon), as well as the memory of the so-called letter of divorce that Moses introduced, which permitted under certain conditions dissolving a legally contracted marriage.

But Christ definitely opposed these customary traditions by emphasizing the original institution of marriage and the original thought of the Creator linked to it (" . . . but at the beginning it was not so").[4] This thought, the idea of a monogamous marriage living in the mind and will of the Creator, was distorted also among the "chosen nation." The polygamy of the patriarchs is often explained by their will to possess numerous progeny, and in this way regard for procreation as the objective end of marriage would justify polygamy within the Old Law and analogically also anywhere else where polygamy was to serve this very purpose. At the same time, however, the books of the Old Testament provide sufficient proof that plural marriage (*polygynia*) contributes in practice to a man treating a woman as an object of use, and as a result impairing her and lowering the level of morality of the man himself, which is indicated, e.g., by the history of Solomon.

The elimination of polygamy and the restoration of monogamy and of the indissolubility of marriage remain closely connected with the commandment to love understood in the way we have understood it from the beginning—as the personalistic norm. Since all the interaction and relations between persons of different sex are to live up to the requirements of this norm, they must be formed in accordance with and around the principle of monogamy and indissolubility—"around" inasmuch as this principle sheds light on many other details related to the coexistence and interaction between a man and a woman. (The commandment to love, as it is contained in the Gospel, is more than the "personalistic norm" itself, since at the same time there dwells in this commandment the fundamental law of the whole supernatural order, the supernatural relation to God and people. Nonetheless, the "personalistic norm" dwells in it with all certainty and is in a sense a natural content of the commandment to love, the content which we also comprehend without faith, by reason alone. Let us add that the norm constitutes a condition for understanding and realizing the full, i.e., supernatural, content of the commandment to love.)

Polygamy and also the dissolution of a legally contracted marriage (so-called divorce), which in fact leads in practice to polygamy, clash with the demands of the personalistic norm. These things—especially as an expression of treating the person of the other sex as an "object representing merely a sexual value," and treating marriage as an institution based only on this value, serving only this value, and not serving the personal union of persons—go hand in hand.[5]

Man is a being that has the capacity for conceptual thinking, and hence the ability to be guided by universal principles.[6] In light of these principles, i.e., holding fast to the personalistic norm, we must accept that in those cases where the life of the spouses together becomes impossible due to some truly serious causes (especially due to marital infidelity), only a possibility of separation exists, that is, a parting of the spouses without breaking the marriage itself. Of course, even separation is a ("necessary") evil with respect to the essence of marriage, as marriage should be a durable unity of a man and a woman. Nonetheless, this evil does not cancel the personalistic norm itself: none of the persons, and especially the woman, is basically put in the position of an object of use for the other one. But that would be the case if, despite the fact of belonging by way of marriage to another person (within a validly contracted marriage), a person abandoned that other person and during his lifetime joined somebody else by way of marriage (*po małżeńsku*). However, when they simply withdraw from conjugal intercourse and from the whole conjugal-familial partnership of life without being joined by marriage to other persons, then the personal order itself is in no way violated. The person is not pushed to the rank of an object of use, and marriage retains the character of an institution serving the personal union of a man and a woman, and not only their sexual intercourse.

We must accept that while having conjugal relations a man and a woman unite as persons, and thus the union endures as long as these persons are alive. We cannot accept, however, that this union endures only as long as the persons themselves want this, for precisely this would contradict the personalistic norm: for this norm takes as its basis the person as a being. From this point of view, a man and a woman who had conjugal relations within a validly contracted marriage are objectively united to each other in a way that is not dissoluble other than by the death of one of them. And nothing is changed by the circumstance that over time one or even both of them cease to want it, as this can by no means remove the fact that they are objectively united to each other as husband and wife. It is possible that one or both of them may fall short of the subjective justification for this union, and it is also possible that a subjective state may arise that opposes this union psychologically or psycho-physiologically. This state explains their division "from bed and table" (precisely this is a separation), but cannot annihilate the fact that they are objectively united—and united as spouses. Precisely the personalistic norm, which stands above the will and above the decision of each concerned party, requires a durable, lifelong preservation of this union. Presenting the matter otherwise would place the person essentially in the position of an object of "use," which is equivalent to frustrating the objective order of love in which the supra-utilitarian value of the person is affirmed.

This order, however, is implicated in the principle of strict monogamy, which is identified with the indissolubility of a validly contracted marriage. This principle is difficult, but at the same time indispensable if the relationship between persons of different sex (and indirectly also all of human life, which, after all, is based to an enormous extent on this relationship) is to stay on the level of the person and be situated within the dimensions of love. The point here of course is love in its full, objective sense, love as virtue, and not love merely in a psychological-subjective sense. The difficulty contained in the principle of monogamy and indissolubility of marriage originates from the fact that "love" is at times understood and realized too exclusively in the latter and not in the former sense. The principle of monogamy and indissolubility of marriage necessitates the integration of love (see the chapter devoted to the analysis of love, especially its third part). Without it marriage is an enormous risk.[7] A man and a woman whose love has not thoroughly matured, has not crystallized as a fully-mature union of persons, should not marry, for they are not prepared for the life test of marriage. In any case, the point is not for their love to be already definitively mature at the moment of contracting marriage, but to be mature for further maturation within marriage and through marriage.

For it is impossible to relinquish the good that is monogamy and indissolubility not only from the supernatural standpoint, from the position of faith, but also from the rational, human standpoint. For the point is the primacy of the value of the person over the value of *sexus* itself and the realization of love in the field in which love can be easily ousted by the utilitarian "principle of utility," which in fact conceals the affirmation of the attitude to use directed toward another person. Strict monogamy is an exponent of the personal order.

## *The value of the institution*

The above reflections prepared us to understand the value of the institution of marriage. For marriage cannot be understood merely as the very fact of sexual intercourse of some human couple, a man and a woman, but we must see in marriage an institution. However, whereas it is beyond doubt that the fact of bodily intercourse between given persons, Y and X, really determines the institution (hence the old Latin adage: *matrimonium facit copula*), intercourse itself outside the frame-work of institution is not yet marriage.[8] The word "institution" means the same as "establishment" or "organization" that results from the order of justice. As it is known, the order of justice concerns inter-personal matters and social matters (commutative justice, social justice). Now, marriage is an inter-personal and a social matter.

The very fact of sexual intercourse between two individual persons, a man and a woman, possesses an intimate character due to reasons already described in the previous chapter (in the analysis of shame). Nevertheless, both persons taking part in it belong to society, and for many reasons they should justify their intercourse with respect to society. Precisely the institution of marriage constitutes this justification. The point here is not merely justification in the sense of legalization, in the sense of conforming to the law. To "justify" means to "make just." It also has nothing in common with making excuses, with providing extenuating circumstances in an attempt to vindicate a consent to something that is in fact evil.[9]

The need to justify intercourse between a man and a woman with respect to society occurs not only because of the ordinary consequences of this intercourse, but also due to the very persons partaking in it, and particularly the woman. The ordinary consequence of sexual intercourse between a man and a woman is progeny. A child is a new member of society—and society must accept him, and even register him (presuming an adequately high organization of society). The birth of a child causes the union of a man and a woman based on sexual intercourse to become a family. The family itself is already a community, a small society, on which the existence of every large society depends, e.g., a nation, a state, the Church. It is understandable that this large society tries to watch over the process of its continuous becoming through the family. The family is the most elementary institution connected with the foundations of human existence.* It inheres in a large society, which it constantly creates, but at the same time it is distanced from that society; it possesses its own character and ends. Both, i.e., the immanence of the family in society as well as its specific autonomy and inviolability, must be reflected in legislation. The starting point here is the law of nature— the objectivization of the order that follows from the very nature of the family.

The family is an institution that has marriage at its foundation. It is impossible to order the family correctly within the life of a large society without correctly ordering marriage. This does not mean, however, that marriage ought to be treated only and exclusively as a means to an end, to that end which is the family. For although in a natural way it leads to the existence of the family and should be open to the family, *marriage* nonetheless *by no means loses itself in the family*. It preserves its distinctness as an institution whose interior structure differs from that of the family. The family possesses the structure of a society in which the father and also the mother—each of them in his own way—hold sway, to which the children are subject. Marriage does not yet possess the structure of a society, but it possesses an inter-personal structure: it is a coming together and union of two persons.

---

* *"The family is the place in which every man appears in his uniqueness and unrepeatability* [emphasis original]. It is—and should be—a particular system of forces in which every man is important and needed due to the fact that he is and who he is—a system most profoundly 'human,' built on the value of the person and comprehensively oriented to this value" (K. Wojtyła, "Rodzina jako '*communio personarum*'" [The Family as '*Communio Personarum*'], *Ateneum Kapłańskie* 66, vol. 83 [1974], 348).

This distinct character of the institution of marriage is also preserved when marriage grows into a family. This, however, may not occur due to various reasons, yet the lack of the family does not in any way deprive marriage of its proper character. For the interior and essential *raison d'être* of marriage is not only to become a family, but above all to constitute a durable personal union of a man and a woman based on love. First and foremost, marriage serves existence—as was indicated by reflections contained in chapter I—but is based on love. The full value of the institution is also enjoyed by a marriage that is childless due to no fault on the part of the spouses. On the other hand, marriage serves love, so to speak, more fully when it serves existence, when it becomes a family. This is the way to understand the thought contained in the statement that procreation is the primary end of marriage. Marriage that cannot achieve this end by no means loses thereby its meaning as an institution of an interpersonal character. Furthermore, the realization of the primary end of marriage demands that this inter-personal character be most fully realized in it, that the love of the spouses be as mature and creative as possible.[10] It must be added that if this love is already mature in some measure, it matures all the more through procreation.

Marriage then constitutes a distinct institution that has a clearly delineated inter-personal structure. This institution grows into a family, becomes it, and in a sense is even identified with it. However, it must be said that inasmuch as the family proceeds through marriage, marriage proceeds through the family, confirming itself through the family and in it, and achieving for itself the needed fullness. Thus, for example, old spouses who live surrounded not only by their children but also by the families of those children and sometimes even of grandchildren constitute among this multigenerational family an "institution," simultaneously a unity and a whole that exists and lives by its own laws in accordance with its fundamental, interpersonal character. Therefore it is an institution. The laws upon which its being is based must proceed from the presuppositions of the personalistic norm, for only this is able to ensure the truly personal character of the union between two persons. The social constitution of the family is good when it enables and supports precisely this character of marriage. And therefore, in the case, for instance, of a family that grew out of polygamy, even though being as a family more numerous and materially speaking a more powerful society (as, e.g., the families of the patriarchs of the Old Law), its moral value is nonetheless fundamentally lower than that of a family that grew out of a monogamous marriage. The value of persons and the value of love as a durable union of these persons are much more strongly manifested in the constitution of the latter (which in itself bears a significant educational importance), whereas in the constitution of the family that originated from polygamy, biological fertility itself and quantitative development are manifested more than the value of the person and the personal value of love.

The significance of the institution of marriage lies in this, that it justifies the fact of sexual intercourse between a given couple, Y and X, within the whole of social life. This is important not only with regard to the consequences of this fact—of which we have already spoken—but also with regard to the persons themselves taking part in it. This is also important with regard to the moral qualification of their love, as their love demands some orienting toward other people, toward a more proximate society and a society at large. And perhaps nowhere else but here, where actually all happens between two people as some function of their love, it turns out that man is also a social being. The point is that this "love," which for both (for Y and X) psychologically justifies and legitimates, as it were, their intercourse, should in addition acquire the right of citizenship among people.

At first it may seem to them (i.e., to Y and X) that this is not the point, but in due time they must perceive that without this right their love lacks something very essential. They feel that their love should mature enough so that it could be manifested before society. The need to conceal sexual intercourse proceeding from love is one matter, whereas the need for love as the union of persons to be acknowledged by society is yet another. Love needs this acknowledgment, without which it does not feel fully itself. And the difference in meaning associated with the words "lover," "concubine," "mistress," etc., and with the words "wife" or "fiancée" (all these words signify a woman, but also pertain to a man) is not in the least simply conventional. Rather, the blurring of this difference is something conventional and secondary, whereas the very difference is something original, natural, and fundamental. For instance, the word "lover" (*kochanka*) in its contemporary semantic tint indicates that the relation of a given man to "this" woman remains on the level of using an "object" in sexual relations and intercourse, whereas the word "wife" or "fiancée" ("bride") speaks of the co-subject of love having a full personal, hence also social, value.

This is the meaning possessed by the institution of marriage. Amid a society acknowledging healthy ethical principles and living in accord with them (without pharisaism and prudery), this institution is needed in order to bear witness to the maturity of the very union of a man and a woman, to love that durably joins and unifies them. In this function, the institution of marriage is needed not only with regard to society, with respect to "other" people who belong to it, but also—and even above all—with respect to the very persons who constitute marriage. Even if there were no other people around them, they would still need the institution of marriage (and perhaps even some "form" of it, that is, some rite that determines the creation of this institution by both interested parties, Y and X). And although the institution could arise by way of facts themselves, among which precisely the facts of sexual intercourse would be decisive, it nevertheless would definitely differ from them. The facts of sexual intercourse between a man and a woman demand the institution of marriage as their natural setting, for the institution legitimates these facts above all in the consciousness of the very persons partaking in sexual intercourse.

Our consideration of this matter can be also facilitated by the fact that the Latin word *matrimonium*, which is the equivalent of the word "marriage," emphasizes in a particular way the "state of the mother," as if it wished to suggest a particular responsibility for the motherhood of this woman with whom a given man has conjugal relations. The responsibility for motherhood is a problem we will return to in this chapter. For the time being it is sufficient to state that the fact of sexual intercourse definitely demands the framework of the institution of *matrimonium*, in fact due to the very relation of a person to another person. Sexual intercourse outside marriage *ipso facto* places one person in the position of an object of use for another person. Which for which? It is not ruled out that the man is also placed in this position in relation to the woman; however, it is always the case that the woman is placed in this position in relation to the man. This is easily inferred (by contrast) at least from the very analysis of the word *matri-monium*. Sexual intercourse outside the institution of marriage is always objectively speaking detrimental to the woman. This is always the case, even when she herself permits it, or, what is more, when she herself strives and longs for it.

Therefore, "adultery" in the broadest sense of the word is morally evil. It is actually used in this sense in Holy Scripture, in the Decalogue and the Gospel. The point is not only the fact of sexual intercourse with a woman who is "somebody else's wife," but also the fact of having relations with any woman who is not "one's own wife," regardless of whether or not she has a husband.[11] Concerning a woman, the point is having relations with a man who is not "her husband." In accordance with the analysis of chastity that we conducted in the previous chapter, some derivatives of "adultery" comprehended this way are also present in interior "deeds" such as "desire" itself (see the sentence from Matthew 5:28, which has been already cited several times). Clearly, adultery is committed especially when these "deeds" concern a person who is "somebody else's wife" or "somebody else's husband," and then it contains in itself moral evil that is all the greater because it proceeds from a violation of the order of justice, from crossing the boundary between "my own" and "somebody else's." Nonetheless, this boundary is crossed not only when one reaches for what is clearly "somebody else's," but always also when one reaches for what is "not his own."* In this case,

---

* What lies at the foundation of the interpersonal *communio* is "a capacity for giving oneself, for becoming a gift for others," a capacity that is proper to man as a person (presupposing the structures of self-possession and self-governance). (See K. Wojtyła, "O znaczeniu miłości oblubieńczej," *Roczniki Filozoficzne* 22, fasc. 2 [1974], 166; see p. 282 in this book.) However, "if this disinterested gift of self is to remain a gift and be realized as a gift in the interpersonal relation, ( . . . ) it must be not only '*given,*' but also '*received*' in its *whole truth and authenticity* [emphasis original]." (See K. Wojtyła, "Rodzina jako '*communio personarum*'" [The Family as '*Communio Personarum*'], *Ateneum Kapłańskie* 66, vol. 83 [1974], 355.) This truth includes the fact that by giving himself (which does not mean in the least: "by depriving himself of the ontic incommunicability"—see "O znaczeniu miłości oblubieńczej," 165–168; see also pp. 280–285 [although the editors probably meant pp. 165–166, i.e., pp. 280–281 in this book — Trans.]), man in a sense loses the right to himself in favor of the person to whom he gave himself. Thus, both "reaching for somebody else's property" (for somebody else's husband or wife) and giving oneself (by a spouse) to a third person are acts of specific theft that strike at the interpersonal community of love as deeply as the disinterested gift of self constitutes this community. "A person may not be deprived of the gift he brings; in this self-giving he may not be robbed of who he really is and what he really intends to express by his action" ("Rodzina jako '*communio personarum,*'" 355).

the institution of marriage determines the possession—the reciprocal belonging of persons to each other. Let us add what has been substantiated previously, namely that that institution is fully-mature only on condition of monogamy and indissolubility.

All that has been said here to demonstrate the moral evil of "adultery" permits us to state that every fact of sexual intercourse of a man and a woman outside the institution of *matrimonium*, hence including both pre-marital and extra-marital relations, is morally evil. The so-called deliberate "free love" is all the more morally evil, for it includes a rejection of the institution of marriage or a reduction of its role in the sphere of sexual relations between a man and a woman. According to the program of "free love" the institution of marriage plays in this sphere a nonessential and contingent role. The previous analysis aimed to demonstrate that marriage plays precisely a role that is most essential and necessary. For without the institution of *matrimonium* a person engaging in sexual intercourse is, as a matter of fact, pushed to the position of an object of use for another person (X for Y), and this fully contradicts the demands of the personalistic norm, without which we cannot in any way imagine relations between persons on a truly personal level. Marriage as an institution is indispensable to justify the fact of conjugal relations between a man and a woman, first of all regarding themselves, but also regarding society.[12] Since we speak about "justification," it is evident that the institution of marriage proceeds from the objective order of justice.

In addition, there occurs *the need to justify* the fact of sexual relations between a man and a woman with respect to God the Creator. This is also demanded by the objective order of justice. Indeed, a thorough analysis leads us to the conviction that justification of the fact of conjugal relations between a man and a woman with respect to the Creator is the basis for any justification of it, both "from within"—between the persons—and "from without"—with respect to society. It is another matter that only a religious man—that is, a person who acknowledges the existence of God the Creator and accepts the fact that all beings in the universe that surrounds us are creatures of this God, and that among them man-person is also a creature—is able to conduct such an analysis and to accept its conclusions. The concept of "creature" entails a particular kind of dependence on the Creator, namely dependence for existence (to be created means to be dependent for existence).[13] In turn, this dependence is the basis for a special right of ownership with respect to all creatures (*dominium altum*) that belongs to the Creator. The Creator most thoroughly possesses each creature, for since each of them is ultimately determined by existence that comes from the Creator, then in a certain way "all is his," because also whatever the creature "created" in and by itself is based on existence. The activity of creatures progresses by developing what is really contained in each of them thanks to the fact that they exist.

Man differs from all other creatures of the visible world by the fact that he is able to grasp all this by reason. At the same time rationality (*rozumność*) constitutes the basis of personhood; it conditions the "inwardness" and spirituality of the being and life of the person. Thanks to his rationality man comprehends that he possesses himself (*sui iuris*), and at the same time that he as a creature is a possession of the Creator, and experiences (*przeżywać*) the Creator's right of ownership with respect to himself. This state of consciousness eventually develops in man whose reason is enlightened by faith. Reason also allows him to perceive and commands him to acknowledge the same fact in another man, in every other person: that he possesses himself and at the same time as a creature is possessed by God. What is therefore born here is the twofold need to justify the sexual intercourse of a man and a woman by the institution of marriage. For the fact of intercourse makes a person (X) become in a certain way a possession of another person (Y), and this at the same time occurs in the opposite direction: Y is a possession of X. Thus, if a need exists to justify this fact of the reciprocal relation of Y-X and X-Y, then at the same time an objective need exists to justify it with respect to the Creator. Another thing is that this need is understood only by religious people. For "a religious man" means not merely "someone capable of religious lived-experiences" (as is most often thought), but above all "someone who is just with respect to God the Creator."

Here we find ourselves at the threshold of understanding the "sacramentality" of marriage. According to the teaching of the Church, it is a sacrament from the beginning, i.e., from the moment of creation of the first human couple. The "sacrament of nature" was later, in the Gospel, even more fully manifested through the institution, or rather through the revelation of the sacrament of grace linked with it. The Latin word *sacramentum* means the same as mystery, and mystery in the most common sense of the word is what is not yet fully known due to not being fully seen, for it does not lie in the field of immediate sensual experience. Now, outside the field of this experience, in the sphere of "understanding" alone, there exist both the right of ownership, which each person possesses in relation to himself, and all the more this *dominium altum*, which the Creator possesses in relation to each person. But if this supreme right of ownership is accepted—and it is accepted by every religious man—then marriage must seek to be justified above all in his eyes; it must suppose his approval. It is not sufficient for a woman to give her person through marriage to a man, and for him to do so with his person to her. If each of these persons is at the same time a possession of the Creator, then he also must give him to her, and her to him, or in any case he must approve their reciprocal self-giving that is contained in the institution of marriage.*

This approval cannot be subjected to the senses, as it can only be "understood" on the basis of the order of nature. Marriage as a *sacramentum naturae* is nothing else but the institution of *matrimonium* based already on some understanding of the right of the Creator with respect to persons entering it.[14] Marriage as a *sacramentum gratiae* presupposes above all the full understanding of that right.[15] Besides this, however, the sacrament of marriage develops on the ground of the belief

---

* "Each time we follow attentively the whole liturgy of this sacrament [of marriage, —Ed.], two people stand before us, a man and a woman, who come to express before God precisely this, that they constitute an objective situation, in which both are to become a gift for each other as spouses. Conjugal intercourse also belongs to the essence of this situation, which is then expressed, and thereby ultimately matures and is constituted as a sacrament. This intercourse *is included in the totality of their life's vocation that they both confess before God* as 'their share with Jesus Christ' in the community of the Church. And through this confession they, in a sense, *receive each other from the hands of God the Creator and Redeemer.* They receive each other in order to be a gift for each other as husband and wife. This includes the sacramental confirmation of the right to sexual intercourse, which only in the marital covenant can be the correct form of realizing the general 'law of the gift' inscribed by God in the very being of the person [emphasis original]" (K. Wojtyła, "O znaczeniu miłości oblubieńczej" [On the Meaning of Spousal Love], *Roczniki Filozoficzne* 22, fasc. 2 [1974], 174; see p. 294 in this book).

we owe to the Gospel, that the justification of man with respect to God is accomplished fundamentally through grace.* And man receives grace through the sacraments imparted by the Church, which Christ endowed for this end with power in the supernatural order. Therefore, only the sacrament of marriage fully satisfies the need for justification of the fact of conjugal intercourse with respect to God the Creator. This explains the fact that its institution came hand in hand with the definitive revelation of the supernatural order.

## *Reproduction and parenthood*

The value of the institution of marriage consists, among other things, in that it justifies the fact of sexual intercourse between a woman and a man. The "fact" we understand here not as one-time, but as continuous—as many facts. Therefore, human marriage is a "state" (the married state), that is, a stable institution that creates for a lifetime a framework for the coexistence of a man and a woman. Of course, this framework is not filled with facts of sexual intercourse alone. The point is a whole group of facts from very diverse fields, both from the economic as well as cultural or religious fields. All of them together create a rich and fairly comprehensive community of life of two people, first as a marriage and later as a family. They possess their own specific weight, and in some way they condition the development of the love of a man and a woman in marriage. Among them the facts of sexual intercourse

---

* "Justification through grace," i.e., the release of man from the "original" debt, is accomplished fundamentally and principally by *Baptism.* The rebellion of the first parents, however, damaged the physical and moral nature of man itself, so that, as a rule, human individuals are inclined to incur numerous faults and personal debts with respect to one another, and above all with respect to God, the owner of every being. People, who on that account need and long for justification, find it in Christ, because only through him and in him can man be "quite all right" with respect to his Creator. This is principally accomplished through the *sacrament of Penance,* but also through other sacraments, hence also through *Christian marriage.*

These two kinds of "justification" should not be confused with the "justification" of the fact of sexual intercourse itself that occurs within the objective and durable framework of the institution of marriage as a *sacramentum naturae,* hence on the ground of honorableness designated by the natural law.

possess their own specificity and distinct meaning, for they remain particularly connected with the development of the love of persons. The institution of marriage, as we have stated, justifies the sexual intercourse of a man and a woman. The institution of marriage justifies the sexual intercourse of a given man with a given woman in the sense that it creates the objective framework in which a durable union of persons can be realized (of course, on condition of monogamy and indissolubility).

However, the realization of this union between the persons Y and X in each distinct act of conjugal intercourse constitutes a separate moral problem, an interior problem of marriage. The point is that every such act, every conjugal act, has to possess its interior justice, for without justice we cannot speak of the union of persons in love. Thus, a distinct problem exists—one immensely important from the viewpoint of morality and the culture of the person—of conforming conjugal intercourse itself to the objective demands of the personalistic norm. Precisely in this sphere the realization of the demands of this norm is particularly important, and at the same time—let us not conceal this—particularly difficult, for a whole nexus comes to light of interior factors and exterior circumstances that facilitate the reduction of this act of the reciprocal love of persons to the level of "using." If anywhere, it is particularly here that we ought to speak of responsibility for love. Let us at once add that this responsibility for the love of the person is complemented here by responsibility for life and also for health—it is a whole nexus of fundamental goods that together determine the ethical value of each fact of conjugal intercourse. Hence, one can form a view concerning this value by starting from each of these goods separately and from responsibility for them. In this book, in accordance with its presupposition and the main direction of reflections, we will start from the good that is constituted by the person and love truly understood. For it seems that this good lies most deeply in this whole nexus and conditions the relation to the other ones.*

---

* The personalistic norm refers above all to the attitude of the subject (*benevolentia*): the good of the person-object ought to be strived for, or at least the person-object must not be completely subordinated to the subject's own ends. However, by bringing this postulate into action (*beneficentia*), one cannot affirm the person-object in any other way but only by realizing particular pre-moral goods (life, health, etc.), which possess value inasmuch as they serve the person. Hence, it can be stated that all norms concerning the realization of these goods (the category of rightness—see footnote, p. 146) have a teleological character: they bind because (and inasmuch as) observing them brings the person-object

A man and a woman who as spouses unite themselves in full sexual intercourse thereby enter into the orbit of the order that should be rightly called the order of nature. In chapter I we observed that the order of nature cannot be identified with the "biological order," for the former is first and foremost the order of existing and becoming—of procreation. Now, we have in mind the word *procreatio* in its full meaning when we state that the order of nature tends to reproduction by way of sexual intercourse. This is the natural finality of conjugal intercourse— every fact of sexual intercourse between a man and a woman stands intrinsically in the orbit of that finality.[16] Thus, the conjugal act considered with complete objectivity is not only a union of persons, of a man and a woman, in their reciprocal relation, but also is by its nature (essence) a union of persons in relation to *procreatio*. The word *procreatio* expresses more fully the content of the problem, whereas the word "reproduction" (*rozrodczość*) possesses a meaning that is rather purely "biological."* It is evident that in this case the point is not merely the beginning of life in a purely biological sense, but the beginning of the existence of the person; hence it is better to say "procreation."

Thus, a meeting of two orders takes place in the conjugal intercourse of a man and a woman, namely of the order of nature, which aims at reproduction, and of the personal order, which is expressed in the love of persons and strives to realize this love as fully as possible.†

---

more good than not observing them. From the fact, however, that the value of the person supersedes the value of all pre-moral goods, it does not follow that all norms commanding their realization permit exceptions. Even more so, it is not the case that the subject in virtue of his decision can institute which norm binds him in a given situation. Precisely due to the way pre-moral goods are linked with the good of the person, one can discover a certain hierarchy of these goods, which is stable to the extent that human nature is stable. Hence, the effective affirmation of the person-object demands from the subject a careful discernment of the rank of the pre-moral goods at hand. The respect for the goods that are essentially linked with the good and with development of the human person manifests the degree in which the attitude of the subject is actually an attitude of love.

* See footnote, p. 41.

† The encyclical *Humanae Vitae* (see especially par. 12) emphasizes the interconnection between these two orders that is essential for the meaning of conjugal intercourse. The discussion evoked by the encyclical proves how difficult it is to grasp this particular twofold meaning of the conjugal act, which is based on a certain vision of the human person and of conjugal love—a vision identical in its fundamental features in both the encyclical and *Love and Responsibility*. Without going into the details of this discussion, it is worthwhile to underscore the structural difference between both of these orders, as communicated by

It is impossible to separate these two orders; one depends on the other, and particularly the relation to reproduction (*procreatio*) conditions the realization of love. In the animal world there is only reproduction, which is realized by way of instinct. There are no persons there, hence there is neither the possibility for nor the demands of the personalistic norm proclaiming love. But in the world of persons instinct alone does not solve anything, and the sexual drive, so to speak, enters the gates of consciousness and the will, providing not only the conditions of fertility but at the same time the specific "material" for love. If the issue is to be solved on a truly human level, on a personal level, one cannot be realized without the other. Both, i.e., procreation (reproduction) as well as love, are realized on the basis of the conscious choice of

---

Karol Wojtyła: the order of nature (here understood as a group of relatively autonomous dynamisms dwelling in man and serving the transmission of life) tends toward reproduction, whereas the personal order is expressed in the love of persons. The order of nature contains the relation to the given effect of the conjugal act (the birth of man), whereas the point in the personal order is directly and above all the expression of love by a person to another person. However, because the body belongs integrally to the human person ("by touching your hand, I touch you"), and because through it the person expresses his attitude toward other people, the way of manifesting love must therefore respect this "interior logic" by which nature governs itself in man. For precisely the capacity for introducing the order of nature into the framework of the personal order is a property of the human person—as Karol Wojtyła shows in *Love and Responsibility*, and even more clearly in his study *Person and Act* (see especially the part *Integration of the Person in the Act*). The moral right to manipulate nature arbitrarily does not by any means follow from the superiority of the personal order; quite the contrary, observing nature's basic laws constitutes an indispensable condition for the possibility of a true and full realization of the personal order. (See supra and also the separate articles of the author: "Zagadnienie katolickiej etyki seksualnej," *Roczniki Filozoficzne* 13, fasc. 2 [1965], 5–25; and "Osoba ludzka a prawo naturalne" [The Human Person and the Natural Law], *Roczniki Filozoficzne* 18, fasc. 2 [1970], 53–59.)

The consequence of such anthropological presuppositions in relation to conjugal ethics is, among others, a negative assessment—contained in both *Love and Responsibility* and *Humanae Vitae*, and causing particularly sharp controversies—of all methods for regulating conceptions that attempt to separate the two orders from each other and to realize interpersonal love through distorting that logic of nature.

The difference between the order of nature and the order of the person indicated by the author recalls the differentiation of acts into "acts of fulfillment" (*Erfüllungshandlungen*) and "acts of expression" (*Ausdruckshandlungen*) that is known in more recent theological and moral literature. However, contemporary authors are willing to treat both of these categories separately, whereas according to the conception of Karol Wojtyła—especially in relation to conjugal love—one should rather speak of two "dimensions" of an act, namely the "effective" (proper to the order of nature) and the "expressive" (specifically personal). Both dimensions should be, as has been mentioned, in an appropriate way harmonized with each other.

persons. When a man and a woman within marriage consciously and freely choose sexual intercourse, then together with it they choose at the same time the possibility of procreation; they choose to participate in creating (to apply the proper meaning of *procreatio*). Only then do they place their sexual intercourse within marriage on the truly personal level, when they consciously unite in their conduct the one and the other.*

The problem of parenthood arises precisely here. Nature tends only to reproduction (let us add that the very word "nature" comes from the verb *nascor*: to be born, hence nature = what is determined by the very fact of birth). Reproduction is connected with biological fertility, by the power of which the mature individuals of a given species become parents by bringing into the world their offspring, i.e., new individuals of that species. The case is similar within the species *Homo sapiens*. Man, however, is a person, and, therefore, a simple natural fact of becoming a father or a mother possesses a deeper meaning: not only "biological," but also personal. This fact finds—should find—its thorough reflection in the "interiority" of the person. This reflection is contained precisely in the content of the concept of "parenthood" (*rodzicielstwo*). For human parenthood presupposes the whole process of consciousness and of the choice of the will linked with marriage, and in particular with the conjugal intercourse of persons. And because conjugal intercourse is—and should be—a realization of love, and on the personal level at that, then precisely in love we must look for the proper place for parenthood. The sexual intercourse of a man and a woman in marriage possesses its full value of a personal union only when it contains the conscious acceptance of the possibility of parenthood. This is a plain result of the synthesis of the two orders: the order of nature and the order of the person. A man and a woman in conjugal intercourse do not remain only and exclusively in a reciprocal relation

---

* "Of course, it is impossible to accept that a man and a woman (except for cases of acquired or innate infertility) join themselves in marriage first and foremost for the purpose of reciprocal complementing (*uzupełnić się*) or supplementing each other (*mutuum adiutorium*), for this is not in accordance with the plan of the Creator both in the order of nature, i.e., in the light of reason, and in the light of Revelation and the order of Grace." (K. Wojtyła, "Zagadnienie katolickiej etyki seksualnej," *Roczniki Filozoficzne* 13, fasc. 2 [1965], 16.)

to each other, but, as a matter of fact, they remain in relation to the new person who can be created (*procreatio*) thanks precisely to their union.*

What must be particularly emphasized here is the word "can," for it indicates the potential character of this new relation. The conjugal act of both persons "can" give new life to a new person. So, when a man and a woman who are capable of procreation unite themselves in conjugal intercourse, the following state of consciousness and of the will must accompany their union: "I can be a father," "I can be a mother." Without this their reciprocal relation is not interiorly justified, but, in fact, unjust. Reciprocal spousal love demands the union of persons. However, the very union of persons is something different from the persons' union in sexual intercourse. The latter rises to the personal level only when it is accompanied in consciousness and the will by this "I can be a mother," "I can be a father." This moment is so important, so decisive, that without it we cannot speak about the realization of the personal order in conjugal intercourse of a man and a woman. What would remain in place of the truly personal union is only a sexual coming together that is not fully-mature personally. If we wish to be thorough and consistent to the end, this coming together would be based merely on the value of *sexus*, and not on the affirmation of the value of the person. For the affirmation of the value of the person may not be separated in both, in a woman and a man, from this state of consciousness and the will: "I can be a mother," "I can be a father."

If this attitude is missing, then their sexual intercourse does not find fully objective justification with regard to themselves (not only in the eyes of a third person who considers this situation theoretically and abstractly). If the potential parental moment is positively excluded from the conjugal act, the reciprocal configuration of the persons partaking in this act is thereby changed. This change progresses from a

---

* "*Parenthood is an interior fact* in husband and wife as father and mother, who begin to take part in a new property and a new state once their child is conceived and born" [emphasis original]. (K. Wojtyła, "Rodzicielstwo jako '*communio personarum*'" ["Parenthood as '*Communio Personarum*'"], *Ateneum Kapłańskie* 67, vol. 84 [1975], 17.) "Children enter into the conjugal community of husband and wife also in order to confirm, strengthen, and deepen this community. Thus, their own inter-personal participation, *communio personarum*, is here enriched" (ibid., 21).

union in love to a shared or, rather, merely mutual "use."* Although this change happens inevitably, it possesses different varieties and shades. We will attempt to penetrate them later in this chapter, for this problem requires a more detailed analysis. At any rate, we must indicate that this change of configuration, in which the persons Y and X remain in relation to each other once the parental moment is excluded *in potentia* from their conjugal intercourse, shifts their reciprocal relation beyond the sphere of objective demands of the personalistic norm. In the conjugal act in which a man and a woman completely cancel this "I can be a father," "I can be a mother," when they positively exclude parenthood, a danger occurs that—objectively speaking—nothing else remains in this act but the use, the object of which, of course, is a person for another person.

This formulation possesses an overtone that can evoke a great deal of resistance, both in theory and in practice. Therefore, it is necessary to recall all that was an object of our reflections, especially in chapter I. The proper relation of the person to the sexual drive lies in this: on the one hand, to employ the drive consciously in the direction of its natural finality, and, on the other hand, to resist it inasmuch as its consequence was to place the relation of the persons Y and X below the level of love, since in love the value of the person is reciprocally affirmed in the union possessing a truly personal character. The sexual (conjugal) act has this character; it is a truly personal union insofar as a certain parental readiness is not positively excluded from it. This results from a conscious relation to the drive: to master the sexual drive means precisely to accept its finality in the conjugal act.

At this point a thought can arise that this position submits the man-person to "nature," when, after all, in so many fields man wins a victory over nature and masters it. This is an ostensible argument, for everywhere man masters nature by adapting to its immanent dynamic.[17]

---

* The relation of the Creator to this kind of behavior imposes itself on reason in an unequivocal way, just as we can foresee without difficulties the reaction of a father upon seeing that the child to whom he gave, e.g., a slice of bread with jam, eats only the jam and throws the bread away. If the child must not reach only for what brings a pleasant *lived-experience* when it is connected with what serves *life*, how much less proper it is for adults to do so!

There is no victory over nature in the sense of violating it. Mastery of nature can result only from a thorough knowledge of its finality and the regularity that governs it. Man masters nature by the fact of ever more fully taking advantage of the possibilities hidden in it. The application to our problem seems relatively clear, and we will penetrate it in more detail later in this chapter. Concerning the sexual drive, man also cannot win a victory over "nature" by violating this nature, but only through adapting to its immanent finality thanks to understanding the laws that govern that drive and taking advantage of the possibilities hidden in it. Hence proceeds the passage into love. Since sexual intercourse is based on the drive and draws the other person into the totality of the fact and lived-experience, then the relation to that person regarding his moral value is formed indirectly through the way of engaging the drive in sexual intercourse. Man can remain faithful to the person in the order of love proper to him insofar as he is faithful to nature. When he violates nature, he also "violates" the person by making him an object of use instead of an object of love.[18]

Parental readiness in the conjugal act guards love and is an indispensable condition of a truly personal union. The union of persons in love does not have to be realized through sexual intercourse. However, when it is realized this way, then the personalistic value of sexual intercourse cannot be protected without parental readiness. Thanks to it, both of the united persons act in conformity with the interior logic of love; they respect the interior dynamic of love and open themselves to the new good, which in this case is an expression of the creative power of love. Parental readiness serves here the purpose of breaking bilateral egoism (or at least, due to a consent of one person, unilateral egoism), behind which always hides the use of the person.

It is evident that all this is based on the presupposition according to which there is a close link between the order of nature and the person as well as the realization of human personhood. We must admit that it is difficult for man to understand and acknowledge the order of nature as a certain "abstract magnitude" (ordinarily it is then confused with the "biological order," and precisely thereby annihilated).* It is much easier

---

* See footnote, p. 41.

to comprehend the power of the order of nature, which is constitutive for morality, and thus also for the realization of human personhood, inasmuch as behind this order one perceives the personal authority of the Creator. Hence, the totality of our reflections bears the title "Justice with Respect to the Creator." This concept will be later analyzed separately.

In practice the problem is not that easy since love in connection with sexual intercourse, and in general in connection with all the interactions between persons of different sex, very easily undergoes subjectivization. As a result, what is taken for love is the ephemeral amorous (erotic) lived-experience alone. The reasoning then is as follows: there is no love without amorous lived-experiences. This reasoning is not totally erroneous; it is only incomplete. For when we grasp the problem integrally, it must be said that there is no love without the reciprocal affirmation of the value of the person, since the personal union of a man and a woman is based on it.[19] Amorous lived-experiences serve this union (i.e., love) insofar as they do not contradict the value of the person. Thus, not all amorous (erotic) lived-experiences truly serve the union of the persons Y and X in love. Certainly, the lived-experiences that, objectively speaking, in some way cancel the value of the person do not serve it. But precisely the erotic lived-experiences connected with sexual intercourse of a man and a woman that positively exclude the parental moment ("I can be a father," "I can be a mother") cancel the value of the person. For the value of the person is manifested, on the one hand, in action that is fully conscious and fully harmonized with the objective finality of the world (the "order of nature"), and, on the other hand, by excluding the person from any "use." A thorough contradiction exists between "to love" and "to use" in relation to the person.

At this point, it is beneficial to refer to the analysis of shame and to the phenomenon (the law) of the absorption of sexual shame by love, which were discussed in the previous chapter. In conjugal intercourse both shame and the process of its correct absorption by love are linked to letting the readiness for parenthood speak, this "I can be a mother," "I can be a father." In the case of a positive, tendentious exclusion of this eventuality, sexual intercourse acquires the characteristics of shamelessness. The circumstance that this intercourse is realized within a legitimate marriage does not usually efface the characteristics of shamelessness in the awareness of people who exclude the possibility of parenthood in this way. It is another matter that this awareness does not arise in all persons equally. It may seem sometimes that in women it arises more easily than in men. On the other hand, it must be underscored that conjugal shame (which constitutes the foundation of conjugal chastity) encounters strong resistance in the consciousness of both a man and a woman. This resistance proceeds from the fear of parenthood, of motherhood and fatherhood. A man and a woman "are afraid of a child," as a child is not only a joy, but also a burden, which cannot be denied in any way. However, when the fear of a child is excessive, it paralyzes love, and directly contributes to the suppression of the reaction of shame. A correct solution worthy of persons is by way of abstinence (*wstrzemięźliwość*), but this requires a mastery of erotic lived-experiences. It also requires a thorough culture of the person and the "culture of loving." Authentic conjugal abstinence grows out of shame, which reacts negatively to every manifestation of "using" the person. On the other hand, however, the more authentic abstinence exists, and together with it the culture of the person and the "culture of loving," the stronger the reaction of shame turns out to be.

This is a natural reaction, an elementary factor of natural morality. The following sentences from Gandhi's *Autobiography* can attest to this:[20]

> In my opinion the statement that the sexual act is an unprompted activity similar to sleeping or satisfying hunger is a summit of ignorance. The existence of the world depends on the act of reproduction, and due to the fact that the world is a realm governed by God and constitutes a reflection of his power, the act of reproduction should come under the control that has the development of life on earth as its end. Whoever understands this will strive by all means to master his senses and will arm himself with knowledge, which is indispensable for the physical and spiritual flourishing of his progeny, and he will bestow the fruits of this knowledge on posterity and for its benefit.

Elsewhere in his *Autobiography*, Gandhi admits that twice in his life he yielded to propaganda recommending artificial means in order to exclude the possibility of conception. However, he reached a conviction that "one must rather act with the help of interior impulses, self-mastery or self-control ( . . . )." Let us add that this is the only solution to the problem of conscious parenthood, conscious fatherhood and conscious motherhood, on the level worthy of persons. When solving this problem, however, one cannot ignore the fundamental fact that man, a woman and a man, is a person.

In connection with all the reflections devoted to reproduction and parenthood, two concepts demand a separate and detailed analysis. The first one is "parenthood *in potentia*," and the second one is the "positive exclusion of procreation." They are so closely linked that without understanding the first one, it is impossible to understand the second.

1) When writing about the moral rectitude of sexual intercourse in marriage we constantly emphasize that it depends on including in the consciousness and will of a man and a woman the readiness for parenthood—"I can be a father," "I can be a mother"—without which the conjugal act itself of persons unaffected by innate or acquired infertility loses the value of a union in love, and becomes merely a mutual sexual use. Sexual intercourse of a man and a woman entails the possibility of biological conception and procreation; this is a natural effect of the conjugal act. This effect, however, does not always have to occur. It depends on a whole nexus of conditions, which man can recognize, and with which he can comply in his conduct. We have no basis to identify each act of sexual intercourse with the "necessity" of conception. The biological laws established even with scientific accuracy are always based on incomplete induction, and they do not exclude a certain contingency regarding the connection between one specific act of sexual intercourse of a given couple and biological conception. Hence, the spouses must not be required to positively will procreation in every act of intercourse. In connection with this, the following position in ethics would be excessive: the conjugal act is permissible and honorable only on condition that X and Y want progeny by it. This position would be incompatible with the order of nature, which expresses itself precisely in a certain contingency with regard to the connection of sexual intercourse with reproduction for particular married couples. Of course, it is right to strive for some mastery of this contingency and for grasping with the greatest certainty the connection between a given conjugal act and the possibility of conception—this striving constitutes the very core of "conscious motherhood" properly understood.

Returning once more to the aforementioned position that the conjugal act is permissible and honorable only on condition that X and Y intend to bring about procreation by it, we must observe that this position may contain in itself concealed utilitarianism (the person as a means to an end—which has been already discussed in chapter I), but then this would collide with the personalistic norm. Conjugal intercourse proceeds and should proceed from reciprocal spousal love. It is needed for love, and not only for procreation. *Marriage is an institution of love, and not only of fertility.* By itself conjugal intercourse is an interpersonal relation, is an act of spousal love, and therefore the intention and attention should be directed toward the other person, toward the person's true good. It is not proper to direct this intention and attention toward the possible (*in potentia*) consequence of the act, especially if this means turning attention and intention away from the spouse. Therefore, certainly the point is not the attitude: "We perform this act exclusively in order to be parents." The following attitude is perfectly sufficient: "By performing this act we know that we can become a father and a mother, and we are ready for it." Only this attitude is in conformity with love and enables its shared lived-experience. Becoming a mother and a father is accomplished in virtue of the conjugal act, which itself should be an act of love, an act of uniting persons, and not merely a "tool" or a "means" of procreation.

2) However, if some overemphasis on the intention of procreation itself seems to clash with the proper character of conjugal intercourse, what clashes with it all the more is the *positive* exclusion of procreation (or rather of the possibility of procreation). A certain overemphasis on the intention of procreation is perfectly understandable in marriages that remained childless for a long time. There, it does not constitute a distortion of the act of love, but rather merely manifests the natural connection of love with parenthood. However, the positive exclusion of the possibility of conception directly deprives conjugal intercourse of this potential parental character, which fully justifies this intercourse above all with respect to the very persons partaking in it, and which makes them consider it modest and chaste. When a man and a woman who have conjugal relations together positively exclude the possibility of fatherhood and motherhood, then *eo ipso* the intention of each of them turns away from the person and is directed toward the use alone:

the "person co-creating love" disappears and what remains is a "partner of an erotic lived-experience." And this most thoroughly contradicts the proper orientation of the act of love. The attention and intention in connection with this act should be directed to the very person, the will should be concerned with his good, and the affection should be full of affirmation of his proper value. By positively excluding the possibility of procreation in conjugal intercourse, a man and a woman inevitably shift the whole lived-experience toward sexual pleasure alone. Then the content of the lived-experience becomes the "using," whereas it should be precisely the "loving," while the using (in the second meaning of the verb "to use") should merely accompany the conjugal act.

By the very fact of positively excluding parental possibilities from conjugal intercourse the intention is directed toward "use" alone. It is enough to realize that what we call here the "positive exclusion" of the possibility of procreation consists simply in an exclusion of this possibility in an artificial way. Man as a rational being can direct his conjugal life in such a way that it does not cause procreation. He can do so by conforming to the periods of the woman's fertility and infertility, that is, by having intercourse during the infertile periods and abstaining from intercourse during fertile periods. Procreation is then excluded in a natural way. A man and a woman employ no "artificial" procedure or treatment for the purpose of avoiding conception. They only conform to the very regularity of nature, to the order that governs it—the fertility cycle in the woman is an element of this order. Procreation is naturally enabled in the period of fertility and naturally excluded in the period of infertility. However, the positive exclusion of procreation by man acting against the order and regularity of nature is another matter. It is necessary to speak about the positive exclusion of procreation when a man and a woman (the man himself with the woman's approval, or the woman herself with the man's approval) employ "artificial" procedures or treatments that aim at preventing procreation. Because these means are artificial, this way of excluding procreation contradicts the "naturalness" of conjugal intercourse, which cannot be admitted about the exclusion of procreation when it results from conforming to the periods of fertility and infertility. That is fundamentally "in accordance with nature." But does this not in itself already constitute the "positive" exclusion of procreation, which possesses precisely a negative moral qualification? In order to answer this, it is necessary to consider quite thoroughly from an ethical perspective the problem of so-called periodical abstinence. We shall do this in the next section.

Drawing from all that we have concluded in the most recent analysis, we must state that a close connection occurs between natural reproduction and the culture of parenthood in conjugal life. Sexual intercourse of the spouses carries with itself the possibility of procreation, and therefore their love in this act of intercourse demands the inclusion of the possibility of parenthood, of motherhood and fatherhood. The positive exclusion of this possibility contradicts not only the order of nature, but at the same time love itself—the union of a woman and a man on a truly personal level. For this exclusion makes sexual "use" itself the only content of the conjugal act. It must be emphasized that only the positive exclusion of the possibility of procreation evokes such a consequence. For as long as a man and a woman in marriage, having sexual relations together, do not employ any procedures and artificial means that aim at excluding procreation *in potentia*, they retain in their consciousness and will this "I can be a father," "I can be a mother." It is enough that they are ready to accept the fact of conception, even if they "do not wish" it in a particular case. It is not necessary for them to will procreation explicitly. They can also have conjugal relations despite permanent or periodic infertility. For infertility itself does not exclude this interior basis of "I can," i.e., "I am ready" to accept the fact of conception, should it occur. It is another matter when conception does not occur because it is excluded by nature. After all, even old spouses who physically are unable to become parents have relations—in this case procreation is excluded by nature. However, leaving aside such circumstances, which man cannot influence with his will, it must be accepted that the interior attitude indicated above justifies sexual intercourse of a man and a woman in marriage (justifies, i.e., "makes just"), justifying it with respect to themselves reciprocally and with respect to God the Creator. The proper greatness of the human person is expressed in the fact that sexual life needs such a thorough justification. It cannot be otherwise. Man must reconcile himself to his natural greatness. But precisely when he so deeply enters into the order of nature, when he immerses himself, as it were, in the vehement processes of nature, he cannot forget that he is a person. Instinct alone will not solve anything in him, for everything appeals to his "interiority," to reason and responsibility. What appeals to him in a particular way is this love that stands at the cradle of the coming to be of human kind. Responsibility for love—to which we paid particular attention in these reflections—is bound most closely with responsibility for procreation. Therefore, by no means can love be separated from parenthood, the readiness for which constitutes a necessary condition of love.

## Periodic abstinence: The method and interpretation

The previous reflections lead to the conclusion that sexual intercourse of a man and a woman in marriage has the value of love, i.e., of a truly personal union, only when both of them do not positively exclude the possibility of procreation, when in their consciousness and will this intercourse is accompanied by this "I can be a father," "I can be a mother." If this is missing, then a man and a woman should refrain from intercourse. Thus, they ought to refrain from it when they "cannot," "do not want to," or "should not" be a father and a mother. Various situations exist that fit the categories indicated by the quotation marks. However, whenever it is proper for a man and a woman to refrain from conjugal intercourse and from the amorous lived-experiences of a sensory-sexual character that accompany this intercourse, abstinence (*wstrzemięźliwość*) must come to light, for it conditions love, i.e., the reciprocal relation between a man and a woman (especially of a man toward a woman) demanded by genuine affirmation of the value of the person. Let us recall that the problems of abstinence were discussed in the previous chapter in relation to the virtue of temperance (*temperantia*). This virtue is difficult in its own way, for it requires one to master the movements of sensuality, which reveal a powerful drive, and also at times the affective sensibility, which remains in close connection with the very love of a man and a woman, as we saw in the analysis of this love.

Conjugal abstinence is more difficult than abstinence outside of marriage because the spouses get used to sexual intercourse in accordance with the nature of the state, which they have consciously chosen.

From the moment they begin conjugal life together, a wont and a constant inclination are created; a reciprocal demand for intercourse arises. This demand (*zapotrzebowanie*) is a normal manifestation of love, not only in the sensory-sexual sense, but also in the personal sense. A man and a woman in marriage belong to each other in a particular way—they are "one flesh" (Gen 2:24), and the reciprocal demand of one person for another is expressed also in the need for sexual intercourse. With regard to this, refraining from intercourse must encounter certain resistance and difficulties. On the other hand, without refraining from conjugal intercourse they can cause an excessive increase of their family in number. This problem is extraordinarily relevant. For against the background of the prevailing relations nowadays, we observe some crisis of the family in the traditional sense—the numerous family, supported above all by a job held by the father and sustained interiorly by the mother—the heart of the family. The necessity or even the very possibility of professional jobs held by married women seems to be a main symptom of this crisis, a symptom that is of course not isolated from others, since many factors of various natures contribute to this situation.

Leaving aside a more extensive discussion of this problem—a problem distinct from the main theme of our book, even though undoubtedly closely related to this theme—it is necessary to indicate that precisely with respect to the aforementioned circumstances the demand to limit children is at times put forth with great insistence. As we mentioned in chapter I, this demand is connected with the name of Thomas Malthus, the author of the book *An Essay on the Principle of Population*. Hence we speak of Malthusianism, according to which economic reasons argue for the necessity of limiting births because the means of subsistence grow with arithmetic progression, and, therefore, do not keep up with population growth, which progresses geometrically.* The view thus formulated found favorable conditions in a mentality molded by sensualist empiricism and the utilitarianism linked to it, and on this soil bore fruit in the form of so-called neo-Malthusianism. From chapter I (the

---

* Of course, this is not entirely precise, since when a new man is born, not only a new "stomach to fill" is born, but also a new worker and sometimes an inventor and creator of devices that multiply the efficiency of labor.

section "Critique of utilitarianism") we know the view according to which the task of man's reason is to calculate for man's entire life the maximum of pleasure with the minimum of pain, for this is synonymous with "happiness" superficially understood. Since sexual intercourse brings to a man and a woman such a great deal of pleasure, or even delight, then it is necessary to find means so that they do not have to refrain from it also when they do not want to bear offspring, when they "cannot" be a father and a mother (in the meaning described above). Here we stand at the origin of many neo-Malthusian "methods." For human reason, by being aware of the whole process of sexual intercourse and the reproduction connected with it, can in fact find various means that positively exclude procreation. Neo-Malthusianism indicates above all the means that in some way violate the normal, "natural" course of the whole process of sexual intercourse between a man and a woman.

Clearly, in that case we find ourselves in conflict with the principle introduced in the previous section of this chapter ("Reproduction and parenthood"). Sexual intercourse of a man and a woman in marriage remains on the level of a personal union in love only on the condition that they do not positively exclude the possibility of procreation and parenthood. When this "I can be a father," "I can be a mother" is positively excluded in the consciousness and will of a man and a woman, then what is left (objectively speaking) in the conjugal act is sexual use alone. In that case, a person (e.g., X) becomes an object of use for another person (Y), which contradicts the personalistic norm. Man possesses reason not first and foremost so that he can calculate the maximum of pleasure in his life, but above all so that he can know the objective truth, ground the principles possessing the absolute meaning (norms) in that truth, and in turn live by them. Then he lives in a way worthy of who he is—he lives in an "honorable" way.* Human morality cannot be based on utility alone, but must extend to honorableness (*godziwość*). And honorableness demands the supra-utilitarian value of the person to be acknowledged: right here "honorableness" is most clearly against "utility" itself. Especially in the sexual sphere, it is not enough to state that a given way of conduct is "useful," but it is

---

* See footnote †, p. 183.

necessary to state whether it is "honorable." However, if we are to remain consistently on the ground of honorableness and of the personalistic norm connected with it, then the only "method" of regulating conceptions in conjugal intercourse can be abstinence (*wstrzemięźliwość*). Whoever does not want the effect, avoids the cause. Since the cause of conception in the biological sense is sexual intercourse of the spouses, if they exclude conception, they should also exclude intercourse itself; they should refrain from it. The principle of conjugal abstinence under the ethical aspect is clear. Now, the point is the problem of so-called periodic abstinence.[21]

It is generally known that the biological fertility of a woman is periodic. By nature the periods of infertility that occur in her can be relatively easily discerned. Difficulties arise in the case of applying general rules to particular women. This, however, is a separate issue, for at this point we are interested in the purely ethical problem: if a woman and a man conform their conjugal abstinence to the aforementioned periods of infertility, so that they have conjugal relations precisely when they foresee on the basis of biological laws that they will not become parents, can it be then stated that they bring into their conjugal intercourse parental readiness, precisely this "I can be a father," "I can be a mother"? After all, they have conjugal relations precisely with the thought of not becoming a father and a mother, and therefore they choose the period of presumed infertility in a woman. Do they not then "positively" exclude the possibility of procreation? Why does the natural method in the moral aspect differ from artificial methods since all aim at the same end: to exclude procreation in conjugal life?

In order to answer this question, it is necessary above all to be freed from many associations that accompany the expression "method." When speaking of the natural method, the same point of view is often applied to it as to the "artificial methods," thus, deriving it from utilitarian presuppositions. In this perspective, the natural method would also be merely one of the means aiming at securing maximum pleasure, but using a different way than the artificial methods. Here lies the fundamental error. It turns out that it is not sufficient in this case to speak of a method, but it is absolutely necessary to attach its appropriate interpretation. Only then can we answer the questions posed above. And so, periodic abstinence as a way of controlling conceptions (1) is permissible on the grounds that it will respect the demands of the personalistic norm, and (2) its permissibility presupposes certain qualifications.

Regarding the first point (1), the demands of the personalistic norm, as has been stated previously, go hand in hand with preserving the order of nature in conjugal intercourse. As opposed to artificial methods, the natural method in striving to regulate conceptions takes advantage of the circumstances in which biological conception cannot naturally occur. Hence, the very "naturalness" of conjugal intercourse is not violated, whereas artificial methods violate the very "naturalness" of intercourse. In the former case, infertility is derived from the very principles of fertility; in the latter case it is imposed against nature.* Let us add that this issue is closely linked to the problem of justice with respect to the Creator (this problem will be further analyzed in order to explicate its personalistic sense). This personalistic asset of periodic abstinence as a method of regulating conceptions is manifested not so much in preserving the "naturalness" of intercourse, but in the fact that its basis in the will of the involved persons must be an appropriately mature virtue. Precisely here the significance of interpretation is made visible: the utilitarian interpretation distorts the essence of what we call the "natural method." For the essence of this method is its reliance on abstinence as a virtue, which—as has been demonstrated in the previous chapter—is very closely connected with love of the person.

The essence of abstinence as a virtue is linked to the conviction that the love of a man and a woman loses nothing by temporarily relinquishing amorous lived-experiences; on the contrary, it gains: the union of persons becomes more profound, grounded fundamentally on affirmation of the value of the person, and not merely on sexual attachment. Abstinence as a virtue cannot be comprehended as a "contraceptive." The spouses who practice it are ready to refrain from sexual intercourse also from other motives (e.g., religious ones), and not only for the purpose of avoiding offspring. Self-interested, "calculated" abstinence raises

---

* It is worthwhile to recall that nature here is not understood biologistically. Thus, the point here is above all that the initiative of human persons falls within the framework of the "initiative" whose expression is the creative order established by God. The initiative of people "technically frustrating" conjugal intercourse does not, quite clearly at that, fall within that framework.

doubts. Just like any other virtue, it should be disinterested, concentrated on "honorableness" itself and not only on "utility." Without this it will find no place in the true love of persons. As long as it is not a virtue, abstinence represents an "alien being" to love. The love of a man and a woman must reach maturity with respect to abstinence, and abstinence must acquire for them a constructive meaning as a love-forming factor. Only then does the "natural method" find justification in persons, for its secret lies in practicing virtue; "technique" alone solves nothing here.

We have indicated above (in the second point) that the natural method can be permitted only with certain qualifications. What we mean here is the relation to parenthood. If abstinence is to be a virtue and not merely a "method" in the utilitarian sense, it cannot contribute to the destruction of parental readiness itself in a man and a woman who as spouses have conjugal relations. For this "I can be a father," "I can be a mother" justifies the fact of conjugal intercourse, raising it to the level of a true union of persons. Therefore, we cannot speak of abstinence as a virtue when the spouses take advantage of the periods of biological infertility only for the purpose of not having children at all, when for the sake of convenience they have intercourse only and exclusively in these periods. This would amount to using the "natural method" against nature—both the objective order of nature and the very essence of love oppose positing the matter this way.[*]

Therefore, if we can treat periodic abstinence as a "method" in this case, we can do so only and exclusively as a method of regulating conceptions, and not as a method of avoiding a family. Without understanding the essence of the family there is no way of grasping the ethical rectitude of this problem. The institution of the family is closely connected with the parenthood of a man and a woman who have conjugal relations. The family is a natural community, which in its being and acting remains directly dependent on parents. Parents create the family as a complement and expansion (*dopełnienie i rozszerzenie*) of their love. To create a family means to create a community, as by nature

---

[*] This concerns conduct deprived of a sufficient moral rationale, that is, without objectively important reasons dictated by the dignity of the person. This condition is worthy of being underscored, for it protects against a hasty conclusion that conjugal intercourse of infertile persons cannot be virtuous.

the family is a community—indeed a society, for if it is not a society, it is not itself. But in order to be a society, the family needs a certain size. This is manifested the most with regard to the education of children. For the family is an educational institution within which a new man forms his personhood.[22] In order to form this personhood correctly, it is of utmost importance for him not to be alone but to dwell in a natural society. It is said sometimes that "it is easier to raise a few children rather than an only child," and also that "two children are not yet a community but two only ones." In education the parents possess a leading role. However, under their parents' guidance the children educate themselves, especially by the fact that they dwell and develop within a community of children, a cluster of siblings.

This moment must be taken into account above all with regard to the regulation of conceptions. Every society—the state, the nation, in which the family happens to exist—should take care so that the family can truly be a community. At the same time, the parents themselves should take care that by limiting conceptions they do not harm their family and society, which, after all, also has an interest in an appropriate family size. A minimalistic attitude of the spouses, the principle of convenient life, must harm morally both their family and the whole society. In any case, limiting conceptions in conjugal life cannot be equivalent to canceling the parental attitude. From the viewpoint of the family, periodic abstinence as a method of regulating conceptions is permissible insofar as it does not clash with a genuine parental attitude.

Nonetheless, circumstances occur in which precisely this attitude demands a relinquishment of parenthood, and a further increase of the family would be incompatible with that attitude. In that case, moved by true concern for the good of their family and by a full sense of responsibility for the procreation, support, and education of their children, a man and a woman limit their conjugal intercourse; they refrain from it in the periods when it could bring a new conception that would be inadvisable in the concrete conditions in which the marriage and family exist.*

---

* "Avoiding parenthood in a concrete fact of intercourse cannot be equivalent with avoiding or even canceling parenthood in the perspective of the whole marriage. This should be above all taken into consideration" (K. Wojtyła, *Miłość i odpowiedzialność* [*Love and Responsibility*], 1st edition [Lublin, 1960], 185).

Parental readiness is also expressed in the fact that the spouses do not attempt to avoid conception at any price, but they are ready to accept it if it takes place contrary to expectations. This readiness of "I can be a father," "I can be a mother" permeates their consciousness and will even when they do not wish for conception, when they decide to have intercourse precisely in the period in which it is expected that conception will not occur. This readiness within the scope of a concrete conjugal act in connection with the general (i.e., within the scope of the whole marriage) parental attitude determines the moral value of the "method" of periodic abstinence. Here we cannot speak of some mendacity, a falsification of the true intention. One cannot claim that a man and a woman do not want to be a father and a mother in opposition to the Creator, since they do not do anything to positively exclude this possibility on their part (and it is evident that they could do that). In this case they do not employ any means aimed at a given end, namely those that explicitly clash with the parental attitude, thereby depriving conjugal intercourse of the value of love, and leaving only the value of "use."

# Part Two

# Vocation

## *The concept of "justice with respect to the Creator"*

Our whole reflection so far has remained on the plane of the personalistic norm. By stating that the person cannot be an object of use, but only an object of love (hence the commandment to love), the personalistic norm indicates what is due to the person solely on account of his being a person. In this way love presupposes justice. A need exists to justify the whole conduct of one person with respect to another person in the sexual sphere, a need to justify various manifestations of sexual life with respect to the human person. This has been the main theme of our reflections thus far. Concerning them, we could speak of justice in the horizontal direction. But a separate problem remains: justice in the vertical direction—a need to justify all conduct in the sexual sphere with respect to God. We have already mentioned this in the first part of this chapter in the section "The value of the institution." The point now is to confirm and expand even more on this aspect of the whole problem.

It is generally held that justice is a cardinal and fundamental virtue, for without it the ordered coexistence and relationships of persons is impossible. By speaking about justice with respect to God we state that he is a Personal Being, with whom man also should have some sort of relationship. Clearly, this position presumes, on the one hand, the knowledge and understanding of God's rights, and, on the other hand, of man's obligations. These rights and obligations proceed above all from the fact that God is the Creator and man a creature. Faith based on Revelation unveils still further spheres of dependence between man and God: God is the redeemer of man and his sanctifier through grace. Revelation allows us to know the work of redemption and sanctification, through which it is manifested most fully that God relates to man as a person to another person, that his relation to man is "loving." In the reciprocal relation of God and man, the "personalistic norm" has in a sense its fullest *raison d'être*, there lies its first source. At this point, it is worthwhile to recall the commandment to love in its full reading: "You shall love the Lord, your God, with all your heart, with all your soul, with all your strength, and with all your mind, and your neighbor as yourself."[23] However, it is known that it is precisely justice that stands at the basis of this norm (which instructs us to love the person). Hence, it follows that the more fully man knows the love of God toward himself, the more fully he also comprehends the rights that God has with regard to his person and his love. So, he sees how far-reaching human obligations are in relation to God and tries to realize them. True religion (*religijność*) consists in justice thus understood with respect to God—according to St. Thomas the virtue of religion[24] constitutes *pars potentialis iustitiae*.[25]

The point of departure for this justice is the fact of creation. God is the Creator, which means that all beings in the universe, all creatures and among them man in particular, owe their existence to him. God is not only the Creator, i.e., the unceasing Giver of existence, but the very essences of individual creatures come from him as well; they constitute a reflection of the eternal thought and plan of God. In this way, the whole order of nature has its source in God, for this order is based directly on the essences (i.e., natures) of beings existing in the world; hence proceed all dependencies, relations, and connections between them. In the world of beings inferior to man, irrational beings, this order of nature is realized by nature itself, by way of instinct, and eventually with the contribution of sensory cognition (the animal world). In the human world, the order of nature must be realized differently, namely on the basis of understanding it and acknowledging it rationally. Now, this understanding and rational acknowledgment of the order of nature is at the same time the acknowledgment of the Creator's rights. That is then the basis of the elementary justice of man with respect to God. With respect to God the Creator, man is just by acknowledging the order of nature and preserving it in his action.

However, the point is not simply a mere preservation of the objective order of nature. By knowing it with reason and preserving it in his actions, man becomes a partaker of God's thought, *particeps Creatoris*; he has a share in the law which God eternally imparted to the world by creating it.[26] So this is an end for itself: the value of man, of a rational being, is most manifested by the fact that he is *particeps Creatoris*, that he participates in the thought of God, in his law. Justice with respect to the Creator, thoroughly understood, consists in this. With respect to the Creator, the rational creature, man, is just by striving in his action toward precisely this human value, by conducting himself as *particeps Creatoris*. This position is contradicted by so-called autonomism: man manifests his value above all by the fact that he himself is the legislator for himself, that he feels himself to be the source of all law and all justice (Kant).[27] This position is erroneous; man himself could be the ultimate legislator for himself only if he were not a creature, if he himself were his ultimate cause. But since he is a creature, since he depends for existence on God, to whom man with all other creatures ultimately owes his nature, then reason should serve him to discern correctly the laws of the Creator that are expressed in the objective order of nature, and in turn only then to establish human laws in conformity with the law of nature. First and foremost, however, human conscience, the direct guide of acts, should remain in conformity with the law of nature. Only then will man be just with respect to the Creator.

Evidently, justice with respect to the Creator on the part of man comprises two elements: the preservation of the order of nature and the manifestation of the value of the person.[28] The value of the created person (i.e., of a creature who is a person) is most fully manifested through participation in the thought of the Creator, through the fact that the created person is *particeps Creatoris* in his thinking and acting. This causes him to possess a correct relation to the whole of reality in all its constituent parts, in all elements. This relation is a kind of love, and not only a love of the world, but also a love of the Creator.[29] It is another matter that love of the Creator is included in this relation only in an indirect way, though real all the same. The man who has a correct relation to the whole created reality by that very fact indirectly has a proper relation to the Creator, is simply and fundamentally just with respect to him. In any case, we cannot speak of justice with respect to the Creator if this correct relation toward creatures is missing. In particular, the point is the correct relation toward other people—and here we find ourselves already in the orbit of the personalistic norm. Man can be just with respect to God the Creator insofar as he loves people.

This principle is particularly applicable in the sphere of coexistence and relationships between persons of different sex, of men and women. The whole reflection devoted so far to this problem, i.e., concentrated around the issue of "love and responsibility," was at the same time an analysis of the obligations of justice with respect to the Creator. It is out of the question that a man and a woman act justly with respect to God the Creator if their reciprocal conduct does not live up to the demands of the personalistic norm. God in a particular sense is the Creator of the person, for the person particularly reflects his essence. By being the Creator of the person, God is the source of the whole personal order, which rises above the order of nature thanks precisely to the person's capacity for understanding the latter and for his conscious self-determination within it. Justice with respect to the Creator demands from man above all the preservation of the personal order. A more particular expression of this order is love, in which the essence of God is reflected in an unusual way since Revelation tells us that "God is love" (1 Jn 4:8).

In entire nature (*przyroda*), the domain of sex is connected with reproduction. In having conjugal relations a man and a woman mediate the transmission of existence to a new human being. Here, too, sexual life is connected with reproduction, but because a man and a woman are persons, they have a conscious share in the work of creation (*procreatio*)— in this sense they are *participes Creatoris*.[30] Therefore, it is difficult to compare their conjugal life to the sexual life of animals remaining under the power of instinct. But precisely therefore, both in conjugal life as well as in general in the whole coexistence and relationships between persons of different sex, a problem occurs of justice with respect to the Creator, a problem most closely connected with responsibility for love. This leads to the very institution of marriage, and hence requires reproduction to be joined correctly with parenthood within the framework of marriage itself. For man, or rather two people, a man and a woman, does not fulfill the obligations of justice in relation to the Creator merely by effecting reproduction. The person transcends the world of nature (*przyroda*), and the personal order is not completely contained in the order of nature. Therefore, a man and a woman who have conjugal relations fulfill their obligations with respect to God the Creator only when they place all these relations on the level of love, i.e., on the level of a truly personal union. Only then are they *participes Creatoris* in the proper meaning of the word. And precisely for this reason conjugal intercourse itself must be permeated with a readiness for parenthood. The point here is not so much reproduction alone, but precisely love. For a lack of parental readiness in a man and a woman deprives their intercourse of the value of love, i.e., the value of a union on a truly personal level, leaving only intercourse itself, or rather shared sexual use.

## Virginity and intactness

Monogamous and indissoluble marriage solves the problem of intercourse between persons of different sex in a just way with respect to the Creator. Within marriage, justice with respect to the Creator demands a correct connection of reproduction with parenthood, for without this a man and a woman preserve neither the order of nature nor the personal order, which requires that their reciprocal relation is based on true love. In this way justice with respect to the Creator is realized by the fact of rational creatures acknowledging the supreme right of the Creator in the sphere of nature and in the sphere of the person, and conforming their conduct to it. However, the very concept of "justice" opens even further perspectives. To be just means to give to another person all that is rightly due to him. God is the Creator, that is, the unceasing source of the existence of every created being. And existence determines all that the given being is and what it has in itself. All properties, attributes, and perfections of a given being are what they are, have the value they have, by the fact that this being exists, and that they exist in it. For this reason the rights of the Creator reach very deeply in the creature, which is completely a possession of the Creator, for also what it "created" in and by itself is based on the fact of existence—if it did not exist, the creature's own creativity would be impossible. When man reflects on all this from the point of view of justice with respect to the Creator, the following conclusion arises: if I want to be fully just with respect to God the Creator, I should direct toward him all that is in me, my whole being, for he has the first right to all this.[31] Justice demands equalization; it is realized when what is due is given *usque ad aequalitatem*.[32]

However, the possibility of perfect equalization occurs where a fundamental equality of parties exists, an equality of persons. From this point of view, the full realization of justice with respect to the Creator by man is impossible. A creature will never be able to pay its debt to God, as it is not equal to him. It will not be able to face him as an equal "partner" or "contracting party."*

The relation to God, a religion (*religia*) based on justice alone, is in its foundation indeed incomplete and imperfect, since the realization of justice in the relation of man to God remains impossible as a rule. Christ provided a different solution. The relation to God cannot be based on justice alone, as man is not able to give him all that is his, so that he can face God as a "partner" or "contracting party" who has paid his debt in full. However, he can give himself to him relinquishing the attitude afforded within pure justice by the sense "I gave all back," "I owe nothing." Self-giving springs from a different root, not from justice alone, but from love. What Christ taught mankind was religion based on love, which facilitates a way from one person to another, from man to God (but without disregarding the problem of repayment by the debtor).[33] At the same time, love places the relation of man to God on a higher level than justice alone, for the latter does not go toward a union of persons at all, whereas love tends precisely to it.†

Against the background of the relation of man to God thus understood, the idea of virginity acquires its full meaning. The concept of virginity (*dziewictwo*) is associated with the concept of intactness (*dziewiczość*); "virginal" (*dziewiczy*) means the same as "untouched" (in this sense one can speak, for instance, of a "virgin forest").[34] This concept finds a particular application with respect to man, to a woman or a

---

* Let us consider that man is an object not only of "material" benefits provided by God, for the very commitment of the Creator in creating him, in imparting existence and freedom to him, is a certain kind of personal benefit. Insofar as purely material equalization does not depend on the dignity of contracting parties, equality concerning the exchange of personal benefits is closely connected with that dignity.

† Clearly, the point here concerns "commercial" justice (of the *do ut des* type); justice in the deeper, integral sense tends, however, at the same time to some "equalization" in reciprocal loving, in "giving of self." [*Do ut des*: I give so that you may give. — Trans.] The divergence of principles (of justice and love) would disappear here, but equalization with respect to this matter between the creature and the Creator turns out to be unthinkable: simply, we are not able to love God as we are loved by him.

man. A "virgin" (*dziewiczy człowiek*) means somebody untouched by another, sexually intact. Intactness finds its expression even in the physiological constitution of a woman. Conjugal intercourse removes this bodily intactness of a woman; from the moment she gives herself to her husband, she ceases to be "virginal." However, because the conjugal act is realized between persons, the problem of intactness possesses a deeper meaning, not only physiological. The person as such is nontransferable (*alteri incommunicabilis*), is a master of himself, belongs to himself, and besides that belongs only to the Creator on the basis of being a creature. Bodily intactness is an exterior expression of the fact that the person belongs only to himself and to the Creator. When he gives himself to another person, when a woman gives herself to a man in conjugal intercourse, then this giving should have the full value of spousal love. A woman then ceases to be "virginal" in the bodily sense. And because the self-giving is reciprocal, then a man also ceases to be "virginal." It is another matter that this self-giving can be experienced (*przeżywać*) as "giving" only by a woman; a man experiences (*przeżywać*) it rather as "possessing." In any case, marriage is based on reciprocal spousal love, for without it the mutual bodily self-giving of a woman and a man would not possess full justification in persons.

Within the relation of man to God that is understood as a relation of love, there can—or even should—develop an attitude of self-giving to God. This attitude is understandable especially when the religious man is aware that God in a divine and supernatural way gives himself to him (the mystery of faith, which was manifested to mankind by the revelation of Christ). Here the possibility of reciprocal spousal love appears: the human soul, being the bride of God, gives itself to him exclusively. This exclusive and total self-giving to God is the fruit of a spiritual process accomplished inside the person under the influence of grace. It constitutes the essence of virginity: virginity is spousal love directed to God himself. The word "virginity" is closely associated and connected with intactness.[35] The intactness of the human person, of a woman or a man, is the state in which he exists through total exclusion from sexual intercourse, from marriage. For the person choosing the total and exclusive self-giving to God binds it with intactness, which he decides to preserve. The intactness of the person signifies that he is a master of himself, and that he belongs to no one but God the Creator.

Virginity emphasizes even more strongly this belonging to God: what was the state of nature becomes an object of the will, an object of a conscious choice and decision.

Virginity is closely connected with intactness. When a person living in marriage, or who used to live in marriage but later became a widow or a widower, gives himself—in a particular way—to God, we do not call this virginity, although the very giving of oneself to God may be an act of spousal love analogically to the one that constitutes the essence of virginity. However, we should not think that the essence of virginity lies merely in bodily intactness or in the unmarried state. Intactness is only, on the one hand, a disposition to virginity and, on the other hand, its effect. One can remain in the virginal state until the end of life and never turn this intactness into virginity.[36] On the other hand, however, a person who has chosen virginity remains in it as long as he preserves intactness.

Also the unmarried state itself (*bezżeństwo*), i.e., celibacy (from the Latin word *coelebs*: unmarried) is not the same as virginity.[37] Celibacy is only refraining from marriage, and can be dictated by various reasons or motives. Thus, those persons intending to devote themselves to research or creative work in general, public service, etc., refrain from marriage. Persons who are sick, who are incapable of marriage, also refrain from it. Apart from this there are many persons who by no means wanted to refrain from marriage, but nonetheless remained single. Priestly celibacy in the Catholic Church is a separate phenomenon. It stands, so to speak, on the border line between the unmarried state dictated by the motives of public service (a priest is a pastor of souls; he should live and work for many people, for the whole community, e.g., of a parish) and virginity proceeding from spousal love toward God. Priestly celibacy, which is so closely linked with dedication to the things of God's kingdom on earth, seeks to be complemented with virginity, even though the sacrament of Holy Orders can be imparted to people who previously lived in marriage.

In general, a problem exists when the spiritual attitude constituting the interior essence of virginity, the will for total and exclusive self-giving to God, develops later—later, that is, when a given person is no longer intact in the bodily sense. It often happens that this attitude grows from an interior search among various circumstances in life: somebody tries to solve the problem of his life's vocation in the direction of marriage, but then, failing to find the solution there, he gives up. However, the very relinquishing of marriage is a solution merely in a negative sense. A need for spousal love dwells in man, a need to give himself to another person. The purely negative fact of failing to find such a person may be understood as a clue of sorts: after all there is a possibility of giving oneself to God alone. A psychological difficulty that arises here is not without significance: is it possible for someone to give to God what he "failed" to give to man? This is a psychological difficulty inasmuch as marriage, and especially virginity linked with spousal love, should be, according to popular belief, a fruit of "first love," i.e., of the first choice. In order to accept the possibility of "secondary virginity" it is necessary to remember that human life can and should be a search for a path to God, a path that is ever better and ever closer.

In accordance with the teaching of Christ and the Church, virginity is such a path. By choosing virginity, man chooses God himself, although this does not mean that by choosing marriage he chooses man and not God. Marriage and man's spousal love connected with it, the giving of self to another human person, solve the problem only in the scope of earthly life and temporality. The very union of one person with another is then realized in a bodily and sexual manner—in conformity with the bodily nature of man and the natural direction of the action of the sexual drive. Nevertheless, the very need to give oneself to another person is deeper than the sexual drive and is connected above all with the spiritual nature of the person. It is not sexuality that evokes in a woman and a man the need for reciprocal self-giving but, quite the contrary, the need for self-giving, which is latent in every person, is unfolded in the conditions of bodily existence and on the substratum of the sexual drive through the bodily and sexual union of a man and a woman in marriage. However, the very need for spousal love, the need to give oneself to a person and to unite with him, is deeper, is connected with the spiritual being of the person.[38] It does not find its final and total satisfaction in the union with man alone. Marriage considered in the perspective of the person's eternal being is only a certain attempt to solve the problem of the union with a person through love. The fact is that the majority of people choose precisely this attempt.

Virginity considered in the perspective of the person's eternal being is another attempt to solve this problem. Its going toward the final union with the personal God through love is more explicit than in marriage; in a sense it precedes marriage in the conditions of the temporal and bodily existence of the human person. In this lies the lofty value of virginity. We should not see it in the negative fact itself, i.e., in the relinquishing of marriage and family life. Very frequently the essence of virginity is distorted by regarding virginity as a solution imposed on man by fate, a lot destined for people who are disappointed or incapable of married and family life. Furthermore, the proper value of virginity is not determined by, as is often thought, the very superiority of spiritual values over the bodily ones. According to this understanding, conjugal life would mean choosing the bodily values, or at any rate these values would hold predominance in marriage, whereas virginity would serve to emphasize the primacy of spirit over the body and matter. Here, a certain element of truth can be easily confused with the Manichaean opposition of spirit and matter. Marriage is not in the least a mere "affair of the body." If it is to possess full value, marriage, just like virginity or celibacy, must consist in the genuine mobilization of man's spiritual energies.

The proper criterion of recognizing the value of the one and the other does not lie in the fact of the greater or lesser "ease" of marriage or virginity. Generally speaking, marriage is "easier" for man than virginity, as it seems to be located nearer man's natural development, whereas virginity is rather something exceptional. Nonetheless, undoubtedly there are times when it is easier to live in virginity than in marriage. At the very least let us consider the sexual side of life: virginity from the beginning removes man from sexual life, whereas marriage introduces him into it, although with this introduction a certain wont and demand for this life also arise. Hence, the difficulties of the person who must cultivate abstinence in marriage (if only periodic abstinence) may be greater for the time being than those of someone who from the beginning moved away from sexual life. If there are such moments when it is easier for man to live in virginity than in marriage, then certainly people exist who can live in virginity more easily than others, and who would find it more difficult to live in marriage. On the other hand, there are people who rather have dispositions toward married life while having firm indispositions toward virginity. In truth, however, dispositions and indispositions themselves do not yet ultimately determine anything. A man thoroughly absorbed by motives based on an ideal can sometimes bring out from himself a way of life toward which he does not possess distinct dispositions by nature, and toward which he at times acquired indispositions (for example, the person of Charles de Foucauld or St. Augustine comes to mind).

Therefore, it must be concluded that the value of virginity is due to a reason different from the one concerning the primacy of spirit over the body and matter. The value of virginity, indeed, its superiority over marriage—the superiority that is distinctly emphasized in the Gospel, in the epistle to the Corinthians (1 Cor 7), and has constantly been upheld in the teaching of the Church—lies in the fact that virginity fulfills an exceptionally important function in the realization of God's kingdom on earth. The kingdom of God on earth is realized by this, that particular people prepare themselves and mature for the everlasting union with God. In this union the objective development of the human person reaches its summit. Virginity—as the giving of the human person to God himself, the giving that proceeds from spousal love—explicitly advances toward this eternal union with God and shows a path to it.

## *The problem of vocation*

At this point, it is proper to sketch, at least in a few words, the problem of vocation (*powołanie*).[39] This concept is closely connected with the world of persons and the order of love. It does not make sense in the world of things, for we hardly speak of a vocation of some thing, but only of functions performed by individual things serving this or that end. Also, there are no vocations in the very order of nature, which is governed by determination, and which lacks the capacity for choice and self-determination. Therefore, in relation to animals, for instance, it is difficult to say that they fulfill some "vocation" by keeping their species in existence, through reproduction, for this happens by way of instinct. When we speak of vocation, we presuppose a capacity for personal commitment with respect to an end, and only a rational being is capable of that. So, "vocation" belongs exclusively to persons—through this concept we enter into a very interesting and profound sphere of the interior life of man. Perhaps this link with it is not manifested so clearly at first glance, for the word "vocation" is often applied in an administrative and legal sense. In this sense we speak, for instance, of being called to military service or to some office. Since in this case an institution stands behind "vocation," man is ignored, especially his interior life. Even in the case of a priestly vocation, this institutional-social moment plays a great role. This vocation is understood as a call by a given religious community, e.g., a diocese, to perform priestly functions, and is expressed in the decision of the superior of this community, i.e., a bishop who permits the given candidate to be ordained.

Besides this meaning of the word "vocation," the external, social-institutional meaning, another one exists: an interior, personal one. We must consult it when discussing the problem of vocation. In this meaning, the word "vocation" indicates that there exists a proper direction of every person's development through commitment of his whole life in the service of certain values. Every person should accurately discern this direction by understanding, on the one hand, what he carries in himself and what he could give of himself to others, and, on the other hand, what is expected of him. To discern the direction of one's own possibilities of acting, and to make a commitment in accord with this direction is one of the decisive moments in the process of the formation of personhood—not simply concerning the person's external position among people, but above all his interior life. The very discernment of this direction, of course, is not everything. The point is to commit oneself actively in this direction with one's whole life. And, therefore, vocation always means some main direction of love in a given person. Where one is called (*powołany*), one must not only love someone, but also "give himself" out of love. While analyzing love we have stated that such a gift of self can be most creative for the person: he realizes himself the most precisely by giving himself the most.[40]

The process of self-giving remains most closely connected with spousal love. A person then gives himself to another person. Therefore, understood in a deeply personalistic way, both virginity and marriage are vocations. Speaking of marriage, we must emphasize the world-view basis according to which we refer to it, for this basis determines whether we will perceive a vocation in marriage or not. This, after all, pertains not only to marriage, which according to materialistic, purely "biological" presuppositions can be nothing else but an understanding of a certain necessity rooted "in the body and sex." Also, any other vocation loses its *raison d'être* in a perception of reality that actually has no place for the person. According to non-personalistic presuppositions, virginity will be understood as a simple consequence of physiological and psychological conditions-dispositions (or rather indispositions) and of the external socio-economic situation. Vocation has its *raison d'être* only within the personalistic vision of human existence, where a conscious choice made by persons gives direction to their life and action.

In the evangelical vision of human existence the vocation of the human person is not only justified from within. The need proceeding from the person's interiority to discern the main direction of his development through love encounters God's objective call. This is the fundamental appeal of the Gospel expressed in the commandment to love and in the sentence "Be perfect . . ."—a call to perfection through love.[41] This call is universal. The task of every man of good will is to apply it to himself and by this to concretize it, precisely by discerning the main direction of life. What is my vocation? This means: in which direction should the development of my personhood proceed in light of what I have in myself, what I can give of myself, what others—people and God—expect from me? A believer thoroughly convinced of the veracity and reality of the evangelical vision of human existence is also aware that this development of personhood through love is not accomplished merely by the power of his own spiritual assets. By calling to perfection, the Gospel at the same time presents the truth about grace for us to believe. The action of grace places man in the orbit of the action of God, who is inscrutable in his personal life, and in the orbit of his love. The point is so that by discerning the proper direction for the development of his personhood, and together with it the main direction of his love, each man knows at the same time how to enter into God's action and respond to his love. The fully-mature solution of the problem of vocation depends on this.

The Gospel has explicitly put forth the problem of the relation of virginity to marriage (Mt 19:8, 1 Cor 7). According to the constant teaching and practice of the Church, virginity realized as a life's vocation consciously chosen, supported by the vow of chastity, and bound with two other vows, namely of poverty and obedience, creates particularly favorable conditions for achieving evangelical perfection. This group of conditions originating from the application of the evangelical counsels in the life of particular people, especially in their life together, is called the state of perfection. The "state of perfection," however, differs from perfection itself, which every man realizes in a way proper to his vocation by striving to fulfill the commandment to love God and his neighbor. Thus it may also happen that somebody who is situated outside the "state of perfection" is effectively more perfect thanks to fulfilling this greatest commandment than someone who chose that state.[42] In the light of the Gospel every man solves the problem of his vocation in practice above all through his efforts for a conscious personal relation to the greatest demand contained in the commandment to love. This relation is first and foremost a function of the person, the state (marriage, celibacy, even virginity understood only as a "state" or as its element) plays in this a secondary role.

## Fatherhood and motherhood

The theme of fatherhood and motherhood was already covered when we discussed the relation of reproduction to parenthood. Parenthood is not only a mere exterior fact connected with generation, especially with the birth and the possession of a child, but it is also a certain interior fact—an attitude that should characterize the love of a woman and a man when they engage in conjugal relations with each other. Thus, parenthood—motherhood in a woman, fatherhood in a man—considered on the personal and not merely "biological" plane, is in a sense a new crystallization of the love of persons that grows on the substratum of their already mature union. It does not, however, grow unexpectedly, but is deeply rooted in the whole being of a woman and a man. It is sometimes held that especially a woman by nature shows maternal inclinations to such an extent that in marriage she seeks a child rather than a man. The longing for a child is in any case a manifestation of potential motherhood. If it occurs in a man, it constitutes a manifestation of potential fatherhood. It seems that a man is generally further from this longing than a woman, which can be easily explained by the fact that her very organism is from the beginning formed for the sake of motherhood. Although it is true that physically a woman becomes a mother by a man, "interiorly" (psychically and spiritually) a man's fatherhood is formed thanks to a woman's motherhood. A man's physical fatherhood has a lesser place in his life, especially in his organism, than a woman's physical motherhood has in her life and organism. Therefore, fatherhood must be specially molded and educated so that it constitutes in the interior life of a man a position as important as motherhood is in the interior life of a woman: the biological facts themselves in a sense impose this on her.

We are now speaking about fatherhood and motherhood above all in the bodily, biological sense. It consists in possessing a child to whom life has been given, existence transmitted (*procreatio*). In this fact a certain natural perfection of a being is expressed: that it can give life to another being similar to itself in a certain sense manifests its own value, according to the well-known Latin saying: "*bonum est diffusivum sui,*" which was readily invoked by St. Thomas and other Christian thinkers.[43] Therefore, this longing for a child, which comes to light not only in a woman but also in a man, is perfectly understandable. A man expects a child from a woman, and, therefore, he takes her under his protection (*matris-munus*) through marriage. In parenthood they both find a confirmation not only of their physical but also of their spiritual maturity and a foreshadowing of extending their own existence. Once each of them ends this life with the death of the body, their child will still live—the "flesh of their flesh," but above all the man-person whom they both formed also from within; they formed in him what chiefly determines personhood. For the person is, in a sense, more "interiority" than a "body."

At this point we reach the essence of a new problem. Fatherhood and motherhood in the world of persons are definitely not limited to the biological function, to transmitting life. They reach much deeper—as deep as they must reach, since the one who transmits biological life, i.e., a father or a mother, is a person. Fatherhood and motherhood in the world of persons are the mark of a particular spiritual perfection, which always consists in some "generation" in the spiritual sense, in forming souls. And, therefore, the scope of this spiritual fatherhood and motherhood is much broader than that of bodily fatherhood and motherhood. The father and mother who gave biological life to their children must in turn complement their parenthood with laborious effort by spiritual fatherhood and motherhood through education. Other people apart from parents, however, also take part in the latter. Parents must here, in a sense, share with others, or, rather, skillfully incorporate in their education all that their children can receive from others in a bodily, spiritual, moral, and interior sense.

Spiritual fatherhood and motherhood is a distinctive characteristic of a mature interior personhood of a man and a woman. This spiritual fatherhood is much more similar to spiritual motherhood than bodily fatherhood is to bodily motherhood. The sphere of the spirit stands beyond the scope of sex. Having in mind his spiritual fatherhood with respect to Galatians, the apostle Paul did not hesitate to write: "My children, to whom I give birth suffering . . ." (Gal 4:19). Spiritual generation is a symptom of the person's maturity and of some fullness, both of which one wills to give to others (*"bonum est diffusivum sui"*). So, it seeks "children," i.e., other people, especially younger, who will receive what it wants to give. And those who receive become an object of a particular love—similar to the love of parents for their children—again, in a sense, because what became mature in the spiritual father or mother will live on in them. Thus, we can observe various manifestations of this spiritual fatherhood and various crystallizations of the love connected with it, e.g., the love of souls by priests and the religious, or the love of pupils by teachers. Spiritual kinship based on the bonds of souls is often stronger then the kinship that results from the bonds of blood alone. Spiritual fatherhood or motherhood contains some transmission of personhood.[44]

Spiritual fatherhood and motherhood as a manifestation of interior maturity of the human person is an end to which every man, a man and a woman, is called in some way (and the ways will be quite diverse), even outside marriage. This vocation is implicated, in a sense, in the evangelical call to perfection, which indicates the "Father" as its supreme model. Thus, man attains a likeness to God the Creator particularly when this primarily spiritual fatherhood-motherhood, whose archetype is God, is also formed in him. It is necessary to say this at the end of a book connected quite closely with the problems of generation and parenthood. The "father" and "mother" in the world of nature (*przyroda*) are two individuals of different sex to whom a new individual of the same species owes its biological life. The "father" and "mother" in the world of persons are, in a sense, two realized ideals, models for other persons, namely for those who are to be formed personally and develop within the sphere of their influence. In this way the order of nature stops at the facts, which within its realm are finite and ultimate, but in the world of persons they are opened anew, reaching for a new content—one that they do not find in the order of nature alone. The Gospel teaches that they are to draw this content from God himself.

However, every attempt to deprive the elements of spiritual fatherhood and motherhood of their human greatness, as well as every attempt to push fatherhood and motherhood outside the margin of social importance, is contrary to the natural paths of man's development.

CHAPTER V

# Sexology and Ethics: A Supplementary View

# Introductory remarks

Books are usually accompanied by footnotes. They do not constitute a separate chapter of a book; they do not belong to the totality of thoughts, views, and notions developed "inside" the book, which remain a close possession of its author. They are in a sense situated "outside," being a manifestation of dependence on someone else's thought and on other books; at the same time, they witness to the author's erudition and research. This book has no author's footnotes, and the following remarks have a different role to perform. They are not situated "outside" the book, but they are indeed woven into its fabric; they constitute an aspect of its content, which was not adequately brought to light in the previous chapters. It is time to supplement this lack. Therefore, this chapter serves not so much to supply footnotes to the previous four chapters, but, as the subtitle indicates, as a "supplementary view" of the totality of the matters that concern us in this book.

As is known, these matters pertain to persons: the love of a man and a woman is above all an affair of persons. In the previous chapters we attempted to explicate this truth as the fundamental problem. Therefore, the viewpoint of all sexual ethics is personalistic and cannot be otherwise. The proper object of sexual ethics does not consist in the affairs of the "body and sex," but in the affairs of persons and the problems of the personal love between a woman and a man that are bound closely with the affairs of the "body and sex." Love in the sense understood here can only and exclusively belong to persons. The affairs of the "body and sex" participate in love through the fact that they are subordinated to the principles enframing the order that should govern the world of persons.

Therefore, sexual ethics cannot be sexology, i.e., a view of woman and man and of love that posits the whole problem exclusively or above all from the viewpoint of the "body and sex." This way of seeing is characteristic of "pure" sexology, which deals with problems in sexual life from the side of bio-physiology and medicine. The sexologist-biologist is also aware that a woman and a man are persons, but this fact does not constitute the point of departure for his inquiries and for his whole view on the problem of their love.[1] As a result, his view is true, but at the same time only partial; hence, it is only partly true. The only fully true view is the one that proceeds from a thorough analysis of the fact that a woman and a man are persons, and that their love is a reciprocal relation of persons. Only then can the knowledge of the sexologist-biologist contribute a great deal to the detailed understanding of the principles of sexual ethics. Without moving the person to the fore-ground and without connecting him to love, we deprive ourselves of the essential basis of discernment in this difficult sphere of human morality. Thus, the proper point of view should be personalistic, not sexological. Sexology can only provide a supplementary view.

Biological sexology is ordinarily bound with medicine, hence becoming medical sexology. The viewpoint of medicine—and medicine is not only a science but also an art (an art of healing based on the bio-logical view on the human body)—is not identified with the viewpoint of ethics. Medicine is oriented toward the health of the body, in which it sees its proper object and end. Ethics, instead, sees its proper object and end in the moral good of the person. The very health of the body is not yet identified with the moral good of the whole person. It is only a partial good in relation to the moral good. After all, it is known that healthy but evil people exist, just as there happen to be sick and weak individuals of a remarkable moral value. It is another matter that respect for health and the protection of biological life is one of the fields of morality (the commandment "You shall not kill"), but not the only one. The viewpoint proper to medicine ("one ought to strive for health and avoid sickness") is in principle merely incidentally connected with sex-ual ethics, in which the personalistic viewpoint dominates. The point is what is due to a woman from a man, and to a man from a woman, on account of the fact that they are both persons, and not merely what is beneficial to their health. The viewpoint of medical sexology is thus only a partial viewpoint, which should be subordinated to ethics and, in it, to the objective demands of the personalistic norm. Clearly, in the field of vision of this norm, the norm that excludes treating the person as an object of use and demands that the true good of the person be sought, also lies concern for the biological life and health of the person, as one of his goods. This, however, is neither his only good nor the supe-rior or "ultimate" one.[2]

The pre-scientific statement that sex is a property of the human individual opens far-reaching horizons to us. For the human individual is a person, and the person is the subject and the object of love, a love that is born precisely between persons. This love is born between a woman and a man not because they are two sexually differentiated systems, but because they are two persons. The sexual differences themselves comprehended in a purely biological way indicate only one end: reproduction. The difference of sex is immediately and directly for the sake of reproduction. The fact that reproduction should find its basis in love by no means follows from the biological analysis of sex, but from the metaphysical (i.e., "extra- and supra-biological") fact of being a person. Only as a property of the person does sex have a share in the coming to be and development of love; by itself sex does not yet create a sufficient basis for that.[3]

When analyzing love in the psychological aspect in the second part of chapter II, we paid attention to the value of the "body and sex," which is the proper object of reactions of sensuality, while at the same time stating that these reactions provide, so to speak, the material for love between a woman and a man. Yet, a biological analysis of particular factors of sex and sexual life manifests to us neither this value nor its lived-experience. The facts of somatic nature and physiological processes, which belong to the vegetative sphere, condition merely "from without" this lived-experience of the value of the "body and sex." Even though being conditioned by biological facts, this lived-experience is not in the least identified with them. That this lived-experience can have significance for love, as we indicated in previous chapters (especially in chapter II), derives from the fact that sex is a property of the human person.[4]

## *The sexual drive*

In chapter I we defined the sexual drive as a specific direction (*skierowanie*) of the whole human being resulting from the division of the species *Homo sapiens* into two sexes. This drive turns not toward sex itself as a property of man, but toward the human being of the other sex.[5] The ultimate end of the sexual drive is the existence of the human species. The existence of somatic differences and the activity of sexual hormones evoke and condition the sexual drive, which nonetheless cannot be completely reduced to anatomical-somatic and physiological factors. The sexual drive is a separate force of nature, which is only based on these factors. Let us take a brief look at the developmental stages of the sexual drive.

The majority of physiologists and sexologists consider the period of puberty as the moment of the proper awakening of the sexual drive.[6] This period occurs in girls between the ages of 12 and 13, and somewhat later in boys. It is preceded by the period of pre-pubescence (*praepubertas*). Physiological sexual maturity is identified in girls with the appearance of menstruation and the ability to conceive, whereas in boys with the ability to produce semen. This is accompanied by characteristic psychical phenomena: a period of animation and, so to speak, acceleration of reactions is then followed by a period of their deceleration and sluggishness, which is particularly visible in girls, who usually experience (*przeżywać*) it more deeply.

Before the period of puberty, the sexual drive exists in a child in the shape of an unspecified and even unconscious interest, which only gradually reaches consciousness. The period of puberty brings a rapid growth of the drive, some eruption of it, so to speak. Next, the drive is stabilized in the period of physical and psychical maturity, then it undergoes a phase of pre-senile (climacteric) stimulation, and sooner or later slowly vanishes in old age.

Speaking about the drive, its awakening, growth, and diminishing, we have in mind various manifestations of sexual, urge-related reactions. We think of these when we indicate the difference in the intensity of this type of reaction in particular persons, at different ages or in varying circumstances. Sexology is supplementary here, especially with respect to the analysis of sensuality that was conducted in the second part of chapter II. The fact that we encounter a different "threshold of sexual excitability" in different people means that they react differently to the stimuli evoking sexual arousal. The grounds for this, among others, exist in man's somatic constitution and physiology.

Thus, sexual arousal itself can be described from a bodily perspective. It emerges by way of a neural reflex. It is a state of tension evoked by stimulating the nerve endings of the sensory organs either directly or in a psychogenic way through imaginational associations. Sexual stimuli can be received by various sensory organs, especially [as] touch and sight, but also hearing and taste, and even smell. They cause the state of a particular tension (tumescence) not only in the genital organs, but also in the whole organism. This finds its expression in vegetative reactions, but it is characteristic that the state of a certain tension is demonstrated by both the sympathetic and the parasympathetic systems.

Sexual stimuli proceed automatically and involuntarily by means of neural reflexes (the reflex arc on the S2–S3 nerve level). Concerning the physiological and somatic side, it must be pointed out that places exist in man that transmit sexual stimuli with a particular ease—the so-called erogenous (erogenic) zones, of which a woman possesses more than a man. The degree of arousal depends directly on the quality of the stimulus and on the receiving organ. Various factors among physiological conditions can increase or diminish sexual excitability; thus, for instance, fatigue contributes to its decrease, whereas excessive fatigue, as well as insomnia, may act in quite the opposite direction. Sexual arousal itself precedes the act of sexual intercourse, but can also exist outside it.

Sexology introduces us in a much more detailed way into this group of somatic and physiological conditionings of sensuality, for it is in sensuality that the action of the sexual drive is manifested in man. However, in connection with chapter II it is worthwhile to recall that what in itself must be acknowledged as a manifestation of the drive can become a real factor of love once it is transformed in the interior life of persons.

## *The problem of marriage and intercourse*

In the two preceding sections of this chapter, the view supplementing the matters already discussed in the previous chapters focused more or less on information from the sphere of biological sexology. What will come more to light in the following sections is medical sexology. Being a part of medicine, it possesses a normative character, for it directs the action of man with regard to his health. As has been mentioned earlier, health is a good of man as a psycho-physical being. Our further reflections will deal with indicating the principal moments of the convergence between the moral good, which is defined by sexual ethics, and that precise good around which the recommendations of medical sexology concentrate, and which constitutes the basis for its pronouncements and norms. It is known that sexual ethics does not proceed from biological facts alone, but from the concept of the person and love as a reciprocal relation of persons. Can ethics be contrary to the hygiene and health of a man and a woman? In an ultimate and thorough analysis, can regard for the physical health of persons remain in conflict with their moral good, thus with the objective demands of sexual ethics? We sometimes encounter such questions. Therefore, this theme, too, must be undertaken in some measure. We refer thus to chapters III and IV (on chastity and marriage).

The proper substantiation of a monogamous and indissoluble marriage is, as we stated in the first part of chapter IV, the personalistic norm together with the acknowledgment of the objective order of the ends of marriage. What proceeds from that norm is the prohibition of adultery in the broad sense of the word, thus also the prohibition of pre-marital relations. Only a deep conviction about the supra-utilitarian value of the person (of a woman for a man, and of a man for a woman) allows us to substantiate fully, in a profound and compelling way, this position in ethics and to seek its realization in morality. Is sexology able to second it somehow and thus in a sense provide additional substantiation for it? For this reason we must turn our attention to certain very essential moments of sexual intercourse. As has been stated in chapter IV, this intercourse preserves its personal dimension exclusively in marriage, whereas outside the institution of marriage it places the person exclusively and wholly in the position of an object of use for another person (it does so especially with a woman in respect to a man).

Sexual intercourse (the sexual act) is not merely a simple consequence of sexual arousal, which can arise generally without the act of the will, i.e., spontaneously, and only then it secondarily encounters the will's consent or opposition. It is known that this arousal can even reach the climax, which sexology calls orgasm (*orgasmus*). However, this climactic sexual arousal is not interchangeable with sexual intercourse (although it is generally not reached without a consent of the will and without some "action"). We have stated already in the analysis of the concupiscence of the flesh (in the first part of chapter III) that the reactions of sensuality have their own dynamic in man, which is most closely connected not only with the value of the "body and sex" but also with the reflexive dynamic of the sexual spheres of the human body, with the physiology of sex. Nonetheless, the sexual act or sexual intercourse between a man and a woman is unthinkable without the act of the will, especially on the part of the man. The point here is not the decision alone, but also the physiological potency of performing sexual intercourse, of which a man is not capable in the states that disengage his will, e.g., during sleep or unconsciousness. What results from the nature of the act itself is that in it a man plays an active role, he has the initiative, whereas a woman is rather a passive party disposed to receiving and experiencing.[7] Her passivity and lack of resistance suffice to such an extent that the sexual act can take place even without the participation of her will, that is, in the state that wholly disengages her consciousness, e.g., when unconscious, fainted, or asleep. In this sense, sexual intercourse depends on a man's decision. Because this decision is at times evoked by his sexual arousal, which does not have to correspond to an analogical state in a woman, a problem thus emerges of great practical significance, both medical and ethical. Sexual ethics, conjugal ethics, must penetrate here the structure of certain facts well known to medical sexology. We defined love as striving for the true good of the other person, thus as the opposite of egoism. Since a man and a woman in marriage are united also through sexual intercourse, this good should be sought in this field as well.

From the viewpoint of loving another person, from the position of altruism, it must be required that the conjugal act should serve not merely to reach the climax of sexual arousal on one side, i.e., that of a man, but happen in harmony, not at the other person's expense, but with that person's involvement. This follows precisely from the position of the principle already thoroughly analyzed, which excludes use and demands love in relation to the person. And love demands in this case that the reactions of the other person, of the "partner," be taken fully into consideration.

Sexologists state that the curve of sexual arousal in a woman differs from that of a man: it rises more slowly and subsides more slowly. Anatomically, this arousal proceeds just as in a man (the center of the stimulation is situated in the nerves S2–S3). The organism of a woman, as has been mentioned above, reacts with a greater ease by arousal from various places of the body, and that, in a sense, compensates for the fact that the arousal in her case rises more slowly than in a man. A man should be aware of that, not because of hedonistic but of altruistic motives. In this sphere there is some rhythm bestowed by nature itself, and this rhythm should be sought and found by both spouses, so that the climax of sexual arousal takes place both in a man and in a woman, and that it occurs inasmuch as possible in both spouses at the same time. The subjective happiness they then suffer together possesses plain characteristics of that *frui*, i.e., the joy proceeding from the conformity of actions with the objective order of nature. On the other hand, egoism—in this case we mean rather the egoism of a man—is most closely associated with that *uti*, in which one party strives only for one's own pleasure at the other's expense. It is evident that the elementary recommendations of sexology converge with ethics.

A failure to observe these recommendations of sexology in conjugal intercourse is contrary to the good of the spouse and to the durability and cohesion of marriage itself. We must take into account the fact that a natural difficulty exists concerning the adaptation of a woman to a man in conjugal intercourse, a certain natural inequality of the bodily-psychical rhythm. Hence, there is a need for harmonization, which is impossible without good will, especially in a man, and without a careful observation of a woman. If a woman does not find this natural happiness in sexual intercourse, then a danger emerges that she will experience (*przeżywać*) the conjugal act in a way that is not fully-mature, without the commitment of her whole personhood.[8] This way of experiencing (*przeżywać*) particularly facilitates the evoking of a neurotic reaction, e.g., secondary sexual frigidity. At times this frigidity (*frigiditas*) is a result of some inhibition on the part of the woman herself, some lack of involvement on her part, for which she is sometimes culpable. Most often, however, it is a result of egoism on the part of the man, who fails to acknowledge the woman's subjective longings in intercourse and the objective laws of the sexual process that takes place in her, and who seeks merely his own satisfaction in a way that is at times even brutal.[*]

---

[*] It is known that the normal course of sexual intercourse is at times disturbed by an egocentric focus of attention on one's own lived-experiences. The spouses should remember that their bodily intercourse constitutes at the same time a mystery of their spiritual union in love and reverence. The complete absorption of their consciousness by (especially one's own) sensual satisfaction turns out to be dangerous and equally harmful to the biological, psychical, and moral sides of the act.

In a woman, this generates unwillingness for intercourse and sexual aversion, which is equally or even more difficult to master than the sexual drive. This also causes neuroses and sometimes even organic disorders (which derive from the fact that the hyperemia of the genital organs during sexual arousal causes inflammation in the area of the so-called little pelvis when the arousal does not end with relaxation, which in turn is closely connected with an orgasm in a woman). Psychologically speaking, this situation evokes not only indifference, but often even hostility. It is with great difficulty that a woman forgives a man for the lack of happiness in conjugal sexual intercourse. This becomes difficult for her to bear, and over time it can amount to a completely incommensurate traumatic reaction. All this may lead to a breakup of the marriage. In order to prevent this, we need appropriate sexual education—*not merely instruction concerning the matters of sex, but precisely education*. For it should be emphasized again that physical aversion does not exist in a marriage as an original phenomenon, but is in general a secondary reaction: in women it is a response to egoism and brutality, whereas in men to frigidity and indifference. But this frigidity and indifference in a woman are often caused by mistakes in a man's conduct, when he leaves the woman unsatisfied while searching for his own self-satisfaction. This, *nota bene*, even clashes with masculine ambition. However, the innate ambition itself may not be sufficient in the long run in certain, especially more difficult, situations: it is known that, on the one hand, egoism makes one blind by removing ambition, whereas, on the other hand, it generates an unhealthy excess of it. In both cases the other person is disregarded. Similarly, the natural goodness of a woman cannot suffice in the long run when she sometimes "simulates an orgasm" (as claimed by sexologists) in order to satisfy a man's ambition. All this, however, does not correctly solve the problem of intercourse, but may suffice only temporarily. What is needed in the long run is sexual education, and one that is constant at that. The most important point of this education is to shape the following conviction: *the other person is more important than I*. This conviction will not appear all of a sudden and out of nothing, purely on the basis of bodily intercourse alone. It can be only and exclusively a result of integral education in love. *Sexual intercourse alone does not teach love; but love, if it is a true virtue, will also turn out to be such in conjugal sexual intercourse.* Only then can the "sexual formation" provide proper benefits, for without education it can even be detrimental.

The culture of conjugal relations is reduced to and connected precisely with that. Not the technique alone, but precisely the culture.[9] Sexology (van de Velde) often pays principal attention to the technique, which is rather something secondary, and perhaps often even contrary to what it should in principle lead. The drive is so strong that it creates in a normal man and a normal woman, in a sense, instinctive knowledge as to "how to have intercourse." An artificial analysis (which is linked precisely with the concept of "technique"), instead, can spoil the whole thing, for there the point is a certain spontaneity and naturalness, of course subordinated to morality. Thus, this instinctive knowledge must mature for the culture of intercourse. At this point, it is proper to refer to the analysis of tenderness, especially "disinterested tenderness," which was conducted in the third part of chapter III. Precisely this ability to feel directly another person's states and lived-experiences may play a great role in harmonizing conjugal intercourse. It grows from affectivity, which is oriented more toward man, and hence can soothe and equalize both the vehement reactions of sensuality oriented merely toward the body and the unrestrained impulses of the concupiscence of the flesh. Precisely due to the longer and slower increase of the sexual reaction so characteristic of a woman's organism, the demand for tenderness in physical intercourse, both before it begins and after it concludes, is explained almost biologically. In this way, the act of tenderness by a man grows within conjugal intercourse to mean an act of virtue—and precisely of the virtue of abstinence, and indirectly of love (see the analysis in the third part of chapter III)—when we take into consideration the short and more vehement "curve of stimulation" on the part of a man. Marriage cannot be reduced to physical relations, but needs an affective climate without which virtue, both love and chastity, becomes difficult to realize.

What we mean here is not a shallow affective climate or superficial love, which has little in common with virtue. Love should help in understanding man, in feeling for him, as this is the way to educate him, or to co-educate him as is the case in conjugal life. A man must take into account that a woman is a "world different" from him, not only in the physiological, but also the psychological sense. Since he is to play an active role in conjugal intercourse, he should get to know this world, and even empathize with it as much as possible. This is precisely the positive function of tenderness. Without it a man will attempt merely to subordinate a woman to the demands of his body and his psyche, at times acting to her detriment. Of course, a woman, too, should attempt to understand a man and at the same time to educate him in relation to herself, for one is not less important than the other. Neglect with respect to one of them can be equally a fruit of egoism. It is precisely sexology, though not alone, that advocates this formulation of demands concerning morality and conjugal pedagogy.

Does all this, which medical sexology contributes to the problem of sexual intercourse between a man and a woman, directly advocate the principle of monogamy and the indissolubility of marriage? Does all this advocate against adultery and pre- and extra-marital relations? Perhaps not directly, for, after all, this cannot be demanded from sexology, which directly deals with the sexual act itself as a certain physiological or at most psycho-physical process, and with its conditionings in the organism and psyche. Indirectly, however, sexology itself constantly advocates for natural sexual and conjugal morality on account of concern for the most thoroughly understood psycho-physical health of a woman and a man. And so, harmonious sexual relations are possible only when they are free from a sense of conflict with one's own conscience, when they are not disturbed by an interior reaction of fear. Concerning a woman, for instance, she can certainly experience (*przeżyć*) complete sexual satisfaction in extra-marital intercourse, although the conflict with conscience may contribute even to disturbing the natural biological rhythm. Peace and certainty of conscience have a decisive influence even on the organism. By itself, this cannot amount to an argument for monogamy and conjugal fidelity, and against adultery; rather, here there is a certain consequence of the natural rules of morality. Sexology does not have to provide grounds for deducing the latter; it is enough that it incidentally confirms the rules already known from elsewhere and substantiated in another way. Certainly then, marriage as a stable institution that protects the eventual motherhood of a woman (*matris-munus*) frees her in some fundamental measure from the anxiety reactions that not only take revenge on her psyche, but also contribute to the disturbance of her natural biological rhythm. This remains closely connected with the fear of a child—the main source of female neuroses.

A harmonious marriage solves these situations.[10] However, we have demonstrated that this harmony cannot be merely a function of some technique, but precisely a function of the culture of intercourse, i.e., in the last analysis, of the virtue of love. By its essence such a marriage is a fruit not only of sexual compatibility, but also of an ethically fully-mature choice.

From the viewpoint of bio-physiology itself, it is impossible to discern and formulate laws that would determine the grounds according to which a man and a woman decide to marry. It seems that no such "purely" biological factors of attraction exist, although, on the other hand, the persons who bind themselves in marriage also take sexual interest in each other. People feeling physical aversion to each other from the beginning will not enter into matrimony. The laws of reciprocal attraction can only sometimes be defined by the psychological principle of likeness or, on the contrary, of contrast; in general, however, the matter is more complicated. Although the fact is that at the moment of choice the sensual-affective factors are at work in a very powerful way, the rational analysis should nonetheless be of decisive importance.

It must be stated that the promoted "trials" of sexual intercourse before marriage constitute no test of "compatibility," for the specificity of conjugal relations is different from that of pre-marital ones. Incompatibility in marriage is something more than simple physical incompatibility, and certainly cannot be tested in advance by pre-marital intercourse. Married couples who later consider themselves incompatible very often have at the beginning a period of perfect sexual intercourse. It turns out that the breakup occurs for another reason. Positing the matter this way closely converges with the ethical principle that excludes pre-marital relations, and although it does not in fact confirm this principle directly, it nevertheless leads to the abrogation of the principle that permits or even recommends such relations.

If the point is not so much compatibility, but the choice of the spouse, then especially concern for the offspring requires us to observe the principles of healthy eugenics. Medicine gives contraindications regarding marriage in the cases of certain illnesses, but this is a separate problem, which we do not present here, for it pertains not so much to sexual ethics itself, but to ethics of health and life (the Fifth, not the Sixth Commandment).[11]

The conclusions reached by medical sexology do not at any point speak against the chief principles of sexual ethics: monogamy, conjugal fidelity, a mature choice of the person, etc. The principle of conjugal shame analyzed in the second part of chapter III also finds its confirmation in the existence of neuroses, well known to sexologists and psychiatrists, which are a consequence of sexual intercourse experienced (*przeżywać*) in an atmosphere of fearing to be surprised by some unwelcome factor from outside.[12] Hence, there is a need for an appropriate place, one's own house or at least an apartment, where conjugal life can "safely" carry on, i.e., in accordance with the demands of shame, where a man and a woman, so to speak, "have the right" to experience (*przeżywać*) matters most intimate to them.

## *The problem of conscious motherhood*

The reflections on conjugal intercourse conducted from the perspective of sexology (in order to supplement the viewpoint of ethics) necessarily place before us the problem of conscious motherhood. This problem is so closely joined with the previous one that in a sense it only complements the other one as its continuation. The very concept of "conscious motherhood" (*świadome macierzyństwo*) can be understood in a variety of ways. It can thus mean the consciousness of what motherhood is (and by analogy what fatherhood is)—we have devoted a good amount of space to this problem in the reflections of chapters I and IV. Nonetheless, "conscious motherhood" usually signifies something else. It could be briefly summarized in the following sentence: "Know the way in which a woman becomes a mother in conjugal intercourse, and act this way so that you can become one only when you want it." Although this sentence is addressed to a woman, it actually concerns a man as her "partner" in sexual (conjugal) intercourse, for he is the one who makes decisions here in the majority of cases.

This instruction or program—for nowadays conscious motherhood is already an explicit program—stated as above may raise no reservations. After all, man is a rational being, and thus striving for the fullest possible participation of consciousness in all that man does is in conformity with his nature. The striving to consciously become a mother or a father, for one cannot be in any way separated from the other, is also in conformity with it. The consciousness of when and how a woman and a man can become parents by having conjugal relations should direct their intercourse. For they are responsible for every conception both with respect to themselves and to the family that they create or augment by such a conception. We have already spoken of this in chapter IV (in the sections "Reproduction and parenthood" and "Periodic abstinence: The method and interpretation"). The present reflections clearly relate to those there.

The program of conscious motherhood can easily step down to the level of utilitarian presuppositions, where a conflict emerges with the supra-utilitarian value of the person—in this whole book, perhaps more space has been devoted to this problem than to any other. The only way out of this conflict, the way in conformity with the character of the person, and thus fully honorable, is the virtue of abstinence, whose framework is designated in a sense by nature itself. However, understanding this accurately again requires a fuller elucidation from the perspective of sexology.[13]

As is known, the nature of a woman regulates the number of conceptions in a precise and, so to speak, "frugal" way, for throughout the whole menstrual cycle, a mature ovum, an object of possible fertilization, emerges only once. On the part of a man, however, every conjugal intercourse involves potential fertility. Thus, the determinant of the number of offspring is the woman's organism. Fertilization can take place only at a moment when a woman's organism permits it, that is, once the organism has been prepared for it by a whole series of preceding biochemical reactions. It is possible to discern the time of "fertility," though not in a general and routine way, but individually, for each woman separately. Every woman can observe changes that occur in her in the appropriate phase of the cycle.[14] Besides, there are objective scientific medical-biological methods that provide indicators for marking the moment of ovulation, i.e., the period of fertility.

However, let us begin by elucidating the positive side of the problem. Sexology speaks of the "maternal and paternal instincts." Insofar as the former usually arises in a woman even before the birth of the baby, and often even before the baby's conception, the latter ordinarily develops later, sometimes even with respect to children a few years old. The maternal instinct can already be developing in girls during puberty, for it is biologically dependent on the working of hormones, whereas the sexual rhythm of a woman prepares her every month for receiving a baby and orients her organism exactly to that end. Hence, the disposition toward the child arises, which sexology calls the maternal instinct because this disposition is caused to a large extent by the states of a woman's organism that recur monthly. In conjugal intercourse, this disposition does not dominate the consciousness of a woman, and especially of a man, and does not in the least have to dominate it (according to what we concluded in the reflection on reproduction and parenthood in chapter IV). It is understandable, however, that together with marriage and conjugal intercourse, a desire to have a child arises as a natural phenomenon, whereas an attitude contrary to this in the will and consciousness is precisely something unnatural. And this fear of conceiving, the fear of a child, is a moment of great importance in the problem of conscious motherhood. It is, in a sense, a paradoxical moment. For, on the one hand, it is precisely what evokes the whole problem of "conscious motherhood" in the form: "What to do in order to have a child only when one wants him." On the other hand, however, the very same fear of a child principally impedes taking advantage of the possibilities provided in this sphere by nature itself.

Here lies a fundamental difficulty with respect to the regulation of conceptions that is correct from the medical-biological and ethical viewpoints. This difficulty does not dwell in nature itself, which regulates the number of conceptions in a clear way that is fairly easy to discern.[15] The factors disturbing the biological regularity in a woman are above all of a psychogenic nature.[16] We encounter their effects much more often than disorders of an organic nature.[17] Concerning psychogenic factors, precisely this fear of conceiving, the fear of pregnancy, moves to the foreground.

It is known that physical fatigue, a change of climate, states of stress, and especially fear can check or accelerate menstruation. Thus, fear is a powerful negative stimulus that can destroy the natural regularity of a woman's sexual cycle. Clinical practice also confirms the thesis that precisely the fear of pregnancy deprives a woman of the "joy of spontaneously experiencing (*przeżywać*) love," the joy that is brought by action in conformity with nature.[18] This fear, as a dominant affection, overwhelms all other sensations and leads to unpredictable reactions.

All this indicates indirectly how decisive in this case is precisely that moral attitude analyzed in chapter IV.[19] This moral attitude is reduced to two elements, namely the readiness for parenthood during intercourse ("I can be a mother," "I can be a father") and the readiness to abstain that proceeds from virtue, from loving the closest person. Only in this way can biological equilibrium, without which it would be impossible to think of and realize the natural regulation of conceptions, be achieved in a woman.[20] "Nature" in man is subordinated to ethics: the correct biological rhythm of a woman and the possibility of the natural regulation of conceptions resulting from it are most closely connected with love, which is revealed, on the one hand, in the readiness for parenthood and, on the other hand, in the virtue of abstinence, in the ability to relinquish and sacrifice one's own "I."[21] Egoism is a denial of love; it is manifested in contrary attitudes and constitutes the most dangerous source of that dominating fear that paralyzes healthy processes of nature.

Almost no one speaks about it.[22] We must state clearly that at the basis of natural methods lies the fundamental one: the "method" of virtue (love and abstinence). Once it is presupposed and accepted in practice, then all knowledge about sexual and reproductive processes can turn out to be effective. For once man realizes that fertilization is not an "accident" or a coincidence, but a biological fact carefully prepared by nature, and that the preparations can be investigated in full, then the possibilities of directing conception in a rational way and in conformity with nature increase.[23]

Conscious motherhood is reduced to two kinds of "methods," which we have already analyzed from the ethical perspective in chapter IV. These are, on the one hand, the so-called natural methods, and, on the other hand, the artificial methods that consist in using contraceptives.[24] Contraceptive means are by nature detrimental to health.[25] Besides temporary barrenness, biological means can cause far-reaching and irrevocable changes in man's constitution. Chemical means are by their nature cellular venoms, as otherwise they would not have the strength to kill reproductive cells, and thus they are physically harmful. Mechanical means not only cause local damage in a woman's reproductive tract, but in addition violate the spontaneity of the sexual act, which is unbearable especially for a woman.[26]

Most often spouses use *coitus interruptus* (the withdrawal method) without immediately being aware of its evil effects. These effects, however, are inevitable.[27] Disregarding the fact of this method's unreliability in preventing fertilization, a question arises why people use this method at all. At first glance it seems that this behavior proceeds exclusively from a man's egoism. However, a deep analysis demonstrates that a man by interrupting intercourse often thinks that in this way he "protects the woman." Indeed, even though in this behavior various goods are destroyed, such as depriving a woman of orgasm or upsetting her nervous equilibrium, her fundamental biological capacity, namely fertility, remains nonetheless intact. Hence, even women themselves at times hold the conviction that this "does no harm." A man then has the sense that he controls the situation and decides about it, whereas a woman retains the attitude of sexual passivity proper to her, leaving the responsibility to the man. Precisely in this attitude of both one can perceive a certain good, although they seek it by an improper way. For if the spouses arrived at the justified conclusion that they should postpone conception, then the man—instead of interrupting the act already started—should not undertake it presently, but instead wait responsibly until his spouse's biological infertility. For this reason they both should get to know the organism of the woman and base their decision on accurate knowledge of its operation. But thereby we return precisely to the issue of periodic abstinence.

Natural methods are ways of controlling fertility through periodic abstinence.[28] Using natural methods demands accurate knowledge of the organism of a given woman and of her biological rhythm, and, furthermore, it demands peace and biological equilibrium, of which much has been said previously. However, above all there is a need for a certain renunciation and abstinence, a need that is immediate, especially on the part of women. For naturally, the sexual drive makes itself heard most strongly in a woman at the moment of ovulation and in the period of fertility (the intensification of the drive is one of the indicators of so-called ovulatory syndrome)—and precisely in this period conjugal intercourse should be forsaken. Periodic abstinence does not present this difficulty for a man, for in him the sexual drive is not subject to such fluctuations as in a woman. A man's abstinence must be then accommodated to the signs provided by a woman's organism. A more important task for a man than merely accommodating to a woman's biological cycle is the creation of a psychical climate for their reciprocal intercourse, a climate without which the effective use of natural methods is out of the question.[29] This does demand regular abstinence on the part of a man, and thus the problem of regulating conceptions in conformity with nature appeals in the last analysis to his masculine moral attitude. Conjugal intercourse demands tenderness on his part, i.e., an understanding for the lived-experiences of a woman. In this sense, conscious motherhood appeals to his abstinence, without which it is impossible to grasp the correct biological rhythm in marriage.

This is a rhythm of nature, and therefore conjugal intercourse in conformity with it is at the same time hygienic, healthy, and free from all those neuroses caused by the aforementioned artificial methods of avoiding pregnancy. However, the natural methods cannot be used without grasping the whole biological rhythm—they fail if used *ad hoc* and mechanically. It could hardly be otherwise in light of the facts presented above. But if a man and a woman use them with full understanding of these facts and with the simultaneous acknowledgment of the objective finality of marriage, then the natural methods leave them with the sense of conscious choice and of the spontaneity in lived-experience ("naturalness"). Most importantly, they leave them with the possibility of consciously controlling procreation. The effort put in using these "methods" is above all ethical in nature, as has already been indicated in chapter IV. Without the appropriately comprehended and cultivated virtue of abstinence, it is impossible to think of the natural regulation of conceptions, of motherhood and of fatherhood as truly conscious.

A separate study should be devoted to the problem of abortion. Here, it is proper to touch on this theme, at least in a few words. The fact of artificially terminating pregnancy is in itself, apart from its ethical qualification, highly "neurotogenic," it displays all the marks of experimental neuroses. After all, it is an artificial interruption of a natural biological rhythm with far-reaching effects.[30] Together with this, an enormous injury arises in the psyche of a woman, incomparable with anything else. She can neither forget this fact nor rid herself of her grievance toward the man who led her to it. Besides somatic reactions, abortion evokes an anxiety-depressive neurosis with a predominant sense of guilt and sometimes even with a deep psychotic reaction. With regard to this, the statements of women suffering from depression in the climacteric period are remarkable. Sometimes after ten or more years they recall their abortions with regret, and on that account they have a belated sense of guilt. For there is no need to add that abortion is from the ethical point of view a very grave fault. Due to substantive concerns, reflecting on this problem in connection with conscious motherhood (conscious parenthood) would be completely improper.

## Sexual psychopathology and ethics

A broadly disseminated idea exists that a lack of sexual intercourse is harmful to human health in general, and in particular to a man's health. However, no one has described a pathological syndrome that would confirm the rightness of that thesis. The previous reflections demonstrated that sexual neuroses are above all a consequence of abuses in sexual life, that they result from not conforming to nature and its processes. It is not abstinence itself, but precisely its lack that causes genuine disorders. This lack can also consist in an improper suppression of the sexual drive and its manifestations in man. This is mistakenly considered to be abstinence and—as has been demonstrated in chapter III—has little in common with the true virtue of abstinence and chastity.

The sexual drive in man is a fact that should be acknowledged and affirmed by him as a source of natural energy; otherwise it can cause psychical disorders. The urge-related reaction itself, which is called sexual arousal, as a vegetative reaction is largely independent from the will, and a lack of understanding this simple fact often becomes a cause of serious sexual neuroses. Man is then faced with a conflict situation: he is troubled by two ambivalent tendencies that he does not know how to reconcile— hence the neurotic reactions. A significant part of sexual neuroses is constituted by neuroses connected with irregularities concerning conjugal intercourse, which we spoke of in the previous section.

So-called sexual neuroses have a clinical image similar to other neuroses and usually are not manifested solely in the sexual sphere.[31] It happens that the cause of a neurosis dwells completely elsewhere, with anxiety and disorders in the sphere of sexual life being secondary effects, because it is precisely a neurosis that impedes man's control of himself.

This is not the place to account for disorders in detail, but rather the point is an integral view of man's sexual life.[32] What seems to be necessary for the sake of rectitude and health is to educate man from his childhood onward, on the one hand, in truth and, on the other hand, in respect for matters of sex as the matters most closely connected with the highest values of human life and love. Sexual reactions can be evoked at any age, already in early childhood. The sexual drive that is awakened early, in an improper period of life, can become a source of neurotic disorders when it is suppressed in an inappropriate way. Therefore, sexual education based on genuine biological information is so important. A lack of information, and especially a lack in formation of attitudes, may cause aberrations of various kinds (such as onanism in children and youth). This problem is educational rather than medical, although, as a rule, where incorrect attitudes of man exist, a neurotic reaction occurs as a response of the organism and of the nervous system to constant tension.

## Therapy[33]

Without presently analyzing the clinical symptoms of various possible aberrations, we would rather like to recommend ways of preventing such reactions.[34] These general recommendations can be reduced to a few principal ones:

a) It is necessary to remove the often widespread conviction among people that the sexual drive is something evil by nature, something that must be combated in the name of the good. On the contrary, it is necessary to introduce the conviction, in conformity with the proper conception of man, that sexual reactions are by all means natural and in themselves do not yet contain any ethical value. They are neither morally good nor evil, but one can make morally good or morally evil use of them.

b) In order for man to acquire the conviction that he is capable of controlling his reactions, first of all he must be freed from the idea that sexual reactions are necessarily determined and are completely independent of the human will. He must be convinced that the body can be "obedient" to him, if it is habituated by him to be so.

c) It is necessary to free man, especially young people, from the conviction that sexual matters constitute a sphere of nearly catastrophic, unintelligible phenomena that in some mysterious way absorb man and threaten his equilibrium; instead, they should be reduced to the level of phenomena that, though great and beautiful, are nonetheless fully intelligible and, so to speak, "ordinary." This requires correct biological information provided in the proper time.

d) The most important thing is to convey to man the proper hierarchy of values and to show what position the sexual drive holds in that hierarchy. Its use will be then subordinated to the end it is to serve. Furthermore, man must be convinced about the possibility and necessity of conscious choice. It is necessary to "restore" to man, as it were, the consciousness of the freedom of the will and of the fact that the sphere of sexual lived-experiences is fully subject to this will.

e) Of course, there are cases of disorders in which the help of a professional sexologist or psychiatrist is needed, although the advice offered by these professionals should take into account the totality of human aspirations, and above all the integral, personalistic conception of man.[35] For sometimes precisely the advice of a doctor "makes" the patient a neurotic by openly contradicting who man really is. The biologistic attitude of some doctors, often formed under the influence of the "myth of orgasm," leads them to give advice that is quite contrary to the human understanding and experience (*przeżywać*) of sexual matters.

The psychotherapy of sexual neuroses differs from sexual pedagogics, for it has for its object not the people who possess a normal and healthy sexual inclination, but some perversion or disorder of the drive. Therefore, the methods of influence must be more particular than those used in ordinary sexual pedagogics. Sick persons are less capable of "love and responsibility," and psychotherapy aims at restoring this capability to them. When we carefully analyze the recommendations it follows, we arrive at the conclusion that what it attempts above all is to free these persons from the overwhelming idea about the determining power of the drive, and to cultivate in them the conviction of the capacity in every man for self-determination within the drive and with respect to the impulses born of it. This is precisely the point of departure for all sexual ethics. Psychotherapy, and through it medical sexology, relates in this way to the supra-material energies in man. It attempts to shape appropriate convictions, attitudes based on them, etc., and thus it attempts, in a sense, to regain man's "interiority" in order to guide his "exterior" conduct in this way. The truth about the drive plays a fundamental role in forming this "interiority." This method presupposes the conviction that only the man who thinks correctly about the object of his action can act correctly (i.e., at once truly and well).

As we know from this whole book, this object is not merely the drive, but the whole person connected with the force of nature that is the drive. Therefore, all correct sexual education, including the one that must assume the form of therapy, cannot move solely on the "biological" plane of the sexual drive, but on the plane of the person, with whom the whole problem of "love and responsibility" is linked. And it seems that in the last analysis here no other remedy exists, nor other pedagogical means. Thorough knowledge of the bio-physical sexual processes is very important, expedient, and valuable. However, it will not lead to the proper end, either in education or in sexual therapy, if it is not genuinely embedded in the objective vision of the person and his natural (and super-natural) vocation to love.

# Appendix

# On the Meaning
# of Spousal Love

# (Concerning the discussion)[1]

A discussion between Fr. Karol Meissner, OSB and Fr. Andrzej Szostek was published in *Roczniki Filozoficzne KUL* (the ethical booklet).[2] Because the discussion concerned the book *Love and Responsibility*, as indicated by the subtitle of Fr. Meissner's statement, therefore in turn the author of that book wishes to speak concerning that discussion. After all, in a certain sense both debaters invite him to do so. Thus, at first, I wish to formulate some *remarks* concerning both texts published in *Roczniki Filozoficzne*. Then, taking advantage of the discussion that has arisen, I wish to take up anew certain themes that were previously treated in *Love and Responsibility* in order to elaborate on them more completely and elucidate them more extensively. What comes to mind at this point is the term "*retractatio*" that was used by St. Augustine when he intended to express a different view regarding an issue he had presented earlier. However, the very term "*retractatio*" does not necessarily mean a change of views, but rather simply *speaks about another consideration of a problem*. And in this sense one can also understand the following statement as "*retractatio*."

# 1. Spousal love and marriage

The problem that Fr. Meissner deals with in his statement is certainly very significant and fundamental for conjugal ethics and for the entire so-called sexual ethics. However, I have doubts whether the method of extracting this problem from the text of *Love and Responsibility* is quite correct. Fr. Szostek speaks here about a certain reinterpretation of that book and declares that the reinterpretation rendered by Fr. Meissner "is slightly simplified and his conclusions due to that fact are insufficiently substantiated." Even if we disregard this assessment, at any rate we have to agree with Fr. Szostek's formulation of "the *obligation to read the intention of the author in the most 'integral' way possible*, and to interpret unclear formulations in light of other formulations contained either within the discussed work or outside it."

Personally, it seems to me that when Fr. Meissner, after having arranged several texts from *Love and Responsibility*, poses the question:

"Is marriage the source of these rights [to conjugal intercourse—KW]—as suggested by some statements—or is the source located somewhere else, and thus marriage constitutes an institution conditioning the honorable use of these rights?" then the above formulated principle seems to apply.[3] Besides, the question posed this way does not pertain to two different issues but to *one and the same issue under two aspects*, exactly as do the excerpts from *Love and Responsibility* referred to by Fr. Meissner. For one could say both that marriage is the source of conjugal rights and that it is the institution conditioning the use of these rights, thus indicating by these two formulations one and the same thing. Therefore, the problem posed in that way suggests somewhat artificially that *Love and Responsibility* contains a certain "lack of unequivocalness" concerning this matter.

Thus, at this point, Fr. Meissner's *discussion* with the theses of my book seems to me rather *ostensible*. This is indicated at the very least by the final result of that discussion. For at the end of his reflections, and even in light of the excerpts he quoted, Fr. Meissner arrives at the same [truth] that is contained precisely in *Love and Responsibility*. When he writes: "Thus spousal love as an attitude is indeed the only motive fully corresponding to the personalistic norm both in contracting marriage as well as in conjugal life. However, the rights to the person can be granted exclusively by the marital covenant—the act that is materially different from the act of conjugal love, and which originates in the Divine institution ( . . . )," he then proclaims the same that anyone can learn from *Love and Responsibility*. This "marital covenant" is the sacrament of marriage, which Fr. Meissner rightly defines as an act originating in the Divine institution and "granting participation in his [that is, God's—KW] rights to human persons for the purpose of accomplishing tasks foreseen in his creative and salvific plan."

We will return to the latter issue in a moment. Presently, it must be noted that the *dispute* between Fr. Meissner and Fr. Szostek concerns precisely the way of understanding this participation of people, spouses, in the rights that God alone possesses with respect to human persons as their Creator and also as their Redeemer. Fr. Szostek states outright that "Fr. Meissner's propositions implicate in a disturbing way" a non-personalistic "concept of the person and marriage." I think personally that in this aspect of his critical reflections on the study he analyzed (and we must admit that this is the central aspect), Fr. Meissner has not read "the intention of the author in the most integral way possible." For, first of all, *Love and Responsibility* is an ethical study, in which *the point is the substantiation of the fundamental norms* of Catholic conjugal ethics (and even more widely, sexual ethics) on the ground of rational principles, which in the fundamental measure do coincide with the commandment to love contained in the Gospel. The personalistic norm is such a principle. In this respect the remark of Fr. de Lubac in the introduction to the French edition of *Amour et responsabilité* is characteristic. He writes there as follows: "*L'auteur, toutefois, ne s'adresse pas uniquement aux croyants; du moins ne fait-il pas appel d'abord à leur foi. Il ne procède pas d'après les enseignements de l'Ecriture, mais par les voies de l'argumentation rationnelle.*"[4]

Besides this aspect, which after all possesses a practical and accidental meaning, one needs to consider the fundamental and substantial aspect to which Fr. Szostek draws attention, and the securing of which he rightly demands in his statement. For if it is a strict truth of faith, which obliges in the conscience of every Christian and of every theologian, that through marriage *God realizes his creative and salvific plan* in the history of mankind, then the truth that God desires this plan to be realized *in a way proper to man* and corresponding to his dignity is in no way less obliging. What was defined in *Love and Responsibility* as "spousal love" speaks at the same time about a certain truth that is both important on the part of man and revealed by God. On the part of man, spousal love denotes a particular dimension of the relation in which two persons, namely the spouses, "mutually give and accept each other" (according to the formulation of *Gaudium et Spes*, 48).[5] At the same time, entire Divine Revelation, from the words of Genesis to the words of the marital vow in the sacrament, not only confirms precisely this dimension of that inter-personal relation, but also decidedly postulates and demands it.

In this light, it seems that the very positing of the issue in the article of Fr. Meissner diverges from the fundamental intention of the author of *Love and Responsibility*. For the latter did not pose the problem in the way that spousal love alone is the source of the reciprocal right to each other, and concretely the right to conjugal intercourse between a man and a woman, *but* in his entire study he expressed the view that *the full rectitude of this intercourse* in marriage, which for Christians is a sacrament of faith, *demands spousal love*, both on the part of God the Creator and Redeemer and on the part of man, both in light of reason and of Revelation.

Clearly, the work of Fr. Meissner refers to a selected problem, which constitutes only a part of my study titled *Love and Responsibility*. Nevertheless, it seems that precisely this important and central part critiqued in Fr. Meissner's article does not adhere quite correctly to the whole. In that critique, the thought axis of the entire study has been slightly shifted, which certainly occurred inadvertently, but which nonetheless negatively affects the very gist of the issue raised by Fr. Meissner. No one doubts that this issue in itself is of great importance.

## 2. Spousal love and the human person

However, the above remarks, which come to mind concerning the discussion published in *Roczniki Filozoficzne*, are not the most important aim of our present statement. What is more important is the attempt to reconsider the problem indicated by both Fr. Meissner's article and the reply to it contained in Fr. Szostek's article. The point here is *the proper meaning of spousal love* and indirectly *the very conception of the human person* on the basis of Christian philosophy and also theology. First of all, it must be stated that the problem has already been discussed to a considerable extent in the mentioned articles, so that we must only determine the *status questionis*, that is, compare the positions of disputants. Only then will we be able to take our own position and do so, as I have said, as "*retractatio*," as considering the problem again. Fr. Szostek sees this need, above all, as concerning precision of language. We will see whether the point concerns only that.

Remaining on the ground of the discussion itself, we must state that Fr. Szostek perhaps rightly demonstrates on the part of Fr. Meissner the lack of differentiation between the ontic and the moral orders. What is at stake here? Fr. Meissner criticizes the notion of spousal love not only on account of terminology, which the author of *Love and Responsibility* employed to express it, but also on account of what was expressed in that notion and what is contained in it within the boundaries of the study under discussion. In particular he criticizes the view *that a person can authentically give himself to another person* and that this giving should take place in the reciprocal relation between a man and a woman in marriage. Fr. Meissner writes: "( . . . ) The dignity of the human person ( . . . ) and above all the belonging to the Creator, not only as to the source of the person's existence but also as to the person's final end, constitute the basis of the *inalienable* right by virtue of which no person is able to belong to any other person. Consequently, no person can acquire any rights to another person, even if the latter consents to it out of spousal love. Love gives man no rights to anyone. The social character of human existence cannot change this fact as well ( . . . )."

It is evident that Fr. Meissner does not deny the human person the right to give himself to another human person as much as he denies the right to such giving that would entail the relation of ownership toward the person who gives himself, that is, by virtue of which the latter would belong to the former as his possession. According to Fr. Meissner, the basis for this is both the dignity of the human person and above all his belonging to the Creator as the source of the person's existence and his final end. "Precisely for this reason," he writes, "it does not also seem right to place the self-giving of the human person to God on the same level with the self-giving of the human person to another person," because in the former case there exists "the giving to God what is rightly due to him," whereas "one can in no way assert that the self-giving to another person in marriage is rightly due to that person."

But in my opinion, the distinction of Fr. Szostek rightly applies to all those formulations. Among other things he writes: "The person is incommunicable without exception *in the ontic sense*: nobody, not even the Creator, can decide about the person instead of the person himself. However, the person is 'communicable' *in the moral sense*: he can accept that someone else governs him. He does not violate his personal dignity in this way because in 'giving himself' to somebody he wills the same thing that somebody wills. He violates this dignity (he acts unworthily), however, only when he makes an improper decision, and this improperness can pertain to the choice of the person-object to whom he gives himself as well as to the end or the way in which he does it. In this case, he opposes the intentions of the Creator ( . . . )."

Fr. Szostek continues: "( . . . ) As the Creator and the End of human life, God possesses a particular right of ownership in relation to man, a right that nevertheless does not rescind man's freedom ( . . . ). Thus, the fact that the human person is *sui iuris et alteri incommunicabilis* does not prevent (on the personal-moral plane) self-giving to another person, and in some sense it even constitutes the basis for this giving." At this point, Fr. Szostek refers to analyses from *Person and Act* and, in turn, continues his thought with the following words: "( . . . ) Marriage in this context can be (logically and not chronologically) nothing else but a consequence of spousal love and of the decision to give oneself to each other forever. Its sacramental character emphasizes God's particular share in what will be taking place between people ( . . . )."

However, concerning the issue of the human person *giving himself to God* and *to man* that Fr. Meissner raised, Fr. Szostek takes it up with the following words: "The self-giving to God and the self-giving to man is accomplished (thus) on different planes: the self-giving to man should constitute a certain stage and a way of self-giving to God, which will be fully realized in heaven where nobody will marry nor be given in marriage anymore."

Even if the issue has not been fully discussed, in any case the clear distinction of the ontic order and sense from the moral order and sense possesses the key meaning for explaining the essence of spousal love and the problems connected with it. The person as a being is "*sui iuris*" and "*alteri incommunicabilis*"—his essential "incommunicability" remains in close connection with the power of self-determination proper to him. Such is the person in virtue of the act of creation, thus by the will of the Creator. Being such, the person is—on the basis of that very same act and the very same will—a possession of God. He belongs to God in the ontic sense. He nonetheless belongs to him as a being who is "*sui iuris*" and "*alteri incommunicabilis*." In this belonging to God the Creator—one could say in the status of possession resulting from the fact of being created—the human person possesses himself and determines himself. The Creator's ontic status of possession contains, without being violated, the status of self-possession proper to man as a person, which means that at the same time man is his own possession, and the status of self-governance, which means that if he is to determine himself, he consequently must also govern himself. And as self-possession in the ontic status of the person *does not abolish his creatureliness*, that is, that as a creature he is a possession of the Creator, so also self-governance *does not abolish* the supreme *authority of the Creator* over the man-person. At the same time, with all metaphysical certainty, we state that both the possession of man by the Creator and his governance over man are closely suited to the nature of the creature, which is man, that is, to self-possession and self-governance proper to him as a person, both of which are expressed in their own way in human self-determination. (This was more widely and more thoroughly analyzed by the author of *Love and Responsibility* in another study titled *Person and Act*.)

All the above clarifications within the ontic sense are indispensable in order to cross correctly into the ethical order. The ontic order speaks about what is, whereas the ethical order speaks about what can and should be. What can and should be correctly follows—should follow—from what is.[6] Ultimately, this is the point in *Love and Responsibility* as well as in both statements that appeared in *Roczniki Filozoficzne*.

## 3. *The "law of the gift" inscribed in the being of the person*

From what man is as a person, that is, a being that possesses itself and governs itself, follows that he can "give himself," he can make himself a gift for others, without thereby violating his ontic status. The "law of the gift" is inscribed, so to speak, in the very being of the person. The entire tradition of Christian thought, for which the Gospel is and always remains the source of inspiration, convinces us about that. We find a concise expression of this thought in the teaching of Vatican II, in the Pastoral Constitution on the Church, where among other things we read the following sentence: "Man, *who is the only creature on earth which God willed for itself, cannot fully find himself except through a sincere gift of self*," *Gaudium et Spes*, 24 (the Constitution refers at this point to Luke 17:33).[7] The Creator inscribed in the nature of the personal being the potency and power of giving oneself, and this potency is closely joined with the structure of self-possession and self-governance proper to the person, with the fact that he is "*sui iuris et alteri incommunicabilis.*" What is rooted precisely in this ontic "incommunicability" is a capacity for giving oneself, for becoming a gift for others. Only and exclusively a being that possesses itself is able to "give itself," that is, to make itself a gift. The quoted conciliar text, which expresses the thought of the Gospel, bids us to accept that precisely by this the man-person fully finds himself.

It is clear that this self-giving, this becoming a gift for others, possesses here a moral meaning. It does not signify and cannot signify a relinquishing of the ontic status of the person. Fr. Meissner rightly observes that certain formulations that appear in *Love and Responsibility* should be stated more precisely. Fr. Meissner has in mind expressions such as "self-giving," "possession," and "relinquishing of the right to self-reliance and incommunicability" used in the context of reflections on spousal love. In turn, however, Fr. Szostek observes no less correctly that these formulations were employed in that context in a metaphorical sense. He lists a few examples: "Love, *so to speak*, snatches the person from this ( . . . ) incommunicability ( . . . ). He wants, *so to speak*, to stop being his own exclusive possession ( . . . ). It signifies a *certain* relinquishing of that *sui iuris* ( . . . )" (all these quotations from *Love and Responsibility* were provided in footnotes. See footnote 6 on p. 295). In this case, the call for a more precise language is justified, and so we want to satisfy it by this treatise. However, the most essential thing is the very understanding of the reality in question.

The sentence from the Pastoral Constitution on the Church of Vatican II quoted above indicates clearly that the "law of the gift" is inscribed in the being of the person as the principle that *confers sense on human existence*, and thereby it also *explains the action of man* in the most fundamental way. Man is not only a being given to himself ("the only creature on earth which God willed for itself"), but at the same time he is a being entrusted to himself, for he must keep finding himself, and indeed he tries to "fully find himself."[8] Such is the deepest vector of the dynamic of being and acting, the dynamic proper to man as a person. And precisely here the category of the gift appears. Man "cannot fully find himself except through a sincere gift of self." What is this gift? In light of the teaching of Vatican II, it is certainly not a frustration of the ontic status of the person; it is not and cannot be a denial of the person's proper self-possession and self-governance. Rather, it is its particular confirmation, a revelation of richness. If in

*Love and Responsibility* it is somewhere stated that spousal love, "so to speak, snatches the person from his proper incommunicability," this expression is metaphorical. Through the gift of self, through "a sincere gift," the person confirms and, so to speak, deepens the self-possession and self-governance proper to himself. Through the gift of self in the moral sense, the person does not lose anything, but becomes richer instead.

Of course, the precision of language that we can afford here is conditioned by the order of phenomenological thinking, which is different from the order of metaphysical thinking. Nonetheless, *the truths about the person that we formulate here in two different languages are coherent and explain each other.* Thus, the statement *"persona est sui iuris et alteri incommunicabilis,"* expressed in metaphysical categories, and the statement about self-possession and self-governance as the essential properties of the person are coherent, even though the latter is an expression of the direct experience of man, experience in the phenomenological sense. We are convinced that the "phenomenon" in this case "carries in itself" a being and reveals it fully, conditioning the precision of metaphysical formulations.

By these explanations concerning the precision of language we do not wish to close the way to a further and more penetrating analysis. For what still remains to be explained is how the being of the person and the "law of the gift" inscribed in it are related to each other. At the end of these reflections the problem must emerge of what ultimately determines the person: substance or relation. We do not intend to take up this analysis within the framework of this statement. However, it is worthwhile to note that the previously quoted sentence of Vatican II seems to link quite clearly one with the other: man is the creature (i.e., a being) that God willed "for its own sake," and at the same time this being finds itself fully "through a sincere gift of self." *In order to explain the reality of the human person,* both senses, *the ontic and the moral* (referring to Fr. Szostek's expression), *must be unified.* They must be properly correlated, that is, coordinated. By accepting that the person becomes a gift in the moral sense, that he gives himself, we indicate the very being of the person, his essential properties, self-possession and self-governance, that he is *"sui iuris et alteri incommunicabilis,"* and ultimately we at last indicate his substantiality.

By this we also indicate the organic link of ethics with metaphysics that is formed in the person; it emerges from the person's efficacy and subjectivity. This is also a vast problem, which we do not take up here. It is nonetheless proper to note that this "gift of self," which the person can and should perform, not only must be understood in the moral sense, but also constitutes a particular category that is located at the crossing from metaphysics to ethics, and it also constitutes, *so to speak, a synthetic expression of human morality*. In turn, this synthetic expression could be subjected to an analysis. Then, it would become evident how this gift of self, which man can and should make in order to fully find himself, is realized through particular virtues and through each of them. It would also become evident how this gift of the person is ruined and frustrated through man's particular vices and sins. It would be a new and perhaps more personalistic *grasp of entire aretology*.[9]

However, we do not take up this topic here, for this problem is in itself very vast and diverse. Nevertheless, this problem needs to be mentioned and at least initially positioned, if only in consideration of Fr. Szostek's statement included in his polemic with Fr. Meissner:

> ( ... ) Giving oneself to somebody else, serving the other, dedicating oneself, etc., express different forms and degrees of love, yet the moment of giving, of sacrificing oneself, as the expression of affirming the one to whom it turns, is contained in every act of love. Questioning the right to self-giving in spousal love at the same time undermines man's right to self-giving in any other form ( ... ). Although, in fact, a difference exists regarding the degree of the "fullness" of this giving among different forms of love, the structure of the action of the subject is always similar and depends on the same principle: the principle of man's freedom and the right to govern himself.

Referring to the analyses included in *Love and Responsibility*, these sentences speak of the "law of the gift," which, as we state here, is inscribed in the being of the person, and which is realized in various forms *through every act of love* (in order to avoid all misunderstandings, we could say: through every act of true love). Indirectly, the act of every virtue is such an act because all virtues find in love their common root, their full sense and ultimate expression.

While granting the correctness of the understanding indicated by Fr. Szostek's text quoted above, it is nevertheless necessary to consider whether the law of the gift, which is somehow realized in every true act of love, is realized in the same way *in spousal love*. It is known that an act of love can be a provisional and one-time act, whereas spousal love *is linked to the choice of a vocation in the dimension of the whole life*, as has been indicated by both the analyses conducted in *Love and Responsibility* and the discussion between Fr. Meissner and Fr. Szostek concerning that book. So, is there a difference here as to the degree of the "fullness" of giving, as Fr. Szostek suggests, or rather a more fundamental difference? Without anticipating the conclusions concerning this matter, we must agree on one thing, namely that what comes to light both in a one-time act of love and also in spousal love is the same "law of the gift" which is inscribed deeply in the very being of the person. Based on this law, man is able to perform provisional acts of love in which self-giving sometimes reaches the summits of heroism (it is sufficient to recall the act of Bl. Maximilian in Auschwitz).[10] Based on it, man can also choose a vocation for his whole life, a vocation that will continuously demand acts of love from him. In the latter case, self-giving, the gift of the person, becomes, so to speak, the common denominator of many acts—insofar as of the possibility of them all—on the path of this vocation. In any case, the degree of the fullness of the gift can be considered *both in the intensive as well as the extensive meaning*. An ethicist and, above all, a moral theologian will easily agree that in both cases, that is, in the case of a provisional act of love and in the case of the choice of a vocation for one's whole life, ultimately the point is the maturity of the very virtue of love, which must be expressed and tested one way or another. However, the problem still remains open as to how much and to what extent the "law of the gift" inscribed in the being of the person can constitute the basis for the right to the person. This is an essential problem of spousal love.

## 4. Spousal love and the "law of the gift"

It seems that in many points the previous analyses specify and deepen the position taken in *Love and Responsibility*. According to that position, the full ethical rectitude of a man and a woman's union and intercourse in marriage, which for Christians is a sacrament of faith, requires spousal love. The sacrament of marriage constitutes the basis of the right to the person in the reciprocal relation between a man and a woman. Fr. Meissner links this sacrament with the right possessed by God alone to every human person when he writes: "Rights to the person can be granted exclusively by the marital covenant, which is an act materially different from an act of conjugal love and originating from the Divine institution as granting participation in his rights to human persons for the purpose of accomplishing the tasks foreseen in his creative and salvific plan." However, this creative and salvific plan as well as the Divine institution *find their full justification in human personal dimensions*. This justification is precisely the "law of the gift" inscribed in the being of the person, and in this case, of two persons, a man and a woman. By virtue of precisely this law, the spouses "mutually give and accept each other" as the Second Vatican Council teaches (*Gaudium et Spes*, 48). By virtue of precisely this law, marriage achieves at the same time—in the Divine dimension of the sacrament—*the full human profile of spousal love*. The vocation to such love is inscribed in the very nature of human persons, of a man and a woman, together with the "law of the gift," as we have attempted to demonstrate thus far.

In this case, the point is the gift of self in a different meaning than in the case of any one-time or even recurring act of love. The point is the gift of one person for another person, the gift which in this case is indispensable *for the union of persons*, so that they, a man and a woman, constitute a particular community and unity. Christ speaks of this unity, referring to the words of Genesis: "So they are no longer two, but one flesh" (Mt 19:6). In turn, Vatican II does not hesitate to describe this unity with the phrase "*communio personarum*" (*Gaudium et Spes*, 12). All this testifies indirectly about the meaning of spousal love and about the "law of the gift," thanks to which this love—this reciprocal self-giving of persons and their reciprocal belonging to each other—is possible. If the spouses are to be united as persons, with self-possession and self-governance being the properties of each, they must give themselves to each other in this sacrament, they must in a sense *take advantage* of this "law of the gift" in their relation to each other, for this law is inscribed by the Creator himself in the being of the person together with the fundamental law of belonging to him.

In the human profile of spousal love, the "law of the gift" constitutes above all the foundation of the durable, indissoluble union of persons. Such a union cannot exist without their reciprocal and durable belonging to each other. At this point, the following sentence of Fr. Meissner must be verified once more: "The dignity of the human person ( . . . ) and above all the belonging to the Creator, not only as to the source of the person's existence but also as to the person's final end, constitute the basis of the *inalienable* right by virtue of which no person is able to belong to any other person ( . . . )." The belonging of the human person to God as his Creator and Redeemer does not abolish the "law of the gift," which he himself inscribed in the personal being of man, as the teaching of Vatican II reminds us, and as we have attempted to demonstrate in the preceding analysis. The man-person cannot become a possession of another man in the same way that things become his possessions. No man possesses such a right of ownership to a woman and vice versa. It can be said that *precisely the "law of the gift" inscribed in the being of every person protects against the right of ownership so understood in relation to the human person.* If in the history of humanity such social systems existed or exist in which through marriage a woman becomes a man's possession (or vice versa), whom the man could own and use like a thing, these social systems—of course—are not in conformity with the dignity of the person and the institution of the Creator.

The conjugal belonging of a woman to a man in the community of persons, "*in communione personarum*," is indeed something different. Clearly, such belonging generates reciprocal rights to the person. The words of the sacramental marriage vow express the quintessence of these rights. Both such belonging and the reciprocal rights to the person derived from it by no means violate the belonging of each person, a man and a woman, to God alone, the belonging through the mystery of creation and redemption. Quite the contrary, this belonging of persons, who are spouses, to each other finds its source and its confirmation in the belonging of each of them to God alone.

The "*law of the gift*," which God as the Creator inscribed in the being of the human person, of a man and a woman, and the meaning of which was confirmed and deepened by him as the Redeemer in the consciousness of every man, *constitutes the proper basis of that* "*communio personarum,*" of which the previously quoted text of Vatican II speaks. From the very beginning, the Creator wills that marriage is this "*communio personarum*" in which a man and a woman realize day by day and in the dimension of their whole life the ideal of the personal union by "giving and receiving each other" (see *Gaudium et Spes*, 48). Spousal love can be understood as the realization of this ideal. In such a union, "*in communione personarum,*" the precise point is so that the person is always and in every situation treated as a person, that is, as "the only creature on earth which God wills for itself" (*Gaudium et Spes*, 24)—so that the woman is treated this way by the man and the man by the woman, especially that each of them brings into their marriage that "sincere gift of self," of which Vatican II speaks (*Gaudium et Spes*, 24).[11] Each of them brings this gift in a particular and irrevocable way. The gift of self, which is expressed among other things by conjugal giving and union, creates particularly many occasions for violating the "law of the gift," which is written not merely in the body alone and its sexual distinctness, but in the very person. And therefore it must be protected.

The consciousness of the "law of the gift," the law inscribed in the very being of the person, *must protect from any appropriation of the person*, from imposing upon him the non-personal status of possession. Wherever the "law of the gift" exists, there the right of ownership is out of the question, although there we can and must speak of the belonging and the union of persons. Indeed, only by virtue of this law is this union able to be an authentically personal union. This truth is fundamental for understanding the reality of marriage, its Christian and also human ethics, and finally for understanding many other principles of all so-called sexual ethics. The dignity of the person, both of a woman and of a man, lies at the center of these principles. Therefore, in *Love and Responsibility* the *personalistic norm* was placed in the foreground. A thorough analysis demonstrates that this norm in no way obscures "the finality of the marital covenant," that is, these "intentions of God the Father and Creator, which the persons who give themselves to each other in marriage enter into" (quoted from Fr. Meissner's article). Instead, this norm reveals in depth the personalistic meaning and value of Divine intentions in human persons and for these persons.

At this point, one more issue remains, namely *the issue of the analogous meaning of spousal love*. Everyone who has attentively read Sacred Scripture is fully aware of that. Fr. Meissner writes: "It does not seem right to place the self-giving of the human person to God on the same level with the self-giving of the human person to another [human, of course—KW] person," because what happens in the former case is the "giving to God what is rightly due to him," whereas "one can in no way assert that the self-giving to another person in marriage is rightly due to that person." Already in *Love and Responsibility* it was quite extensively stated that the matters treated here cannot be considered under the principle of that "*debitum*" which mere justice administers (see the sections "The Concept of 'Justice with Respect to the Creator'" and "Virginity and Intactness" [in chapter IV, part 2]).

The revelational meaning of the Gospel (revelational in the literal sense since *revelare* means "to reveal") consists in introducing a consistent order of love in the relations of man-God and man-man. The point of departure is love in the relation God-man. It seems that what was already outlined in this way in *Love and Responsibility* can be elucidated and complemented even more by relying on the category of the gift inscribed in the personal being.

The Gospel poses very clearly the issue of man's *vocation to the exclusive self-giving to God*, which entails relinquishing marriage. This particular spousal self-giving to man, brought by marriage, gives place, as it were, to a different spousal self-giving. Sacred Scripture of both the Old and New Testaments does not separate or oppose these two forms of spousal love but brings them together and compares them. We must distinguish this comparison from texts such as Ephesians 5:21–23 where the love of Christ for the Church is portrayed in the likeness of conjugal love, although we must also introduce them to that comparison as a third element. This is done by the Dogmatic Constitution on the Church, which, while speaking about the religious vocation, indicates that one's dedication to God's service brought by this vocation "will be the more perfect, in as much as the indissoluble bond of the union of Christ and his bride, the Church, is represented by firm and more stable bonds" (*Lumen Gentium*, 44).[12] And so, the entire tradition, which we do not present here in its full extent, but rather limit ourselves to mentioning it, advocates ascribing an analogous meaning to spousal love. In accordance with Christ's teaching, this love is realized *in one way* in the exclusive self-giving to God alone, and in another way in marriage through the reciprocal self-giving of human persons, of a man and a woman. The Gospel and the Church's teaching that follows it emphasize continuously the superiority of the former vocation over the latter (also see *Love and Responsibility* [in section "Virginity and Intactness," chapter IV, part 2]).

At the same time, however, it is necessary to emphasize that although God as the Creator possesses the "*dominium altum*," the supreme right in relation to all creatures and thus also in relation to man, who is a person, *the total self-giving* "*to God loved beyond all things*" (*Lumen Gentium*, 44), which is expressed in the religious vocation, by the will of Christ himself is left to the free choice of man under the action of grace.[13] Therefore, in this case, indeed above all here, the self-giving of the person must find its basis and *justification* in that "*law of the gift*," which is inscribed by God in the being of the person. Although on the part of man as a creature this vocation, in a sense, confirms the supreme right, the "*dominium altum*" of God the Creator in relation to him, this is nevertheless accomplished (and by nature of the religious or priestly vocation it follows that this must be accomplished) not above all according to the principle of "*debitum*" alone, but in the spirit of love, which seeks the union with the most beloved God, with Christ the Bridegroom. The Magisterium of the Church, including that of the last council, and the theology of vocation and religious life explain extensively *the eschatological dimension of spousal love* expressed in this vocation and the place of this dimension in the Church.[14]

Finally, we must take particular care not to cause yet another, certainly unintended, effect by understanding the issue too radically. This effect could arise if the distinction of these two forms of spousal love, of which we speak here in relation to the religious and marital vocations, created an impression that the reciprocal self-giving of persons in marriage, of a man and a woman, in a sense takes away these people from God, precludes their self-giving to God, or severs them from him. The entire tradition of Christian thought, which draws its inspiration from the Gospel, does not allow such an understanding. By "reciprocally giving and receiving each other" (*Gaudium et Spes*, 48) in this shared vocation of theirs and in its realization throughout their whole life, *the spouses at the same time realize*, together and each of them separately, *that gift of the person which is directed to God alone.* The condition of this realization is the fulfillment of the tasks "foreseen in his creative and salvific plan" (quoted from Fr. Meissner's article), that is, the consistent acceptance of the full finality of marriage. The full respect of this "law of the gift," which forms the community of marriage and also of the family as the authentic "*communio personarum*," is implicated in this acceptance and determines its human level.

# 5. Substantiation of ethical demands for premarital chastity

Returning at the end of these reflections to their beginning, and even more so to the discussion between Fr. Karol Meissner and Fr. Andrzej Szostek, it must be acknowledged that, not without reason, Fr. Meissner is apprehensive about an erroneous interpretation of spousal love and, above all, the consequence of that interpretation in the field of sexual morality. This apprehension must prompt us *to such clarifications that will exclude consequences of this kind.* The effort of ethics and of moral theology can proceed in our field only in this way. This effort cannot be fragmentary or merely casuistic; it is necessary to reach the full truth about man, for it contains the substantiation of the Creator and Redeemer's moral demands.

Therefore, it seems that as the thorough understanding of the reality of the person and of the "law of the gift" inscribed in him constitutes the very framework for substantiations in the field of conjugal ethics, explains the rightness of unity, of indissolubility, of fidelity, of responsible parenthood, and demonstrates the moral evil of adultery, of divorce, of contraception (all this found its expression in *Love and Responsibility*)— the very same principle stands at the basis of all sexual morality. Thus, particularly in the light of this principle we ought to decidedly exclude the ethical permissibility of sexual intercourse before marriage, or treating the issue more broadly, outside of marriage. The latter problem, i.e., the issue of extra-marital relations, seems to be already included in the totality of the previously mentioned principles of conjugal morality. However, we must pay attention to the former problem, for it seems that regarding the area of pre-marital relations *the concept of spousal love can be made shallow with a particular ease and the "law of the gift" abused with a particular inconsideration.*

Precisely here, it is necessary to treat with extreme accuracy the whole truth about man as a person and apply it very responsibly both in speech and in writing on these themes as well as in making decisions, which are never just private and one-sided, but always concern another person. Many reasons call for demanding here a "greater" responsibility on behalf of the man, which does not mean that the woman's responsibility is "lesser." It is only "different." The "law of the gift," which the Creator so deeply and subtly inscribed in the totality of the being of the person, ought to be understood here as the "right to such a gift," that is, to the reciprocal self-giving of a man and a woman in a sexual way.[15] If we consider this concrete issue in its whole truth, which means in complete objective reality as well, then we must acknowledge that *sexual intercourse can be honest and honorable only as a conjugal act.*[16] *Outside of marriage, and thus also before marriage, sexual intercourse is always an abuse* of the "law of the gift," it is—to state this with other words and more within the terminology of *Love and Responsibility*—treating the person as a means of use. Such is the objective qualification of this act, and it cannot be otherwise.

It is known that, regarding this point, conflicts of a subjective character often occur, which can be understood differently and differently qualified. For these conflicts are certainly very often influenced by affection, which imparts its own subjective shape to reasoning and expression. Then, it also seems that the demand for marriage to be a factor that conditions the honorableness and honesty of intercourse between a man and a woman is marked with juridicism and signifies the primacy of an institution over man with his "interior truth." We already tried to elucidate this problem in *Love and Responsibility*, especially in the section titled "The Value of the Institution" [in part 1 of chapter IV]. A thorough analysis of this problem must each time lead us to the conclusion that *marriage as an institution is not something merely "external" in relation to the whole truth of persons*, of a man and a woman, when their love and self-giving are to be expressed with the "*right to such a gift*."

Marriage as an institution does not only proceed from the juridical-social order or a religious order as "external" in relation to the person and his love. Indeed, as an element of this order, marriage proceeds from the very "interiority" of this love, for the shape of the reciprocal self-giving of a man and a woman demands it. When they give themselves to each other in sexual intercourse, such self-giving is fully justified; it corresponds to the truth of love and mutually safeguards the dignity of the person, only if both a man and a woman perform it as spouses, as husband and wife. Otherwise, an abuse of the "law of the gift" takes place. Marriage is not only a social and religious discernment of the whole rectitude of being and action of persons, of men and women, but, above all, it is *a discernment of this rectitude in persons*, in a woman and a man, in the essential meaning of the action of sexual intercourse for both of them. Thus, it is at the same time the correct discernment of the moral law and of the voice of one's own unfalsified conscience. Precisely the "law of the gift" cannot be falsified in this voice because this law covers the sphere of great and in a sense the greatest values. These values are correctly experienced (*przeżywać*) subjectively within the totality of human acts only if these acts manifest their real, objective meaning.

Premarital relations do not manifest this great meaning, which is hidden in the personal "law of the gift," because, strictly speaking, they do not undertake it. For on the one hand, let us say, on the part of the man, there is no basis then to receive "this gift;" whereas, on the other hand, on the part of the woman, there is no basis to offer it. Both, the man and the woman, *have not yet constituted in themselves and between each other such an objective situation, such a "state," in which the sexual act, which is conjugal in its essence, would be fully justified*. Furthermore, the point concerns justification (as we also read in *Love and Responsibility*) with respect to society in the lay and religious sense. Above all, however, the point concerns these two concrete persons. They themselves, in themselves and between each other, must constitute the objective situation, the state, in which sexual intercourse—conjugal in its essence—can be the true and reciprocal gift of the person for another person. Because this intercourse is in its essence conjugal, this objective situation and state is called and is marriage.

What belongs to the essence of this objective situation constituted by a man and a woman in a conscious and free way so that conjugal intercourse could be mutually and reciprocally a free gift of persons is *the full responsibility for the acts of this intercourse*, for their full meaning, that is, also *for their parental sense and procreative finality*. Without accepting this responsibility, the reciprocal sexual self-giving of a man and a woman does not fulfill those inviolable demands that are posed by the dignity of the person understood precisely on the basis of that "law of the gift" inscribed by the Creator in the being of the person. Therefore, a violation then occurs of that law and of the dignity of persons closely linked to it.

This whole ethical truth can be proved or shown to be evident on the basis of reasoning alone, as Fr. de Lubac emphasized in the introduction to the French edition of *Love and Responsibility*. However, *this truth becomes particularly transparent through the sacrament of marriage*. Each time we follow attentively the whole liturgy of this sacrament, two people stand before us, a man and a woman, who come to express before God precisely this, that they constitute an objective situation, in which both are to become a gift for each other as spouses. Conjugal intercourse also belongs to the essence of this situation, which is then expressed, and thereby ultimately matures and is constituted as a sacrament. This intercourse *is included in the totality of their life's vocation that they both confess before God* as "their share with Jesus Christ" in the community of the Church. And through this confession they, in a sense, *receive each other from the hands of God the Creator and Redeemer*. They receive each other in order to be a gift for each other as husband and wife. This includes the sacramental confirmation of the right to sexual intercourse, which only in the marital covenant can be the correct form of realizing the general "law of the gift" inscribed by God in the very being of the person.

Without a doubt, the sacrament of marriage is the institution of the divine law that is very closely guarded in the law of the Church. However, penetrating into the essential structure of this "institution" unveils its deeply personalistic character. One can say that *the sacrament of marriage*, while revealing "the love of God the Father, the grace of our Lord Jesus Christ, and the gift of unity in the Holy Spirit" *at the same time proclaims the full truth about man*, about the vocation of persons. It is necessary to read and to accept this truth in its entire content in order to take up the community of life and of reciprocal self-giving in the dimensions of the sacrament, the sacrament St. Paul described as "great."[17]

# Translator's Notes

## Editors' Introduction to the Polish Edition (1979)

1. *Twenty years ago*: This introduction was written in 1979, that is, nineteen years after the first publication of the book in 1960.

2. *Habent sua fata libelli*: Books have their own fate.

3. *Tolle et lege*: Take and read!

4. *Vide*: See!

5. *Ten years after the appearance of the encyclical* Humanae Vitae: The encyclical was released on July 25, 1968.

6. *In the notes we placed below the text of* Love and Responsibility: The editors' notes were probably placed in that edition (from 1979) as endnotes. However, the most recent Polish editions place the editors' notes as footnotes, which is how they appear in this translation. Let me stress that these footnotes were not written by Wojtyła himself but by the Polish editors.

7. *Medium quo*: Literally "the means by which."

8. *Using a hyphen (-) instead of forming compound words*: The list below contains examples of hyphenated words used by Wojtyła in the book (the words marked with an asterisk are found in the deleted material from the 1962 edition). These words are not normally hyphenated in Polish. Sometimes in different places Wojtyła may use both the hyphenated and compound versions, e.g., inter-personal and interpersonal.

co-create (*współ-tworzyć*)
co-creator (*współ-twórca*)
co-subject (*współ-podmiot*)

dis-integration (*dez-integracja*)
ego-centric (*ego-centryczny*)
extra-marital (*poza-małżeński*)

in-communicable (*nie-odstępny*)
inter-personal (*między-osobowy*)
inter-subjective (*inter-subiektywny*)
meta-cognitive (*poza-poznawczy*)
meta-intellectual (*poza-rozumowy*)
non-transferable (*nie-przekazywalny*)
non-visual (*nie-oglądowy*)
over-excitability* (*nad-pobudliwość*)
pre-marital (*przed-małżeński*)
pre-scientific* (*przed-naukowy*)

psycho-physical (*psycho-fizyczny*)
sex-appeal (*sex-appeal*)
super-natural (*nad-naturalny*)
supra-consumer (*ponad-konsumpcyjny*)
supra-material (*ponad-rzeczowy*)
supra-utilitarian (*ponad-użytkowy*)
supra-subjective (*ponad-podmiotowy*)
trans-subjective (*trans-subiektywny*)
two-sidedness (*obu-stronność*)

## Author's Introduction to the First Polish Edition (1960)

1. *Love between a man and a woman*: Throughout the text, the Polish words denoting a female (*kobieta*) and a male (*mężczyzna*) have been translated with the indefinite article "a" as "a man" and "a woman" respectively. I have not used the words "male" and "female" because they can also be applied to animals, whereas the Polish words *mężczyzna* and *kobieta* are reserved for human beings only.

The meaning of the Polish word *człowiek* corresponds perfectly to that of "man" in English, and means basically the human person. "Man" includes not only that by which man is man (i.e., humanity) but also his bodiliness, and for this reason "man" indicates either a man or a woman. Therefore, as a rule, no article preceding "man" is used when translating that Polish word. Nonetheless, in keeping with the classical usage (which fully agrees with Polish—Wojtyła does not use so-called inclusive language), any pronouns or possessive adjectives referring to "man" are masculine.

There are a few exceptions to the above rule, but the immediate context makes clear whether "man" means "a man" (a male), as in the phrase "man and woman," or the human person, as in the phrase "another man."

In rare instances, however, when the rendering of "man" would produce an erroneous reading due to associations of the word "man" with "a man" (a male), I translated the word as "a human being" or "a human person," as in the following sentence: "The sexual drive in the human person is always by nature turned toward another human person."

2. *Priests, the religious . . .* : Wojtyła uses here the plural form of one word (*duchowny*), which can signify either a priest or a religious person (e.g., a monk or nun).

3. *Raison d'être*: Reason for being. This French phrase is never used by Wojtyła in this book, but is my translation of the corresponding Polish expression (*racja bytu*).

4. *Conduct*: The Polish word *postępowanie* is consistently translated as "conduct" instead of "behavior," which is expressed by the word *zachowanie*. In *Person*

*and Act* (section 10 of chapter VI), Wojtyła explains that "conduct" indicates man's action as a result of his efficacy (self-determination). On the other hand, "behavior" signifies the perceptible "way" a given person handles himself while acting. Behavior accompanies action but is not identified with it.

5. *Introduction of love into love*: By distinguishing the evangelical love (the love commanded by the Gospel) from the "sexual" love between a man and a woman, Wojtyła does not advance a dualistic conception of love. Quite the contrary, he calls for a greater awareness that authentic human love is a reflection of and participation in the divine love, the origin and fulfillment of human love. See the profound cry he puts in the mouth of the Mother in his play *Radiation of Fatherhood*: "Do not divide love. Love is one" ("*Promieniowanie ojcostwa*" in *Poezje i dramaty* (Kraków: Wydawnictwo Znak, 1979), 235 or I.5). The unity of love presupposes that man's likeness to God is manifested and realized not only in his relationship to the Creator and Redeemer, but also in and through his relation to human persons and even, in a radically different way, to nature in general. For this reason Wojtyła can say, for instance, that "man can be just with respect to God the Creator insofar as he loves people" (see part II of chapter IV).

6. *Eo ipso*: Literally "by itself" meaning "this way" or "by the same token." This is the only instance of this Latin phrase in the Polish text.

7. *Sex*: Here and elsewhere in the book this word (*płeć*) does not denote sexual intercourse, but the distinct manner of being man. It is worth noting that Wojtyła does not separate sex (typically taken as the biological-physiological reality) from gender (often seen as the human-psychological reality). Sex is intrinsically united to gender. See Wojtyła's statements in chapter V of this book (especially his description of genetic sex, somatic sex, and physiological sex in the deleted material from chapter V provided in the notes below).

## Author's Introduction to the Second Polish Edition (1962)

1. *Eph 5:22–33*: The Polish text has Ephesians 5:22–23, but judging by the context and the previous introduction of the author, Ephesians 5:22–33 is meant.

2. *An ethical study*: This subtitle is not used in the most recent Polish editions.

3. *Nota bene*: Note well.

## Chapter I: The Person and the Drive

1. *The word "object" in this case signifies more or less the same as "a being" (byt)*: The Polish word *byt*, which means some individual thing that exists (equivalent to Latin's *ens*, or *hoc ens* in this case), is always rendered by me with an article, e.g., "a being."

2. *Individua substantia rationalis naturae*: An individual substance of a rational nature. This definition is found in chapter III of Boethius' *Liber de persona et duabus naturis* (*Patrologia Latina* 64, 1343C–D).

3. *The contact ( . . . ) is not merely "biological" (przyrodniczy), physical, as is the case with all other creations of nature (przyroda)*: There are two distinct Polish words usually translated as "nature," namely *natura* and *przyroda*. *Natura* (nature) with its adjective *naturalny* (natural) refers rather to the essence of things possessed by them because of and since birth (as Wojtyła explains later on or in section 4, chapter II of *Person and Act*). This essence determines the functions of a given being and the direction of its growth. Therefore, Aristotle defines nature as the principle (ἀρχή καὶ αἰτία) of motion and rest that is *inherent* in things, i.e., does not belong to them *per accidens* (see *Physics* 192b20).

On the other hand, the noun *przyroda* (nature) with its adjective *przyrodniczy* (biological) denotes strictly the material environment with its phenomena. Thus, properly speaking, *przyroda* is the visible subset of *natura*, or, so to say, the observable effect of it. Modern empirical science tends to reduce *natura* to *przyroda* and views the operation of the latter as acting in accordance with laws external to it.

In order to distinguish between these two concepts in English (i.e., *natura* and *przyroda*), the word *przyroda* always accompanies its English rendering, whereas the adjective *przyrodniczy* is translated as "biological."

However, it is worth pointing out another distinction used by Wojtyła, who distinguishes between the metaphysical and phenomenological meanings of nature (see sections 4 and 5 in chapter II of *Person and Act*). According to the metaphysical sense (which coincides with the Aristotelian view mentioned above), nature is the basis of the entire dynamism proper to man. In other words, nature is the basis of the essential coherence between who acts and his acting, between the subject of the dynamism and the entire dynamism of the subject. According to the phenomenological understanding, nature is understood as a certain moment of the entire dynamism of man, a moment that has to do with what happens in man, and not with man's (voluntary) actions. In this sense, the personal (what man does consciously) is opposed to nature (a spontaneous dynamism in man).

Wojtyła distinguishes and accepts both views without rejecting one or the other. Nonetheless, he indicates that the metaphysical aspect provides the basis for the phenomenological one, i.e., the integration between nature and person is achieved on the basis of the metaphysical subjectivity (*suppositum*).

4. *The person possesses a body and even in a sense "is a body"*: By frequently using phrases such as "in a sense," "so to speak," "as it were," "as if," etc., or simply by employing quotes Wojtyła indicates that what is stated is true, but not without qualification. The two statements that man *has* a body and that he *is* a body are not contradictory for Wojtyła. Quite the contrary, they are complementary. First and foremost, Wojtyła stresses that the fact that man is a body does not reduce him to the visible world (see John Paul II, *Man and Woman He Created Them: A Theology*

*of the Body* [Boston: Pauline Books & Media, 2006], 2:4, 8:1. Herein after cited as TOB). The only reason Wojtyła at times would observe that man "is not" his body is in order to prevent the materialistic identification of the person with his body (see *Person and Act*, section 5 of chapter V, including the last footnote of that section). It is precisely because man expresses himself with the means of his body that we can say he "is a body" (see TOB 55:2, 10:4). Wojtyła can state elsewhere that man "is" a person inasmuch as he "possesses" himself, including his body, by which he expresses himself (*Person and Act*, section 5 of chapter V). In that case, the "possession" has a very specific meaning for Wojtyła, as it is taken as a basis for the integration that is an indispensable aspect of the transcendence of the person in the act (see more in *Person and Act*).

The last point worth mentioning is that Wojtyła's understanding of the body is not derived from the Gnostic or Cartesian dualism between the material element (the "body") accidently connected with the proper man (the "soul"). It seems that he rather relies on the Aristotelian and Pauline visions of the body. The concept of form (*Gestalt*) developed by Hans Urs von Balthasar also seems to be compatible with Wojtyła's concept of the body. See Hans Urs von Balthasar, *The Glory of the Lord: A Theological Aesthetics*, vol. 1: *Seeing the Form*, trans. Erasmo Leiva-Merikakis (San Francisco: Ignatius Press; New York: Crossroad Publications, 1982), e.g., 117–119.

5. *This power [of self-determination] is called free will*: The Polish word for power here is *władza* (*potentia* in Latin), which could also be translated as faculty (*facultas* in Latin). In *Summa Theologiae* I 83.2 ad 2 (herein after cited as STh) St. Thomas Aquinas explains that "by a power man is as if empowered to act, and by a habit he is apt to act well or ill."

However, Wojtyła explains more explicitly that self-determination is a power only secondarily. Primarily, it is a property (*właściwość*) of the whole person, so it should not be viewed as an element responsible only for some partial function in man's action. See, for instance, chapter III, section 1 in *Person and Act*.

6. *Sui iuris*: Literally "of one's own law," which in legal language indicates the competence to manage one's own affairs independently, i.e., autonomy.

7. *Alteri incommunicabilis*: Literally "incommunicable to the other." Being a counterpart to *sui iuris*, this phrase indicates that, due to his interiority, the person is inviolable by an other not only in his ontological structure but also in his operation.

8. *No one else can will in my stead*: This could also be translated "No one else can want in my stead," as the Polish word *chcieć* can be translated as "to will" or "to want." The context and suitability determined the rendering of this word in each case.

9. *I am and should be self-reliant in my actions*: This exigency to act on one's own initiative and responsibility is only one side of the coin, as it were. Wojtyła

recognizes the human person's incommunicability and self-determination as an inalienable element of his dignity. This is what is acknowledged by the Second Vatican Council as being willed for one's own sake by God (cf. *Gaudium et Spes*, 24 and also 36) or by the Scriptures as being left in the power of one's own counsel (cf. Sir 15:14).

However, self-determination does not denote for Wojtyła an absolute independence or autonomy, precisely due to the creaturely status of man. In all that man is and does, he depends on God and his truth (cf. *Person and Act*, chapter III, section 7; *Veritatis Splendor*, 41). Man's vocation to a life of happiness with God is fundamental for his human dignity.

The proper integration of the two aforementioned anthropological principles results in the correct concept of human relationality. Man finds his fulfillment as a person in communion through love. This is attested by the words of *Gaudium et Spes* 24 that man, being an image of God, cannot find himself unless through a sincere gift of self in the communion of persons.

10. *Education*: This word translates *wychowanie* (and also *wykształcenie*), which does not simply mean schooling or training, especially in the sense of specializing within one area, but rather an integral formation or cultivation of the whole person with full respect for his dignity (hence, owing to the fact that the object of education is the person-subject, Wojtyła calls this formation "creativity"— see the section "The religious interpretation" in part 2 of chapter I). Because education advocates the full maturity of the person, it is the cultivation of the form of man, or, in other words, education is culture. At this point, we could conveniently integrate the thought of Martin Heidegger in our reflections and describe education as the engagement with beings in their unconcealment (ἀλήθεια), in their becoming what they are (what they are called to be!) by neither abandoning them nor controlling or manipulating them. Wojtyła simply sees education as helping man achieve his true ends.

It is important to remember that for Wojtyła the education of the person is above all the education of love: man's education in love and to love. The education of man's love, as overcoming various shapes of egoism, becomes fully adequate when man cooperates with the "grace of love." The education of love must proceed from the truth that "God is love" and that "love is from God." See the section "The problem of the education of love" in chapter II and Wojtyła's article "Wychowanie miłości" (The Education of Love) published in *Znak* 21 (1960). The form of man is implicated in man's vocation to love.

11. *For man is not only the subject of action, but he also at times is its object*: The sentence immediately following this one makes it clear that at this point Wojtyła's context is the man-man relation. Nonetheless, it is important to keep in mind that first and foremost a human subject has himself as the object of his actions. The personal property of self-determination together with the lived-experience of it is

the basis for the person's "self-creation" (i.e., becoming a good or bad person) through his acts. See chapter II, section 2 in *Person and Act*.

12. *Fully-mature (pełnowartościowy)*: No English word adequately translates the Polish word *pełnowartościowy*. Literally it means "of full value." But since being of "full value" presupposes maturity or perfection, I decided to translate this word as "fully-mature" instead of using a more literal construct. This word simply indicates being an end in itself, thus consequently being a good that is both desired by others and self-giving to them for the sake of their perfection.

13. *Personhood*: The Polish word *osobowość* can be translated either as "personhood" or as "personality." In translating it as "personhood" I keep with the ontological depth conveyed by the English word, quite in conformity with the profound and integral view of the human person presented by Wojtyła in this book. Using the word "personality" throughout could be viewed as restricting the meaning to only one dimension of the person, e.g., solely affective or behavioral. However, because the word *osobowość* is not used univocally, it is translated as "personality" when the meaning demands it.

14. *Every person is capable by his nature to define his ends himself*: Of course, this "defining" is not arbitrary, simply dependent on the individual subject, but performed in conformity with rational human nature and man's striving for his final and beatifying end, which is God. In this sense, what Wojtyła calls here "ends," although contributing to man's fulfillment as a person, are in a sense means related to the final end of man, that is, God. Man does not "choose" God as his final end, but is created intending him, i.e., being already implicitly directed or inclined to him by his nature. It is only with the help of grace that man can explicitly know that God is his last end and his beatitude, can love him fully, and is capable of attaining him. See St. Thomas in STh I–II 5.8, 109.3.

15. *He lets him know*: Although Wojtyła follows the Polish rules of style and capitalizes personal pronouns when they refer to God or any of the Divine Persons, I follow modern English usage, which keeps such words in lowercase.

16. *The decision to strive for this end, its choice, is left to man's freedom*: Of course, Wojtyła is not semi-Pelagian, as is evident from the whole context of his statements. He simply wants to indicate that human freedom allows saying no to God and his grace. In other words, the conscious yes to God does not imply that it is wholly initiated by man or that it is not a response to God's initiative performed with God's help.

17. *Immanuel Kant formulated this elementary principle of the moral order in the following imperative*: Kant formulates his practical imperative as follows: *Handle so, daß du die Menschheit sowohl in deiner Person, als in der Person eines jeden anderen jederzeit zugleich als Zweck, niemals bloß als Mittel brauchst* ("Act in a way so as to use humanity—both in your person and in the person of anybody else—never as

a mere means [to an end] but always at the same time as an end"). See Immanuel Kant, "Grundlegung zur Metaphysik der Sitten," in *Kritik der praktischen Vernunft und andere kritische Schriften* (Cologne: Könemann, 1995), 226.

18. *The person himself has or at least should have his end*: By reformulating Kant's practical imperative, Wojtyła does not intend to oppose Kant's understanding of the human person as an end in himself. According to Kant, a person as a rational being possesses existence that is an end in itself, hence he cannot be used merely as a means. In a sense, this truth is confirmed by the Church's recognition of man as the only being that is willed by God for its own sake (see *Gaudium et Spes*, 24). However, Kant disregards the teleological moment, which Wojtyła emphasizes in his reformulation of Kant's practical imperative: the relation to another man does not merely depend on the fact of him being an end in himself, but also on him being ordained to ends outside of himself that are perfective of him (and of his freedom), and ultimately to God as his final end. Wojtyła's formulation of the personalistic principle encompasses the ontological depth of man, his dignity as a creature called to beatific union with God.

Finally, Wojtyła's formulation is deeply personalistic and not merely "objective." Loving the other person demands a recognition of not only his final end and his vocation to it, but also his capacity (interiority) and responsibility to order his conduct toward that end (through his self-determination) and to become good (or evil) in this conduct.

19. *Love is first of all a principle or an idea, which people must live up to, so to speak, in their conduct*: Wojtyła here speaks of the need for people literally to "pull up" their conduct to the idea of love.

20. *They become in a sense "one flesh"*: The Polish word *ciało* can be translated as either "flesh" or "body" depending on the context.

21. *Science*: Here, the word science (*nauka*) does not necessarily refer to particular sciences (e.g., physical/natural sciences, social sciences, or humanities), but to science in general (i.e., knowledge obtained by reasoning from demonstration).

22. *Lived-experience*: Wojtyła employs two Polish words that could be translated in English as "experience." The first one is *doświadczenie* (with its corresponding infinitive *doświadczać*). This word is quite properly translated by the English "experience," and pertains broadly to living beings capable of apprehension. In Polish, *doświadczenie* probably derives from *wiedzieć* (to know), which is also constitutive of words like *świadek* (witness), *świadomość* (consciousness), and *wieść* (news). Conveniently, then, the Polish word expresses the truth that experience is also some understanding, since the mind is always involved in the experienced object itself, and not in the object's "image" fashioned by the mind from the sensory contents of experience. See *Person and Act*, chapter I, section 2.

The other word for experience is *przeżycie* (with its infinitive *przeżywać*), which is hard to translate in English in contradistinction to *doświadczenie/ doświadczać*. The root of this Polish word (*życie*) means "life," and the prefix (*prze*) "through." Hence, the words are conveniently translated by the German words *Erlebnis* and *Erleben*. I decided to translate the noun as "lived-experience" and its corresponding verbal form as "to experience" at the same time providing the Polish original in the text.

Lived-experience (*przeżycie*) seems to express a more subjective reality than experience (*doświadczenie*), being an integral, experiential fact rooted in the spiritual depth of man. Depending on the experienced value, Wojtyła can speak of various types of lived-experience (such as sensory, affective, erotic, of truth, or of freedom).

The context of lived-experience for Wojtyła is man's experience of himself. When man experiences anything (even an object outside of himself), man also experiences himself, and precisely this experience (lived-experience) helps us understand man in himself. For this reason, lived-experience is a truly personalistic category (see *Podmiotowość i to co nieredukowalne w człowieku* [*Subjectivity and the Irreducible in Man*]). In *Person and Act* (chapter I, section 4) Wojtyła explains that the fundamental function of consciousness is to form lived-experience, by which man can experience his own subjectivity, hence he can experience (*przeżywać*) his acts not only as acts, but as his own acts. In a sense, through lived-experience man subjectivizes what he knows objectively.

23. *The whole moral problem of using as the opposite of loving is linked to this consciousness*: The pronoun replaced in the translation with "this consciousness" may also refer to morality or finality, but the sense of the sentence justifies the chosen rendering as best.

24. *Normalizing human acts*: The words translated in this book as "to normalize" (*normować*) and "normalizing" or "normalization" (*normowanie*) have a specific philosophical meaning. In general, normalization means regulating human action by reason according to the true good. In other words, normalization consists in introducing conformity with reason into every human act. The goal of normalization is to perfect the human being through his action so that man can attain and realize his good. Normalizing closely depends on valuating (see n. 28 on valuation below). Wojtyła describes the difference in the last section of his article titled "O metafizycznej i fenomenologicznej podstawie normy moralnej. Na podstawie koncepcji św. Tomasza z Akwinu i Maxa Schelera" [On the metaphysical and phenomenological basis of the moral norm. Based on the conception of St. Thomas Aquinas and Max Scheler]:

> It is clear that normalizing (*normowanie*) differs from assessing (*ocenianie*) or valuating (*wartościowanie*). Nonetheless, both include the fundamental

moment—the moment of the truth about the good. And in this sense assessing or valuating is so to speak already normalizing, although not in the full sense of the word. What we call normalizing in the full sense of the word is not solely to determine the truth about the good of a human act, but to direct that act in accordance with that truth.

25. *From egoism inherently concealed in it*: That is, from egoism inherently concealed in subjectivism.

26. *A concrete man X and in a concrete woman Y*: Henceforth, however, Wojtyła consistently uses X in reference to a woman and Y in reference to a man.

27. *Honorableness (godziwość)*: The Polish adjective *godziwy* (which I translated as "honorable"), like its nounal form *godziwość* (honorableness), has no adequate English rendering. I met with others translating this word as "noble," "virtuous," "praiseworthy," "of rectitude," "honest," or "just." Its Latin equivalent is *honestus*, a rendering of the Greek word καλός, which is commonly translated as "beautiful" or "good." Perhaps the rendering of the Greek word as *honestus* has been influenced by Cicero, who in his *De finibus bonorum et malorum* (book II, 45) defines *honestum* as that which can be praised for its own sake apart from all utility and rewards or enjoyments. According to Aristotle, the honorable is something beautiful, something chosen for its own sake (*Nicomachean Ethics*, book X, 1176b5–10). In part 3 of chapter III of this book, Wojtyła simply states that "honorable" (*godziwe*) is precisely what is in accord with reason, thus what is worthy of a rational being, of a person.

By presenting all of the above meanings I wish to indicate that Wojtyła's use of this word is in full conformity with its classical meaning. Therefore, my own translation of *godziwy* as "honorable" does not make Wojtyła an adherent of timocracy (a system based on honor), but rather aristocracy (a system based on virtue or excellence).

Also, see my note on the honorable good, i.e., *bonum honestum*, below (n. 19, p. 317).

28. *Valuating*: The words translated in this book as "to valuate" (*wartościować*) and "valuating" or "valuation" (*wartościowanie*) are not commonly used in the Polish language. What Wojtyła means by them is the rational perception and acknowledgment of goods and their hierarchy in reality. The discovery of things' value based on their participation in the universal good (*ratio boni*) is based on the contemplative subordination of perceived beings to truth, on seeing them in the light of truth. Therefore, although this discovery is constituted by reason, valuation is not an arbitrary assignment of value to beings based on some subjective (ultimately utilitarian) criterion chosen by man. Valuation seems to be closely related to the method of objectivization described by Wojtyła in chapter III of this book (in part 3: "Problems of Abstinence"). Valuation, which closely follows upon apprehension, naturally precedes directing human acts according to reason, that is, normalization. See my note on normalization above (n. 24).

29. *Uti and frui*: To use and to enjoy. St. Augustine explains these two concepts in his *De doctrina christiana*, book I, chapters 3–4, and also in *De Civitate Dei*, book XI, chapter 25. Man is placed among things he should use, enjoy, or both use and enjoy. To enjoy means to delight in a thing for its own sake, whereas to use means to employ a thing for the sake of something else. St. Augustine realizes that in this world we happen to enjoy things we use, although he also recognizes a disordered enjoyment of things (an abuse), namely when a thing to be used is enjoyed for its own sake. Ultimately, the true object of enjoyment is the Triune God, and all other things are to be used or used and enjoyed. (See n. 14 [p. 301] on "defining ends.")

Wojtyła's point seems to be this: in order to properly enjoy the other person, one must respect his nature with its inclination to procreation. Enjoying sexual pleasure through another person for the sake of pleasure alone (disregarding the objective finality of sexual use as intrinsically open to procreation) constitutes an abuse. On the other hand, rejecting pleasure in favor of procreation alone leads to another form of abuse (namely rigorism, covered in part 2 below), for the lived-experience of pleasure is an integral part of authentic *frui*.

30. *Instinguere*: Other meanings of this word include "to urge onward," "to incite," and "to impel." See Latin *instigare*.

31. *Drive is a certain natural direction of tending, innate in every man*: Wojtyła speaks about the sexual drive (as well as the drive for self-preservation) in terms of drive instead of instinct because of its orientation or direction toward some goal. According to *Person and Act* (section 8, chapter V), "instinct" (*instynkt*) indicates a way of dynamization proper to nature itself, whereas "drive" (*popęd*) is a certain dynamic orientation of that nature in a given direction. Instincts correspond more to reflexes; they operate within the somatic reactivity of the body. Drives, on the other hand, even though deeply inhering in the body and its natural reactivity, are not purely somatic, but share in the psychical dynamism open to values outside of the subject. Both, drives and instincts, although each in its way, contribute to the development of the person.

32. *From birth belonging to one of the two sexes*: The statement that man belongs to one of the two sexes from birth does not conflict with Wojtyła's later statements, especially in chapter V, that sex is determined from the moment of fertilization (cf. genetic sex). Here Wojtyła simply makes a reference to nature, which, as he explains, takes its name from the word "birth" (*natus*). Hence, birth here means man's beginning.

33. *Complemented*: The two Polish verbs used by Wojtyła to convey the notion of complementing are *uzupełnić* and *dopełnić* (with all their derivatives). Both are translated by "to complement" because they are synonymous in Polish. Both express the idea of making something complete, of bringing things to completion. Perhaps the word *uzupełnić/uzupełniać* indicates more explicitly the

lack of completeness being remedied, and therefore it could be translated as "to supplement." However, both words have basically the same meaning, and therefore I believe that they do not convey any significant difference. In any case, all the instances of *uzupełnić/uzupełniać* are marked in the text, so the reader can discern which Polish word stands behind the English rendering (the instances of *dopełnić/dopełniać* are not accompanied by the Polish original words).

34. *A human being of the other sex*: This phrase translates the Polish phrase *człowiek drugiej płci*, which literally means "man of the other sex." Wojtyła uses this phrase 33 times in this book although he prefers the phrase "the person(s) of the other/same sex," which he uses about three times more often.

Also, I must note that never in Wojtyła's works in Polish have I met with the phrase "opposite sex" (as in "the person of the opposite sex") even though such a construct exists in Polish (*płeć przeciwna*). Instead Wojtyła uses the phrase "the other sex" (*druga płeć*) or "the different sex" (*odmienna* or *różna płeć*), by which he seems to highlight the complementarity of the sexes and eventually a certain unity of men and women in humanity despite or even partly because of their sexual difference.

35. *Existence*: The Polish noun *istnienie* can also be translated as "being."

36. *Per accidens*: Literally "accidentally." What is *per accidens* (accidental) is distinguished from what is *per se* (essential or substantial). As understood traditionally, an accident inheres in a substance, without which it cannot exist on its own. To use a simple example, the color of hair or even hair itself is an accident of a human person.

37. *Per se*: Literally "in itself" or "by itself." See my note above on *per accidens* (n. 36).

38. *Conservatio est continua creatio*: Preservation is continued creation.

39. *The human being*: The 1962 edition (p. 45) has "the beginning of human personhood" instead of "the human being."

40. *Education*: See my comments on education (n. 10).

41. *Sexus*: This is the Latin equivalent of the Polish word *płeć* and the English word "sex." Therefore, in the given sentence, Wojtyła does not mean three realities but two, namely *sexus* (sex) and the sexual drive.

42. *Sui generis*: Literally "of its own kind."

43. *Sexual use without treating the person....*: This sentence is also ambiguous in the Polish (in both the 1962 and 2001 editions). On the one hand, it can mean that the sexual use in separation from the personalistic norm is ethically or morally problematic. This seems to be the meaning that the 2001 edition seems to emphasize by its slight modifications of the sentence structure from the 1962 edition. This meaning is also supported by the context. On the other hand, the sentence can also mean that the sexual use in accordance with the personalistic

norm is ethically problematic, although this sense is excluded by the context. Finally, it can additionally mean that sexual use (either in conformity with or in separation from the personalistic principles) is an issue to be dealt with by ethics.

44. *The "libidinistic" interpretation*: The 1962 edition (p. 51) has "Libido and Neo-Malthusianism" as the title of this section.

45. *Extrema se tangunt*: Extremes touch each other—or simply "extremes meet."

46. *The whole urge-related life in man*: Since Wojtyła explicitly distinguishes between instinct and drive, I wished to keep this distinction in adjectives and adverbs as well. As could be expected, the words "instinctive" and "instinctively" correspond to "instinct" (*instynkt*). However, due to the lack of adjectival forms for "drive" (*popęd*) in English, I have employed the adjective "urge-related," and hence "urge-related life" or "urge-related reactions."

47. *Development of the relation*: The Polish word used here for "development" is *rozwiązanie*, which literally means "untying" or "solving." In this context, however, the word means a way of unfolding or cultivating the subject's relation to an object.

48. *The providence, which man as a rational being must also be . . .* : See St. Thomas in STh I–II 91.2.

49. *The person is the most proximate good for all mankind*: Another possible, but not probable, reading is "the value of the person is the most proximate good for all mankind."

50. *The objective, ontological order*: In general, Wojtyła distinguishes the objective (ontological) order pertaining to the very being of beings and the subjective (psychological, axiological) order in connection to some value experienced by man. This distinction is not dialectical, and, hence, Wojtyła declares that "being and value together must constitute the principle of the hermeneutics of man." See *Antropologia Encykliki Humanae Vitae* (Anthropology of the Encyclical *Humanae Vitae*).

There seem to be no grounds for sharply delimiting Wojtyła's use of the words "ontological" and "ontic," as has been done, for example, by Martin Heidegger. For Heidegger, there exist, so to speak, two realms of reality: the primary (transcendental) and secondary (positive). Words like "existential" or "ontological" correspond to the former one, as it pertains to being itself. Words like "existentiell" or "ontic" relate to the latter one, as it refers to beings. See, for instance, Martin Heidegger, "Phenomenology and Theology" in *Pathmarks*, ed. William McNeill (Cambridge: University Press, 1998), 39–62. Wojtyła, on the other hand, tends to use the two words interchangeably, although preferring to use "ontic" over "ontological" when discussing the (objective) structure of a being. Wojtyła certainly understands God's transcendence with regard to the created things in light of the knowledge he acquired studying St. Thomas Aquinas and St. John of the Cross.

51. *Mutual co-education*: This Polish phrase used here by Wojtyła (*wzajemne współwychowywanie*) denotes continuous educating of each spouse by the other spouse in marriage. Both spouses contribute to this education and both benefit from it. In the same paragraph Wojtyła also speaks of co-education in terms of cooperation.

## Chapter II: The Person and Love

1. *Univocal*: There are three ways in the predication of things: univocal, equivocal, and analogical. The things predicated univocally have the same meaning, or, in other words, they share in the same, common nature. Equivocal predication means that the natures of the predicated things have nothing in common, hence equivocal words, even having the same spelling, can denote completely different things depending on the context. Finally, analogical predication always refers to something common in the predicated things, either in respect to something third (not predicated) or some relation between the predicated things. According to St. Thomas Aquinas, only the latter form of analogy is applicable when speaking of God. For a more extensive treatment of the threefold predication, see *Summa Contra Gentiles* I.34, *De Potentia Dei* 7.7, and STh I 13.5.

2. *Love as fondness*: In the 1962 edition, this section bears the title: "Fondness and the lived-experience of value."

3. *Fondness*: Henceforth Wojtyła begins to describe various aspects of love. The first of them is fondness (*upodobanie*), in which the subject has been faced with an object and finds it pleasing, but does not yet desire to possess it exclusively. As Wojtyła indicates in what follows, fondness corresponds to the Latin word *complacentia*. The Polish word *upodobanie* is derived from the verb *upodobać* or *podobać się*, which basically means "to take a liking to something" or "to find something pleasing or interesting." It is noteworthy to point out that the Polish word *upodobanie* also implies liking something or somebody more than others, hence, it stands, so to speak, on the threshold of a choice. Although it indicates an elementary stage of love, fondness is also an established situation affording an insight *in medias res* (into the midst of things), as it were. For this reason, I see fondness bearing a profound ontological and theological significance for understanding the human person as being from the beginning in the fundamental relation to God and to God's creation, especially to other human persons.

The next aspects of love to be examined are "desire" (*pożądanie*) and "benevolence" (*życzliwość*). Wojtyła concludes these reflections with the concept of spousal love (*miłość oblubieńcza*). The order of presenting these aspects suggests them to be stages in the development of the love between a man and a woman, from the initial fondness toward each other up to their mature union in spousal love. That is correct, and in this context the English word "attraction" instead of "fondness" could possibly work if qualified correctly. Nonetheless, Wojtyła does not use for fondness the Polish word for attraction, namely *atrakcja* or *atrakcyjność*, which he uses in another part of this book. The reason seems to be not only that the concept of fondness already includes a sense of attraction, but most importantly that the word "attraction" does not sufficiently express the personalistic character of human love. Furthermore, Wojtyła insists that all these aspects of love are analogical, i.e. present in some way in all forms of love between persons, not simply between a man and a woman. He also observes that not all of these aspects have to take place for love to exist, thus indicating their relative independence from one another.

4. *Passion*: This word is used here with a general meaning denoting more or less passive reception or experience of something.

5. *Affective life*: I understand the subject of the last two sentences of this paragraph to be "affective life." However, due to the pronouns used in the sentences, the subject may also be "the tint of the content of affective life," the tint that gives emotional color to affective life. In that case, it would be the tint that comes to light in individual emotional-affective reactions and that conditions the direction that fondness will follow.

6. *When, for instance, a concrete Y [he]* . . . : In the 1962 edition (p. 65), this sentence was followed by another: "Then we ought to take into account that not only will he react differently to some concrete X [her], but also in general he will more likely react to different X [women] than the former Y mentioned above."

7. *Logique du coeur*: The logic of the heart.

8. *A man needs a woman as if to complement his being, and in a similar way she needs a man*: See n. 33 (p. 305) on the two Polish words conveying the idea of complementing. In this case, we need to remember that the use of the "as if" indicates a qualified sense, especially that the complementarity spoken of here pertains to the ontological level, the level of being. Since each of them, a man and a woman, constitutes an ontologically complete, integral being in a fundamental relation to God through the act of creation, the sense is not absolute. At the same time, Wojtyła does not exclude the fact of man's, so to speak, ontological relationality, in which man needs the other not only for the preservation of his existence but also for his personal fulfillment or perfection. Such thinking is probably grounded (at least to some extent) in the Biblical account of the creation of the first man and woman in Genesis 2 (see especially verses 2:21–23).

9. *This objective, ontic need*: See my note on the ontological order above (n. 50 [p. 307]).

10. *Love ( . . . ) most fully develops the existence of the person*: Or below, Wojtyła says: "[T]rue love perfects the being of the person and develops his existence." This profound statement conveys the ontological dimension of love. On the one

hand, Wojtyła recognizes that something must first exist in order to act. This is one way of understanding the adage that action follows upon being/existence (*operatio sequitur esse*). On the other hand, however, action, broadly speaking, reveals being and fulfills it in this communication (when we presuppose good action). Thus we can speak of action making man good or evil. In this sense, action perfects being. This is problematic for those who consider action strictly as an accident of substance. But if human action is only an accident, how can a human act make *the person* performing it good or bad? Furthermore, human love as an act of the person would not be able to fully express the person, but only to express him in a fragmentary way. In other words, the human person would not be capable of the gift of self in this case, but always of some partial gift. For Wojtyła, however, love perfects the person himself.

11. *Amor benevolentiae, or benevolentia for short, which corresponds in our language, not quite accurately, by the way, to the concept of benevolence (życzliwość)*: Of course, Wojtyła refers to the Polish language here. In fact, the Polish word *życzliwość* is associated more with kindness or politeness then benevolence, and hence Wojtyła notices a certain discrepancy between the Latin and Polish words. The English translation of *życzliwość* as benevolence conveys more fully the meaning of the Latin original concept.

12. *It is worthwhile to pay attention to this preposition*: In Polish Wojtyła says "adverb" (*przysłówek*) instead of "preposition" (*przyimek*). However, from the context it is clear that he means the preposition "between."

13. *This "I" possesses its interiority thanks to which it is, so to speak, a little world, which depends on God for its existence, while at the same time being self-reliant within the proper limits*: Here we have a clear recognition of the primacy of the relation to God, within which self-determination (freedom) is constituted. In other words, man's freedom expressed in his self-determination is not arbitrary, indifferent, or neutral toward God, but is in a sense an element of man's relationship to him, of his very existence. Hence, the "introduction of love into love," of which Wojtyła speaks in the Introduction as his task, is most natural for man.

At the same time, the very act of creation on the part of loving God indicates that love between God and man contains an inherent reciprocity, that it is inherently relational. For this reason, it is evident how unfounded is the critique of Christianity by Friedrich Nietzsche, who claims in *The Gay Science* (book III, 141) that true love does not look for reciprocity: "*Wenn ich dich liebe, was geht's dich an?*" (If I love you, what is it to you?). Indeed, true love does not need to look for reciprocity because reciprocity, so to speak, already resides in its essence. Hence, Wojtyła is justified to state that "love is by its nature reciprocal" (see the section "The belonging of a person to another person" in part 3 of this chapter).

14. *To suffer*: "To suffer" (*doznawać*) in this sense means to undergo or experience any action, process, or condition, and not specifically to endure pain, distress, or injury. The word is used in this sense a number of times in this book.

15. *Sympathy means as much as "co-passion"*: Certainly, the word "co-passion" (*współ-doznawanie*) is not equivalent to compassion or a feeling of sorrow for another. Rather, co-passion here denotes sharing something together, experiencing it together, which in itself is pleasant. Therefore, Wojtyła speaks of sympathy as accompanied by a "positive affective overtone."

16. *Something to consume*: In order to describe love here Wojtyła uses the adjective *konsumpcyjny*, by which he indicates either that it is love that consumes or is consumed (or both). Although both interpretations make sense, I based my translation on the more common meaning of the adjective in Polish.

17. *The complete, specific weight of persons*: Wojtyła uses the phrase "specific weight" (*ciężar gatunkowy*) a fair number of times in his writings. The phrase denotes one's own worth, a very concrete and comprehensive significance due to simply what somebody or something is, including his or its proper connections or relations with others. Take for example a passage from Wojtyła's play *Przed sklepem jubilera* (In Front of the Jeweler's Shop) (II.3.III): "Love is not an adventure. It has the flavor of the whole man. It has his specific weight. And the weight of the whole fate."

Very rarely Wojtyła uses the phrases "proper weight" (*ciężar właściwy*) and "one's own weight" (*ciężar własny*) (see *Przed sklepem jubilera*, I.4, or *Myśl— przestrzenią dziwną*, III.3). These, however, seem to be synonymous to "specific weight."

18. *Ars amandi*: The art of loving.

19. *Unum velle*: To will one thing.

20. *Spousal love (miłość oblubieńcza)*: The adjective *oblubieńczy* is derived from *oblubieniec*, which can mean in Polish either a person engaged to be married or simply a married person. Therefore, the rendering "betrothed love" instead of "spousal love" is also acceptable. In turn, the word *oblubieniec* derives from *luby* or *lubić*, i.e., to love, to like. At the same time, it also directly relates to the derivative of *lubić*, namely *ślub* (vow or wedding). Accordingly, the word *oblubieńczy* expresses not only the subjective aspect of love but also its objective character manifested in the consent concerning "the dimension of the whole life."

21. *Whoever wants to save his soul . . .* : Since Wojtyła probably cites the Scriptures from memory, the Bible citations are translated as quoted by him.

22. *Nontransferable and incommunicable*: This is one example of the "inconsistent" use of hyphens with some words (Wojtyła used hyphenated versions of these words earlier in this paragraph). However, it is difficult to tell whether the lack of hyphens is intended by the author or is simply an omission of the editors/publisher. The 1962 edition has "nontransferable and in-communicable" here instead (p. 86).

23. *Impressions are most closely linked to the specific property and power of the senses, which is cognition*: Wojtyła here speaks of sensory cognition, which differs

from intellectual cognition. In his *Summa Theologiae* (II–II 8.1), St. Thomas briefly outlines the difference between the senses and the intellect. He states that sensory cognition concerns exterior sensible qualities, whereas intellectual cognition penetrates the essence of things, which lies, so to speak, under the accidents, because the object of the intellect is what something is. Also see St. Thomas' *De Veritate* 2.7 ad 5 as well as Aristotle's *De Anima* III.6.

24. *The interior senses*: To learn more about the interior and exterior senses, see STh I 78.3–4.

25. *Emotions are something separate, different from impressions*: Here the Polish text identifies *wzruszenie* with *emocja*, both meaning emotion, by indicating that the former has the Polish origin, whereas the latter has the Latin one. Thus in *Love and Responsibility* both Polish words are translated as emotion (Wojtyła uses the noun *emocja* only a few times in this book). However, in *Person and Act* Wojtyła states explicitly that the meaning of the Polish word *emocja* does not fully correspond to the word *wzruszenie* (see section 6 of chapter VI). His reflections suggest that *emocja* has a broader meaning than *wzruszenie* by including more affective states as well. The Polish word *wzruszenie* is derived from *ruszać*, i.e., "to move," thus meaning some movement or stirring in man, however, a movement or stirring that is affective (psychical) rather than bodily or sensual. Although having some relation to the bodily dynamism, *wzruszenie* inheres more in man's psyche than in sensuality, and constitutes the emotive core of affection.

26. *It even has the body as a factor*: See section 4 of chapter V in *Person and Act*, in which Wojtyła says: "And so, for instance, the eyesight or affective emotions are not in themselves bodily, but demonstrate a certain dependence on the body and an interconnection with it."

27. *These processes . . .* : In the 1962 edition (p. 95), this sentence is followed by another: "We will devote to this the last chapter of our book."

28. *Sensuality itself is not in the least identified with the sexual vitality of a woman's or a man's body, a vitality which in itself possesses a merely vegetative and not yet sensual character*: In identifying sexual vitality with the vegetative functions of the organism, Wojtyła follows Aristotle, who in his *De Anima* (see book II, chapters 3–4) observes various powers of the soul as distinguished by the manifestations of life in nutrition, growth and decay, locomotion and rest, perception (i.e., sensation that is accompanied by appetite), and thinking. Respectively, Aristotle distinguishes the vegetative (or nutritive), the sensitive, and the intellective powers (or "parts") of the soul. The vegetative soul, being most primitive and most widely distributed in living things, manifests itself under two fundamental aspects: reproduction (generation of another like oneself) and the use of food. Of course, in man the intellectual soul, the sensitive soul, and the nutritive soul are numerically one soul since the intellective soul "contains" in itself the other two (cf. STh 76).

29. *Reciprocal nearness, and the coming together of both individuals*: Wojtyła here speaks neither about a nearness of the bodies nor about a nearness of persons, for he uses the word *postać* (individual, shape, figure) instead of the word *osoba* (person). Perhaps he means to indicate that the nearness at question is neither fully bodily nor yet fully personal.

30. *Characteristic processes*: This is based on the 1962 edition. The 2001 edition has "changeable" (*zmienne*) instead of "characteristic" (*znamienne*), which is probably a typo.

31. *Unification*: A similar explanation for the meaning of the Latin word *integer* or the Polish word *scalanie* (here translated as "unification") can be found in *Person and Act* (in section 1 of chapter V).

32. *Freedom together with truth, and truth together with freedom*: Wojtyła indicates the unity of freedom and truth here, and for this reason he repeats himself by emphasizing first freedom and then truth, instead of simply saying "freedom and truth."

33. *Veracity*: All the instances of the Polish word *prawdziwość* were translated here as "veracity," in distinction from the word *prawda*, i.e., truth. Due to denoting an adherence to objective truth or a rootedness in it, veracity could also be rendered "truthfulness." In *Person and Act* Wojtyła understands veracity (*prawdziwość*) as the human mind's effort directed toward truth (see section 3 of chapter IV). The adjective *prawdziwy*, which refers to both nouns, was translated as "true."

34. *Too rigid and essential*: The word "essential" translates the Polish adjective *esencjalny*, and basically refers to the essence of a thing, i.e., to its form. Therefore, one could say "formal" instead of "essential" in this case.

35. *Situationism and existentialism, which supposedly in the name of freedom reject duty objectively substantiated*: The reason for this rejection seems to be the unwillingness to submit to heteronomy, a law of the other. Instead, what is sought is a peculiar autonomy that transcends the categories of good or evil. As should be clear by now, such an approach is out of the question for Wojtyła, precisely due to the creaturely status of man. God, being *interior intimo meo* (more interior to my innermost) with respect to man, does not simply impose a law that is heteronomous. Even though God's divine law and grace come from him, the Other, the existence does as well. As a result, man is inherently open to all of God's gifts, expects them, so to speak, and receives them as his own.

36. *In the metaphysical analysis of love*: The 1962 edition (p. 114) has "in the general analysis of love" instead.

37. *Which here comes to light*: The most probable reading of the relative clause whose subject is "light" is that it is the "form of love" that comes to light, although it also would be grammatically possible for the antecedent of "which" to be "the nature" or simply "love."

38. *One must "give the soul"*: Perhaps Wojtyła has in mind passages such as Mt 22:37, 1 Thess 2:8, or Eph 6:6.

39. *Responsibility for love is reduced, as is evident, to responsibility for the person, proceeding from it and also returning to it*: Another possible reading of the pronouns employed in the sentence is that the responsibility for love proceeds from the person and returns to him.

40. *For man is always, above all, himself (a "person")*: Wojtyła uses a play on the words "to be oneself" (*być sobą*) and "person" (*osoba*), hence indicating that self-possession and self-governance are a fundamental dimension of the person. In other words, the person can be described as *sui iuris et alteri incommunicabilis*. However, in the same sentence, Wojtyła ties this dimension with another, namely with the person's inherent relationality and his fulfillment in the communion of persons.

41. *The purely subjective truth of affection yielded its place to the objective truth of the person, who is the object of the choice and of love*: My reading is that "the person" is the object of choice, not "the . . . truth of the person," even though the latter reading is also grammatically possible.

42. *This is the essential basis for the primacy of love in the moral order*: The sense and context indicate that the pronoun "this" refers to "love," not "freedom," although the latter reading is also grammatically possible. Hence, Wojtyła speaks of the primacy of love, not the primacy of freedom, in the moral order.

43. *Fait accompli*: Literally "an accomplished fact," or to speak colloquially, "a done deal." This expression is not used in the original Polish.

44. *To whom it turns*: That is, to whom the love turns.

45. *When love . . .* : I kept this sentence as originally printed in the 1962 edition, which places a comma after "the 'absolute.'"

46. *In that case love remains only a psychological situation, which is (as if against its nature) subordinated to the demands of objective morality*: Undoubtedly, Wojtyła speaks of moralism here.

47. *Love is guided by a norm*: Another possible translation is "Love conducts itself by a norm."

## Chapter III: The Person and Chastity

1. *The right of citizenship*: To be a citizen of a country means to belong to it as a proper member, not as an alien. For Wojtyła, virtue to the human soul is like a citizen to his country.

2. *Resentment*: *Ressentiment* in German.

3. *Sloth*: Laziness is another name for this capital vice.

4. *St. Thomas defines sloth (acedia) as "sorrow proceeding from the fact that the good is difficult"*: This definition is probably presented from memory as a summary of St. Thomas' teaching on sloth. See STh II–II 35. Sometimes sloth (*acedia*) is translated in Polish as *zniechęcenie*.

5. *The word "chastity" (czystość) speaks of being free from all that "makes dirty"*: The Polish word for chastity used here by Wojtyła, namely *czystość*, corresponds to the adjective *czysty*, which means "clean" or "pure." Hence, the word *czystość* could possibly also be translated as "purity" or "cleanliness." See n. 23 on the sense of shame to learn about the interchangeability and difference between chastity and purity.

6. *In general it has a different application in the Polish language*: Wojtyła must be referring to the fact that the Polish word *akt* can also mean a piece of art depicting a person or persons in the nude, an official or legal document, or a part of a theatrical play.

7. *Directional character*: The word "directional" expresses a natural, inherent ordering of something toward something else outside of it. This ordering is an openness to a thing or action in the sense of being directed or tending toward it implicitly. This directional stage (as distinguished from the other two, namely desire and willing) seems to correspond to the state of fondness (*complacentia*).

8. *The concupiscence of the flesh*: Although the Polish word *ciało* can be translated as "body" or "flesh," I decided to translate the phrase as "the concupiscence of the flesh" in order to retain the scriptural references to 1 Jn 2:16, so apparent in Polish. The phrase "the concupiscence of the flesh" stands as *concupiscentia carnis* in Latin or ἡ ἐπιθυμία τῆς σαρκὸς in Greek.

9. *He clearly distinguished the concupiscible power (appetitus concupiscibilis) from the irascible power (appetitus irascibilis)*: In general, St. Thomas Aquinas distinguishes a twofold appetite in man, namely the intellective appetite (i.e., the will, which is in reason) and the sensitive appetite (also called sensuality by St. Thomas), which is divided into the irascible and concupiscible powers. The object of an appetite is a good. See STh I 81.2.

10. *The sensitive soul*: Other possible renderings in English include the sensual, sensory, or sensible soul. Also, as was indicated above (n. 28 [p. 312]), in man the intellectual soul, the sensitive soul, and the nutritive soul are numerically one soul. See STh 76.3.

11. *Passiones animae*: The passions of the soul. See STh I–II 22.1 where St. Thomas explains in what sense we can speak of passions belonging to the soul.

12. *Whether the deeds are exterior . . .* : In the 1962 edition (p. 141), this sentence is followed by another: "And so, in the persons whose sensuality is dominated by 'touch' (*tactus*) there will be a tendency toward exterior deeds, whereas interior

deeds prevail in the persons in whom sight and all the more imagination (the interior senses) dominate."

13. *One of the persons wills the good of the other as much as his own*: Again, the meaning is "willing the good *to* or *for* the other," and not simply wanting to appropriate the good of the other. The context of the sentence and other places in the book explicitly confirm this meaning.

14. *Suffering*: Again, suffering here is taken in the broad sense, i.e., as undergoing an experience.

15. *The will lacks love*: This phrase (in Polish: *miłości brakuje woli*) can also be translated "love lacks the will," although this translation is not supported by the context.

16. *Not only one's own person* . . . : In the 1962 edition (p. 157), the sentence continues: "Let us add that good love often heals the 'evil love' of the other person, but the evil love may at times lead the good one into ruin."

17. *Perfectioristic*: In his article "W poszukiwaniu podstaw perfekcjoryzmu w etyce" (In Search for the Basis of Perfectiorism in Ethics) (first published in *Roczniki Filozoficzne* 5, fasc. 4 [1955–57], 303–317), Wojtyła explains that perfectiorism denotes a certain principle of perfection in beings: since every being strives to be perfect (to "be" in the fullest sense), every being thus strives for the good by which it is perfected. In fact, the statement of St. Thomas that the good in general is that which all desire (*bonum est quod omnia appetunt*) (see, e.g., STh I 5.1) could refer both to the good of the subject himself and to the good of the desired objects. In any case, something is desired as good in the first place precisely because it is perfect (cf. STh I 5.5). Therefore, the good denotes for St. Thomas not only that which is perfect in itself (STh I 5), but also that which communicates itself to another, and in this way is perfective of another after the manner of an end (cf. STh I 19.2). In this sense, the being that achieves its perfection, its full goodness, also becomes an end for others.

Returning to our point, speaking of perfectiorism in ethics we speak of the fact that a good act essentially perfects the person performing it. At the beginning of the aforementioned article, Wojtyła distinguishes between perfectiorism and perfectionism, although he does not find a significant difference between the two concepts. The former stresses the betterment of man through every good act, whereas the latter speaks in a general way about man's growing in moral perfection.

18. *The value of sexus*: This is one of the few instances of the expression used in the singular ("the value of *sexus*"). Usually, Wojtyła uses the expression "the values of *sexus*" although sometimes it is in the genitive, which is the same in singular and in plural. Since Wojtyła uses the plural expression more often, I translated the genitive form in plural when ambiguous.

19. *The true good (bonum honestum)*: The distinction into the honorable, useful, and pleasant good has been received by Christian thinkers from the Greeks. For example, Plato mentions this distinction in his *Republic* (book II, 357) and Aristotle does so in *Nicomachean Ethics* (book II, 1104b and book VIII, 1155b). In STh I 5.6 St. Thomas explains the three kinds of the good (also see his *De Veritate* 21.1):

a) *the honorable good* (*bonum honestum*): something that is an end in itself;

b) *the useful good* (*bonum utile*): something that is the means to achieve an end;

c) *the pleasurable good* (*bonum delectabile*): something that follows upon attaining the desired end.

Wojtyła calls *bonum honestum* the true good precisely because it is perfective of man as a rational being, as a person. In fact, *Love and Responsibility* as a whole can be interpreted as Wojtyła's endeavor to affirm and regain the primacy of the honorable good in human life and interaction. We see that the focus on utility or pleasure (see the two meanings of the verb "to use") in separation from the objective good of man is always detrimental to him as a person. The affirmation of the honorable good demonstrates Wojtyła's emphasis on cultivating the contemplative attitude, which he also advanced as John Paul II (for instance, see his encyclicals *Evangelium Vitae*, 83 and *Fides et Ratio*, 81).

20. *Blessed are the pure of heart, for they see God*: Both the Greek and Latin manuscripts use the future here, i.e., "they shall see" (ὄψονται, *videbunt*). Wojtyła probably writes the Scripture passages from memory.

21. *Max Scheler, Franciszek Sawicki*: Perhaps Wojtyła has in mind Scheler's work *Über Scham und Schamgefühl* (Halle, 1914) and Sawicki's *Fenomenologia wstydliwości* (Kraków, 1949).

22. *We often feel shame for the good*: In other words, "I did something good, and I feel shame about it." Of course, as Wojtyła explains, this "shame" pertains to the fact of the visibility of the good act rather than to the goodness of the act itself. The general point Wojtyła makes about shame is that it is not simply a pejorative concept. This is affirmed by the fact that the Polish phrase "to feel shame" (*wstydzić się*) does not have as strongly negative connotations as its English rendering may. Because of its strong connection with modesty or purity, the phrase could be also translated as "to be embarrassed," "to be shy," or "to be bashful."

23. *The sense of shame*: The word used by Wojtyła translated here as "the sense of shame" is *wstydliwość*, whose root is the noun *wstyd*, i.e., shame. Wojtyła's concept of the sense of shame as the constant readiness to feel shame for indecent or shameful things (especially concerning the sexual sphere) more or less corresponds to St. Thomas' notion of *verecundia*. According to St. Thomas, *verecundia* means that by which one shies away from what is contrary to the virtue of temperance

(cf. STh II-II 143.1). The sense of shame is also closely related to *erubescentia*, i.e., some fear of a disgraceful deed not yet committed (cf. STh I-II 41.4). In English, "*wstydliwość*" is at times translated as "modesty."

Wojtyła considers the sense of shame compatible with chastity: a chaste person also feels shame for a disgraceful act, even if he did not commit it but is faced with it in one manner or another. We can see the etymological reflection of this compatibility in the Latin word *pudicitia* (purity), which is derived from *pudor*, i.e., shame. Speaking of purity (*pudicitia*), St. Thomas distinguishes it from chastity (*castitas*) by the fact that chastity properly moderates pleasures pertaining to the conjugal act itself, whereas purity concerns pleasures circumstantial to the conjugal act as contained in kissing, embracing, etc. (cf. STh II-II 143.1). Nonetheless, because purity is an aspect of chastity, St. Thomas recognizes that the two words (chastity and purity) are often used interchangeably (see STh II-II 151.4). Under the name of chastity (*czystość*), Wojtyła certainly includes both meanings conveyed by the Thomistic understanding of chastity and purity explained here.

Lastly, we must always remember that, as is clear from Wojtyła's description of shame in his text above, the sense of shame (just like chastity) is not merely a negative and reactionary concept, but above all an integral one, first and foremost affirming the person and his value.

24. *The law of nature*: Besides the phrase "the law of nature," in his various articles and books Wojtyła also employs the phrase "the natural law" (see especially "Osoba ludzka a prawo naturalne" [The Human Person and the Natural Law], *Roczniki Filozoficzne* 18, fasc. 2 [1970], 53–59 and "Prawo natury" [The Law of Nature] in *Aby Chrystus się nami posługiwał* [Kraków: Wydawnictwo Znak, 1979], 146–149). It is safe to state that Wojtyła employs the two phrases interchangeably. In both cases Wojtyła stresses that the law he refers to does not have a merely mechanistic character or express simply a biological regularity. The law of nature is a group of norms or "codex" of the Creator that is inscribed in the very being of man and the world, the "codex" that man is able to read and realize in his life. Wojtyła spoke of this when discussing the concept of *particeps Creatoris* (see the section "The concept of 'justice with respect to the Creator'" in part 2 of chapter IV). See TOB 124:6. Hence, that law enables the correct understanding of two correlated orders: of being (the metaphysical or ontological order) and of value (the axiological or moral order) (see K. Wojtyła, *Człowiek w polu odpowiedzialności* [Man in the Field of Responsibility] [Rzym-Kraków: Instytut Jana Pawła II KUL, 1991], 82–84). Also, Wojtyła considers the personalistic norm as complementary to the law of nature. While the law of nature pertains to man's action in the world, the personalistic norm regulates the relation to man as a person, emphasizing his distinctness and transcendence (cf. ibid., 85, 87).

25. *A woman rather wants to suffer love so that she can love. A man rather wants to love so that he can suffer love*: Here as in other places (e.g., in the section

*Spousal love* in part 1 of chapter II) Wojtyła indicates that love between the husband and the wife has a very specific character: although being equal in dignity, each spouse loves the other in a different way. Such is the specificity of spousal love as well as of other relationships in the family built on that love (cf. Eph 5:21–6:9). This specificity reaches back to the creation of the first man and the first woman (cf. Gen 2) and thus to God's plan for marriage to experience, reveal, and also share in the Mystery of Divine Love. See the relevant sections of TOB on the subject of sacramentality (e.g., chapter I of part II: *The Dimension of Covenant and of Grace*). Therefore, the language of love (ἀγαπᾶν) and subordination (ὑποτάσσειν) used by St. Paul in Ephesians 5 and Colossians 3 concerning the reciprocal relation of the spouses excludes a dynamic of domination (master-slave) or of interchangeable equality (partner-partner), and instead expresses a dynamic of an authentic communion of persons based on the gift of self and the reception of that gift. See, for instance, TOB 92:6. For an insightful and exegetical reflection on the reality of marriage see Fr. Francis Martin, "Marriage in the New Testament Period" in *Christian Marriage: A Historical Study*, ed. Glenn W. Olsen (New York: Crossroad Publishing Company, 2001), 50–100.

26. *When he posits this attitude*: Other possible readings, which do not change the meaning of the sentence, are: "When he posits the lived-experiences" or "When he posits the sensory-sexual use."

27. *The unprompted reaction of sensuality*: "Unprompted" (*samorzutny*) is synonymous with "instinctive" or "spontaneous," i.e., not being a result of man's efficacy (self-determination). Wojtyła understands this word in this sense in his *Person and Act* (e.g., section 7 in chapter V and section 7 in chapter VI).

28. *Pornography*: For a more detailed description see TOB 60–63. Apart from a variety of detrimental psycho-physiological effects in the subject, the problem with pornography (pornovision) is its failure to portray man in the whole truth of his personal being and vocation. Pornography not only shows a fragment, but distorts the truth about the human person and his body by presenting the body devoid of its proper meaning in the order of gift (love), i.e., to form the "communion of persons" and to participate in it (cf. TOB 61:4). Instead, man is reduced to the level of an anonymous object used to gratify one's concupiscence.

29. *A tendency to distort this truth*: Another possible reading is: "A tendency to distort this sphere."

30. *For concerning this point . . .* : In the 1962 edition (p. 185), this sentence is followed by another: "But exactly for this reason, in many cases of alleged pornography, the responsibility ought to be placed on a lack of mature chastity, a lack of the shame of lived-experience."

31. *He subjects himself to it*: See St. Augustine in *In Epistolam Joannis* VIII.7: *Si autem non agnoscis illum qui supra te est, superiorem contemnis, subderis inferiori*

(But if you do not acknowledge him, who is above you, you scorn the superior; you shall be subject to the inferior).

32. *Because we have distinguished* . . . : In the 1962 edition (p. 187), this sentence is followed by another:

> Positing the issue this way presupposes that natural sensual excitability and natural affective sensibility also admit a certain oscillation up and down: one or the other can be more or less intensive for different people and even for the same person in different moments and periods—although they cannot cross normal boundaries.

33. *Abstinence*: The Polish word *"wstrzemięźliwość"* is also translated elsewhere as "temperance" when the context speaks of the cardinal virtue. Normally, in *Love and Responsibility* Wojtyła uses the word *"umiarkowanie"* for temperance.

34. *By a value in the objective sense we mean* . . . : The 1962 edition has simply: "By a value we mean . . ."

35. *Principatus politicus*: Literally, from Latin, "the political dominion or rule." In his *Politica* (book I, chapter 1, 1254b2–5), Aristotle distinguishes in living beings the despotical rule (*principatus despoticus*), by which the soul rules the body, and the political or diplomatic rule (*principatus politicus*), by which the intellect rules the appetites. See STh I 81.3 ad. 2. Wojtyła observes that the political rule, which employs virtues (habits) to attain its goals, is not meant to extinguish or disregard the sensual and affective energy (as the Stoics or Kant wished), but to take advantage of it instead. Reason and the will are able to assimilate that energy, so to speak, thus making it fully their own. However, exercising the political power also includes employing it in an absolute, "despotic" way whenever suitable. See *Person and Act*, section 9 of chapter VI.

36. *Connection and union*: The two Polish words used here are *związek* and *zespolenie*, respectively. Although *zespolenie* does not fully convey the concept of unity or oneness *(jedność)*, it means the operation of being joined into a certain whole (*zespół*) or the effect of such an event.

37. *Whoever wishes to come after me* . . . : See Mt 16:24, Mk 8:34, or Lk 9:23.

## Chapter IV: Justice with Respect to the Creator

1. *Widowhood*: The Polish word for widowhood used here (*wdowieństwo*) can mean either widowhood or widowerhood, although it seems clear that Wojtyła means both.

2. *The praise of widowhood and of absolute monogamy*: See, for instance, 1 Cor 7:8, 26–27, 32, 39–40.

3. *What God has joined together* . . . : See Mt 19:6 or Mk 10:9.

4. *But at the beginning it was not so*: See Mt 19:8.

5. *These things . . .* : In the 1962 edition (p. 206), this sentence is followed by this paragraph:

> Although the breakup of a marriage linked to simultaneous bigamy takes place in time, i.e., after some duration of that marriage, it nevertheless in a moral sense acts retroactively and, so to speak, beyond time. In the case we discuss, the woman X does not become for the man Y a mere "object representing a sexual value," and marriage does not become for him anything more than an institution ordered to taking advantage of that value, only at the moment of divorce or bigamy—this X [she] and marriage were nothing more for Y [him] but that from the beginning. Substantively speaking, since Y [he] permits divorce or bigamy, then X [she] remained for him from the beginning in the position of an object of use, and marriage signified for him only an institution of sexual use—and in general they have for him only that sense. Of course, the matters are the same when X [she] conducts herself in an analogical way toward Y [him].

6. *Man is a being . . .* : In the 1962 edition (pp. 206–207), this sentence is followed by others (the subsequent sentence starting with "In light of these principles" began a new paragraph):

> Thus, in view of subsequent facts the true essence and value of earlier facts often comes to light. Just as in our case, in view of the subsequent (even after many years) breakup of a marriage contracted validly and ratified (*dopełniać*) with conjugal intercourse, in connection with simultaneous bigamy, the fact comes to light that what previously united Y [him] with X [her], and what in his (and her) eyes appeared as love, was in fact not true love of the person; it did not possess the objective force of the personal union of persons, the objective profile of love. It could then contain a very rich subjective content, be based on a full awakening of sensuality and affectivity in both persons, but nonetheless it had not matured to the objective value of the personal union of a man and a woman—and perhaps it was not oriented in that direction at all (for it is known that marriage must continuously mature to the value of the personal union, and therefore the orientation in this direction is so important).

7. *Without it marriage is an enormous risk*: The Polish is not unequivocal here, although the context indicates that "it" means the integration. To take "it" to mean the principle is also grammatically possible.

8. *Matrimonium facit copula*: Sexual intercourse (*copula carnalis*) makes marriage.

9. *Making excuses*: At least one reason why Wojtyła distinguishes justification (*usprawiedliwienie*) from making excuses (*usprawiedliwiać się*) is the similarity of pronunciation in Polish.

10. *That this inter-personal character be most fully realized in it*: That is, realized in the end or in marriage—both readings are grammatically possible. However, the sense indicates the latter reading as intended by Wojtyła.

11. *The point is not only the fact of sexual intercourse with a woman who is "some-body else's wife," but also the fact of having relations with any woman who is not "one's own wife," regardless of whether or not she has a husband*: This whole statement becomes clearer once the Polish etymology of the word adultery (*cudzołóstwo*) is explained. The word literally refers to "somebody else's bed" (*cudze łoże*). Wojtyła broadens the concept of adultery (*cudzołóstwo*) to include acts of fornication as well. In this sense, for example, sexual intercourse of a married man with an unmarried woman would also constitute an act of adultery.

12. *Marriage as an institution is indispensable to justify the fact of conjugal relations between a man and a woman*: This, of course, does not mean that every sexual act or even intention performed by the spouses within marriage is morally good. In his Wednesday audiences on the Theology of the Body, Blessed John Paul II permits a possibility of committing adultery in one's own heart with one's own wife (TOB 43:2–3). The point is the way a man looks at a woman, regardless of whether she is his wife or not. A man who lusts after a woman, who is for him but an object to satisfy his concupiscence, commits adultery with her in his heart, in accordance with the words of our Lord Jesus in Matthew 5:28. At this point, Blessed John Paul II refers to St. Augustine's expression "*adultor uxoris*" (the adulterer of his own wife) as used in *De nuptiis et concupiscentia*, XV.

In *Love and Responsibility* we encounter an indirect confirmation of this possibility, for instance, when Wojtyła treats of shamelessness in the sexual relations of spouses, in which the possibility of procreation and parenthood is positively excluded. It seems worthwhile to ask about the meaning of belonging to one's spouse so that he or she becomes "one's own," so to speak. Perhaps, once the other person is viewed as an object of use, the boundary between "my own" and "some-body else's" is crossed (my wife then in a sense ceases to be "my own"), thus enabling an act of adultery to be committed.

13. *To be dependent for existence*: That is, to be dependent for existence on somebody else.

14. *Sacramentum naturae*: Sacrament of nature.

15. *Sacramentum gratiae*: Sacrament of grace.

16. *This is the natural finality of conjugal intercourse—every fact of sexual intercourse between a man and a woman stands intrinsically in the orbit of that finality*: This sentence is a direct translation from the second Polish edition of *Love and Responsibility* from 1962 (p. 219). The 2001 Polish edition reads: "The natural finality of conjugal intercourse, every fact of sexual intercourse between a man and a woman stands intrinsically in the orbit of that finality." I used the older version because I found it more intelligible in English.

17. *Man masters nature by adapting to its immanent dynamic*: This statement might seem to resemble Francis Bacon's assertion in his *Novum Organum* that nature is not commanded or overcome except by being obeyed (book I, aphorisms

III and CXXIX). Wojtyła, however, is no Baconian. As is clear from the context of his statement, Wojtyła acknowledges and respects the objective finality of nature, that is, the finality that nature possesses on its own accord (*per se*). This finality needs to be acknowledged, but also integrated and cultivated in man's life. It is clear that for Wojtyła the natural finality, or teleology, does not enslave but, on the contrary, serves the person and his fulfillment. Such an approach honors nature, its creator, and its possessor or user alike. Bacon, on the other hand, learns about the structure and workings of nature in order to use them exclusively as a means for self-appointed ends. He acknowledges no inherent finality of nature (or at least considers such a finality as useless) and sees no need to cooperate with it.

These two separate ways of relating to nature by the human person indicate two different concepts of nature held by the two thinkers. What is necessary for recognizing the finality of nature is, first, the contemplative attitude—the ability and readiness to see the beauty of the world, of nature. It is because, in beauty, man is capable to see and love both nature and the mystery that reveals itself in it.

18. *When he violates nature, he also "violates" the person*: Since in Polish the word *gwałcić* means not only to violate but also to rape, Wojtyła may be using quotes here to indicate that the violation does not literally mean the act of raping the person. By using the word here, he may be nevertheless also establishing an analogy with an act of rape.

19. *The personal union of a man and a woman is based on it*: The Polish text is not unequivocal as to what is the basis of the personal union, as this "it" may refer either to love, to the affirmation, to the value, or even to the person. Nonetheless, the sense of the sentence indicates that Wojtyła speaks of the affirmation of the value of the person as the basis of love (love understood as the personal union of a man and a woman).

20. *Gandhi's* Autobiography: Wojtyła does not cite any references here, but the first quotation is from part III, chapter VI of the autobiography. The second quotation is probably a paraphrase of a thought taken from part III, chapter VII. The quotations are translated directly from Polish. In TOB 129:2, however, where he cites the same material in a footnote, Wojtyła gives the following reference: M. K. Gandhi, *Autobiografia. Dzieje moich poszukiwań prawdy*, trans. Józef Brodzki (Warsaw, 1958), 242, 244.

21. *Periodic abstinence*: This phrase could also be rendered as "periodic continence," although without suggesting that the virtue of continence is practiced only periodically. The virtue of continence is to be practiced at all times, and only sometimes as abstinence.

22. *Personhood*: As I mentioned previously, the Polish word *osobowość* can be translated as "personhood" or "personality." Since Wojtyła's reflections always have ontological depth, I translated the word as "personhood." Thus, in this case, the family is not only a place where man's character or temperament is molded, but

where a new person is formed in love and to love. In other words, according to Wojtyła, personhood is not a static reality, but "grows" with the person, and thus needs to be properly cultivated in the proper environment.

23. *You shall love the Lord . . .* : Cf. Mk 12:30–33, Mt 22:37–39, and Lk 10:27.

24. *Religion*: The Polish word used here (*religijność*) could also be translated as "religiosity." However, due to negative connotations of that English word and owing to the fact that Wojtyła refers here to a virtue, which has a customary rendering in English, I chose "religion" as the best translation.

25. *Pars potentialis iustitiae*: A potential part of justice.

A potential part of a principal virtue (as religion is to justice, for instance) is a virtue that has something in common with the principal virtue but lacks the perfection of that virtue. In a sense not having the full power of the principal virtue, the potential parts of it are directed to certain secondary acts or matters. See STh II-II 48.1 and 80.1.

St. Thomas discusses the moral virtue of religion in his *Summa Theologiae* II–II q. 81, its acts in qq. 82–91, and the vices opposed to it in qq. 92–114. Also see STh II–II 80.1 and 80.1 ad 2 for some perspective on the relation between religion and justice. Basically, since all moral virtues pertaining to operations have the character of justice (*ratio iustitiae*), St. Thomas associates various kinds of debt with different virtues. Hence, religion (*religio*) is that through which debt is paid to God, piety (*pietas*) is that through which debt is paid to one's parents or country, and gratitude (*gratia*) is that through which debt is paid to benefactors (STh I-II 60.3).

26. *Particeps Creatoris*: Literally "a partaker of the Creator." This phrase has nothing to do with pantheism since, as Wojtyła explains, it means man as a sharer in God's thought, in God's law, which he realizes and reveals through culture (the cultivation of himself and the world).

27. *Autonomism*: Indeed, Kant advocated the separation from anything empirical in order to foster the rational (objective and free) principles of morality. Since, properly speaking, freedom for Kant was independence from the determined causes of the natural world, it is understandable that the Kantian concept of justice could not be based on the order of nature. (See Kant's *Groundwork of the Metaphysics of Morals* for more detailed exposition of his views on that subject.)

Wojtyła, on the other hand, is not afraid to base his concept of justice on the natural order, since he sees this order as an expression of God's wisdom. Hence, man's acting in conformity with that order is not derogatory but rather manifests and fulfills his value as a person, at the same time appreciating the value of nature. Such relation to the world is an expression of man's love toward the world and its Creator (see the following paragraph in Wojtyła's text).

28. *The preservation of the order of nature and the manifestation of the value of the person*: This seems like a precursor of *Gaudium et Spes*, 24.

29. This relation is a kind of love, and not only a love of the world, but also a love of the Creator: See my note on the unity of love above (n. 5 [p. 297]).

30. *Participes Creatoris*: The plural of *particeps Creatoris*. See n. 26.

31. *I should direct toward him all that is in me, my whole being*: Here is an indication that love of God implicates the whole being of man, and not just one of his powers—otherwise Wojtyła would not be able to speak of directing the "whole being" of man toward God in love. A valuable resource on understanding love as an order of reality is Dr. David L. Schindler's book *Ordering Love* (Grand Rapids, MI: William B. Eerdmans, 2011).

32. *Usque ad aequalitatem*: Until equality [is attained].

33. *What Christ taught mankind was religion based on love, which facilitates a way from one person to another*: It is grammatically unclear whether "which" refers to religion or love. Both readings make sense.

34. *"Virginal" (dziewiczy) means the same as "untouched"*: The adjective *dziewiczy* may refer to both "virginity" (*dziewictwo*) or "intactness" (*dziewiczość*), hence it could be translated as either "virginal" or "intact." Nonetheless, I translate *dziewiczy* as "virginal" and *nienaruszony* as "intact" for the sake of consistency and better intelligibility in English.

35. *"Virginity" is closely associated and connected with intactness*: It is evident in the Polish language on account of the same word root, i.e., *dziewica* (virgin).

36. *The virginal state*: Here the adjective "virginal" refers to intactness (*dziewiczość*) rather than to virginity (*dziewictwo*).

37. *Coelebs*: Same as *caelebs*.

38. *The very need for spousal love, the need to give oneself to a person and to unite with him, is deeper, is connected with the spiritual being of the person*: Marriage and virginity for the Kingdom of God are thus fundamentally spiritual affairs. By no means does Wojtyła claim that marriage is simply a bodily affair. On the other hand, virginity is not purely spiritual, as the gift of self to God encompasses the body and life in this world. Wojtyła warns us not to see the traditional primacy of virginity as resulting from a false primacy of the spiritual over the material. Both marriage and virginity involve the whole man and his ultimate destiny, though virginity "prepares" man for the beatific vision in a more direct manner.

39. *Vocation (powołanie)*: Just as in English (and Latin), the Polish word *powołanie* derives from the word "to call" (*wołać*, or *vocare* in Latin).

40. *A gift of self can be most creative for the person: he realizes himself the most precisely by giving himself the most*: Here we see another precursor of *Gaudium et Spes*, 24.

41. *Be perfect . . .*: Cf. Mt 5:48.

42. *Somebody who is situated outside the "state of perfection" is effectively more perfect . . .*: See STh II-II 184.4 where St. Thomas states that because Christian perfection consists in charity, nothing hinders a person from being perfect without being in the state of perfection, and, conversely, from being in the state of perfection without being perfect. Also see TOB 78:3.

43. *Bonum est diffusivum sui*: The good is self-diffusive.

It is true that this adage is generally understood as referring to efficient causality. However, Wojtyła is aware that most properly the good is diffusive after the manner of the final cause since the good has the character of an end, as has been affirmed in previous notes. See Wojtyła's *Wykłady Lubelskie* (Lublin Lectures) (Lublin: Towarzystwo Naukowe KUL, 2006), 128, and St. Thomas' *De Veritate* 21.1 ad 4 and STh I 5.4 ad 2. For this reason, in this same section below Wojtyła speaks of the maturity and fullness of the person engaged in spiritual generation as well as of the mother and father as the ideals or models for others.

44. *Spiritual fatherhood or motherhood contains some transmission of personhood*: In the 1962 edition (p. 255), this sentence appears as follows: "Spiritual fatherhood or motherhood contains some (intentional, above all) transmission of entire personhood in what constitutes it most basically. We can, of course, speak here about 'transmission' only in the sense of analogy of attribution, for it is known that precisely personhood is by all means nontransferable (*alteri incommunicabilis*)."

# Chapter V: Sexology and Ethics: A Supplementary View

1. *Persons*: The 1962 edition (p. 260) has the word "persons" in quotes.

2. *This, however, is neither his only good nor the superior or "ultimate" one*: In the 1962 edition (pp. 261–266), this sentence is followed by a few pages of text, most of which have been presented under the section titled *Sex*. The next sentence in the 2001 edition, starting with "The pre-scientific statement" is here duplicated (due to being slightly different in the 1962 edition):

> What is then the sense of this "supplementary view"? Because some matters discussed in this book from the personalistic position can and should be at the same time elucidated from the position of biological and medical sexology, despite my lack of personal education in that field and using the knowledge of others as a basis, I shall attempt to include this elucidation in the totality of personalistic reflections. I emphasize the word "include," for this position is not often included in the framework of ethical personalism, but remains on its own—indeed, by itself it introduces certain rules and norms that acquire the force of proper ethical norms due to the meaning that people generally attach to the value of health (and of biological life).

## Sex

The first problem that possibly demands elucidation from the side of sexology is the very concept of sex. In chapter I of our book, where sexual drive constitutes a particular object of reflections, sex was defined as a property of the whole human being, of the whole person. What entitles us to positing the matter this way is the simple pre-scientific recognition, which in an enormous majority of cases is something completely easy and obvious. However, the attempt to define sex presents difficulties on the scientific-biological grounds due to the fact that many factors come into play. None of the factors constitutes the definitive criterion of recognition, but only their very complicated totality explains the fact of sexual distinctness. This distinctness dates from the moment of fertilization, for then the sex of a given individual becomes determined, and determined in a fundamentally irrevocable way at that. Thus, first of all there is a need to speak of genetic sex.

*Genetic sex* can be recognized by the presence of the so-called sex chromatin (a Barr body) positioned differently in the cells of males and females. The characteristic chromatin follicles occur in 4–5 percent in the former and in 50 percent in the latter. However, it is difficult to establish what determines genetic sex—there are a number of contradictory theories on that subject (for example, the theory of the X and Y chromosomes, according to which sex is determined by sperm, and the opposing theory of Schöner claiming that the ovum determines genetic sex). In any case, genetic sex conditions the development of further sexual features, that is, so-called somatic (morphotic) sex.

*Somatic sex* is designated by somatic (i.e., bodily) sexual features that can be arranged into three orders. The primary features are gonads, that is, sexual glands (testis and ovary), which in turn condition the development of the secondary features. The further reproductive organs serving either the transmission of sexual cells in a man and a woman or the implantation of a new embryo in a woman (in the womb—*uterus*) belong to the secondary features. The tertiary features (e.g., the distinct skeleton structure, the characteristic hair growth, the mammary glands in a woman, the difference in the voice pitch, etc.), which are least essential for the development of somatic sexual distinctness, are most conspicuous.

At this point it is worthwhile to note that the so-called psychical sexual features do not depend directly on somatic sex but rather on "physiological sex," i.e., on the presence of active sexual hormones (which we shall cover soon). We also need to add that the very differences in psyche constitute the least certain criterion for the recognition of sex. According to the generally accepted views, what is characteristic to the masculine psyche is its tendency toward activity, expansion, or even aggression, whereas an attitude that is passive, expectant, and inclined to subordination is rather manifested in women. It is well known, however, that there are persons who are described as "masculine women" or "effeminate men," thereby indicating precisely the psychical characteristics, for their sexual belonging in the somatic and physiological regards raises no doubts. Those are our grounds to qualify a given person as "a woman" or "a man," since the psychical characteristics cannot serve as the basis for this qualification.

Hermaphroditism constitutes a pathological manifestation precisely in the sphere of somatic sex, brought about only in the fetal period of life. Subsequent harmful influences of a various nature (alcoholism of the parents, infectious diseases in fetal development, toxic factors, or labor injuries) can lead to various abnormalities concerning sexual development manifested in the lack of secondary sexual features or their underdevelopment, and even in the lack of certain organs, e.g., *agenesia uteri*. In turn, the underdevelopment or also the defective development of sexual glands impairs hormonal action and disturbs the further development of the individual. At this point, we already touch the problem of the physiology of sex.

*Physiological sex* is conditioned by the presence of the formed sexual gland able to produce hormones. Masculine hormones, that is, the androgenic bodies, not only determine the development of secondary and tertiary sexual features, but also condition the rise of the sexual drive (which we shall speak of in the next section), although this is not a simple and direct quantitative dependence, and that is proved by the fact that the sexual drive also exists in eunuchs (Kinsey). Androgens exist in equal quantity both in boys and in girls up to seven to ten years old. Then, this quantity in boys increases greatly, whereas in girls it remains the same or rises only slightly. On the other hand, the masculine sexual gland produces feminine hormones, which, until the period of puberty, have the same quantity in boys as in girls; this relation undergoes a change only later.

Feminine hormones produced by the woman's sexual gland constitute two kinds of bodies, which create a specific system. In this system, the mentioned bodies act on each other and occur one after the other so that in a woman's organism a characteristic cycle of changes emerges called the sexual cycle. In the first phase of the cycle the feminine sexual gland produces so-called folliculin—the most potent estrogenic compound. In children, before puberty, estrogenic bodies occur in a small quantity, and only in puberty does their level in girls suddenly rise. After puberty the sexual rhythm of a physically mature woman displays three phases that depend on changes taking place in the uterus:

a) The follicular period, i.e., the proliferative phase (*stadium proliferationis*), in which estrogens act on the endometrium, evoking in it growth changes (*hyperplasia*). This first phase lasts about 14 days in the 28-day cycle and concludes with ovulation, during which the so-called graafian follicle develops, releasing a mature ovum able to be fertilized, which moves in the direction of the uterus. Ovulation is accompanied by a whole group of symptoms that can be observed—this is important for determining the fertility period in a woman and hence important for the problem of conscious motherhood, of which we shall speak in a subsequent section of this chapter. From the moment of ovulation, the level of estrogen drops and the second phase of a woman's sexual cycle begins.

b) The secretory period (*stadium secretionis*), in which the endometrium undergoes further changes and in the ovary the so-called *corpus luteum* (the yellow body) emerges, which produces the second feminine hormone: progesterone. This is a body that adapts a woman's organism to a possible pregnancy, and therefore it evokes specific changes in the uterus that enable the implantation of the ovum; it decreases the activity of the uterus (it slows down its contractions); and finally it helps to maintain the pregnancy if one occurs. The progesterone-producing *corpus luteum* exists about 10 days, after which it begins to decay. The peak of production of progesterone occurs at about two days before menstruation (seven to ten days after ovulation), but then its quantity quickly drops and vanishes completely in day 23–24 of the cycle. If the ovum does not undergo fertilization, the third phase of a woman's sexual cycle begins.

c) The degenerative or desquamative period (*stadium desquamationis*). Here, the mucosa of the uterus, softened and prepared to receive pregnancy, is excreted. The peeling of the mucosa is linked to bleeding (*menses*), and together with blood the dead ovum is also discharged. After menstruation a period of regeneration follows, and the cycle begins anew.

In a healthy and biologically fully-mature woman all the changes take place regularly and are accompanied with psychical changes dependent on the activity of hormones. In the period preceding menstruation these changes are manifested in the form of intensified irritability and excitability, fatigue, and also a number of somatic ailments.

Since we are talking about the secretory activity of the sexual glands, we ought to pay attention to the fact of so-called *hormonal correlation*. For the secretory activity of the sexual glands remains directly connected with the activity of other endocrine glands, although in a particular way it depends on the action of the pituitary gland, which constitutes a superior gland in relation to sexual glands. It makes the so-called gonadotropins FSH (follicle-stimulating hormone) and LH (luteinizing hormone), which induce gonads to produce their proper hormones but also stimulate the production of reproductive cells. Besides the pituitary gland, the thyroid gland is also of serious importance for man's sexual life. Its lack causes an inhibition of the development of the sexual glands, for the thyroid hormone makes the glands sensitive to the action of the pituitary gland hormones. Besides this, all glands of internal secretion influence one another.

In addition, there is the central nervous system, which regulates the activity of glands. It seems that the centers controlling sexual life are found in the *tuber cinereum* of the hypothalamus. Besides that, the superior centers lie in the cortical cortex, although the ways of their action have not yet been discovered.

A correlation also occurs between the sexual hormones of both sexes— namely, it seems that estrogens strengthen the action of androgens. The normal sexual rhythm demands a certain level of hormones (the measure of their presence is the level of 17 ketosteroids in man's blood). Harmful factors also exist that disturb the normal sexual rhythm, which allows the production of reproductive cells and conditions the ability to react to sexual stimuli. These factors can work in the direction of so-called sexual overexcitability or, on the contrary, in the direction of lowered sexual excitability. The pathophysiology of sex deals with that, whereas sexual psychopathology studies sexual disorders of neurogenic and psychogenic origin. The above account of elementary information from the field of biological and medical sexology does not properly give us a deeper understanding of the very concept of "sex," but it also does not at all overthrow the conviction drawn from the pre-scientific observation that sex is a property of the human individual. If we were content with a biological analysis alone, then the following conclusion would present itself: sex is connected directly and immediately with reproduction; this is indicated most strongly by the physiology of sexual life. Nothing more can be said on the basis of the biological analysis. But precisely here the "pre-scientific" statement that sex is a property of the human individual opens far-reaching horizons to us.

3. *Sex*: Again, this word (*płeć*) does not denote sexual intercourse, but a property of the body and of the person (see nn. 4 below and 7 on p. 297).

4. *Sex is a property of the human person*: This profound statement seems to stand in opposition to Wojtyła's earlier pronouncements that sex is a property of the body and is manifested in the body (see the section "The concupiscence of the flesh" in chapter III, part 1) or that sex is merely a property of a being, not linked with the whole being of the person (see the section "Affirmation of the value of the person" in chapter II, part 3). These statements are indeed contradictory, but only if one presupposes a dualism between the person and the body, between the person and his nature. These statements present Wojtyła's call for a renewed reflection on the whole person including his bodiliness, which in fact he continues in his famous Wednesday audiences, also called the Theology of the Body. See John Paul II, *Man and Woman He Created Them: A Theology of the Body*, trans. Michael Waldstein, second edition (Boston: Pauline Books & Media, 2006).

5. *This drive turns . . .* : In the 1962 edition (p. 267), this sentence is followed by another: "We can presently complement our knowledge about the sexual drive in the 'biological' way, having before our eyes all that was said in the previous section on the theme of sex itself, especially in the somatic and physiological sense."

6. *The majority of physiologists and sexologists consider . . .* : The 1962 edition (p. 267) has: "The majority of physiologists and sexologists, contrary to the theory of pansexualism (Freud), consider . . ."

7. *What results from . . .* : In the 1962 edition (p. 271), this sentence is followed by another: "Exceptionally, this can occur in some states of hazy consciousness, e.g., in some mental illnesses (the hypomanic syndrome, the confusional state), although at least partial consciousness is always necessary."

8. *If a woman does not find . . .* : In the 1962 edition (pp. 272–273), this and the next sentence have the following form:

> If a woman does not find in sexual intercourse this natural satisfaction, which is linked to the climactic sexual arousal (*orgasmus*), then a danger emerges that she will experience (*przeżywać*) the conjugal act in a way that is not fully-mature, without the commitment of her whole personhood (according to some authorities, this often is a cause of prostitution). This way of experiencing (*przeżywać*) makes it particularly easy to fall into neurotic

reactions and secondary sexual frigidity, i.e., the inability to experience (*przeżyć*) arousal especially in the climactic phase.

9. *Not the technique alone, but precisely the culture*: In the 1962 edition (p. 274), the sentence uses quotation marks around "technique" and "culture."

10. *A harmonious marriage solves these situations*: In the 1962 edition (p. 276), this sentence has the following form: "The correct way out of this situation is only marriage, and a 'perfect marriage' at that, i.e., marriage physically harmonized (as van de Velde wants)."

11. *The Fifth, not the Sixth Commandment*: Wojtyła refers to the Catholic numbering of the Ten Commandments, where the Fifth Commandment is "You shall not kill" and the Sixth Commandment is "You shall not commit adultery."

12. *The principle of conjugal shame . . .* : The 1962 edition (p. 277) adds at the end of this sentence: "(*vaginismus* in women; in men: *eiaculatio praecox* and a frequent cause of impotence)."

13. *However, understanding this accurately . . .* : In the 1962 edition (pp. 279–280), this sentence is followed by two paragraphs:

> Sexual intercourse itself signifies a nexus of a man's and a woman's actions determined by the will of the man and by the consent of the woman (the intercourse should not take place against her will) and proceeding from sexual arousal, which develops and increases during intercourse until the climax (*orgasmus*). In the name of the psycho-physical health of a woman and a man, sexologists require that the sexual lived-experience reaches that climax by both parties and more or less at the same time—we have spoken of this already.
>
> The center of the sexual movement on the part of a man is located in the core S2–S3; the stimulus proceeds via *nervus pudendus* to the posterior radicles of the core and then returns through the erectile nerve, evoking cavernous bodies to be filled and the erectile reflex. The same stimulus by way of extension radiates to L1 and L3, where the core center of ejaculation is located. The lumbo-sacral sympathetic fibers are the descending path for ejaculation. In the correct conditions ejaculation (literally: "the expulsion of sperm") in a man is linked to orgasm (only exceptionally these two functions are at times dissociated under pathological conditions), and this is manifested by a number of simultaneous vegetative reactions. This simultaneity is to prove that sexual stimulation is carried via neurons and not, as was supposed earlier, in a humoral way. In this moment symptoms occur simultaneously on the part of the sympathetic and parasympathetic nervous system, the respiratory system (the accelerated breathing), the circulatory system (the increase of blood pressure and tachycardia), etc. Ejaculation serves procreation directly, because in every ejaculate there are millions of sperm—the male germs of life. In this way, a man in sexual intercourse always serves procreation by providing the germs of life in abundance.

14. *Every woman can observe changes that occur in her in the appropriate phase of the cycle*: In the 1962 edition (p. 280), this sentence has the following form:

"Every normal woman can observe in herself the time of ovulation by listening at least to her own instinctive reactions, which in a way conforming to the funda- mental end of nature ('reproduction') make a woman's sexual drive manifest itself most strongly in the fertile period."

15. *This difficulty does not dwell* . . . : In the 1962 edition (p. 281), this sentence is followed by others:

> In fact, there is only one day a month when a woman is capable of becoming pregnant, including a few probable days besides that. The calculation of the day of ovulation and of the whole "fertile period" is the object of the Ogino- Knaus theory and the Smulders method based on that, a method that can be considered as verified. The newer method of Holt is joined to it—a thermal method and observation of the so-called ovulatory symptoms syndrome to- gether with a histological study. However, all these methods are reliable only for women with a harmonious and undisturbed sexual rhythm.

16. *The factors disturbing* . . . : The 1962 edition (p. 281) has: "The fundamental factors disturbing . . ."

17. *We encounter their effects* . . . : The 1962 edition (p. 281) adds at the end of this sentence: "such as women's illnesses, general diseases, and mechanical injuries."

18. *Clinical practice also confirms* . . . : In the 1962 edition (p. 282), this and the next sentence have the following form:

> Clinical practice confirms the thesis that precisely the fear of pregnancy paralyzes the regulatory activity of nature the most. Not only does it de- prive a woman of the "joy of experiencing (*przeżywać*) love," the joy that should be brought by action in conformity with nature, and as a dominant affection overwhelms all other sensations, but it also leads to unpredictable reactions, often exactly by bringing forth the pregnancy that the woman fears so much and that would not have taken place in the case of normal intercourse free from this overpowering anxiety reaction. (At this point we can also mention so-called "hysterical pregnancies," when under the influence of the longing for a child or, on the contrary, of the fear of him, a group of symptoms develops imitating a pregnancy without fertilization taking place.)

19. *All this indicates indirectly* . . . : The 1962 edition (p. 282) adds at the end of this sentence: "(Reproduction and parenthood, Periodic abstinence: The method and interpretation)."

20. *Only in this way can biological equilibrium, without which* . . . : In the 1962 edition (p. 282), this has the following form: "Only in this way can biological equilibrium, which so much depends on the psychogenic factors, and without which . . ."

21. *The natural regulation of conceptions*: This concept is equivalent to NFP, i.e., natural family planning.

22. *Almost no one speaks about it*: The 1962 edition (p. 283) has instead: "Almost no one speaks about it, disregarding ethics in favor of 'technique' alone, and thereby impeding the effectiveness of the 'natural methods.'"

23. *For once man realizes . . .* : In the 1962 edition (pp. 283–285), this sentence is followed by three paragraphs:

> In the correct conditions fertilization takes place in a woman's reproductive tract, whence the fertilized cell (the so-called zygote) travels to the uterus where it implants itself and grows. Fertilization is possible only when a mature ovum is in the organism of a woman. The ovum is the biggest cell in the human organism, "laden" with nutritive substances and not too mobile, but which slowly moves toward meeting sperm. The ovum is capable of being fertilized only during a few hours, after which it dies. Sperm, however, the smallest and most mobile cell of the human system, demonstrates enormous vitality and is able to survive a few days (three to four or even sometimes longer) while waiting for the ovum. At the moment of penetration by one spermatozoon, the ovum surrounds itself wholly with membrane, as it were, so that it becomes resistant to other spermatozoa, and after that, as a "zygote," travels and implants itself in the uterus. Implantation takes place outside the uterus only in exceptional cases (hence extrauterine pregnancy). In the correct conditions in the pregnant uterus, the so-called placenta develops—a formation that takes over the internal-secretory function of the *corpus luteum* and produces the gonadotropic hormones and progesterone, which is indispensable to maintain pregnancy. Through the placenta the child receives nourishment from the blood of the mother—if the mother does not provide the child with certain substances from food, the child picks up the substances from her organism, which is, of course, to the detriment of the mother. Thus in this period the mother must be cared for in a particular way.
>
> Inasmuch as the whole life of a woman is very strongly biologically dependent on the sexual rhythm, the period of pregnancy is in this regard particularly privileged. In normal conditions, i.e., with the full acceptance of the conceived child, a pregnant woman experiences (*przeżywać*) her motherhood as a period full of joy, joy that counterbalances the physical hardships. This is a period of biological equilibrium that is produced on the basis of the hormonal correlation—turbulent rhythmical changes disappear for the benefit of the child, to whom everything in the mother's organism is subordinated. The gonadotropic hormones maintain pregnancy until the moment of childbirth, when their level in the blood suddenly drops, thus automatically giving the advantage to the hormones of the pituitary gland (oxytocin), which evoke contractions of the uterus and expel the mature to be born fetus. A correct childbirth must be painful, for pain is a psychical equivalent of the contraction of the uterus, without which a woman cannot give birth. The technique of the so-called painless labor does not actually consist in the removal of pain, but only in the active inclusion of the woman, who has been informed about the progress of labor and the role of contractions, in the whole process of childbirth. This

decreases the pain to a minimum, as a calm subjection to the rhythm of nature and the woman's active cooperation, consisting in contracting and relaxing at appropriate moments the muscles she controls, quickens the labor and diverts attention from the very lived-experience of pain.

According to sexologists the maternal instinct of a woman reaches a peak in the lactation period, that is, in the period of breastfeeding the baby. The lactation hormones are in a certain measure the antagonists of estrogens; hence during lactation a certain percentage of women do not menstruate. However, ovulation returns, and so ("accidental") pregnancies then occur, originating precisely in that period. At this point one more characteristic phenomenon must be mentioned. Sometimes there is a negative attitude of the mother to her born child, which usually happens to be some projection of her affections with respect to the father of the child (e.g., in the case of marriages in discord or extra-marital pregnancy, when the appearance of the child foreshadows a number of conflicts and difficulties). However, usually the maternal instinct prevails, and after a period of initial reluctance the mother's reaction to her child becomes more and more positive as the child develops. The cases of infanticide are pathological and in the opinion of sexologists they occur in women either mentally underdeveloped or displaying so-called moral insanity.

That is it about motherhood itself.

24. *These are, on the one hand . . .*:  In the 1962 edition (p. 285), this sentence is followed by another: "We will briefly present an assessment of these methods in light of medical sexology, which accepts only the viewpoint of psycho-physical health and not of the moral good and evil themselves."

25. *Contraceptive means are by nature detrimental to health*: The 1962 edition (p. 285) has: "Contraceptive means do not require a detailed description, although we must state that all of them are by nature detrimental to health."

26. *Mechanical means . . .* : The 1962 edition (p. 285) adds at the end of this sentence: "—the proof is neuroses in women caused by using precisely such brutal means."

27. *These effects, however, are inevitable*: In the 1962 edition (p. 285), this sentence is followed by others:

> The one who falls victim to them is first and foremost the man, whose contribution in conjugal intercourse is linked to the nervous straining of attention and an understandable state of anxiety. This leads to shortening the whole act and to the so-called *eiaculatio praecox*, and in the long run may lead to complete impotence. The effects on the woman are easily recognizable if we remember the fact that her "curve of stimulation" in sexual intercourse is longer and slower. Once intercourse is interrupted, she remains unsatisfied all the more, which, as is known, evokes neuroses and leads secondarily to sexual frigidity. Even in the eyes of the classic advocates of utilitarianism, the unreasonable search for ephemeral pleasure has been assessed negatively, and this is worth recalling here.

What follows until the end of paragraph, starting with the words "Disregarding the fact of this method's unreliability," is absent from the 1962 edition.

28. *Natural methods are ways of controlling fertility through periodic abstinence*: In the 1962 edition (p. 286), this sentence has the following form:

> Natural methods are the ways of preventing pregnancy that aim at recognizing the moment of ovulation for the purpose of avoiding conjugal intercourse in the fertile period. The very calculation of fertile days cannot be general as it requires close observation of the monthly cycle of a given woman to establish in the space of many months what her rhythm is, for this method demands taking into account both the longest and the shortest cycle. The Holt method consists in observing the so-called ovulatory syndrome with its most characteristic so-called center pain, also the thermal changes (the temperature does not rise above a certain level until the moment of ovulation, but then it suddenly jumps up a few degrees and does not drop until menstruation—this temperature jump is connected precisely with ovulation), and furthermore the changes in the epithelium of the external reproductive organs, changes that can be recognized histologically by studying the cells of the epithelium.

29. *A climate without which the effective use of natural methods is out of the question*: Another possible reading instead of "climate" is "intercourse," but the sense of the sentence excludes that.

30. *After all, it is an artificial interruption of a natural biological rhythm with far-reaching effects*: In the 1962 edition (p. 287), this sentence has the following form: "After all, it is an artificial interruption of a natural biological rhythm in the most brutal way possible, because by means of a surgical procedure. This interruption is not only provisional but with far-reaching effects."

31. *So-called sexual neuroses . . .* : Instead of the paragraph starting with this sentence, the 1962 edition (p. 289) has:

> The progress and somatic symptoms of sexual neuroses resemble other neuroses (headaches, insomnia or a change of the sleeping rhythm, dizziness, irritability, anxiety, etc.), although the neurotic reaction is evoked depending on man's characterological features, thus turning into the hypochondriac reaction in some people (more often in men) and into the hysterical and neurasthenic reactions in others. A particularly frequent symptom of sexual neuroses is compulsions, which actually are very often linked to an incorrect orientation of the sexual drive in a given individual. Sexual neuroses in man are at times connected with the problem of "potency," that is, the ability for sexual intercourse. Organic impotence is rather a rare fact (e.g., after a mechanical injury). However, partial or complete impotence is very often conditioned psychogenically without occurring organically. Also, a certain moment of ambition most frequently attaches itself, a moment that can deepen the neurotic situation even more.

32. *This is not the place . . .* : Instead of the paragraph starting with these words, the 1962 edition (pp. 289–290) has:

> The sexual drive can become a source of neurotic disorders when it is prematurely awakened and then suppressed in an inappropriate way. This also pertains to the manifestations of the drive's aberrations ("perversions") such as onanism or homosexuality. We must distinguish accidental onanism, which occurs even in children, from addictive onanism, which is at times connected with a certain fear of normal intercourse with a person of the other sex. In the latter case we deal with the so-called onanistic syndrome, which is characterized among other things by excessive sensibility, an inferiority complex based on a sense of guilt, and also changes in the somatic state. Physicians themselves state that the treatment of the onanistic syndrome, as well as every form of masturbation, does not belong so much to their competence as to the competence of educators. The fixation on masturbation in a child is also often a result of an erroneous pedagogical approach. The error consists in some "overemphasis of evil," which in many cases brings an opposite effect. Namely, it evokes an exaggerated focus on the meaning of the sexual drive and in general of the matters of *sexus*—this is precisely the way complexes arise—when in fact the point should be to divert attention from these matters. There is a need then to introduce intensively into the field of vision of such a person (younger or even older) all other values while directing his organism to the paths of healthy needs and healthy forms of self-relief by means of a hygienic way of life, physical exercise, and sport.

33. *Therapy*: This section title is missing in the 1962 edition.

34. *Without presently analyzing the clinical symptoms . . .* : In the 1962 edition (p. 290), this and the following sentence have the following form: "The general clinical recommendations concerning the treatment of psychical afflictions with respect to disorders in the sexual sphere can be reduced to the following."

35. *Of course, there are cases of disorders . . .* : In the 1962 edition (pp. 290–291), the paragraph starting with these words has the following form:

> e) What is only sometimes needed is the help of medical means that are simply corroborant in general, because sexual-psychical disorders sometimes have their substratum in general enervation. Particular attention should be paid to the disorders linked to puberty and to a woman's sexual rhythm. The somatic and physiological factors (the hormonal changes) explain a lot here.
>
> These recommendations are almost always important when treating sexual ailments, for most of them have a psychical basis (if not even a psychical character), which must be mastered somehow. This will be the case when "treating" the onanistic complex and even when treating homosexuality. Sexologists more often speak against the existence of congenital homosexuality. It is rather an aberration acquired due to certain predominant relations in the most proximate environment. The sense of guilt and of perversion is at times compensated with some imaginary conviction about the superiority

of precisely these sexual lived-experiences, although sometimes, on the contrary, a sense of inferiority then arises with respect to other people who are "able" to have normal intercourse with a person of the other sex. It must be added that homosexuality at times develops in men in whom an erroneous education resulted in strengthening the conviction that all that is connected with a woman is unclean, is a sin, that she herself is a sin—thus the shift of reaction in relation to persons of the same sex is easily understandable. Homosexuality is generally rarer among women than among men. The basic method of treating it is again psychotherapy based on the goodwill of the patient and which aims first and foremost at breaking in the psyche of the patient the conviction that his state is incurable. By removing him from his previous environment (homosexual men usually create such environments—in contradistinction to women) the physician or educator attempts to produce in him a conviction in conformity with the truth that the sexual drive in every man—so also in him—can be subordinated to the will.

## Appendix: On the Meaning of Spousal Love

1. All three articles were published in the Polemics section of *Roczniki Filozoficzne* 22 (1974) in booklet 2. The article by Fr. Meissner appeared on pages 151–158, by Fr. Szostek on pages 158–161, and by Cardinal Wojtyła on pages 162–174. Wojtyła's article was introduced by the following note:

> In the present ethical booklet, the editors of *Roczniki Filozoficzne KUL* publish a discussion between Fr. Karol Meissner, OSB, and Fr. Andrzej Szostek. Because the discussion concerns Cardinal Karol Wojtyła's ethical study *Love and Responsibility*, the author of that study enters into it as well, taking up anew some problems raised in his book. The statements published here constitute a very important fragment of the discussion, which has been carried on for a number of years among ethicists and moralists in Kraków and Lublin concerning the problems of conjugal morality.

2. *Roczniki Filozoficzne KUL*: The Annals of Philosophy of the Catholic University of Lublin.

3. *KW*: Karol Wojtyła includes his initials in the editorial inserts of his authorship.

4. *L'auteur, toutefois, ne s'adresse pas uniquement aux croyants; du moins ne fait-il pas appel d'abord à leur foi. Il ne procède pas d'après les enseignements de l'Ecriture, mais par les voies de l'argumentation rationnelle*: The author, however, does not address himself only to believers, or at least he does not appeal first to their faith. He does not proceed by presenting the teaching of the Scripture but rather by following the paths of reason.

5. *Mutually give and accept each other*: "*Sese mutuo tradunt atque accipiunt*" in Latin.

6. *What can and should be correctly follows—should follow—from what is*: Here is the first indication of the relation between the ontic and moral orders. Wojtyła

explores this relation in his subsequent reflections on the law of the gift. The gist of his deliberation seems to revolve around the question "What is the contribution of the ontic order in my moral action?" Definitely, such a contribution exists, and he acknowledges it at this point. His task seems to be to explain this contribution in a way that, on the one hand, secures the ontological integrity of the acting person and, on the other hand, shows that that integrity is fully present, expressed, and fulfilled in reciprocal love (self-giving). The point of departure is the correct understanding of that "is," which for Wojtyła cannot be understood without a reference to its origin and destiny in God.

7. *Man, who is the only creature on earth which God willed for itself, cannot fully find himself except through a sincere gift of self:* This has been obviously adapted by Wojtyła, who introduced his own emphasis. This text from *Gaudium et Spes*, 24, in its fuller context runs as follows:

> *Immo Dominus Iesus, quando Patrem orat ut "omnes unum sint . . . , sicut et nos unum sumus," prospectus praebens humanae rationi impervios, aliquam simili- tudinem innuit inter unionem personarum divinarum et unionem filiorum Dei in veritate et caritate. Haec similitudo manifestat hominem, qui in terris sola creatura est quam Deus propter seipsam voluerit, plene seipsum invenire non posse nisi per sincerum sui ipsius donum.* [Indeed, the Lord Jesus, when he prayed to the Father, "that all may be one . . . as we are one" (Jn 17:21–22) opened up vistas closed to human reason, for he implied a certain likeness between the union of the divine Persons, and the unity of God's sons in truth and charity. This likeness reveals that man, who is the only creature on earth which God willed for itself, cannot fully find himself except through a sincere gift of himself (Vatican translation).]

The above excerpt should be accompanied by the following one from *Gaudium et Spes*, 22:

> *Reapse nonnisi in mysterio Verbi incarnati mysterium hominis vere clarescit. Adam enim, primus homo, erat figura futuri, scilicet Christi Domini. Christus, novissimus Adam, in ipsa revelatione mysterii Patris Eiusque amoris, hominem ipsi homini plene manifestat eique altissimam eius vocationem patefacit.* [The truth is that only in the mystery of the incarnate Word does the mystery of man take on light. For Adam, the first man, was a figure of him who was to come, namely Christ the Lord. Christ, the final Adam, by the revelation of the mystery of the Father and his love, fully reveals man to man himself and makes his supreme calling clear (Vatican translation).]

8. *He is a being entrusted to himself:* See n. 11 (p. 300) on "self-creation."

9. *Aretology:* A science about virtues (and vices).

10. *Bl. Maximilian:* Now St. Maximilian Maria Kolbe.

11. *God wills:* Wojtyła uses the present tense, although the text of *Gaudium et Spes*, 24 says "willed."

12. *Lumen Gentium*, 44: The Polish text references *Lumen Gentium*, 45, but paragraph 44 is clearly meant. The fuller context is as follows:

*Per baptismum quidem mortuus est peccato, et Deo sacratus; ut autem gratiae baptismalis uberiorem fructum percipere queat, consiliorum evangelicorum professione in Ecclesia liberari intendit ab impedimentis, quae ipsum a caritatis fervore et divini cultus perfectione retrahere possent, et divino obsequio intimius consecrator. Tanto autem perfectior erit consecratio, quo per firmiora et stabiliora vincula magis repraesentatur Christus cum sponsa Ecclesia indissolubili vinculo coniunctus.* [Indeed through Baptism a person dies to sin and is consecrated to God. However, in order that he may be capable of deriving more abundant fruit from this baptismal grace, he intends, by the profession of the evangelical counsels in the Church, to free himself from those obstacles, which might draw him away from the fervor of charity and the perfection of divine worship. By his profession of the evangelical counsels, then, he is more intimately consecrated to divine service. This consecration will be the more perfect, in as much as the indissoluble bond of the union of Christ and his bride, the Church, is represented by firm and more stable bonds (Vatican translation).]

13. *Lumen Gentium,* 44: Here is the fuller context of the quote:

*Per vota aut alia sacra ligamina, votis propria sua ratione assimilata, quibus christifidelis ad tria praedicta consilia evangelica se obligat, Deo summe dilecto totaliter mancipatur . . .* [The faithful of Christ bind themselves to the three aforesaid counsels either by vows, or by other sacred bonds, which are like vows in their purpose. By such a bond, a person is totally dedicated to God, loved beyond all things (Vatican translation).]

14. *The eschatological dimension of spousal love expressed in this vocation*: The Polish text makes it clear that what is expressed in that vocation is spousal love (and not the eschatological dimension of spousal love).

15. *The "right to such a gift"*: Depending on the context the Polish word *prawo* can be translated either as "law" or as "right."

16. *Honorable*: See my comments on the meaning of "honorable" above (n. 27, p. 304).

17. *The sacrament St. Paul described as "great"*: See Eph 5, especially v. 32.

# Index

# About the Author

Born in 1920 to a devout Catholic family in Poland, Karol Wojtyła was ordained a priest in 1946. He carried out an effective pastoral ministry, continued higher studies, and taught at the university level. Ordained a bishop in 1958, he fearlessly confronted the communist authorities in Poland. He took part in the Second Vatican Council and implemented the Council's reforms at home. After being elected Pope on October 16, 1978, he took the name John Paul II and led the Church for the next twenty-six years in a remarkable and memorable way. He was beatified on May 1, 2011.

Throughout his priesthood Karol Wojtyła was keenly concerned about the problems and possibilities of married love and family life. In *Love and Responsibility* he wrote about the human person's call to love, which enables people to find happiness and fulfillment in the gift of oneself.

# Pauline
## BOOKS & MEDIA

The Daughters of St. Paul operate book and media centers at the following addresses. Visit, call, or write the one nearest you today, or find us at www.pauline.org.

**CALIFORNIA**
3908 Sepulveda Blvd, Culver City, CA 90230    310-397-8676
935 Brewster Avenue, Redwood City, CA 94063    650-369-4230

**FLORIDA**
145 S.W. 107th Avenue, Miami, FL 33174    305-559-6715

**HAWAII**
1143 Bishop Street, Honolulu, HI 96813    808-521-2731

**ILLINOIS**
172 North Michigan Avenue, Chicago, IL 60601    312-346-4228

**LOUISIANA**
4403 Veterans Memorial Blvd, Metairie, LA 70006    504-887-7631

**MASSACHUSETTS**
885 Providence Hwy, Dedham, MA 02026    781-326-5385

**MISSOURI**
9804 Watson Road, St. Louis, MO 63126    314-965-3512

**NEW YORK**
64 W. 38th Street, New York, NY 10018    212-754-1110

**SOUTH CAROLINA**
243 King Street, Charleston, SC 29401    843-577-0175

**TEXAS**
Currently no book center; for parish exhibits or outreach evangelization, contact: 210-569-0500, or SanAntonio@paulinemedia.com, or P.O. Box 761416, San Antonio, TX 78245

**VIRGINIA**
1025 King Street, Alexandria, VA 22314    703-549-3806

**CANADA**
3022 Dufferin Street, Toronto, ON M6B 3T5    416-781-9131

¡También somos su fuente para libros,
videos y música en español!